BUILDING RESPONSIVE AND RESPONSIBLE FINANCIAL REGULATORS IN THE AFTERMATH OF THE GLOBAL FINANCIAL CRISIS

BUILDING RESPONSIVE AND RESPONSIBLE FINANCIAL REGULATORS IN THE AFTERMATH OF THE GLOBAL FINANCIAL CRISIS

Editor:
Pablo Iglesias-Rodríguez

intersentia
Cambridge – Antwerp – Portland

Intersentia Ltd.
Sheraton House | Castle Park
Cambridge | CB3 0AX | United Kingdom
Tel.: +44 1223 370 170 | Email: mail@intersentia.co.uk

Distribution for the UK:
NBN International
Airport Business Centre, 10 Thornbury Road
Plymouth, PL6 7PP
United Kingdom
Tel: +44 1752 202 301 | Fax: +44 1752 202 331
Email: orders@nbninternational.com

Distribution for the USA and Canada:
International Specialized Book Services
920 NE 58th Ave Suite 300
Portland, OR 97213
USA
Tel.: +1 800 944 6190 (toll free)
Email: info@isbs.com

Distribution for Austria:
Neuer Wissenschaftlicher Verlag
Argentinierstraße 42/6
1040 Wien
Austria
Tel.: +43 1 535 61 03 24
Email: office@nwv.at

Distribution for other countries:
Intersentia Publishing nv
Groenstraat 31
2640 Mortsel
Belgium
Tel.: +32 3 680 15 50
Email: mail@intersentia.be

Building Responsive and Responsible Financial Regulators in the Aftermath of the Global Financial Crisis
Pablo Iglesias-Rodríguez (ed.)

ISBN 978-1-78068-179-5
D/2015/7849/8
NUR 828

GPRC
Guaranteed
Peer Reviewed
Content

British Library Cataloguing in Publication Data. A catalogue record for this book is available from the British Library.

PREFACE AND ACKNOWLEDGEMENTS

The global financial crisis that started in the year 2007 has shown how the failures in financial regulation and supervision may have extremely harmful consequences for the protection of investors, the soundness of the financial markets, the stability of the financial system and, ultimately, social well-being.

The architects (scholars, practitioners, policy-makers, legislators, stakeholders ...) of the post-crisis structures of financial regulation and supervision face the highly challenging task of building regulators that effectively tackle the weaknesses of the pre-crisis regimes.

This book aims at re-examining central concepts in the governance of financial regulators, in light of the global financial crisis experience. It does so through both a theoretical analysis of the concepts of accountability and independence of the regulatory function, as well as a critical examination of post-crisis financial regulation architectures in the European Union, the United States of America and Canada. The ultimate goal of this volume is to provide policy-makers with ideas that may help them to build financial regulation architectures which are more responsive to the needs and demands of society and to the challenges of increasingly global financial markets.

I owe an immense debt of gratitude to the contributors to this volume for their excellent work and dedication. They devoted substantial time and effort to writing their contributions and updating them to reflect the latest developments. Working with all of them was a very pleasant, inspiring and rewarding experience.

I am very grateful to Luc Verhey, who strongly supported this project from the outset.

I would also like to thank Tom Scheirs for his advice and assistance throughout the publication process, and the two anonymous reviewers of the book proposal for their invaluable comments.

The Faculty of Law of the VU University Amsterdam and the Global Governance Programme of the European University Institute provided me with very supportive and intellectually rich working environments during successive stages of the editing process. My warmest thanks to them as well.

Pablo Iglesias-Rodríguez
Amsterdam
January 2015

FOREWORD

This book addresses the question of how to build more responsive and responsible financial regulators in the aftermath of the global financial crisis. It provides a insightful and critical analysis of the accountability of key financial regulators in the European Union, the United States of America and Canada, in the post-crisis institutional setting. The book shows that whereas the regulatory overhaul that followed the crisis has generally encompassed a move towards a greater responsiveness of financial regulators, the financial architectures of the post-crisis institutional setting still face important challenges.

The challenges that lie ahead are not of a pure architectural or technical nature; they are closely related to fundamental issues of democratic legitimacy and the rule of law. The financial crisis has shown that financial regulators are powerful actors who have a vital role to play in the global society of the 21th century. They only can effectively contribute to the efficiency and the stability of the financial markets if they are able to fulfil their supervisory and regulatory tasks independent from the one-sided interests of financial enterprises as well as the erratic whims of daily party politics. On the other hand financial regulators should not be isolated from society. They have to give an account on the fulfilling of their mandate to the government, the parliament as well as to the society at large. Experience shows that these vital principles – independence and accountability – are in practice not always easy to reconcile.

This book incisively re-examines the concepts of accountability and independence as the indispensable pillars of the governance of the modern financial regulators. It strongly underlines that the accountability, the independence and, more generally, the good governance of financial regulators, constitute necessary conditions for both the efficiency and legitimacy of the financial regulatory and supervisory functions. A proper accountability framework contributes to the creation, monitoring and enforcement of rules that enhance the soundness of the financial markets, financial stability, investor protection and, ultimately, social development. An important additional value of the book is that its scope is not limited to the European Union and its member states. It also includes the role of financial regulators in leading western countries like the United States and

Canada where the economic circumstances partly seem different from what is at stake in the European Union.

What makes the book even more attractive is that the editor has chosen for a broad perspective. In considering the issues of independence, accountability and governance, this book has sought to encompass the idea that the challenges posed by financial regulation and supervision in global financial markets have a multidimensional nature that can only be understood through and require interdisciplinary analyses. This is reflected in the background of the different contributors, who are economists, lawyers, political scientists and sociologists from both academia and practice. My experience is that confronting the different worlds of different academic disciplines and common sense that is sustained by longstanding practical experience, is the most fruitful method to come to innovative results. This book seems to be a promising example of this multidimensional approach which is undoubtedly necessary to deal with such a complex, sensitive and vital issue as financial regulation.

Luc Verhey
Member of the Advisory Division of the Dutch Council of State and
Kirchheiner Professor of Constitutional and Administrative Law of Leiden University

CONTENTS

LIST OF CONTRIBUTORS

Xosé Carlos Arias is Professor of Applied Financial Economics at the University of Vigo (Spain).

David S. Bieri is Associate Professor of Urban Affairs at Virginia Tech, with a joint appointment in the Global Forum on Urban and Regional Resilience and in the School of Public and International Affairs. His main research and teaching interests are at the intersection of public finance, monetary theory and economic geography. Bieri's research examines spatial features of credit flows, focusing on the dynamics of urbanization and the evolutionary development of the monetary-financial system as a joint historical process. His other research examines regulatory aspects of international finance, global monetary governance, and their role in the process of financialization. He also writes about the history of economic thought.

Prior to joining the faculty at Virginia Tech, Bieri was a faculty member at Taubman College at the University of Michigan, Ann Arbor. From 1999 until 2006, he held various senior positions at the Bank for International Settlements (BIS) in Basel, Switzerland, most recently as the Adviser to the CEO. He was also Head of Business Development in which capacity he was responsible for new financial products and reserve management advisory for central banks. Before his career in central banking, Bieri worked as a high-yield analyst at Bankers Trust in London and in fixed-income syndication at UBS in Zürich.

Bieri received his Ph.D. from the School of Public and International Affairs at Virginia Tech. He holds a M.Sc. in corporate and international finance from the University of Durham and a B.Sc. (hons) in economics from the London School of Economics.

Antón Costas is Professor of Economic Policy at the University of Barcelona (Spain).

Carmine Di Noia is Deputy Director General and Head of Capital Markets and Listed Companies at Assonime – the Association of the Italian Corporations – (Italy).

Nicholas Dorn is a sociologist, inclined to law and politics. His book Democracy and Diversity in Financial Market Regulation was published by Routledge (GlassHouse Press) in summer 2014. He has also published on transnational governance, several aspects of the European Union, public and private policing and economic crime. Until reaching retirement age at the end of 2013 he worked for Erasmus School of Law, Rotterdam, Cardiff University and ISDD/DrugScope.

Dona M. Dunea is an independent researcher affiliated with Glendon College, York University in Toronto (Canada).

Matteo Gargantini is Senior Research Fellow at the Max Planck Institute Luxembourg for International, European and Regulatory Procedural Law (Luxembourg).

Pablo Iglesias-Rodríguez is Senior Researcher at the Faculty of Law of the VU University Amsterdam (The Netherlands) and Honorary Fellow of the Asian Institute of International Financial Law (HKU). Before, he was a postdoctoral researcher at the Faculty of Law, Maastricht University. In 2012/2013 he was a Jean Monnet Fellow (Global Governance Programme) at the Robert Schuman Centre for Advanced Studies of the European University Institute. He has held various visiting positions at European universities and has been a visiting scholar at Columbia University School of Law (New York). He is a graduate of the University of Vigo (LLB and MPhil in Economics) and the EUI (MRes and PhD in Law). He is also a qualified lawyer (Madrid Bar Association).

Rosa María Lastra is Professor in International Financial and Monetary Law at the Centre for Commercial Law Studies of the Queen Mary University of London (UK).

Donato Masciandaro is Professor of Economics and Chair in Economics of Financial Regulation at Bocconi University (Italy).

Hester Peirce is a senior research fellow at the Mercatus Center at George Mason University and program director for the Financial Markets Working Group. Before joining Mercatus, Peirce served on the Senate Committee on Banking, Housing, and Urban Affairs. In that position, she worked on financial regulatory reform following the financial crisis of 2008 as well as oversight of the regulatory implementation of the Dodd-Frank Act. Peirce also worked as an attorney at the Securities and Exchange Commission, the Court of Federal Claims and a Washington, DC law firm. She is the editor of, and a contributor to, the book *Dodd-Frank: What It Does and Why It's Flawed*, published by Mercatus in 2012. Peirce earned her BA in economics from Case Western Reserve University and her JD from Yale Law School.

Guillaume Prache is the Managing Director of BETTER FINANCE, the European Federation of Financial Services Users. He is also one of the experts representing financial services users before the European Commission (as member and vice chair of the Financial Services User Group – FSUG), before the European Securities & Markets Authority (as member and former chair of the ESMA Securities & Markets Stakeholder Group), before the European Insurance and Occupational Pensions Authority (as member of the EIOPA Occupational Pensions Stakeholder Group) and before the French financial regulator AMF.

Ian Roberge is Associate Professor of Political Science at Glendon College, York University in Toronto, Ontario (Canada).

RESPONSIVE-AND-RESPONSIBLE FINANCIAL REGULATION IN THE AFTERMATH OF THE GLOBAL FINANCIAL CRISIS

Pablo Iglesias-Rodríguez

1. INTRODUCTION

The global financial crisis that started in the year 2007[1] sparked several policy and academic debates about the role that Financial Regulation and Supervision Authorities (FRSAs)[2] – the entities entrusted with the regulation and supervision of financial markets and institutions[3] – played in the crisis and, notably, whether, how and why their actions or inactions contributed to the financial meltdown.[4]

---

1 On the structural causes of the global financial crisis see e.g. J. Crotty, 'Structural causes of the global financial crisis: a critical assessment of the 'new financial architecture'' (2009) 33 *Cambridge Journal of Economics* 563. For a summary of the different factors behind the financial crisis see e.g. M. Jickling, 'Causes of the Financial Crisis' (2010) *Congressional Research Service Report for Congress* No. R40173. A timeline of the crisis is available at Federal Reserve Bank of St. Louis, *The Financial Crisis: A Timeline of Events and Policy Actions* <http://timeline.stlouisfed.org/pdf/CrisisTimeline.pdf> accessed 14.10.2014.

2 'A broad, all-embracing definition of FRSAs could be that of entities of a public nature with officially recognized authority to carry out regulation and supervision of the financial sector – financial institutions, markets, and products – in a given jurisdiction' – P. Iglesias-Rodríguez, *The Accountability of Financial Regulators: A European and International Perspective*, Alphen aan den Rijn, Kluwer Law International 2014, p. 5.

3 On the regulatory side FRSAs define – with varying degrees of discretion depending on the legal system under which they operate – rules – e.g. prudential or conduct of business norms – that must be observed by financial market participants. On the supervisory side, FRSAs monitor the functioning of the financial markets and institutions, and enforce the applicable rules; the latter may for example include the suspension or the withdrawal of a financial firm's authorisation. For an overview of the functions of FRSAs in several jurisdictions – and of the different institutional models of financial regulation and supervision – see Group of Thirty, *The Structure of Financial Supervision: Approaches and Challenges in a Global Marketplace*, Group of Thirty, Washington, DC 2008.

4 With respect to the EU see e.g. High-Level Group on Financial Supervision in the EU, *Report of the High-Level Group on Financial Supervision in the EU*, 2009 (Larosière Report) <http://ec.europa.eu/internal_market/finances/docs/de_larosiere_report_en.pdf> accessed 14.10.2014, pp. 39–42. As regards the US, the role of FRSAs in the crisis is critically assessed in The Financial Crisis Inquiry Commission, *The Financial Crisis Inquiry Report: Final Report*

The post-crisis analyses concerning the regulatory and supervisory performance of FRSAs in the years preceding the financial collapse evidenced several failures of FRSAs in the carrying out of their obligations.[5] In some instances, FRSAs performed their duties inappropriately or even negligently by failing to adequately identify and stop financial behaviours and practices that caused harm to consumers of financial services and, ultimately, to the financial system.[6] More generally, it has been claimed that before the crisis FRSAs in countries that were later hit by the crunch followed regulatory and supervisory approaches that acknowledged above all the interest of the financial industry on the one hand,[7] and dismissed to a great extent the objective of financial stability and the interest of the general investing public on the other.[8]

The post-crisis institutional and legal reform-agendas in countries that were severely hit by the crisis have indeed encompassed important changes in the design, governance and organisation of FRSAs. The reforms introduced by the Dodd-Frank Act in the United States of America (US) supervisory institutional framework, the Regulations setting the European Supervisory Authorities in the financial field at the European Union (EU) level as well as the overhaul of financial supervision architectures in jurisdictions with highly sophisticated financial markets – e.g. the creation of the Prudential Regulation Authority and the Financial Conduct Authority in the United Kingdom (UK) – are all examples of this regulatory impetus tackling the functioning of FRSAs and aimed at overcoming some of the shortcomings of the previous regimes.

One of the common elements of the abovementioned post-crisis reforms is that they have brought about profound changes in the accountability of FRSAs and, in consequence, in the way in which they relate to their main account principals, namely political forums and stakeholders in the financial realm. Accountability

---

of the National Commission on the Causes of the Financial and Economic Crisis in the United States, U.S. Government Printing Office, Washington, DC 2011 <www.gpo.gov/fdsys/pkg/GPO-FCIC/pdf/GPO-FCIC.pdf> accessed 14.10.2014. For a summary of literature addressing the failures in supervisory architecture and supervisory governance see D. Masciandaro, R.V. Pansini and M. Quintyn, 'The Economic Crisis: Did Financial Supervision Matter?' (2011) *IMF Working Paper* No. 11/261, pp. 30–31.

5 See e.g. J. Palmer and C. Cerruti, *Is there a need to rethink the supervisory process?,* Paper presented at the International Conference 'Reforming Financial Regulation and Supervision: Going back to Basics', Madrid, 15.06.2009.

6 G. Tabellini – 'Why did bank supervision fail?' in A. Felton and C. Reinhart (eds.), *The First Global Financial Crisis in the 21st Century. Part I: August 2007– May 2008. A VoxEU.org Publication*, CEPR, London 2008, p. 46 – identifies 'bureaucratic inertia together with poor judgement' as two of the reasons of the failure of financial supervision.

7 For instance, some commentators see some links between regulatory capture and the financial crisis – see e.g. S. Johnson, 'The quiet coup', *The Atlantic,* 01.05.2009 <www.theatlantic.com/magazine/archive/2009/05/the-quiet-coup/307364/2/> accessed 14.10.2014.

8 See e.g. P. Iglesias-Rodríguez, *The Accountability of Financial Regulators: A European and International Perspective,* supra note 2, p. 72.

has admittedly been acknowledged as a key condition for the good governance of FRSAs[9] and, its deficit, recognised as one of the factors that contributed to the failures of FRSAs before the financial crisis.[10]

This book addresses topics pertaining to the accountability of FRSAs with a focus on what and how accountability relationships and mechanisms – as well as elements that affect both – foster responsive and effective regulatory and supervisory frameworks that tackle the weaknesses of the previous regimes. It does so in the following manner. First, it re-examines the concepts of accountability and independence as well as the main economic theories underlying financial services policy-making, in light of the crisis experiences. Second, it critically analyses, through case studies, the post-crisis institutional framework of financial regulation and supervision in selected jurisdictions – and the reforms, or lack of reforms therein – with a view to assessing whether and how the FRSAs of the post-global financial crisis era are well-suited to effectively address the challenges and threats that global financial markets pose to the stability, integrity and good functioning of financial systems as well as to the protection of stakeholders affected by financial regulation and of society at large.

This introductory chapter has a threefold mission.

In the first place, it aims at contributing to the discussion about the causes of the pre-crisis failures of FRSAs through the analysis of two concepts: responsiveness and responsibility. It argues that the regulatory and supervisory shortcomings of FRSAs before the global financial crisis reflect flaws in the pursuing of three interrelated variables, namely: a) the statutory objectives and mandates of financial regulation and supervision; b) the interests of stakeholders within the financial realm; and c) social returns. These failures reveal, in turn, weaknesses in two essential legitimacy features of FRSAs: responsiveness and responsibility. Second, it explains how accountability mechanisms and relationships may help to build more responsive-and-responsible FRSAs – and consequently a better regulation and supervision of the financial system. Third, it provides and overview of the structure of the rest of the book.

The remainder of this chapter proceeds as follows. The next section introduces the concept of responsive-and-responsible financial regulation. This is followed by an analysis of its main dimensions – and the provision of examples of pre-crisis failures of FRSAs that concern each of those dimensions. The chapter then turns to the issue of the role of accountability – and related concepts – in the

[9] See e.g. IOSCO, *Objectives and Principles of Securities Regulation*, 1998, p. 10.
[10] P. Iglesias-Rodríguez, *The Accountability of Financial Regulators: A European and International Perspective*, supra note 2.

attainment of responsive-and-responsible financial regulation and supervision. The final section explains the structure of the rest of book.

2. RESPONSIVE-AND-RESPONSIBLE FINANCIAL REGULATORS

The notion of responsiveness within the regulatory sphere has received substantial attention among scholars who address regulatory compliance strategies.[11] Within such context responsiveness essentially makes reference to and focuses on the relationships between regulators and regulatees, addressing the question of what features and characteristics of the latter should determine a regulatory response by the regulator as well as the content of such a response.[12] This notion of responsive regulation is particularly concerned with the issue of how to develop regulatory strategies that foster industry compliance.[13] Responsive regulation strategies have drawn the attention of policy-makers and have indeed been implemented in some jurisdictions, also in the field of financial services regulation.[14]

This book addresses a different concept of responsiveness, which relates to the input and output legitimacy[15] of the FRSAs' regulatory and supervisory decisions.

---

11 See e.g. I. Ayres and J. Braithwaite, *Responsive Regulation: Transcending the Deregulation Debate*, Oxford University Press, Oxford 1992, J. Braithwaite, 'The Essence of Responsive Regulation' (2011) 44 *UBC Law Review* 475, K. Yeung, *Securing Compliance: a principled approach*, Hart Publishing, Oxford 2004, C. Parker, 'The "Compliance" Trap: The Moral Message in Responsive Regulatory Enforcement' (2006) 40 *Law and Society Review* 591.

12 In this respect see the seminal work on responsive regulation: I. Ayres and J. Braithwaite, *Responsive Regulation: Transcending the Deregulation Debate*, supra note 11, p. 4. Ayres and Braithwaite propose a dynamic regulatory strategy that combines punishment and persuasion; in such a system the greater the compliant behaviour by the regulatee the lesser the degree of intervention by the regulator.

13 The notion of responsive regulation has been refined by later works of other scholars, leading to more complex, comprehensive and holistic formulations of the term; see e.g. R. Baldwin and J. Black – 'Really Responsive Regulation' (2007) *LSE Law, Society and Economy Working Paper* No. 15/2007 – who develop a concept of responsive regulation that, in addition to compliance of the regulatee, looks at other elements such as, *inter alia*, the regulated 'firms' own operating and cognitive frameworks' and 'the broader institutional environment of the regulatory regime'.

14 This is for instance the case of Australia – see e.g. G. Pearson, *Financial Services Law and Compliance in Australia*, Cambridge University Press, Melbourne 2008 and C. Wood, M. Ivec, J. Job and V. Braithwaite, 'Applications of Responsive Regulatory Theory in Australia and Overseas' (2010) *RegNet Occasional Paper* No. 15, p. 12 – with regard to the Australian Securities and Investment Commission (ASIC).

15 On the concepts of input-legitimacy and output-legitimacy see F. Scharpf, *Governing in Europe: Effective and Democratic?*, Oxford University Press, Oxford 1999. 'Input-legitimacy is related to the idea of "government by the people" and makes reference to whether policy-outputs reflect the direct or indirect participation, *ex-ante* consensus and will of the persons actually or potentially affected by those policies. Input-legitimacy is therefore concerned, to a great extent, with the inclusiveness and the balance of interests represented in policy-making procedures. Output-legitimacy is linked to the notion of "government for the

This formulation of responsiveness is closer in meaning to the dictionary definition of the term: 'quick to act, especially to meet the needs of someone or something'.[16] The rationale for the legitimacy emphasis of this analysis lies in the pervasive nature of the financial sector[17] – which also bears some relation with the recent financial crisis.[18] In effect, the functioning of the financial markets and institutions, and, consequently, the regulatory and supervisory decisions adopted with regard to them by FRSAs, have an impact on several stakeholders from within the markets – such as industry actors or the general investing public – as well as outside them – e.g. society at large. Therefore, from a legitimacy perspective, it is important that FRSAs' decisions acknowledge the broad spectrum of interests affected by financial phenomena.

We define a responsive financial regulator as one that ideates and puts into practice regulatory and supervisory decisions that acknowledge the needs of the financial system,[19] the financial markets, financial institutions, retail investors and consumers of financial services[20] as well as society at large. This concept of responsiveness goes beyond the generally accepted notions of accountability[21] in the sense that a responsive financial regulator may be responsive to the needs, interests and implicit or explicit demands and desires of actors and forums to which they are not directly accountable. Responsiveness does not only constitute an aspirational ideal encompassed by certain views and policy perspectives about

people" and regards the degree of acceptance of policies by the persons that are affected by them or, in other words, to the degree of matching of the former with the expectations of the latter' – P. Iglesias-Rodríguez, *The Accountability of Financial Regulators: A European and International Perspective,* supra note 2, pp. 24–25.

16 Cambridge Academic Content Dictionary at Cambridge Dictionaries Online <http://dictionary.cambridge.org/dictionary/american-english/> accessed 25.01.2015.

17 The pervasiveness of the financial sector in contemporary societies is related to the process of financialisation, which refers to the growing importance of the financial sector in the economy – see e.g. G.A. Epstein, 'Introduction: Financialization and the World Economy' in G.A. Epstein (ed.) *Financialization and the World Economy*, Edward Elgar, Cheltenham 2005, p. 3 and T.I. Palley, 'Financialization: What It Is and Why It Matters' (2007) *The Levy Economics Institute Working Paper* No. 525.

18 See e.g. L.C. Bresser-Pereira, 'The Global Financial Crisis and a New Capitalism?' (2010) *The Levy Economics Institute Working Paper* No. 592.

19 We adopt the definition of the financial system provided by J. De Haan, S. Oosterloo and D. Schoenmaker – *Financial Markets and Institutions: A European Perspective*, 2nd ed., Cambridge University Press, Cambridge 2012, p. 3: 'The financial system consists of all financial intermediaries and financial markets, and their relations with respect to the flow of funds to and from households, governments, business firms, and foreigners, as well as the financial infrastructure'.

20 Although both terms are often used without distinction, there are however some differences between them; the concept of 'investor' is generally associated with people who put money in a firm in order to make a profit – e.g. the purchaser of stocks of a corporation – whereas the term 'consumer' refers to the purchaser of products, such as retail banking products and services – see P. Iglesias-Rodríguez, *The Accountability of Financial Regulators: A European and International Perspective,* supra note 2, pp. 10–11.

21 The concept of accountability will be further referred in Section 3 below.

how the financial system should be regulated and supervised[22] but also, and to a great extent, a necessary condition for the legitimacy of FRSAs themselves.[23]

Responsive decision-making is a complex task. Sometimes the rights, demands, preferences and needs of different categories of stakeholders within the financial realm[24] differ or are even conflicting. There may also be discrepancies between the maximisation of the interests of some or all stakeholder categories and the attainment of certain endings such as the soundness of the financial markets, the stability of the financial system or even the pursuing of broader social goals. Moreover, in carrying out their duties FRSAs are accountable to multiple principals[25] – both at the national and international levels –[26] with potentially different expectations about the performance of FRSAs. On top of these, FRSAs must balance their regulatory and supervisory decisions against certain statutory mandates that establish a hierarchy of objectives.

Responsive financial regulation and supervision requires a proper assessment and balance of all the conundrums and constraints indicated above with a view to adopting solutions that consider in the best possible manner the rights, preferences and interests of the actors and forums affected directly or indirectly by the functioning of the financial system. In other words, responsiveness requires responsibility, that is, good judgment[27] as regards the optimisation of a complex

---

[22] For instance, some post-crisis policy reactions to the pre-crisis supervisory failures have consisted of a move '... toward more democratically responsive and less technocratically independent regulation' – A.J. Levitin, 'The Politics of Financial Regulation and the Regulation of Financial Politics: A Review Essay' (2014) 127 *Harvard Law Review* 1991, 1994.

[23] At least in pragmatically based forms of legitimacy, in which '... the person or social group perceives that the organisation (e.g. a regulator) will pursue their interests directly or indirectly' – J. Black, 'Legitimacy and the Competition for Regulatory Share' (2009) *LSE Law, Society and Economy Working Paper* No. 14/2009, p. 10.

[24] On the different categories of stakeholders in the financial arena see P. Iglesias-Rodríguez, *The Accountability of Financial Regulators: A European and International Perspective,* supra note 2, p.10.

[25] See E. Hüpkes, M. Quintyn, and M.W. Taylor, 'The Accountability of Financial Sector Supervisors: Principles and Practice' (2005) *IMF Working Paper* No. 05/51, p. 18.

[26] For example, there are certain accountability relationships between national FRSAs and global networks of FRSAs such as the Basel Committee on Banking Supervision (BCBS), the International Organization of Securities Commissions (IOSCO) and the International Association of Insurance Supervisors (IAIS) – see P. Iglesias-Rodríguez, *The Accountability of Financial Regulators: A European and International Perspective,* supra note 2, pp. 314–319.

[27] Responsibility has three main meanings – see Cambridge Academic Content Dictionary at Cambridge Dictionaries Online, supra note 16. The first is related to the concept of 'duty'. FRSAs receive delegations to regulate and supervise the financial markets, actors and institutions, and, therefore, they are intrinsically 'responsible' in the sense of duty-bound. The second refers to the notion of 'blame'; this dimension of responsibility is related to the idea of accountability. As will be explained in Section 3, FRSAs are accountable to political and stakeholder actors and forums; these accountors may censure FRSAs for their actions or inactions. The third – and the most relevant for our analysis – is concerned with the idea of 'good judgment'.

function that embraces those rights, preferences and interests. This function is composed of three main variables:

a) The targets and mandates of financial regulation and supervision – as defined by the legislator in the jurisdiction where an FRSA operates;
b) The interests of stakeholder groups in the financial realm;
c) Social returns.

Responsibility constitutes, in the first place, a necessary condition of responsiveness. In this respect, an FRSA cannot be responsive without being responsible, that is, acting with good judgement as to how to effectively respond to multiple targets, principals and interests. However, in addition to this instrumental function, responsibility is a concept of its own, in the sense that, from a legitimacy viewpoint and within the framework of financial regulation and supervision, responsibility must be primarily directed at the adoption of responsive actions, and, without such a 'responsiveness' focus responsibility would lose its legitimacy rationale. Owing to the entity of both concepts and their interconnectedness, this book refers to responsive-and-responsible FRSAs – or to responsive-and-responsible financial regulation and supervision – as one single term, whose dimensions are analysed in the next sub-section.

2.1. THE DIMENSIONS OF RESPONSIVE-AND-RESPONSIBLE FINANCIAL REGULATION AND THE PRE-CRISIS FAILURES OF FINANCIAL REGULATORS

2.1.1. *The pursuing of the statutory mandates of financial regulation and supervision*

One of the defining elements of a responsive-and-responsible FRSA consists of its willingness and ability to design and adopt regulatory and supervisory actions that pursue and, ideally, effectively achieve the statutory targets of financial regulation and supervision – as defined by the legislator in the jurisdiction where that FRSA operates. These statutory goals – and the corresponding FRSAs' mandates – are normally set in the instruments that establish FRSAs and refer to certain endings pertaining to the financial system, the markets, their participants, investors or society at large. For example, in the US, according to the provisions of the Securities Exchange Act of 1934, the Securities and Exchange Commission (SEC) – the federal securities FRSA – must seek the protection of investors, efficiency, competition and capital formation.[28] In the EU, the legislation instituting the

[28] 15 USC 78c(f): 'Whenever pursuant to this chapter the Commission is engaged in rulemaking, or in the review of a rule of a self-regulatory organization, and is required to consider or

European Securities and Markets Authority (ESMA) – the EU FRSA in the field of securities – binds the authority to the protection of public values, linking the latter to the accomplishment of certain objectives relating to the financial sector: 'The objective of the Authority shall be to protect the public interest by contributing to the short, medium and long-term stability and effectiveness of the financial system, for the Union economy, its citizens and businesses'.[29] In some jurisdictions there is a hierarchy of objectives whereby FRSAs must give priority to certain targets over others; for instance, in the UK, the conduct of business regulator – the Financial Conduct Authority (FCA) – is entrusted with the pursuing of one strategic objective, namely ensuring the good functioning of the markets under its oversight,[30] and of three operational objectives: the protection of consumers, the protection and enhancement of the UK financial system's integrity, and the promotion of effective competition in the interest of consumers;[31] however, the law clearly stipulates that the 'competition objective' must be pursued insofar as compatible with the other two operational targets.[32]

There is a strong link between the mandate and duties of FRSAs and their accountability. In this respect, FRSAs are held to account by their account-holders first and foremost on the basis of their performance with respect to the mandates that they receive from the legislator and, more broadly, of their compliance with their duties. For that very same reason it is important that the objectives and the mandates of FRSAs are defined in a clear and precise fashion so that: a) the latter unambiguously understand their duties and responsibilities and adapt their regulatory and supervisory behaviour accordingly, and b) account-principals and account-holders have precise criteria against which to measure and judge the performance of FRSAs.[33]

---

determine whether an action is necessary or appropriate in the public interest, the Commission shall also consider, in addition to the protection of investors, whether the action will promote efficiency, competition, and capital formation'.

29 Article 1.5 Regulation (EU) No. 1095/2010 of the European Parliament and of the Council of 24 November 2010 establishing a European Supervisory Authority (European Securities and Markets Authority), amending Decision No. 716/2009/EC and repealing Commission Decision 2009/77/EC – ESMA Regulation.

30 Section 6(1B)(2) Financial Services Act 2012.

31 Section 6(1B)(3) Financial Services Act 2012.

32 Section 6(1B)(4) Financial Services Act 2012.

33 In this regards see D.T Llewellyn – *Institutional Structure Of Financial Regulation And Supervision: The Basic Issues*, Paper presented at a World Bank seminar 'Aligning Supervisory Structures with Country Needs', Washington, DC, 06–07.06.2006, p. 16: 'Firstly, regulatory agencies might be most effective and efficient when they have clearly defined, and precisely delineated, objectives and when their mandate is clear and precise. Secondly, accountability might be more effective and transparent when it is clear for what objectives particular agencies are responsible' – in reference to supporters of institutional structures of financial regulation and supervision by 'objectives'.

On the one side, the effective pursuing of the statutory targets of financial regulation and supervision involves, to a certain extent, responsiveness, input-legitimacy and output-legitimacy of the financial regulatory and supervisory decisions. In the first place, the FRSAs' statutory mandates are set in the relevant laws passed by the legislator and, therefore, encompass processes of parliamentary debate and scrutiny by elected representatives. Second, in most jurisdictions the procedure of elaboration of financial services-sector laws entails forms of public engagement and input whereby different categories of stakeholders are given voice in the legislative process.[34] As a consequence, statutorily-set mandates of financial regulation and supervision embrace representative and/or deliberative processes.

On the other side, the maximisation of the statutory targets of financial regulation and supervision by an FRSA does not necessarily lead to output legitimacy – i.e. outcomes that effectively advance the interests of stakeholders in the financial domain or of society at large. For instance, the law may establish regulatory and supervisory priorities – or a hierarchy of them – that dismiss the needs of a group or groups of stakeholders affected by financial regulation and/or supervision. Moreover the process of creation of the laws where the targets of financial regulation and supervision are set may suffer from certain asymmetries – also from an accountability perspective – as regards the engagement, power and influence of different interest groups, that result in the establishment of biased targets that favour the preferences of some actors in the financial field to the detriment of other groups of stakeholders or of society at large.[35]

A notorious pre-crisis concrete instance of the failure of an FRSA to effectively pursue its statutory mandates is the Madoff case. In December 2008 Federal Agents arrested Mr. Bernard Madoff, the owner of a mainstream investment firm in Wall Street, over an alleged – later confirmed – major Ponzi scheme

34 See e.g. H.M. Treasury, *A new approach to financial regulation: the blueprint for reform*, HM Treasury, London 2011 <www.hm-treasury.gov.uk/d/consult_finreg__new_approach_blueprint.pdf> accessed 19.10.2014 – this document included a public consultation on *inter alia* the Draft Financial Services Bill and aspects pertaining to the objectives and scope of the UK FRSAs.

35 For instance, in an Opinion of the year 2012, the European Economic and Social Committee (EESC) saw certain links between the financial crisis and the unbalanced influence of different categories of stakeholders in the political discussions concerning financial regulation: 'One of the reasons for the financial crisis was inadequate and ineffective regulation and supervision of the financial markets. One of the difficulties in financial regulation is how to ensure that differing and contradictory positions are given a balanced hearing. There is no effective counterweight to the legitimate representation of the financial sector's interests. Political debate primarily plays out between the legislator on one side and the financial sector concerned on the other' – European Economic and Social Committee, Opinion of the European Economic and Social Committee on 'How to involve civil society in financial regulation', CESE 172/2012 – ECO/298.

that amounted to USD 65 billion.[36] Since the year 2000, Mr. Harry Markopolos – a chartered financial analyst – had been periodically warning the SEC – with detailed information – about the illegal nature of Madoff's financial activities.[37] Despite these warnings, the US securities supervisor failed to properly investigate and stop Madoff's scheme, which grew in size over the years leading to major investor's losses.[38] A later investigation into the performance of the SEC in the case evidenced the lack of both ability and disposition of the securities supervisor to effectively seek one of its statutory mandates – the protection of investors – through a proper investigation of the Madoff's activities. On the one side, the SEC lacked certain means, such as experienced staff, to adequately examine the Madoff's Ponzi scheme. On the other side, the SEC also suffered from certain apathy towards the investigation of the Madoff's firms; as summarised by the Office of Investigations of the SEC:

> 'The OIG found that the conduct of the examinations and investigations was similar in that they were generally conducted by inexperienced personnel, not planned adequately, and were too limited in scope. While examiners and investigators discovered suspicious information and evidence and caught Madoff in contradictions and inconsistencies, they either disregarded these concerns or relied inappropriately upon Madoff's representations and documentation in dismissing them. Further, the SEC examiners and investigators failed to understand the complexities of Madoff's trading and the importance of verifying his returns with independent third parties.'[39]

2.1.2. *The unbiased pursuing of the interests of stakeholders within the financial realm*

When FRSAs carry out their functions they exercise discretion. Indeed, discretion constitutes an intrinsic and integral element of the decision-making processes of FRSAs and of independent regulatory agencies in general. In this respect, when legislators delegate regulatory and supervisory powers to FRSAs[40] they transfer

---

36 E. Honan and D. Wilchinshttp, 'Bernard Madoff arrested over alleged $50 billion fraud', *Reuters*, 12.12.2008 <www.reuters.com/article/2008/12/12/us-madoff-arrest-idUSTRE4BA7IK20081212> accessed 19.10.2014 and G. McCool and M. Graybow, 'Madoff pleads guilty, is jailed for $65 billion fraud', *Reuters*, 13.03.2009 <www.reuters.com/article/2009/03/13/us-madoff-idUSTRE52A5JK20090313> accessed 19.10.2014.

37 In this regard see H. Markopolos, *No One Would Listen: A True Financial Thriller*, John Wiley and Sons, Inc, Hoboken, NJ 2010.

38 Sec Office of Investigations, *Investigation of Failure of the SEC to Uncover Bernard Madoff's Ponzi Scheme – Public Version*, Report No. OIG-509, 2009 <www.sec.gov/news/studies/2009/oig-509.pdf> accessed 21.10.2014.

39 Sec Office of Investigations, *Investigation of Failure of the SEC to Uncover Bernard Madoff's Ponzi Scheme – Public Version*, Report No. OIG-509, supra note 38, p. 457.

40 The rationale for the delegation to FRSAs lies in *inter alia*, their technical expertise on financial markets' issues and their relative independence from partisan pressures – see e.g. G. Majone,

discretion to the latter,[41] with regard to, among others, the definition of the strategies aimed at the accomplishment of the statutory objectives and mandates of financial regulation and supervision.

Statutory objectives and mandates are rather broad – e.g. 'financial stability' or 'the soundness of the financial system' – and do not necessarily imply or indicate the manner in which the interests and preferences of different stakeholders must be pursued in relation to those objectives; that choice is largely left to the discretion of the supervisor. Therefore, in exercising such discretion through regulation, supervision and enforcement, FRSAs implicitly or explicitly determine whether, how and the degree to which the FRSAs' outcomes will satisfy the interests and preferences of the different categories and subcategories of stakeholders within the financial realm.

Responsive-and-responsible financial regulation – and the notions of input and output legitimacy embedded in this concept – requires that, regardless of their specific content, the FRSAs' regulatory and supervisory decisions reflect an unbiased balance of the interests of the different categories of stakeholders in the financial sphere. To put it differently, it presupposes a weighting of those interests that does not biasedly maximise the preferences of one group to the detriment of other group(s).

A condition for the effective pursing of this dimension of responsive-and-responsible financial regulation is that FRSAs have the ability and willingness to acquire, understand and properly process information concerning: a) the reality and the complexities of the financial markets at both the local and international levels; b) the needs, aspirations and preferences of different stakeholders in those markets and the interactions among them; c) the effects of financial markets institutions, products, activities and behaviours on each category of stakeholders, the financial markets, the financial system as a whole and society at large; and d) the impact of financial regulation and supervision on a, b and c. Responsive-and-responsible financial regulation is not a static concept; it does not only refer to a, b and c at a given point in time but also to their evolution over the time and/or their meaning in different institutional contexts and settings.[42]

'The rise of the regulatory state in Europe' (1994) 17 *West European Politics* 77, 84–85 and M. Thatcher and A. Stone Sweet, 'Theory and Practice of Delegation to Non-Majoritarian Institutions' (2002) 25 *West European Politics* 1, 4.

41 On the relationship between delegation and discretion in the context of administrative law see J.F. Garner, 'The Delegation of Administrative Discretion' (1949) 27 *Public Administration* 115.

42 Responsiveness to changes also constitutes a key element of some concepts of responsiveness developed within the framework of enforcement theories – see e.g. R. Baldwin and J. Black, 'Really Responsive Regulation', supra note 13.

A broad notion of the concept 'stakeholder'[43] that acknowledges the pervasiveness of the financial sector in contemporary societies, would include almost every non-state societal actor. A more specific, financial sector-focused definition essentially distinguishes two main categories of stakeholders, namely financial industry stakeholders on the one side, and non-financial industry stakeholders on the other.[44] The first is composed of physical and legal persons – and their representatives – whose principal activity consists of offering financial goods and services in the markets.[45] The second group gathers actors – and their representatives – that act primarily as purchasers of financial goods and services offered by financial industry stakeholders.[46] Although the stakeholders within each of these two categories – and their respective sub-groups – may share certain common interests, preferences and regulatory expectations, they may tend to have some differing views about how the markets should be regulated and supervised. For instance, non-industry actors may demand rules that protect them against the failure or misconduct of financial institutions, whereas industry players may have a preference for the dismantling of regulatory barriers – e.g. a regulatory and supervisory framework that gives them substantial freedom as regards their governance, the products and services that they are allowed to offer and the markets where they are authorised to operate. In some instances the maximisation of the utility function of a given category or subcategory may be detrimental to the interests of another category – e.g. when the reduction of the regulatory requirements applicable to financial firms leads to lesser investor protection.

The pre-crisis decisions of FRSAs in jurisdictions such as the EU and the US reflected to a large extent biased judgments that tended to favour the industry preferences. The opposition of the Federal Reserve, the SEC and the Treasury to the strengthening of over-the-counter (OTC) derivatives regulation in the late 1990s, the SEC's relaxation of capital requirements of broker-dealer firms in the mid 2000s and the obstruction by federal FRSAs – such as the Office of the Comptroller of the Currency (OCC) and the Office of Thrift Supervision (OTS) – to state laws that prevented predatory-lending, during the last decade, are all examples of this pro-industry *laissez-faire* – and in a way, deregulatory – approach characterised by a lenient regulation and supervision which favoured, above all, the interests of the industry but which ultimately led to costs being

[43] According to the New Oxford American Dictionary (3rd ed.) a stakeholder is: 'a person with an interest or concern in something, especially a business'.

[44] See P. Iglesias-Rodríguez, *The Accountability of Financial Regulators: A European and International Perspective*, supra note 2, p. 10.

[45] This would for instance include banking, insurance and securities firms.

[46] This category comprises, for example, retail investors and consumers of financial services.

imposed on other stakeholder groups and, as will be referred in the next section, on society at large.[47]

2.1.3. *The pursuing of social returns*

When providing goods and services and carrying out their business activities, financial services corporations may intentionally or unintentionally shift part of the costs of their activities to other parties.[48] These 'negative externalities'[49] or 'social costs'[50] lead to welfare-inefficiencies, notably, when the community at large experiences a substantial harm.

Under lax regulatory conditions, financial services institutions are able and may have a tendency to shift costs of their business to third parties or even to society at large. For instance, the credit crunch of the years 2007–2008[51] offers several examples of financial activities that eventually led to considerable negative externalities.[52] In the US, during the years preceding the crisis major

---

47 These and other instances of pro-industry regulation are explained in P. Iglesias-Rodríguez, *The Accountability of Financial Regulators: A European and International Perspective*, supra note 2, pp. 67–73.

48 This cost shifting is related to the idea of 'externality', which was first developed by A.C. Pigou – *The Economics of Welfare*, MacMillan, London 1932 (4rd ed.). Pigou provides some examples of negative externalities, such as those arising: 'when the owner of a site in a residential quarter of a city builds a factory there and so destroys a great part of the amenities of the neighbouring sites; or, in a less degree, when he uses his site in such a way as to spoil the lighting of the houses opposite: or when he invests resources in erecting buildings in a crowded centre, which, by contracting the air space and the playing-room of the neighbourhood, tend to injure the health and efficiency of the families living there. Yet again, third parties – this time the public in general – suffer incidental uncharged disservices from resources invested in the running of motor cars that wear out the surface of the roads' – A.C. Pigou – *The Economics of Welfare,* supra this note, p. 108.

49 A negative externality appears when there is a difference between the private costs of production or consumption of a good or service and the total costs of production or consumption of such good or service – the difference between both being the indirect costs, borne by third parties not involved in the relevant transaction. Positive externalities occur when there is a difference between the private returns of a given activity an the total returns of that very same activity – the difference being in this case an indirect return that benefits third parties. For a clear and concise explanation of the concept of externality see T. Helbling, *Externalities: Prices Do Not Capture All Costs,* <www.imf.org/external/pubs/ft/fandd/basics/external.htm> accessed 24.10.2014.

50 K.W. Kapp – *The Social Costs of Business Enterprise*, Spokesman, Nottingham 1978, pp. 13–14 – defines 'social costs' as: '... all direct and indirect losses sustained by third persons or the general public as a result of unrestrained economic activities' or 'all those harmful consequences and damages which other persons or the community sustain as a result of productive processes, and for which private entrepreneurs are not held accountable'.

51 On the credit crisis see e.g., M.K. Brunnermeier, 'Deciphering the Liquidity and Credit Crunch 2007–08' (2008) *NBER Working Paper* No. 14612 <www.nber.org/papers/w14612.pdf> accessed 20.09.2014, P. Mizen, 'The Credit Crunch of 2007–2008: A Discussion of the Background, Market Reactions, and Policy Responses' (2008) 90 *Federal Reserve Bank of St. Louis Review* 531.

52 On the topic of financial crises and externalities see e.g. M. Miller and L. Zhang, 'Whither Capitalism? Financial externalities and crisis' (2012) *University of Warwick CAGE Online*

investment banks had been leveraging very heavily,[53] in order to, *inter alia*, increase their investments in the highly risky but – back then – profitable sub-prime mortgage market.[54] Some scholars point out that one of the reasons for such behaviour was that the main US investment banks were limited liability corporations.[55] This incentivised them to leverage and adopt risky investment patterns because a substantial part of the resulting risks was shifted to their creditors.[56] The expectation of government bailouts – i.e. the ability to shift risks to the government – also contributed to the behaviour of banks.[57] The burst of the housing bubble and the subsequent credit crisis did indeed affect negatively not only actors within the financial realm, but ultimately and especially society at large, that suffered the consequences of the credit meltdown, in the form of taxpayer-funded bailouts,[58] financial instability, general economic downturn, unemployment,[59] and greater social unrest.[60]

By regulating and supervising the financial markets and institutions, and notably, the behaviour of financial firms, FRSAs influence the ability and willingness of the latter to shift costs of their activities on to third parties or the community. The statutory objectives and mandates of financial regulation and supervision in most jurisdictions encompass either directly or indirectly the idea that when FRSAs exercise their functions they must seek the minimisation of social costs sourcing from financial services activities. In addition, they may also encompass

Working Paper No. 79 <http://wrap.warwick.ac.uk/57780/1/WRAP_79.2012_miller.pdf> accessed 29.10.2014.

53 See e.g. S. Kalemli-Ozcan, B. Sorensen and S. Yesiltas, 'Leverage Across Firms, Banks, and Countries' (2011) *NBER Working Paper* No. 17354 <www.nber.org/papers/w17354.pdf> accessed 29.10.2014.

54 See e.g. A. Blundell-Wignall, P. Atkinson and S.H. Lee, 'The Current Financial Crisis: Causes and Policy Issues' (2008) 95 *Financial Market Trends* 1, 3–4, 8.

55 This argument is extensively developed in H-W. Sinn, *Casino Capitalism: How the Financial Crisis Came About and What Needs to be Done Now*, Oxford University Press, New York 2010.

56 See H-W. Sinn, *Casino Capitalism: How the Financial Crisis Came About and What Needs to be Done Now*, supra note 55, p. 79.

57 See H-W. Sinn, *Casino Capitalism: How the Financial Crisis Came About and What Needs to be Done Now*, supra note 55, p. 84. Some indeed consider that, in the context of financial crises, bailouts are inevitable – see e.g. N. Kocherlakota, 'Taxing Risk and the Optimal Regulation of Financial Institutions' (2010) *Federal Reserve Bank of Minneapolis Economic Policy Paper* N. 10–3, p. 2: 'knowing bailouts are inevitable, financial institutions fail to internalize all the risks that their investment decisions impose on society'.

58 On the issue of crises and bailouts see e.g. B. Ritholtz, *Bailout Nation: How Greed and Easy Money Corrupted Wall Street and Shook the World Economy*, John Wiley & Sons, Inc., Hoboken, NJ 2009.

59 On the economic consequences of the crisis see e.g. European Commission, Directorate-General for Economic and Financial Affairs, *Economic Crisis in Europe: Causes, Consequences and Responses – European Economy 7|2009* – European Communities, Luxembourg 2009.

60 The effects of the crisis on social well-being and unrest are referred in International Institute for Labour Studies, *World of Work Report 2013. Repairing the economic and social fabric*, International Labour Organization, Geneva 2013, pp. 14–16.

general public values and consequently embrace the pursuing by FRSAs of social goals which go beyond the scope of the financial sector. In this respect, in some jurisdictions, the laws applicable to FRSAs make explicit reference to 'third party' or 'societal' interest that must be sought by the relevant FRSAs. For example, in the US, the rules issued by the SEC must be consistent with both investor protection and the public interest.[61] In the EU one of the targets of the ESMA relates to the 'integrity and stability of the financial system', which the EU legislator includes within the overall objective 'protect public values';[62] in effect, a financial system with such features – integrity and stability – will likely reflect less negative externalities being imposed on society.[63]

Responsive-and-responsible FRSAs adopt decisions that, within the scope of their mandates, and after careful consideration of the interests of stakeholders within the financial domain, aim at minimising the social costs related to financial services activities – e.g. deterring financial behaviours that cause negative externalities – and, contemporarily and possibly, maximise social returns – e.g. encouraging financial behaviours and activities that result in positive externalities. This element of responsiveness-and-responsibility is consistent with the legitimacy side of responsive-and-responsible financial regulation and supervision. In this regard, the output-legitimacy of FRSAs is largely built on their ability to contribute through regulation and supervision, to the good functioning of the overall economic system.[64] Otherwise, when FRSAs fail to do so, the public may demand changes concerning the way in which FRSAs operate, their institutional design or even their very same existence.

This dimension of the concept responsive-and-responsible cannot be detached from the legal and institutional framework where an FRSA operates. Responsive-and-responsible financial regulation and supervision indeed presupposes the compliance of an FRSA with the legal framework and, more generally, the observance of the norms emanating from the fiduciary relationships upon which

---

61 See e.g., 15 USC 78c(f) or 15 USC 78c(a)(11).

62 Recital 11 ESMA Regulation.

63 On the relationships between financial stability and negative externalities see H.J. Allen, 'What is "Financial Stability"? The Need for Some Common Language in International Financial Regulation' (2014) 45 *Georgetown Journal of International Law* 929.

64 For instance, during the consultations preceding the reforms of the UK financial supervision architecture some respondents considered that the Financial Policy Committee (FPC) – a committee of the Bank of England created by the Financial Services Act 2012 and primarily entrusted with systemic risk identification, monitoring and mitigation (Section 4 Financial Services Act 2012) – '... should take into account the impact of its actions on economic growth', and the Government recognised '... the importance of the FPC balancing its financial stability objective with the wider consequences of its actions, including on economic growth ...' – H.M. Treasury, *A new approach to financial regulation: summary of consultation responses*, H.M. Treasury, London 2010, pp. 6–7 <https://www.gov.uk/government/uploads/system/uploads/attachment_data/file/190261/summaryofcondocresponses241110.pdf> accessed 24.10.2014.

the authority of FRSAs is built.[65] A regulator that does not obey the law – e.g. its statutory mandate or the applicable rules of regulation and supervision – is, by definition, not responsive-and-responsible. For that very same reason, responsible-and-responsible financial regulation and supervision somehow requires the absence of exogenous constraints of a legal or institutional nature that bind an FRSA to adopt actions that are suboptimal from the point of view of the resulting social consequences.

When FRSAs formulate and implement regulatory and supervisory polices and decisions, they implicitly or explicitly consider not only the potential social costs linked to the activities performed by regulated entities but also their potential social returns. To put it in Coasian terms, FRSAs constantly face the question of whether the value of the benefits resulting from certain activities and behaviours in the financial markets is greater or lesser than the value of the long-term costs related to such activities and behaviours.[66] The global financial crisis provides examples of lack of good judgment of FRSAs as regards such an assessment. For instance, before the year 2007, FRSAs from jurisdictions with highly sophisticated financial markets – such as the US – seemed to encompass the idea that certain innovative financial activities and products that became pervasive in the pre-crisis financial setting – and which, later, proved to be at the heart of the crisis – would lead to positive social outcomes. In this respect, the remarks of the former chairman of the SEC before the American Securitization Forum in June 2006 – less than one year before the start of the credit crisis – reveal the lack of acuity of the SEC about the risks inherent in the massive securitisation process that was taking place in the US:

> 'The increased liquidity that securitization brings means lower credit costs – and that's good for everyone. That's why it doesn't come as a surprise that asset-backed securities are now the largest segment in all of fixed income. Last year, they surpassed U.S. Treasury debt, even in a year with runaway deficit spending.
>
> So there's no doubt that every consumer in America depends on you, and benefits from your work – even if they've never heard of you'.[67]

65 Some scholars define the relationships between FRSAs and their account-principals – e.g., governments, parliaments and, ultimately, society – as fiduciary in nature – see M. Quintyn and M.W. Taylor, 'Robust Regulators and Their Political Masters: Independence and Accountability in Theory' in D. Masciandaro and M. Quintyn (eds.), *Designing financial supervision institutions: independence, accountability and governance,* Edward Elgar, Cheltenham 2007, pp. 12–13.

66 R.H. Coase, 'The Problem of Social Cost' (1960) 3 *Journal of Law and Economics* 1.

67 C. Cox, Chairman of the SEC, Remarks at the American Securitization Forum, New York, 07.06.2006 <www.sec.gov/news/speech/2006/spch060706cc.htm> accessed 24.10.2014.

Securitisation was later acknowledged as one of the 'channels that amplified some of the underlying excesses of the pre-crisis period'[68] and as an indirect source of major negative externalities.[69] In some countries FRSAs were indeed harshly criticised for their passivity towards the pre-crisis securitisation developments; as stated in *The Financial Crisis Inquiry Report*: 'Policy makers and regulators could have stopped the runaway mortgage securitization train. They did not'.[70]

3. THE ROLE OF ACCOUNTABILITY IN RESPONSIVE-AND-RESPONSIBLE FINANCIAL REGULATION

Accountability has long since constituted a key element in the academic and policy debates about the governance of FRSAs.[71] As referred above in Section 1, the financial crisis that started in the year 2007, and, notably, the inconsistencies in the accountability of FRSAs in the pre-crisis institutional setting, increased the attention that both scholars and policy-makers devoted to the analysis of the role of accountability and independence in the performance of FRSAs.

In the context of financial regulation and supervision accountability can be defined as:

> '... a relationship between two or more actors or forums: (1) the accountee(s) – FRSA(s) – on the one side and (2) the accountor(s) – e.g., political or stakeholder forums – on the other side. In this relationship, FRSAs – or persons within them –

---

68 M. Segoviano, B. Jones, P. Lindner and J. Blankenheim, 'Securitization: Lessons Learned and the Road Ahead' (2013) *IMF Working Paper* No. 13/255.

69 Securitization was one of the elements within the mortgage market that led to the real estate bubble and, later, to its collapse, which in turn resulted in certain forms of negative externalities: 'A combination of low interest rates, financial innovation in the form of mortgage securitization, and a global savings glut had led to a boom in U.S. real estate prices that started reversing in 2007. The collapse of the real estate bubble led to the default, or near default, of a number of U.S. financial institutions, most notably Bear Stearns, Lehman Brothers, and AIG. The U.S. government responded with a massive bailout operation in the fall of 2008. Nonetheless, the collapse of the real estate bubble led to one of the longest and deepest recessions in U.S. history' – M.K. Brunnermeier and M. Oehmke, 'Bubbles, Financial Crises, and Systemic Risk' (2012) *NBER Working Paper* No. 18398, p. 11.

70 The Financial Crisis Inquiry Commission, *The Financial Crisis Inquiry Report: Final Report of the National Commission on the Causes of the Financial and Economic Crisis in the United States,* supra note 4, p. xviii.

71 Examples of this early interest in the accountability of FRSAs are V. Grilli, D. Masciandaro and G. Tabellini, 'Political and Monetary Institutions and Public Financial Policies in the Industrial Countries' (1991) 6 *Economic Policy* 342, A. Alesina and L.H. Summers, 'Central Bank Independence and Macroeconomic Performance: Some Comparative Evidence' (1993) 25 *Journal of Money, Credit and Banking* 151, M. Quintyn and M.W. Taylor, 'Regulatory and Supervisory Independence and Financial Stability' (2002) *IMF Working Paper* No. 02/46 <www.imf.org/external/pubs/ft/wp/2002/wp0246.pdf> accessed 27.10.2014.

> may be (a) called to account by their accountors – by being required or requested to give explanations about opinions and plans relevant to the exercise of their authority or about actions or omissions adopted in the exercise of that authority – and/or (b) held to account by those or other accountors for their opinions, plans, actions or omissions, through measures that result in the concerned FRSAs or their officials being subject to some forms of censuring, punishment, disciplining or, more generally, responsibility'.[72]

Accountability essentially concerns relationships between FRSAs on the one side, and political forums, stakeholders and more generally, society, on the other – i.e. the forums around which each of the dimensions of responsive-and-responsible financial regulation gravitates. Accountability has been characterised as a source of independence,[73] democratic control,[74] performance,[75] and also legitimacy of FRSAs.[76] Therefore, accountability provides a highly useful framework for the analysis of responsive-and-responsible financial regulation and supervision. More particularly, it is pertinent to assess whether the nature, content, scope, configuration and actual operation of accountability instruments and relationships have an impact on both the ability and willingness of FRSAs to be responsive-and-responsible, and, therefore, on the quality of their regulatory and/or supervisory policies and decisions. These are questions that are analysed throughout this book.

In the first place, the design of accountability mechanisms and the quality of accountability relationships has an effect on the resources with which FRSAs count to perform their duties and, hence, on their ability to be responsive-and-responsible. Notably, accountability determines to a large degree, the amount and quality of information that an FRSA is able to acquire and process. This information concerns, not only the financial system, markets and institutions – e.g. regulated firms – under the supervisory umbrella of FRSAs but also the demands, needs, preferences and interests of the FRSAs' account-principals.

The mechanisms of accountability of FRSAs towards political actors and forums – e.g. parliamentary appointments of the heads of FRSAs, parliamentary hearings with staff from FRSAs or annual and periodical reporting duties of FRSAs

---

72 P. Iglesias-Rodríguez, *The Accountability of Financial Regulators: A European and International Perspective*, supra note 2, p. 3.

73 E. Hüpkes, M. Quintyn and M.W. Taylor, 'The Accountability of Financial Sector Supervisors: Principles and Practice' supra note 25, p. 8.

74 M. Bovens, 'Public Accountability' in E. Ferlie, L.E. Lynn Jr. and C. Pollitt (eds.), *The Oxford Handbook of Public Management,* Oxford University Press, New York 2005, pp. 192–193.

75 E. Hüpkes, M. Quintyn and M.W. Taylor, 'The Accountability of Financial Sector Supervisors: Principles and Practice', supra note 25, p. 9.

76 M. Bovens, 'Analysing and Assessing Accountability: A Conceptual Framework' (2007) 13 *European Law Journal* 447, 464.

towards political forums – create spaces of debate, discussion and exchange of views between the political accountors – e.g. parliaments and governments – and FRSAs. These instruments primarily constitute a form of political scrutiny aimed at calling FRSAs to account, that is, requesting them to provide explanations about their plans or their performance; the results of such scrutiny may eventually serve as the basis of decisions whereby FRSAs are held to account. However, at the same time, the exchanges – and the debates therein – that these instruments of political accountability encompass constitute a way for FRSAs to receive highly valuable information about the expectations of elected representatives as regards their performance or, for example, clarifications about the meaning of specific mandates and targets of financial regulation and supervision. Moreover, in the framework of those relationships FRSAs may signal to political forums – and/or the latter may spot – deficiencies in the functioning of FRSAs; those political forums may, in turn, use such information to take remedial actions that tackle those deficiencies.[77]

At a broader level, political accountors may hold FRSAs to account through decisions that affect the financial resources at their disposal. This is for instance the case of cuts or freezes affecting the budgets of FRSAs in response to regulatory or supervisory failures of the latter – with respect to FRSAs whose budgets are subject to parliamentary authorisation and appropriations. Budget cuts or freezes may in turn curtail the ability of FRSAs to acquire resources in areas such as staff or technology that are critical for their performance.[78]

Through stakeholder accountability mechanisms – e.g. those providing for the participation of the public in consultations launched by FRSAs or for the engagement of stakeholders in FRSAs' advisory groups – FRSAs receive input from actors and forums with interests in financial regulation, such as the financial services industry or the consumers of financial services. This input may concern general approaches to be pursued by FRSAs in a given field of financial regulation or the specific content of concrete regulatory outputs of the FRSAs' rulemaking process. FRSAs may – and very often are required to – consider such input in the course of their rulemaking procedures. Stakeholder accountability instruments thus also constitute a source of useful information that may be used by FRSAs to produce regulatory and supervisory outcomes that are 'responsive' to the needs of stakeholders.

[77] See e.g. M. Quintyn and M.W. Taylor, 'Robust Regulators and Their Political Masters: Independence and Accountability in Theory', supra note 65, p. 28.

[78] For example, in the US the SEC was subject to budget cuts related to, *inter alia*, its lack of performance in the supervision of Madoff. This was criticised by some commentators who pointed out at the potential negative consequences of those cuts on the ability of the supervisor to perform its duties – notably in light of the expanded responsibilities of SEC after the Dodd-Frank Act; see J.B. Stewart, 'As a Watchdog Starves, Wall Street Is Tossed a Bone', *The New York Times*, 15.07.2011 <www.nytimes.com/2011/07/16/business/budget-cuts-to-sec-reduce-its-effectiveness.html?pagewanted=all> accessed 27.10.2014.

Shortcomings in the design of the FRSAs' accountability may hinder from the onset their ability to think and act responsibly. For example, an accountability framework that enables governments to unduly interfere with the autonomy and independence of FRSAs – e.g. by controlling their decision-making processes so as to maximise political agendas – is more likely to lead to less responsive-and-responsible regulation than systems where FRSAs are accountable to political forums while maintaining, at the same time, their functional, institutional and operational independence from them. Likewise, as regards accountability towards stakeholders, the scope of responsive-and-responsible financial regulation is greater in accountability architectures that effectively enable and foster the symmetric participation of different categories of stakeholders in the activities of FRSAs than in those that give prevalence to input-provision by stakeholders who represent homogeneous sets of interests or only one side of the financial sphere; in the latter case the regulatory and supervisory outputs of FRSAs are more likely to reflect such asymmetric input, and, therefore be less representative of the variety of interests in the financial domain.

Second, the design of accountability instruments and the quality of accountability relationships has an impact on the willingness of FRSAs to act in a responsive-and-responsible manner. In this respect and, as referred above, one of the dimensions of accountability concerns hold-to-account decisions, that is, '... measures that result in the concerned FRSAs or their officials being subject to some forms of censuring, punishment, disciplining or, more generally, responsibility'. Holding FRSAs to account includes measures such as the removal of the heads of FRSAs from office for cause, budget cuts or freezes, judicial decisions that quash the decisions of FRSAs or that acknowledge their tort liability. An extreme form of holding FRSAs to account for their actions or omissions consists of their elimination.[79] The threats to the prestige, resources and, ultimately, very existence of FRSAs that these forms of accountability encompass may deter FRSAs and their staff from behaviours that dismiss the objectives of financial regulation and supervision, the interests of stakeholders and the impact of the financial system on society.

4. CONTENTS AND STRUCTURE OF THE BOOK

This book aims at providing both theoretical and practical contributions to the discussion about the relation between the accountability of financial regulators and the quality of financial regulation and supervision. Whereas the emphasis of

[79] This was for instance the case of the Office of Thrift Supervision (OTS) in the US – see section 313 of the Dodd-Frank Act. On the regulatory failures of the OTS see, *Wall Street and the Financial Crisis: Anatomy of a Financial Collapse, Majority And Minority Staff Report,* United States Senate, Permanent Subcommittee on Investigations, Committee on Homeland Security and Governmental Affairs, Washington, DC, 13.04.2011, pp. 161–242.

the book is to a large extent on accountability relationships and their underlying institutional mechanisms, it also addresses relevant exogenous variables with a potential impact on accountability, such as the prevailing intellectual assumptions and policy paradigms about the financial system and about the economy in the institutional framework where an FRSA carries out its duties – such assumptions and paradigms may influence the perceptions of accountors and accountees about their mutual expectations and therefore affect the content and utilisation of accountability. In different ways the chapters that make this volume relate to the dimensions of the concept of responsiveness-and-responsibility discussed in this chapter and, notably, to the question of whether, what and how accountability relationships and mechanisms foster responsiveness-and-responsibility in financial regulation, responding, at the same time, to the weaknesses of the pre-crisis regimes.

Part I of the book is composed of three chapters that address some key theoretical foundations of responsive-and-responsible financial regulation and supervision, namely accountability, independence and the prevailing economic theories in the institutional settings where FRSAs operate. It examines concepts that are central to the topics and analyses of Part II of the book.

The contributions of Part II of the book tackle specific aspects and institutions of the post-crisis architectures of financial regulation and supervision in the EU (chapters 5, 6 and 7), the US (chapters 8 and 9) and Canada (chapter 10). The rationale for this choice of jurisdictions is twofold. On the one side, the inclusion of the EU and the US in the analysis is motivated by the fact that these are among the jurisdictions where the financial crisis hit particularly hard and in which institutional responses to the pre-crisis failures have been most intense and comprehensive. On the other side, the coverage of Canada – a country with highly developed financial markets that escaped the financial crisis – is of particular relevance to assess whether and how accountability in financial regulation matters for ensuring financial stability.

The chapters of Part II primarily focus on post-crisis institutional developments – e.g. the European Stability Mechanism (ESM) and the European Securities and Markets Authority (ESMA) in the EU, and the Consumer Financial Protection Bureau (CFPB) in the US. However, attention is also paid to supervisory structures that existed before and got through the crisis – e.g. the Financial Industry Regulatory Authority (FINRA) in the US and the Office of the Superintendent of Financial Institutions (OSFI) in Canada; the analysis of the latter is useful to ascertain whether their post-crisis configurations respond to and are consistent with the complexities and challenges of responsive-and-responsible financial regulation in the aftermath of the global financial crisis.

As regards the reasons for the specific choices, Part II.1 (the EU) aims at giving a comprehensive overview of the EU framework by incorporating the main institutional developments at the EU level – the Eurozone mechanisms of the Banking Union on the one side, and the ESMA as one of the three European Supervisory Authorities in the financial field on the other. It also includes a chapter that relates to stakeholder accountability in the EU with the purpose of offering a view about how a specific accountability relationship – i.e. accountability towards stakeholders – operates across EU regulatory levels, institutions and bodies – including the European Supervisory Authorities in the financial field. Among the institutions of the complex US supervisory patchwork this book focuses on the CFPB and FINRA (Part II.2). With respect to the CFPB, its emphasis on consumer financial protection and its cross-sectorial reach make it a particularly interesting case study from a 'responsiveness' perspective. The choice of FINRA – originally a self-regulatory organisation – is based on its accountability singularities: FINRA has a public mandate and performs functions that are very similar in nature to those carried out by government agencies but it is however subject to a less stringent accountability scheme than the latter. The agency examined in Part II.3 – the OSFI – is the Canadian federal prudential regulator, and as referred above, the analysis of its effectiveness and accountability is important to understand the role of institutional aspects of financial regulation in the relative stability of Canada during the global financial crisis.

Overall, these chapters also aim at reflecting diversity of regulatory and supervisory functions – prudential, conduct of business and resolution – as well as of regulated sectors – banking, insurance and securities.

In considering the issues of responsiveness, responsibility, accountability and governance, this book has sought to encompass the idea that the challenges posed by financial regulation and supervision in global financial markets have a multidimensional nature that can only be understood through and require interdisciplinary analyses. This is reflected in the background of the different contributors, who are economists, lawyers, political scientists and sociologists from both academia and practice.

The structure of the book is as follows:

Part I – The contribution of accountability, independence and economic theory to responsive-and-responsible financial regulation – is composed of chapters 2, 3 and 4.

Rosa María Lastra (chapter 2) revisits the theoretical framework concerning supervisory accountability in light of the financial crisis experience. The chapter addresses the notion of accountability – from both legal and economic perspectives – as well as its main components, scope and dimensions. The author also analyses the relationships between accountability and the concepts of legitimacy, transparency and independence, which constitute essential elements in the contemporary policy and academic debates and discussions about the shaping of mechanisms of accountability applicable to both monetary and supervisory authorities. On the normative side, the author proposes a move towards a new accountability policy paradigm that is more inclusive of the interests of civil society stakeholders and more responsive to the global nature of the financial markets.

In chapter 3, Donato Masciandaro addresses one of the main elements in the design of central bank's governance: independence. The author uses a principal-agent model to build a political economy theoretical framework aimed at explaining the evolution of central bank independence. This framework is based on the analysis of two variables, namely the preferences of citizens on the one hand, and the determinants of the behaviour of the policy-makers in charge of the central bank's governance design on the other. The author applies such framework to the analysis of central bank independence before and after the financial meltdown. The chapter shows that the crisis has brought about a shift in the central bank design in several jurisdictions, from independent monetary specialisation and supervisory neglect to a greater allocation of financial supervisory functions to central banks; in the view of the author this trend poses several risks – e.g. political and banking capture – that should be carefully assessed.

Xosé Carlos Arias and Antón Costas (chapter 4) examine the reasons behind and the effects of the pre-crisis overarching and pervasive influence of two economic hypotheses, namely the Efficient Market Hypothesis (EMH) and the Rational Expectations Hypothesis (REH). These scholarly theories expanded their influence far beyond academia, reaching and shaping to a large degree economic thinking and policy-making in the field of financial services as well as financial market's design, from the early 1980s till the 2008 financial meltdown. The authors show that central banks and financial supervisors in several countries were also seduced by the EMH and the REH and this was reflected in light touch regulatory policies that encompassed the ideas of market discipline and self-regulation by the financial industry; this, in turn, contributed to the emergence and development of financial products, structures, practices and behaviours that were among the causes of the financial crash. The authors argue that despite the fact that the 2008 collapse has put into question the validity of the assumptions behind the EMH – and abridged the influence of the latter on policy making and regulatory policies – it is not yet possible to identify a change of paradigm but rather a 'theoretical limbo' where the EMH and the REH still hold certain influence.

Part II – Post-crisis architectures of financial regulation in the European Union, the United States of America and Canada: accountability and responsiveness-and-responsibility – is made of three subparts: II.1, II.2, and II.3.

Part II.1 – The European Union – consists of chapters 5, 6 and 7.

The contribution of Nicholas Dorn (chapter 5) focuses primarily on the post-crisis EU financial markets governance with special emphasis on the Eurozone mechanisms of Banking Union – i.e. the European Stability Mechanism (ESM), the Single Supervisory Mechanism (SSM) and the Single Resolution Mechanism (SRM) – their scope and internal governance, as well as their impact on the behaviour of market conduct regulators. The author defines the post-crisis EU financial markets regulatory governance infrastructure as a 'regulatory cascade', a threefold process in which influence flows from (1) the ESM (an intergovernmental bank resolution mechanism governed by finance ministers, to (2) through the SSM (a eurozone prudential regulator led by ECB staff and national financial regulators), and on to (3) market conduct regulators, whose behaviour may be influenced by the views and positions of the two other actors in the cascade. When it comes to the question of the repercussions of the 'governance cascade' in terms of democratic legitimacy the author contends that some aspects of this new governance structure can be considered as '*ambiguous vis-à-vis* democracy': on the one side, the role of the European Parliament in the new architecture seems to be diluted; there is however, on the other side, scope for national parliaments' activism at the top of the cascade – through their political leverage with regard to finance ministers at the ESM. The chapter concludes with some reflections as regards the implications of the 'regulatory cascade' for European integration.

The European Securities and Markets Authority (ESMA) is one of the three European Supervisory Authorities in the financial field created in the year 2010 as part of the post-crisis financial overhaul in the EU. The contribution of Carmine Di Noia and Matteo Gargantini (chapter 6) discusses the structure, regulatory and supervisory powers, functions and accountability of the ESMA. In their analysis of the governance and of the regulatory and supervisory powers of the ESMA, the authors pay particular attention to the features, role, organisation and accountability of the Securities and Markets Stakeholder Group (SMSG). This body – which introduces innovations with respect to the modes of stakeholder engagement of the previous regime – gives stakeholders from different categories direct representation in the ESMA, institutionalising their participation in the latter's regulatory procedures. The authors characterise the SMSG as a mechanism of 'horizontal accountability' of the ESMA and discuss its potential implications in terms of accountability, legitimacy and effective rulemaking. The chapter also considers the regulatory independence of the ESMA in light of the case law of the Court of Justice of the European Union and, notably, the *Meroni* decision, whose validity has recently been confirmed by the Court in its decision on the case C-270/12, which concerned the powers of the ESMA to take *ad hoc* measures banning short selling in certain cases. The chapter concludes with some recommendations on how to shape the ESMA's powers and governance so as to foster regulatory and supervisory efficiency.

In chapter 7, Guillaume Prache provides an insightful account of the struggles of financial services users and, more generally, non-financial industry stakeholders to make their voice heard in financial services policy-making processes in the EU. The author starts by highlighting and analysing some post-crisis developments that have brought about greater non-financial industry stakeholder engagement and visibility in the creation of financial sector rules in the EU. First, representatives of financial services users have become more active, organised and coordinated; this is reflected in, *inter alia*, the emergence of new associations such as Better Finance and Finance Watch that gather the resources and knowledge of several civil society organisations and which have become very active actors in EU financial services policy-making. Second, some post-crisis legal developments have enhanced the scope and degree of institutionalisation of non-financial industry stakeholder involvement in financial services regulatory processes – e.g. the creation of the Stakeholder Groups of the European Supervisory Authorities in the financial field. The author argues that despite these improvements there remain important asymmetries between the resources and access to EU institutions of non-financial industry stakeholders on the one hand, and of financial industry-stakeholders on the other hand, with the result that the power, influence and engagement of the latter in financial services policy design is substantially greater than that of the former. The last part of the chapter recommends changes in the legal and institutional settings concerning civil society engagement in financial services policy-making as a means to improve the protection of financial services users in the EU.

Part II.2 – The United States of America – comprises chapters 8 and 9.

One of the main institutional responses to the financial crisis in the US consisted of the creation of the Consumer Financial Protection Bureau (CFPB), an independent regulatory agency vested with *inter alia* regulatory and supervisory powers with regard to consumer financial protection. David S. Bieri (chapter 8) analyses the remit, scope, regulatory governance and accountability of the CFPB within the wider context of both the US and global post-crisis regulatory frameworks. In the view of the author 'The creation of the CFPB marks perhaps the most significant change to the post-crisis regulatory institutional landscape in the United States'. On the one side, the CFPB encompasses a shift of policy focus from bank stability towards a wider concept of financial stability that acknowledges the increasing financialisation of household's decision-making.

On the other side, the establishment of the CFPB embodies a departure from the model of de-centralised agencies in the field of financial regulation and supervision, and represents a more holistic institutional approach that gathers within a single structure both micro-prudential and macro-prudential objectives with a view to enhancing overall financial stability. In addition, the chapter claims that, from an accountability perspective, the relative shielding of the CFPB from political processes brings the US system of financial regulation and supervision into a space of greater independence.

In the US, important aspects of the securities markets are regulated and supervised by the Financial Industry Regulatory Authority (FINRA), a non-governmental, not-for-profit corporation incorporated in Delaware and relatively independent from the industry and the government. Hester Peirce (chapter 9) examines the history and responsibilities of FINRA as well as the accountability relationships under which it operates. The author shows that, despite the fact that FINRA is entrusted with a government mandate and vested with regulatory and supervisory powers and tools which are very similar in nature and scope to those of government agencies in the securities field – such as the Securities and Exchange Commission (SEC) – its legal status has enabled it to avoid being subject to the same accountability structures as the latter. As a result, FINRA functions under a much less stricter accountability regime where the SEC plays a key role as an external account-principal. The author questions the validity of such an accountability-independence model, especially in light of the regulatory aspirations of FINRA, which would broaden even more its regulatory and supervisory remit. The chapter closes with some suggestions as regards the role that FINRA should play in the regulation of the US securities markets.

Part II.3 – Canada – consists of chapter 10, in which Ian Roberge and Dona M. Dunea address the effectiveness and the accountability of the Office of the Superintendent of Financial Institutions (OSFI) – the Canadian prudential financial regulator. The chapter starts with the definition and examination of two central concepts in the analysis of the financial sector regulators' performance, namely effectiveness and accountability. With regard to effectiveness, the authors focus on the difficulties of measuring the impact of regulators on market outcomes. When it comes to accountability, the chapter devotes special attention to the relationships and tensions between opacity and transparency in financial regulation, two elements which in the view of the authors '... lie on a continuum, where neither of the extreme is particularly useful'. Concerning the specific analysis of the OSFI, the contribution challenges the widespread contentions about the efficiency of the Canadian prudential regulator and suggests that the resilience of the Canadian financial system during the global financial crisis was the result of a series of factors that include certain aspects of – but are not limited to – the performance of the prudential regulator. In addition, the authors show that the OSFI operates under relatively weak transparency conditions, which, in the opinion of the regulator contribute to its performance and to public confidence. The authors question OSFI's approach arguing that OSFI's opacity makes it difficult to assess its performance and ultimately hinders the normal functioning of the markets. On the policy side, the authors suggest the need for greater public input into OSFI's regulatory processes as well as for a reform of the Canadian financial regulation/supervision infrastructure.

PART I

THE CONTRIBUTION OF ACCOUNTABILITY, INDEPENDENCE AND ECONOMIC THEORY TO RESPONSIVE-AND-RESPONSIBLE FINANCIAL REGULATION

FINANCIAL INSTITUTIONS AND ACCOUNTABILITY MECHANISMS

Rosa María LASTRA

1. INTRODUCTION

The advent of banking union in the EU with the granting of supervisory powers to the ECB, the increased attention given by politicians, legislators and regulators to issues of institutional supervisory design in the US, UK and EU, and the revamping of the financial stability mandate of central banks (with the addition of new macro prudential supervisory powers) are some of the developments that in the aftermath of the financial crisis have brought the issue of accountability back to the fore of legal and economic policy debate.[1]

This paper tries to revisit the theoretical framework for supervisory accountability, an issue which I have amply discussed in earlier writings,[2] in particular in connection with the independence of central banks and other authorities in the discharge of prudential supervision.

The author would like to thank Andrea Miglionico for excellent research assistance.

1 On this discussion see R.M. LASTRA, 'Accountability and Governance–Banking Union Proposals' (2012) Duisenberg School of Finance, Policy Paper No. 30 <www.dsf.nl/home/research/publications> accessed 17.09.2014.

2 See R.M. LASTRA and F. AMTENBRINK, 'Securing Democratic Accountability of Financial Regulatory Agencies – A Theoretical framework' in R.V. DE MULDER (ed.) *Mitigating Risk in the Context of Safety and Security. How Relevant is a Rational Approach?*, Erasmus School of Law & Research School for Safety and Security OMV, Rotterdam 2008, pp. 115–132; R.M. LASTRA, 'Regulating European Securities Markets: Beyond the Lamfalussy Report' in M. ANDENAS and Y AVREGINOS (eds.), *Financial Markets in Europe: Towards a Single Regulator?*, Kluwer Law International, London, The Hague, New York 2003, pp. 211–222; R.M. LASTRA and H. SHAMS, 'Public Accountability in the Financial Sector' in E. FERRAN and C.A.E. GOODHART (eds.), *Regulating Financial Services and Markets in the Twenty First Century*, Hart Publishing, Oxford 2001, pp. 165–188. See also chapters 2, 7 and 11 of R.M. LASTRA, *Legal Foundations of International Monetary Stability*, forthcoming 2nd ed., Oxford University Press, Oxford 2014, and chapter 1 of R.M. LASTRA, *Central Banking and Banking Regulation*, Financial Markets Group, London School of Economics, London, September 1996.

As such, the paper does not intend to dwell on the intricate design of the supervisory structure of the single market in the EU (with the ESAs)[3] nor on the three institutional pillars of European Banking Union,[4] but rather it aims to revisit the theory that surrounds the understanding of these issues.

Any discussion about accountability presupposes the existence of power. Though sovereignty – the organising principle of politics in the Western World since the Renaissance – remains a fundamental principle for allocating power, a new principle based on global governance is becoming increasingly relevant in the last decades. Indeed, we have witnessed how the role of the State and the function of governance have been refined and redefined in recent years. In the current process of increasing globalisation, the state is finding it increasingly difficult to enforce its laws against global actors such as multinational corporations and criminal organisations; tax laws and the opportunities that emerge for regulatory arbitrage or forum-jurisdiction shopping are a case in point.[5] Resolving conflicts requires new mechanisms beyond the state's judicial machinery, hence the crescent popularity of arbitration as an alternative dispute resolution mechanism. Furthermore, the dichotomy between global markets and national institutions has influenced the quest for new mechanisms in the resolution of international financial disputes and conflicts. Even in the area of policing, the state is enlisting the private sector in the fight against crime. Money laundering control systems and

---

3 See J. De Larosière, 'The High-Level Group on Financial Supervision in the EU Report', Brussels, February 2009, pp. 47–48. The major change was the idea of creating a European System of Financial Supervision (ESFS), an integrated network of national and EU supervisors which comprises three European supervisory authorities (ESAs): European Securities and Markets Authority (ESMA), European Banking Authority (EBA) and European Insurance and Occupational Pensions Authority (EIOPA). Principally, the ESAs play the role to coordinate the application of supervisory standards and guarantee strong cooperation between the national supervisors.

4 See European Commission, Communication from the Commission to the European Parliament and the Council: A Roadmap towards a Banking Union, COM (2012) 510 Final, (September 2012) <http://eur-lex.europa.eu/LexUriServ/LexUriServ.do?uri=CELEX:52012DC0510:EN:NOT> accessed 17.09.2014. The design of EU Banking Union has determined a transfer to the European level of the regulatory and institutional framework for safeguarding the robustness and stability of the banking sector. In particular, the EU Banking Union aims to introduce a common platform for regulation of (a) supervision; (b) resolution mechanisms; and, (c) deposit insurance. From an academic view see D. Gros and D. Schoenmaker, 'European Deposit and Resolution in the Banking Union' (2014) 52 *Journal of Common Market Studies* 529; R.M. Lastra, B. Krauskopf, C. Gortsos and R. Smits, 'European Banking Union', Mocomila report to the ILA meeting in Washington DC, April 2014 <www.ila-hq.org/en/committees/index.cfm/cid/22> accessed 17.09.2014; E. Ferran, 'European Banking Union: Imperfect But It Can Work' (2014) University of Cambridge Faculty of Law, Legal Studies Research Paper Series No. 30, p. 17; R.M. Lastra, 'Banking Union and Single Market: Conflict or Companionship?' (2013) 36 *Fordham International Law Journal* 1190; C. Randell, 'European Banking Union and Bank Resolution' (2013) 7 *Law and Financial Markets Review* 30; E. Ferran and V. Babis, 'The European Single Supervisory Mechanism' (2013) 13 *Journal of Corporate Law Studies* 255.

5 See P.G. Cerny, 'What Next for the State' in E. Kofman and G. Youngs (eds.), *Globalization: Theory and Practice*, Pinter, London 1996, p. 126.

the reporting duties they impose on financial institutions are an obvious example of this shift towards private policing and of the need for improved international coordination. Today, the State is neither the sole nor the sufficient holder of the governance function in the society. Power is now diffused. It is exercised by a variety of actors including international organisations, such as the WTO, the IMF and the World Bank, multinational corporations and the civil society.[6]

The question of accountability emerges whenever the question of good governance is examined.[7] With respect to financial markets as holders of power, several loci of accountability may be identified: regulators, market participants, and others, such as auditors.[8] The crisis has also shown that there are many stakeholders that have an interest in the proper functioning of financial institutions (including taxpayers and pensioners).

Though many commentators use the terms interchangeably, there is a significant conceptual difference between supervision and regulation. Regulation is the establishment of rules, while supervision refers to monitoring and enforcement.[9]

Regulation thus refers to the process of rule-making and includes not only legislative acts but also statutory instruments issued by the competent authorities nationally and supra-nationally as well as rules issued by self-regulatory organisations, private bodies and international rules (typically 'soft law' standards).[10] At an

---

6 See e.g. M.K. Brunnermeier, A. Crockett, C. Goodhart, A. Persaud, and H.S. Shin (eds.), *The Fundamental Principles of Financial Regulation*, eleventh Geneva Report on the World Economy, International Center for Monetary and Banking Studies, ICMB, and Centre for Economic Policy Research, CEPR, Geneva 2009, 'Financial Reform – A Framework for Financial Stability', Financial Reform Working Group, G30 ('Volcker's Report'), The Group of Thirty, Washington 2009 <www.group30.org/publications.shtml> accessed 18.09.2014.

7 As discussed in a paper I wrote with Heba Shams, supra note 2, 'if we understand governance as the exercise of power in the management of resources, this function becomes centralised or fragmented inasmuch as the decisions of production, distribution or redistribution are taken by central power or by diffused loci of power. Following the end of the cold war and the spread of neo-liberal economic thinking, the market has become the primary mechanism for the allocation of resources. As a result, the participants in the market have become holders of power and agents of governance. Financial markets share in this power cannot be exaggerated in view of their role in the allocation of the most versatile, mobile and indispensable element of production; namely, capital'.

8 See C Goodhart, 'An Incentive Structure of Financial Regulation' in C. Goodhart (ed.), *The Emerging Framework of Financial Regulation*, Central Banking Publications, London 1998, p. 96.

9 See J. Benjamin, P. Bowden and D. Rouch, 'Law and regulation for global financial markets: markets as rule-makers – enforcement, dispute resolution and risk' (2008) 2 *Law and Financial Markets Review* 321, 322–323; see also J. Benjamin and D. Rouch, 'The international financial markets as a source of global law: the privatisation of rule-making?' (2008) 2 *Law and Financial Markets Review* 78, 82–83.

10 Regulation, defined as set of rules and principles governing a collective organisation, represents the challenge for financial stability and the investor protection system. See J. Black, 'Critical Reflections on Regulation' (2002) 27 *Australian Journal of Legal Philosophy* 1 21–25.

international level, rules that emanate from international organisations suffer from the 'eternal' problem of international law: its effective enforcement. The distinct force and effect of rules – national, regional, international – is important in order to understand the various sources of financial law and regulation and their accountability mechanisms.

Rather than adopting a 'monolithic' approach to the notion of supervision, it is helpful to think about supervision in terms of the functions it involves for the supervisory authorities, from the beginning of the business life of a supervised entity (entry into the market through a licence or authorisation) to its end, which in banking is less straightforward than in other businesses, since bank failures have relevant public policy implications. Supervision in a broad sense can be understood as a process with four stages or phases: (1) licensing, authorisation or chartering (entry into the business), (2) supervision *stricto sensu*, (3) sanctioning or imposition of penalties in the case of non-compliance with the law, fraud, bad management or other types of wrongdoing, and (4) crisis management, which comprises *inter alia* lender of last resort, deposit insurance, resolution and bank insolvency proceedings.[11] Supervision in a narrow sense (i.e., supervision *stricto sensu*) refers to the oversight of financial firms' behaviour, in particular risk monitoring and risk control. Supervision is typically exercised at the national level, though with the advent of Banking Union in Europe, supervision for Eurozone banks will be largely centralized at the ECB level. Internationally, the International Monetary Fund should continue enhance its surveillance of Members' financial sector policies.

The paper first discusses the concepts of accountability, legitimacy and transparency. It then considers the notions of accountability favoured by lawyers (political, institutional, process, focus on inputs) and by economists (technical, performance related, focus on outputs). Following a brief analysis of monetary

---

11 See R.M. Lastra, *International Financial and Monetary Law* (forthcoming 2nd ed. of *Legal Foundations of International Monetary Stability*, to be published by Oxford University Press, Oxford 2015), chapter 3. Because supervision monitors the degree to which a bank or financial institution abides by the rules, there is a connection between the two concepts. The very process of supervision is subject to regulation. The inter-action between supervision and regulation is evidenced in each supervisory stage. For instance, with regard to licensing, the law determines the requirements that a bank needs to fulfil in order to be granted a licence (minimum capital, management competence and integrity, etc.). The adequacy of capital – a key element that supervisors assess to determine the health of a financial institution – is described in detailed rules. Penalties for wrong doing – civil or criminal – are clearly spelt out in the law. In the crisis management stage, most of the tools available to the supervisory authorities are governed by law; this is the case with deposit insurance and with the bankruptcy procedures that apply in the case of liquidation. However, banking law extends beyond the supervisory process and deals with other issues, such as the legal form of the corporation and the bank-customer relationship.

independence versus supervisory independence, the paper finishes with some concluding observations.

2. ACCOUNTABILITY, LEGITIMACY AND TRANSPARENCY

The question of legitimacy pre-exists and is a pre-requisite of accountability.[12] Legitimacy has two aspects: a formal, normative one which refers to legality of the political system and a societal or empirical one, which is determined by the acceptance of or loyalty to the system.[13] In the European Union, the formal legitimacy of the integration process rested initially on the Member States' ratification of the foundational Treaties (and subsequent amendments), while its social legitimacy – its 'popular appeal' – rested upon the benefits in terms of peace and welfare that it promised to deliver to its citizens.[14] The need to combine efficiency (to avoid a cumbersome and unduly complicated decision-making process and excessive bureaucracy) with democratic legitimacy is fundamental for the future of Europe. And since democracy is considered the sole legitimate form of government in the EU, legitimacy equates to democratic legitimacy. The issue of legitimacy is also key in the design of international financial institutions and in the exercise of their powers (rule-making and others).[15]

The creation of a supervisory agency, a central bank or any other type of governmental or inter-governmental entity must be the fruit of a democratic act (an act of the legislator, a constitutional decision or a treaty provision). This first source of legitimisation is essential in a democratic society. It is then in the continuing life of that entity (in particular when such entity is 'independent') that accountability becomes necessary: the process of bringing back (by giving

---

12 See C. Zilioli, 'Accountability and Independence: Irreconcilable Values or Complementary Instruments for Democracy? The Specific Case of the European Central Bank' in G. Vandersanden and others (eds.) *Mélanges en Hommage à Jean-Victor Louis*, ULB, Brussels 2003, p. 403. Zilioli further points out that 'the independent government must be established and the power transferred to it, through a legal act adopted, in accordance with the constitutional framework of the State, by the democratically elected representatives of the people'.

13 See A. Verhoeven, *The European Union in Search of a Democratic and Constitutional Theory*, Kluwer Law International, The Hague 2002, pp. 10–11.

14 Ibid., pp. 63–65.

15 See J. Black, 'Constructing and contesting legitimacy and accountability in polycentric regulatory regimes' (2008) 2 *Regulation & Governance* 137, 149–152. See also See J. Black, 'Legitimacy and the Competition for Regulatory Share' (2009) *LSE Law, Society and Economy Working Paper* No. 14, pp. 22–25. In particular, the author argues that in the competition for regulatory share 'legitimacy should be conceptualized not as an attribute or a resource, but as an endowment', specifically 'legitimacy means social credibility and acceptability, being pragmatically based, morally based and cognitively based'.

account, explaining, justifying or taking measures of amendment or redress) that entity to the procedures and processes of a democratic society.

Accountability[16] can be defined as an obligation owed by one person (the accountable) to another (the accountee)[17] according to which the former must give account of, explain and justify his actions or decisions against criteria of some kind,[18] and take responsibility for any fault or damage.

Four elements are at the core of any understanding of accountability:

- A holder of power (the 'accountable'). Lord Acton's dictum remains true: power corrupts, absolute power corrupts absolutely. Hence, the need for accountability whenever power is exercised. Power cannot be divorced from responsibility.
- An authority to whom accountability is owed (the 'accountee'). Who guards the guardians? Accountability as an obligation must be owed to another party. The latter becomes by virtue of this obligation in a position of authority *vis-à-vis* the accountable. There are various types of accountability according to the authority that exacts it. We speak of judicial accountability (or accountability to the judiciary) when courts are the authority that enforce accountability. An obvious example is the judicial review of administrative actions or decisions. When parliament is the accountee we speak of parliamentary accountability (or accountability to parliament). We speak of accountability to the public, to refer to the general public as the accountee.
- The content of the obligation. The accountable, the holder of power, is under an obligation: (1) to give an account of his decisions or actions, (2) to explain and justify the decision or the course of action taken and, (3) where error is proved or harm inflicted, to own the responsibility and take appropriate measures of amendment or redress. While there is no accountability without a duty to give account and explain, the forms of amends or redress vary from one type of accountability to another. With regard to the content of the obligation, a distinction is often made between 'explanatory accountability' where the obligation is to answer questions, to give account of action, and 'amendatory accountability' where there is an obligation to make amends and grant redress. Amendatory accountability presupposes failure, fault, harm, deviation from a given target. A distinction is also often drawn between ex

16 I have dealt with the concept of accountability in previous writings. See e.g. R.M. Lastra, 'How Much Accountability for Central Banks and Supervisors?' (2001) 12 *Central Banking* 69 and the article I co-wrote with Ms. Heba Shams on 'Public Accountability in the Financial Sector', supra note 2. See also R.M. Lastra and F. Amtenbrink, 'Securing Democratic Accountability of Financial Regulatory Agencies – A Theoretical framework', supra note 2.

17 This usage is borrowed from D. Oliver, 'Law, Politics and Public Accountability: The Search for a New Equilibrium' (1994) *Public Law* 238, 248.

18 Ibid., 246.

ante and ex post accountability. Accountability can either be exercised before/during the process of taking the decision/action, or after the decision/action has been taken.[19]

- Criteria of assessment. Any form of accountability presupposes that there are objectives or standards according to which an action or decision might be assessed. In other words, accountability implies an obligation to comply with certain standards in the exercise of power or to achieve specific goals. The more complex the activity, the more difficult it is to establish clear standards of conduct and specific outcomes. In which case accountability becomes ever more evasive. The more specific the goals and standards the more effective the accountability. This might induce the 'accountees' to resort to economic or other measurable criteria of performance (hence the term 'performance accountability'). Performance accountability is facilitated when:
  (1) there is one goal, rather than multiple goals;
  (2) when that goal is narrowly defined rather than formulated in broad terms;
  (3) if there are multiple goals, a clear and unambiguous ranking is better than no ranking at all.

  The absence of explicit statutory objectives hinders performance accountability.[20]

3. POLITICAL AND TECHNICAL ACCOUNTABILITY

Lawyers and economists tend to give emphasis to different issues when trying to articulate accountability. Lawyers emphasise the political dimension of accountability, i.e., the placing of the institution within the existing system of checks and balances, in relation to the three branches of the State – legislative,

[19] For instance, the appointment procedures of central bank officials, when such procedures require parliamentary approval, and the parliamentary debate of inflation targets (if such a parliamentary debate is required) can be regarded as ways of exercising accountability *ex ante* or through scrutiny. The reporting requirements and the appearances of the central bank chairman or governor in front of parliamentary committees are ways of exercising accountability through control or *ex post*.

[20] The more complex the activity the more difficult it is to identify specific goals and standards and the more evasive accountability becomes. Central bank laws often contain a variety of goals, with price stability ranked as the primary objective in recent years. The mandate of the Federal Reserve System encompasses a variety of objectives with no explicit ranking: stability and growth of the economy, maximum employment, stable prices and the soundness of the financial and payment systems. This lack of explicitly defined priorities means that the Fed can be frequently challenged on its performance accountability when its decisions do not satisfy certain sectors of the public or factions in Congress. A central bank that can choose among potentially conflicting targets must be held accountable for choosing the wrong target or the wrong mix of targets. See H.E. Jackson and E.L. Symons, *Regulation of Financial Institutions* (West Group, St. Paul, Minn.1999, pp. 655–62 and 751–55.

executive and judiciary (the question of who regulates the regulators or who guards the guardians). This political dimension is clearly related to the democratic legitimacy. Accountability – from a legal perspective – should be 'diversified' to include parliamentary accountability as well as judicial review of the agency's acts and decisions, and a degree of co-operation with the executive to ensure consistent overall policy making.[21] In a national context, parliament remains sovereign in its legislative decisions, and one statute proclaiming the independence of an agency can always be removed by another one revoking it. Parliamentary accountability should be exercised through a variety of procedures and mechanisms, including annual reports and appearances in front of parliament of public officials on a regular basis, and also in the case of an emergency situation. Judicial review of the agency's actions and decisions (conducted by an independent and depoliticised judiciary) is essential to prevent and control the arbitrary and unreasonable exercise of discretionary powers. This is a fundamental element of the rule of law. The discretion of public officials should never be unfettered but subject to legal control. Process accountability is fundamental from a legal perspective.

Economists, while accepting the 'institutional' articulation of accountability that I just described, tend to put the emphasis on performance accountability on the one hand (output accountability)[22] and on disclosure on the other. Performance control (the question of how accountability is to be achieved) is concerned with the efficiency of an independent institution and, as I have already pointed out, it is conditional upon the objectives and targets imposed upon the central bank.[23] Performance accountability has a 'technical' rather than a 'political' character.[24] Disclosure (reporting requirements) can be construed as a 'market-based form of accountability', traditionally favoured in Anglo-Saxon countries.

---

21 In terms of accountability, a clear division of responsibilities was set out in the 'Memorandum of Understanding', which allocated the different functions among the UK financial authorities (HM Treasury, the Bank of England and the former Financial Services Authority). See HM Treasury, Bank of England and Financial Services Authority, 'Memorandum of Understanding for Financial Stability', March 2006. In particular, it is made clear that the Treasury is responsible for the entire financial regulation and legislation, the Bank for financial stability maintenance (stability of the monetary system, reducing the systemic risk, monitoring of the system as whole) and the FSA for the supervision of financial markets.

22 See e.g., S. Fischer, 'Modern Central Banking' in F. Capie and others (eds.) *The Future of Central Banking: The Tercentenary Symposium of the Bank of England*, Cambridge University Press, Cambridge 1994.

23 Performance accountability requires that there are objectives or standards (criteria of assessment) according to which an action or decision might be assessed. See L. Garicano and R.M. Lastra, 'Towards a new Architecture for Financial Stability: Seven Principles', infra note 31, 616.

24 M. Draghi, President of the European Central Bank, Speech before the Global Investment Conference, London, 26.07.2012 <https://www.ecb.europa.eu/press/key/date/2012/html/sp120726.en.html> accessed 18.09.2014.

Any recent discussion of accountability often includes a reference to transparency and vice versa. This poses the question of the relationship between the two concepts. Accountability is an obligation to give account of, explain and justify one's actions, while transparency is the degree to which information on such actions is available. The provision of information is clearly an element of accountability.[25] But accountability is not merely about giving information. It must involve defending the action, policy or decision for which the accountable is being held to account. The provision of information (transparency) is hardly ever a neutral account of what happened or of what is happening; hence, the need for an explanation or justification of the agency's actions or decisions (i.e., accountability).

The provision of information in the context of accountability, whether in an ex ante investigation or an ex post requirement of disclosure, facilitates transparency. On the other hand, a transparent economic and political environment enhances the effectiveness of accountability.[26] The two concepts are therefore mutually enforcing, and they both share the provision of information as a common requirement.

4. MONETARY AND SUPERVISORY INDEPENDENCE AND ACCOUNTABILITY

In recent decades, an abundant literature has emerged on the issue of central bank independence, and corresponding accountability.[27] By analogy with this literature, increasing attention is now given to the notion of 'supervisory independence'.[28] Though there are similarities in the analysis, there are important differences as well. To begin, the relative simplicity of 'monetary policy independence' contrasts with the complexity of 'supervisory independence'.[29] The one goal, one instrument, one agency of the former (the goal price stability,

---

25 Transparency is a complement of accountability. It has to do with the availability and relevance of information and with the time framework in which such information is made available. Providing information (transparency) is not sufficient; defending and explaining actions or decision is also necessary. See R.M. Lastra and H. Shams, 'Public Accountability in the Financial Sector', supra note 2, p. 172.

26 See A. Prat, 'The Wrong Kind of Transparency' (2005) 95 *The American Economic Review* 862.

27 Independence and accountability can be seen as opposite sides of a continuum. See R.M. Lastra, 'Accountability and Governance-Banking Union Proposals', supra note 1, p. 9.

28 The issue has also been explored by Marc Quintyn and Michael Taylor of the International Monetary Fund in a paper on 'Regulatory and Supervisory Independence and Financial Stability' published by CESifo Economic Studies, Vol. 49, 2/2003, pp. 259–294 <www.cesifoeconomicstudies.de/> accessed 18.09.2014.

29 See N. Veron, 'Europe's Single Supervisory Mechanism and the Long Journey Towards Banking Union', (2012) Bruegel Policy Contribution No. 2012/16, L. Garicano and R.M. Lastra, 'Towards a new Architecture for Financial Stability: Seven Principles', infra note 31 and R.M. Lastra, *International Financial and Monetary Law*, supra note 11, chapters 2, 3 and 10.

the instrument monetary policy and the agency the independent central bank) contrasts with the several goals, several instruments and, often several agencies of the latter (the goals: financial stability, investor protection, conduct of business and others; the instruments: licensing requirements, prudential supervision, financial stability reviews, lender of last resort operations and others; the agencies: the central bank, the ministry of finance or treasury, the supervisory agency or agencies).

As discussed in the paper I wrote with Luis Garicano:

> 'Performance accountability requires that there are objectives or standards (criteria of assessment) according to which an action or decision might be assessed. The extent to which a particular type of accountability may be preferred can be a function of the type of supervision that is at stake.[30] In the case of supervision, input or process monitoring should be preferred, because as discussed above, performance or outputs on the supervisory activity are hard to measure. The fact that inputs, rather than output monitoring should be chosen also suggests that providing a monetary authority (with a clear performance objective) with independence is not the same as providing independence to a supervisor: if delegation and output measurement cannot be used, then independence must be more restricted with regard to financial supervision than with regard to monetary policy'.[31]

While central bank accountability with regard to monetary policy is typically 'explanatory' (unless the law of the central bank is amended or the governor is removed from office, there is very little room for granting redress with regard to monetary policy decisions), the accountability of the central bank or the supervisory agency in the field of prudential supervision and regulation is some times 'explanatory' and some times 'amendatory'. The liability of financial market supervisors is under discussion in several EU Member States. Several legal scholars have recently explored the issue of (state) liability for loss caused by the inadequate supervision of banks,[32] in the context of the damages action against the Bank of England for the failure of Bank of Credit and Commerce

30 See C. Prendergast, 'The Tenuous Trade-Off between Risk and Incentives' (2002) 110 *Journal of Political Economy*,1071.

31 See L. Garicano and R.M. Lastra, 'Towards a new Architecture for Financial Stability: Seven Principles' (2010) 13 *Journal of International Economic Law* 597, 616.

32 See M. Andenas, 'Liability for supervisors and depositors' rights: the BCCI and the Bank of England in the House of Lords' (2001) 22 *The Company Lawyer* 226; see also M. Andenas and D. Fairgrieve, 'To Supervise or to Compensate? A Comparative Study of State Liability for Negligent Banking Supervision' in M. Andenas and D. Fairgrieve (eds.), *Judicial Review in International Perspective*, Kluwer Law International, The Hague 2000, pp. 333–360.

International (BCCI).[33] The plaintiffs claimed, *inter alia*, that the Bank of England was liable in damages for breach of its supervisory obligations under EU law.

Charles Goodhart[34] points out that providing accountability and transparency for banking supervisors is particularly difficult, since the information that they get is frequently confidential and since 'success' is often measured by the absence of financial failures. The recent financial crisis provides ample evidence about the difficult task supervisors have at hand.

It is important to articulate proper mechanisms of accountability. Since 1992 I have advocated the need for 'accountable independence'.[35] However, given the concerns that arise with regard to the democratic legitimacy and accountability of independent central banks in the conduct of monetary policy responsibilities, it is best to be cautious about granting 'too much' independence to the supervisory authorities. There is a culture of distrust for politicians ingrained in many democratic societies these days that is not healthy for the future of democracy. There is an inherent cynicism that surrounds politicians of all colours. I do not share that cynicism. Though I think that game theory, public choice theory and other theories provide an explanation for the electoral behaviour and incentives of politicians and bureaucrats, I do not necessarily share the overall conclusions that are often reached using such theories. I still believe that there are many politicians that go into office with higher aspirations than to seek re-election or to maximise their own personal benefit and prestige. Indeed, in a democratic community, the checks and balances that are provided by the rule of law and the independence of the judiciary are the framework that many politicians have in mind when they go into office, specially high office. It is important to revitalise the office of the President or Head of State, of the Prime Minister or Head of Government, of the Ministers and Secretaries whose goal is not just to satisfy their hunger for power, but often to serve their country/countries to the best of their abilities.

5. CONCLUDING OBSERVATIONS

I would like to end this paper with a reflection about the framework for legitimacy and accountability in the context of EU financial supervision. The following paragraph extracted from Amaryllis Verhoeven's treatise on *The European Union*

---

[33] See *Three Rivers District Council v. Governor and Company of the Bank of England (No. 3)* (2000) 2 W.L.R. 1220; (2000) 3 All E.R. 1; (2000) Lloyd's Rep. Bank 235, HL.

[34] See C. Goodhart, 'Regulating the Regulator – An Economist's Perspective on Accountability and Control' in E. Ferran and C. Goodhart (eds.), *Regulating Financial Services and Markets in the Twenty First Century,* supra note 2, pp. 162–163.

[35] See R.M. Lastra, 'The Independence of the European System of Central Banks' (1992) 33 *Harvard International Law Journal* 475, 519.

in Search of a Democratic and Constitutional Theory presents some interesting ideas in this regard:

> 'The principle of institutional balance is akin to the age-old ideal of 'trias politica' (...). Institutional balance requires organising the decision-making process in such a way that all interests concerned duly take part in the deliberative process. What is needed then is to develop yardsticks against which the representativity (sic) of the various actors taking part in the decision-making process is assessed. Three issues are of particular concern here. First, while traditional constitutional theory focuses almost exclusively on territorial representation, criteria must be forged in order to ensure functional representation. This, in turn, requires reassessing the role of civic society and the capacity of functional interests to enhance civil society's voice without capturing it. Second, the requirement of representativity does not imply that each and any individual actor must be representative of a particular interest. (...). Third, the whole area of delegated rule-making, which takes place in a constitutional near-void, must be underpinned by clear constitutional rules and principles. Again, an institutional balance approach, focusing on who does what and when and how delegated rule-making can take place, offers a fruitful model of constitutional design'.[36]

It is clear that the issue of accountability remains to be properly designed and that the interests of the institutions and individuals involved in financial supervision ought to be properly represented. This implies a rethinking of the mechanisms of accountability, which should encompass those traditionally included in the old paradigm of accountability as well as new mechanisms (such as advisory panels of practitioners, consumers and others). Globalization is also challenging the accepted wisdom concerning the notions of power and governance, greatly influencing the design and mechanisms of accountability.[37] This is particularly relevant for the proper functioning of the international financial system in the aftermath of the global financial crisis.

---

36 Supra note 13, p. 364.

37 See J. Black and D. Rouch, 'The development of the global markets as rule-makers: engagement and legitimacy' (2008) 2 *Law and Financial Markets Review*, 218, 223–225.

CENTRAL BANK GOVERNANCE, SOCIETY AND POLITICIANS: THE TALE OF INDEPENDENCE

Donato MASCIANDARO

In the modern analysis of monetary policy central bank governance plays a fundamental role. This chapter analyses a pillar of central bank governance – namely independence – and offers three contributions. After a systematic review of the economics of central bank independence, a principal-agent model is used to design a political economy framework that explains how politicians can shape central bank governance in addressing macroeconomic shocks, taking into account both the wishes of the citizens and their own personal interests. The framework is used to interpret the evolution of monetary independence during the Great Moderation – from the eighties to the first decade of the twenty-first century – and then to discuss how it can be shaken by the recent reforms of central bank settings triggered by the global financial crisis.

1. INTRODUCTION

The history of central banks is rich in modifications to their role and functions.[1] Over the last thirty years – before the 2008 crisis – the mandate of central banks has been progressively narrowed. In a large number of countries the central bank mandate has focused on the area of monetary policy and zoomed on the goal of price stability. This narrowing of the mandate has been accompanied by modifications to the bank's governance arrangements. The pillar of central bank governance was identified by increasing the degree of independence.

By the early 2000s an increasing number of countries had adopted a well-defined system of central bank governance: the independent agency becomes increasingly specialised in achieving the monetary policy goals, and consequently its traditional

[1] C. GOODHART, *The Evolution of Central Banks*, MIT Press, Cambridge, Massachusetts 1988 and R. LASTRA, *Central Banking and Banking Regulation*, Financial Markets Group, London School of Economics, London 1996.

responsibilities in pursuing the financial stability became progressively less important. But now that the crisis is posing new challenges to the modern central banking models, where monetary policy is conducted by an independent[2] central bank which follows an interest rate rule-based approach to stabilise inflation and output gaps.[3] A significant number of reforms are taking place concerning in particular the central bank's role in the structure of supervision.

In 2010, the US legislature passed the Dodd-Frank Act, rethinking the role of the Fed as part of the reshaping of financial supervision. Even though during the discussion of the bill US lawmakers debated the possibility of restricting some of the Fed's regulatory powers, as well as increasing political control over the central bank, the Dodd-Frank Act actually ended up increasing the responsibilities of the Fed as a prudential supervisor.[4] In Malaysia, the 2009 Central Bank Law provided for greater involvement by the central bank in supervision.[5] In the current version of the Basel Capital Accord, the activation of countercyclical prudential measures has been put in the hands of central banks.[6]

In Europe, policymakers are moving to finalise reforms concerning the involvement of central banks in supervision at both the regional and national levels. In 2010, the European Systemic Risk Board (ESRC) was established to provide macro-prudential supervision, and this new institution is dominated

---

2 C. Hefeker and B. Zimmer, 'The Optimal Choice of Central Bank Independence and Conservatism under Uncertainty' (2011) 33 *Journal of Macroeconomics* 595.

3 C. Goodhart, C. Osorio and D.P. Tsomocos, 'Analysis of Monetary Policy and Financial Stability: A New Paradigm' (2009) *CESifo Working Paper* No. 2885; V. Curdia and M. Woodford, 'The Central Bank Balance Sheet as an Instrument of Monetary Policy' (2010) *NBER Working Paper* No. 16208; M. Gertler and P. Karadi, 'A Model of Unconventional Monetary Policy' (2011) 58 *Journal of Monetary Policy* 17; F. Giavazzi and A. Giovannini, 'Central Banks and the Financial System' in S.C.W. Eijffinger and D. Masciandaro (eds.), *The Handbook of Central Banking, Financial Regulation and Supervision after the Crisis*, Edward Elgar, Cheltenham 2011; E. Cohen–Cole and J. Morse, 'Monetary Policy and Capital Regulation in the US and Europe' (2010) *European Central Bank Working Paper* No. 1222; B. Aydin and E. Volkan, 'Incorporating Financial Stability in Inflation Targeting Frameworks' (2011) *IMF Working Paper* No. 224; K. Ueda and F.V. Valencia, 'Central Bank Independence and Macro - Prudential Regulation' (2012) *IMF Working Paper* No. 101; O. Issing, *Central Banks - Paradise Lost*, Mayekawa Lectures, Institute for Monetary and Economic Studies, Tokyo, 2012, mimeo; A. Cukierman, 'Monetary Policy and Institutions before, during and after the Global Financial Crisis' (2013) 9 *Journal of Financial Stability* 373; M. Woodford, 'Inflation Targeting and Financial Stability' (2012) *NBER Working Paper* No. 17967.

4 A. Komai and G. Richardson, 'A Brief History of Regulations regarding Financial Markets in the United States: 1789 to 2009' (2011) *NBER Working Paper* No. 17443; G.B. Gorton and A. Metrick, 'The Federal Reserve and Financial Regulation: The First Hundred Years' (2013) *NBER Working Paper* No. 19292.

5 R. Siregar, 'Macro-Prudential Approaches to Banking Regulation: Perspectives of Selected Asian Central Banks' (2011) *ADBI Working Paper* No. 35.

6 C. Goodhart, 'Global Macroeconomic and Financial Supervision: Where Next?' (2011) *NBER Working Paper* No. 17682.

by the European Central Bank (ECB).[7] In June 2012 the heads of state and government of the eurozone started the process of establishing the European single supervisory setting, which will be headquartered in the ECB.

As for individual EU members, in 2011, with the new Banking Act, the German government dismantled its unified financial supervisor (BAFIN) in favour of the Bundesbank, which is now the main banking supervisor. In 2010, the UK government put the key prudential functions of the Financial Services Authority (FSA) within the purview of the Bank of England. In 2010, the Irish Financial Services Regulatory Authority was legally merged with the central bank. Further, an analysis of the reforms undertaken in Bulgaria, the Czech Republic, Estonia, Hungary, Latvia, Poland and Slovakia reveals that the trend towards supervisory consolidation has not resulted in less central bank involvement.[8]

In this respect, it is interesting to note that before the crisis the central bank was the main prudential supervisor in less than half of EU countries (13 out of 27). After the crisis, with the establishment of new supervisory regimes in Belgium, France, Germany and the United Kingdom, the main prudential supervisor is now the central bank in more than half of them (17 out of 27).

These episodes are likely to signal a sort of reversal in central banking governance,[9] given that before the crisis the direction of changes in the supervisory structure had been characterised by the separation of central banking from supervision.[10]

But what could the effects on independence be? The crisis poses new challenges to modern central banking models, under which monetary policy was previously conducted by an independent central bank that followed an interest rate rule-

---

7 M. Salines, G. Glockler, Z. Truchlewski and P. Del Favero, 'Beyond the Economics of the Euro. Analysing the Institutional Evolution of EMU 1999–2010' (2011) *ECB Occasional Paper* No. 127.

8 M. Apinis, M. Bodzioch, E. Csongradi, T. Filipova, Z. Foit, J. Kotkas, M. Porzycki and M. Vetrak, 'The Role of National Central Banks in Banking Supervision in Selected Central and Eastern European Countries' (2010) *ECB Legal Working Paper* No. 11.

9 D. Masciandaro, 'Back to the Future? Central Banks as Prudential Supervisors in the Aftermath of the Crisis' (2012) 12 *European Company and Financial Law Review* 112 and D. Masciandaro, 'Monetary Policy and Banking Supervision: Still at Arm's Length? A Comparative Analysis' (2012) 9 *European Journal of Comparative Economics* 349.

10 D. Masciandaro and M. Quintyn, 'Reforming Financial Supervision and the Role of the Central Banks: A Review of Global Trends, Causes and Effects (1998–2008)' (2009) *CEPR Policy Insight* No. 30; A. Orphanides, 'Monetary Policy Lessons from the Crisis' in S.C.W. Eijffinger and D. Masciandaro (eds.), *The Handbook of Central Banking, Financial Regulation and Supervision after the Crisis*, Edward Elgar, Cheltenham 2011; and B. Eichengreen and N. Dincer, 'Who Should Supervise? The Structure of Bank Supervision and the Performance of the Financial System' (2011) *NBER Working Paper* No. 17401.

based approach to stabilise inflation and output gaps.[11] In other words how should we interpret the ongoing central banking reforms with respect to the never-ending debate on independence?

This chapter offers three contributions. Section 2 discusses the economics of the key feature of the modern central bank governance, i.e. independence, focusing on what the determinants of a given institutional setting could be. The results are used in section 3 to build up a political economy model which highlights the drivers that can explain central bank governance when the policymakers are delegated by the citizens to design the optimal degree of central bank independence. The framework is used in section 4 to evaluate the evolution of central bank governance before and after the crisis in the light of the recent reforms. Section 5 concludes.

2. DESIGNING THE CENTRAL BANK GOVERNANCE AND THE ROLE OF INDEPENDENCE: INSIGHTS FROM THE ECONOMIC LITERATURE

Up to thirty years ago economic theory did not attribute importance to the concept of central bank governance. The institutional arrangements became important when the economic theory started to stress its role in determining the macroeconomic performances, i.e. during the New Classical Revolution; then the role of the central bank design was confirmed in the New Keynesian analysis of the monetary policy.[12]

11 C. Goodhart, C. Osorio and D.P. Tsomocos, 'Analysis of Monetary Policy and Financial Stability: A New Paradigm', supra note 3; V. Curdia and M. Woodford, 'The Central Bank Balance Sheet as an Instrument of Monetary Policy', supra note 3; M. Gertler and P. Karadi, 'A Model of Unconventional Monetary Policy', supra note 3; F. Giavazzi and A. Giovannini, 'Central Banks and the Financial System', supra note 3; E. Cohen-Cole and J. Morse, 'Monetary Policy and Capital Regulation in the US and Europe', supra note 3; B. Aydin and E. Volkan, 'Incorporating Financial Stability in Inflation Targeting Frameworks', supra note 3; C. Hefeker and B. Zimmer, 'The Optimal Choice of Central Bank Independence and Conservatism under Uncertainty', supra note 2; K. Ueda and F.V. Valencia, 'Central Bank Independence and Macro – Prudential Regulation', supra note 3; M. Woodford, 'Inflation Targeting and Financial Stability', supra note 3.

12 For well done reviews see S.C.W Eijffinger and J. De Haan, 'The Political Economy of Central Bank Independence' (1996) *Princeton Special Paper in International Economics* No. 19, A. Cukierman, 'The Economics of Central Banking' in W. Holger (ed.), *Macroeconomic Policy and Financial Systems*, Macmillan, New York 1996, A. Cukierman 'Central Bank Independence and Monetary Policymaking Institutions: Past, Present and Future' (2008) 24 *European Journal of Political Economy* 722, C.E. Walsh, 'Central Bank Independence' in S.N. Durlauf and L.E. Blume (eds.), *The New Palgrave Dictionary of Economics*, Palgrave Macmillan, New York 2008. The inefficient use of the inflation tax by the government seems to be the common feature of the different theoretical explanations of the CBI effectiveness;

The theoretical bottom line can be summarised as follows: policymakers tend to use monetary tools short-sightedly, using inflation tax to smooth out different kinds of macroeconomic shocks, trying to exploit the trade off between real gains and nominal (inflationary) costs. The inflation tax finances the stabilisation policies.

But the more efficient the markets are, the greater the risk is that short-sighted monetary policies only produce inflation. In fact rational private agents anticipate the political incentives of using inflation tax, fully adjusting the nominal variables. In this context the Friedman–Lucas[13] proposition on monetary policy neutrality holds. Furthermore the political inflation bias can dynamically generate greater uncertainty and negative externalities (such as moral hazard risks). The inflation tax is used inefficiently in a systematic way, becoming tendentially high and volatile and then producing only macroeconomic distortions.

The inefficient use of inflation tax was empirically confirmed by the fact that the optimal taxation theory did not find any support in the data.[14] The optimal taxation theory claims that the benevolent policymaker chooses the rate of any taxation – including the inflation tax – to minimise the present value of the social cost; consequently inflation and tax rates have a positive relationship. If the optimal taxation theory empirically fails, it is natural to conclude that the government is not benevolent and that it is affected by inflation biases.[15]

Therefore banning the use of monetary policy for inflation tax purposes becomes the social goal. The institutional setting gains momentum; the relationships

---

S.C.W. Eijffinger and J. De Haan – 'The Political Economy of Central Bank Independence', supra this note – discussed three strands of the literature: the public choice view, the fiscal view and the time-inconsistency view. While the first two views highlight the reasons why the governments in charge might like the accommodative monetary policies, the third one explains their ineffectiveness, using the rational expectations hypothesis. J. Bibow – 'A Post Keynesian Perspective on the Rise of Central Bank Independence: A Dubious Success Story in Monetary Economics' (2010) *Levy Economics Institute of Bard College Working Paper* No. 625 – illustrated the views of Friedman and Keynes on CBI. M. Goodfriend – 'The Elusive Promise of Independent Central Banking' (2012) *Bank of Japan IMES Discussion Paper* No. 2012-E-9 – reviewed CBI as it emerged first under the gold standard and later with fiat money.

13 M. Friedman, 'The Role of Monetary Policy' (1968) 58 *American Economic Review* 1 and R.E. Lucas, 'Some International Evidence on Output Inflation Tradeoffs' (1973) 63 *American Economic Review* 326.

14 For a survey see R.D. Nolivos and G. Vuletin, 'The Role of Central Bank Independence on Optimal Taxation and Seignorage' (2011) *Bocconi University Paolo Baffi Centre Working Paper* No. 2011-103.

15 R.D. Nolivos and G. Vuletin – 'The Role of Central Bank Independence on Optimal Taxation and Seignorage', supra note 14 – reach a different conclusion: the article endogenises the optimal taxation as a function of the CBI, which is the exogenous variable: higher CBI produces lower level of optimal taxation. However the article does not explain why the CBI level is exogenous, i.e. why the social planner does not define at the same time both the optimal taxation and the CBI level.

(governance) between the policymaker – who designs the overall economic policy – and the central bank – which is responsible for the monetary policy – become crucial in avoiding the inflation bias. The more rational the markets are, the more the rules of the game between policymakers and central bankers gain momentum.[16] The optimal central bank governance has to essentially be a two-sided coin.

On the one hand, the central banker has to be independent, i.e. the central bank enjoys the ability to implement non-inflationary monetary policy without any external (political) short-sighted interference. The central banker can veto inflationary monetary policies. On the other hand, the central banker has to be conservative, where conservativeness refers to the importance that he/she assigns to price stability in its relation to other macroeconomic objectives. Conservativeness is necessary to avoid the central banker himself/herself becoming a source of inflation bias. Independence and conservativeness become the conditions for implementing credible non-inflationary monetary policies.[17] Independence can be considered a device to implement conservative monetary policies.[18] But private agents only trust the central banker if effective rules on accountability and transparency hold. In other words, a conservative central banker is credible if he/she works in an institutional setting which guarantees

---

16 R. Barro and D.B. Gordon, 'Rules, Discretion and Reputation in a Model of Monetary Policy' (1983) 12 *Journal of Monetary Economics* 101, D. Backus and J. Driffil, 'Inflation and Reputation' (1985) 75 *American Economic Review* 530, K.S. Rogoff, 'The Optimal Degree of Commitment to an Intermediate Monetary Target' (1985) 100 *Quarterly Journal of Economics* 1169 and S. Lohmann, 'Partisan Control of the Money Supply and Decentralized Appointment Powers' (1997) 13 *European Journal of Political Economy* 225 all explored the role of the rules of the game in determining the outcomes of the overall macroeconomic policy, while T.J. Sargent and N. Wallace, 'Some Unpleasant Monetarist Arithmetic' (1981) 5 *Federal Reserve Bank of Minneapolis Quarterly Review* 1, S. Niemann, 'Dynamic Monetary Fiscal Interactions and the Role of Monetary Conservatism' (2011) 58 *Journal of Monetary Economics* 234, S. Niemann, P. Pichler and G. Sorger, 'Central Bank Independence and the Monetary Instrument Problem' (2013) 54 *International Economic Review* 1031, and F.M. Martin, 'Debt, Inflation and Central Bank Independence' (2013) *Federal Reserve Bank of St. Louis Working Paper* No. 17 focused their attention on fiscal policy.

17 On the relationship between CBI and central banker conservativeness see also S.C.W. Eijffinger and M. Hoeberichts, 'The Trade Off between Central Bank Independence and Conservativeness' (1998) 50 *Oxford Economic Papers* 397, B.T. Mccallum, 'Two Fallacies Concerning Central Bank Independence' (1995) 85 *American Economic Review* 207, and S. Fischer, 'Central Bank Independence Revisited' (1995) 85 *American Economic Review: Papers and Proceedings* 201. On monetary conservativeness and fiscal policy see S. Niemann, 'Dynamic Monetary Fiscal Interactions and the Role of Monetary Conservatism', supra note 16.

18 S.C.W. Eijffinger and M. Hoeberichts – 'The Trade Off between Central Bank Independence and Conservativeness', supra note 17 – and S.C.W. Eijffinger and M. Hoeberichts – 'The Trade Off between Central Bank Independence and Conservatism in a New Keynesian Framework' (2008) 24 *European Journal of Political Economy* 742 – shed light on the trade off between conservativeness and independence: downgrading central bank independence can increase the central banker's conservativeness. The first article used the neoclassic framework while the second one applied a new Keynesian model to obtain the same result.

independence and accountability, and acts in a transparent way[19] and implements an effective communication policy.[20]

The relationship between independence and accountability represents the core of so-called central bank governance.[21] Central bank governance became the institutional setting for implementing day-to-day monetary policy:[22] given the long-term goal of avoiding the risk of inflation, the modern central banker can also smooth out the real business cycles,[23] using monetary policy rules.[24] Monetary policy becomes the final outcome of a complex interaction between three main components: monetary institutions, the central banker's preferences and policy rules.

---

19 On transparency see S.C.W. Eijffinger and P. Geraarts, 'How Transparent are Central Banks?' (2006) 22 *European Journal of Political Economy* 1, and H.A. Hughes and J. Libich, 'Central Bank Independence, Accountability and Transparency: Complements or Strategic Substitutes?' (2006) *CEPR Discussion Paper* No. 5470.

20 On communication see A. Cukierman and A. Meltzer, 'A Theory of Ambiguity, Credibility and Inflation under Discretion and Asymmetric Information' (1986) 54 *Econometrica* 1099, M. Goodfriend, 'Monetary Mistique: Secrecy and Central Banking' (1986) 17 *Journal of Monetary Economics* 63, O. Issing, 'Communication, Transparency, Accountability: Monetary Policy in the Twenty-First Century' (2005) 87 *Federal Reserve Bank of St. Louis Review* 65, and A. Blinder, M. Ehrmann, M. Fratzscher, J. De Haan and D.J. Jansen, 'Central Bank Communication and Monetary Policy: A Survey of Theory and Evidence' (2008) 46 *Journal of Economic Literature* 910.

21 C.B. Briault, A.G. Haldane and M.A. King, 'Central Bank Independence and Accountability: Theory and Evidence' (1996) *Bank of England Working Paper* No. 49, T. Lybek and J.A. Morris, 'Central Bank Governance: a Survey of Boards and Management' (2004) *IMF Working Paper* No. 236, L. Frisell, K. Roszbach and G. Spagnolo, *Governing the Governors: a Clinical Study of Central Banks*, American Economic Association 2007 Annual Meeting, Chicago 2007, mimeo, C. Crowe and E. Meade, 'The Evolution of Central Bank Governance around the World' (2007) 21 *Journal of Economic Perspectives* 69, and I. Hasan and L. Mester, 'Corporate Governance and Effective Central Banking: Cross-Country Empirical Evidence' in P. Syklos, M. Bohl and M. Wohart (eds.), *Frontiers in Central Banking*, Elsevier, Amsterdam 2010.

22 J.B. Taylor – *The Effectiveness of Central Bank Independence Versus Policy Rule*, American Economic Association 2013 Annual Meeting, San Diego 2013, mimeo – cast doubts on the role of the CBI in generating rules-based monetary policies.

23 B. Bernanke and M. Gertler, 'Inside the Black Box: The Credit Channel of Monetary Policy Transmission' (1995) 9 *Journal of Economic Perspectives* 27, R. Clarida, J. Gali and M. Gertler, 'The Science of Monetary Policy: A New Keynesian Perspective' (1999) 37 *Journal of Economic Literature* 1661, M. Woodford, 'Optimal Interest Rate Smoothing' (2003) 70 *Review of Economic Studies* 861, and J. Gali and T. Monacelli, 'Monetary Policy and Exchange Rate Volatility in a Small Open Economy' (2005) 72 *Review of Economic Studies* 707.

24 J.B. Taylor, 'Discretion versus Policy Rules in Practice' (1993) 39 *Carnegie-Rochester Conference Series on Public Policy* 195, D.W. Henderson and W. Mckibbin, 'A Comparison of Some Basis Monetary Policy Regimes for Open Economies: Implications of Different Degrees of Instrument Adjustment and Wage Persistence' (1993) 39 *Carnegie-Rochester Conference Series on Public Policy* 221, T. Persson and G. Tabellini, 'Designing Institutions for Monetary Stability' (1993) 39 *Carnegie-Rochester Conference Series on Public Policy* 53, C. Walsh, 'Optimal Contracts for Central Bankers' (1995) 85 *American Economic Review* 150, and L.E.O. Svensson, 'Optimal Inflation Targets, "Conservative" Central Banks, and Linear Inflation Contracts' (1995) 87 *American Economic Review* 98.

In this chapter the variable we are interested in is the optimal degree of central bank independence (CBI), all other things being equal, including the rules on accountability and transparency.

For our purposes the huge[25] CBI literature can be described as a two-stage process. Initially the scholars involved in the field verified the theoretical conjectures with comparative, institutional and empirical analyses. After constructing indices of independence of the central banks,[26] and bearing in mind alternative historical models of independent and dependent monetary authorities,[27] scholars have

25 G. Vuletin and L. Zhu – 'Replacing a Disobedient Central Bank Governor with a Docile One: A Novel Measure of Central Bank Independence and its Effect on Inflation' (2011) 43 *Journal of Money, Credit and Banking* 1185 – claimed that up to 2011 around 9000 articles had been devoted to the role of CBI on inflation.

26 After the seminal central bank independence indices published by R. Bade and M. Parkin – *Central Bank Laws and Monetary Policy: A Preliminary Investigation*, University of Western Ontario, Ontario 1977 – and by V. Grilli, D. Masciandaro and G. Tabellini – 'Political and Monetary Institutions and Public Financial Policies in the Industrial Countries' (1991) 13 *Economic Policy* 341 – revised in D. Masciandaro and F. Spinelli – 'Central Banks' Independence: Institutional Determinants, Rankings and Central Bankers' Views' (1994) 41 *Scottish Journal of Political Economy* 434 – followed by Cukierman indices – A. Cukierman, *Central Bank Strategy, Credibility, and Autonomy*, MIT Press, Cambridge, Massachusetts 1992 – different indicators were proposed; for a discussion see H. Berger, J. De Haan and S.C.W. Eijffinger, 'Central Bank Independence: an Update of Theory and Evidence' (2000) *CESifo Working Paper* No. 255. A. Cukierman – *Central Bank Strategy, Credibility, and Autonomy,* supra this note – was the first to distinguish legal and de facto indicators of independence. Updates of these indices were proposed in A. Cukierman, S.B. Webb and B. Neyapti, 'Measuring the Independence of Central Banks and its Effects on Policy Outcomes' (1992) 6 *World Bank Economic Review* 353, A. Cukierman, G. Miller and B. Neyapti, 'Central Bank Reform, Liberalization, and Inflation in Transition Economies. An International Perspective' (2002) 49 *Journal of Monetary Economics* 237 and L. Jacome and F. Vasquez, 'Any Link between Legal Central Bank Independence and Inflation? Evidence from the Latin American and the Caribbean' (2005) *IMF Working Paper* No. 75 – for the Cukierman index – and in M. Arnone, B.J. Laurens, J. Segalotto and M. Sommer, 'Central Bank Autonomy: Lessons from Global Trends' (2007) *IMF Working Paper* No. 88 – for the Grilli, Masciandaro and Tabellini index. C. Crowe and E. Meade – 'The Evolution of Central Bank Governance around the World', supra note 21 – developed measures of central bank independence and transparency. G. Vuletin and L. Zhu – 'Replacing a Disobedient Central Bank Governor with a Docile One: A Novel Measure of Central Bank Independence and its Effect on Inflation', supra note 25 – proposed a new de facto index of independence, identifying two different mechanisms embedded in the measure of the turnover rate of central bank governor.

27 G. Toniolo (ed.), *Central Bank Independence in Historical Perspective*, de Gruyter, Berlin–New York 1988, J. Wood, *The Meanings and Historical Background of Central Bank Independence*, 2007, mimeo. On the FED see C. Waller, 'Independence + Accountability: Why the FED is a Well Designed Central Bank' (2011) 93 *Federal Reserve Bank of St. Louis Review* 239, B. Bernanke, A *Century of US Central Banking: Goals, Frameworks, Accountability*, National Bureau of Economic Research Conference 'The First 100 Years of the Federal Reserve: The Policy Record, Lessons Learned, and Prospects for the Future', Cambridge, Massachusetts, 10.07.2013, mimeo, G.B. Gorton and A. Metrick, 'The Federal Reserve and Financial Regulation: The First Hundred Years' (2013) *NBER Working Paper* No. 19292, supra note 4; on the FED and the Bank of England see M. Goodfriend, 'The Elusive Promise of Independent Central Banking' (2012) *Bank of Japan IMES Discussion Paper* No. 2012-E-9; on the Bundesbank see O. Issing, 'Why Did the Great Inflation not Happen in Germany?' (2005) 87 *Federal Reserve Bank of St. Louis Review* 329 and A. Beyer, V. Gaspar, C. Gerberding and

attempted to determine whether the degree of independence could be considered a driver in explaining the most important macroeconomic phenomena: inflation,[28]

O. Issing, 'Opting out of the Great Inflation' (2008) *NBER Working Paper* No. 1496; on the Bank of Italy see E. Gaiotti and A. Secchi, 'Monetary Policy and Fiscal Dominance in Italy from the Early 1970s to the Adoption of the Euro: a Review' (2012) *Banca d'Italia Occasional Paper* No. 141.

28 V. Grilli, D. Masciandaro and G. Tabellini, 'Political and Monetary Institutions and Public Financial Policies in the Industrial Countries', supra note 26, A. Cukierman, 'Central Bank Independence and Monetary Control' (1994) 104 *The Economic Journal* 1437, A. Cukierman, S.B. Webb and B. Neyapti, 'Measuring the Independence of Central Banks and its Effects on Policy Outcomes', supra note 26, A. Cukierman and S.B. Webb, 'Political Influence on the Central Bank: International Evidence' (1995) 9 *World Bank Economic Review* 397, H. Berger, J. De Haan and S.C.W. Eijffinger, 'Central Bank Independence: an Update of Theory and Evidence', supra note 26. See also A. Alesina and L.H. Summers, 'Central Bank Independence and Macroeconomic Performances: Some Comparative Evidence' (1993) 25 *Journal of Money, Credit and Banking* 151, A. Alesina and R. Gatti, 'Independent Central Banks: Low Inflation at no Cost?' (1995) 85 *American Economic Review* 196, E. Gutierrez, 'Inflation Performance and Constitutional Central Bank Independence. Evidence from Latin American and the Caribbean' (2003) *IMF Working Paper* No. 53, L. Jacome and F. Vasquez, 'Any Link between Legal Central Bank Independence and Inflation? Evidence from the Latin American and the Caribbean', supra note 26. J. Klomp and J. De Haan – 'Inflation and Central Bank Independence: a Meta Regression Analysis' (2010) 24 *Journal of Economic Surveys* 593 – performed a meta regression analysis of 59 studies, examining the relationship between inflation and CBI. They still confirmed the existence of a negative and significant relation between inflation and CBI in OECD countries, although the results are sensitive to the indicator used and the estimation period chosen. The legal CBI has been considered a major determinant of macroeconomic performance – A. Cukierman, 'Central Bank Independence and Monetary Policymaking Institutions: Past, Present and Future', supra note 12, J. De Haan, D. Masciandaro and M. Quintyn, 'Does Central Bank Independence still Matter?' (2008) 24 *European Journal of Political Economy* 717, C.T. Carlstrom and T.S. Fuerst, 'Central Bank Independence and Inflation: a Note' (2009) 47 *Economic Inquiry* 182, S. Alpanda and A. Honig, 'The Impact of Central Bank Independence on Political Monetary Cycles in Advanced and Developing Countries' (2009) 41 *Journal of Money, Credit and Banking* 1365, A. Alesina and A. Stella, 'The Politics of Monetary Policy' in B.M. Friedman and M. Woodford (eds.), *Handbook of Monetary Economics Vol. 3,* 2nd ed., Elsevier, Amsterdam 2010, pp. 1001–1054, J. Klomp and J. De Haan, 'Central Bank Independence and Inflation Revisited' (2010) 144 *Public Choice* 445. More recently, the literature has been re-examining the relationship between CBI and the conduct of monetary policy – I. Down, 'Central Bank Independence, Disinflation and Monetary Policy' (2008) 10 *Business and Politics* 1, A. Maslowska, 'Quest for the Best: How to Measure Central Bank Independence and Show its Relation with Inflation?' (2008) *Aboa Centre for Economics Discussion Paper* No. 37, S. Alpanda and A. Honig, 'The Impact of Central Bank Independence on Political Monetary Cycles in Advanced and Developing Countries', supra this note – and the effect of CBI on financial stability – M. Čihák, *Central Bank Independence and Financial Stability,* International Monetary Fund, 2007, mimeo, J. Klomp and J. De Haan, 'Central Bank Independence and Financial Stability' (2009) 5 *Journal of Financial Stability* 321 – as well as on inflation – J. Klomp and J. De Haan, 'Inflation and Central Bank Independence: a Meta Regression Analysis', supra this note, M. Arnone and D. Romelli, 'Dynamic Central Bank Independence Indices and Inflation: An Empirical Exploration' (2013) 9 *Journal of Financial Stability* 385 – and finally on government deficits – C. Bodea, 'Independent Central Banks, Regime Type and Fiscal Performance: The Case of Post – Communist Countries' (2013) 155 *Public Choice* 1.

public debt and interest rates,[29] income and growth.[30]

The aim was to verify whether the existence of the monetary veto player reduces the intended and unintended effects of the misuse of inflation tax and produces additional positive effects for other macro variables. In the first wave of studies central bank independence was essentially considered an exogenous (independent) variable that was useful to explain macro trends.

The step forward in the research was to consider the degree of CBI as an endogenous (dependent) variable[31] that has to be explained. What are the drivers that can motivate the decision of one or more countries to maintain or reform their monetary regimes, i.e. the degree of independence of their central banks? Why and how are policymakers forced to implement monetary reforms that reduce their powers to use inflation tax, increasing the degree of independence of the central bank?

Various interpretative hypotheses were advanced to explain the genesis of the political process that leads a monetary regime to assume certain characteristics. Development in endogenising central bank independence – i.e. its effectiveness – has been the subject of analysis in both economics and political science.[32]

Some scholars maintained the possibility that the degree of CBI depends on the degree to which constituencies that strongly oppose the use of inflation tax are

29 V. Grilli, D. Masciandaro and G. Tabellini, 'Political and Monetary Institutions and Public Financial Policies in the Industrial Countries', supra note 26, A. Alesina and L.H. Summers, 'Central Bank Independence and Macroeconomic Performances: Some Comparative Evidence', supra note 28, A. Cukierman, 'Central Bank Independence and Monetary Control', supra note 28.

30 V. Grilli, D. Masciandaro and G. Tabellini, 'Political and Monetary Institutions and Public Financial Policies in the Industrial Countries', supra note 26, A. Alesina and L.H. Summers, 'Central Bank Independence and Macroeconomic Performances: Some Comparative Evidence', supra note 28, A. Cukierman, P. Kalaitzidakis, L. Summers and S.B. Webb, 'Central Bank Independence, Growth, Investment and Real Rates' (1993) 39 *Carnegie-Rochester Conference Series on Public Policy* 95, A. Cukierman, 'Central Bank Independence and Monetary Control', supra note 28, and H. Berger, J. De Haan and S.C.W. Eijffinger, 'Central Bank Independence: an Update of Theory and Evidence', supra note 26.

31 See D. Masciandaro, 'Designing a Central bank: Social Player, Monetary Agent or Banking Agent?' (1995) 6 *Open Economies Review* 399 and H. Berger, J. De Haan and S.C.W. Eijffinger, 'Central Bank Independence: an Update of Theory and Evidence', supra note 26; note the difference between institutional setting endogeneity and inflationary bias endogeneity. The endogeneity of CBI is systematically reviewed in B. Hayo and C. Hefeker, 'Do We Really Need Central Bank Independence? A Critical Re-examination' (2001) *WWZ Discussion Paper* No. 3.

32 Very good reference books on how central banks policies and their institutional settings have changed, as well as on the causes of these changes are P. Siklos, *The Changing Face of Central Banking. Evolutionary Trends since World War II*, Cambridge University Press, Cambridge UK 2002 and P. Syklos, M.T. Bohl and M. Wohar, *Frontiers in Central Banking*, Cambridge University Press, Cambridge UK 2010.

present, as this drives policymakers to bolster the status of the central bank (*the constituency view*).[33] Others have stressed that the aversion to the use of inflation tax is structurally built into the features of the overall legislative and/or political system, which influence the policymakers to decide whether to have a setting of monetary powers with an independent central bank (*the institutional view*).[34]

---

33 S. Maxfield, *Gatekeepers of Growth. The International Political Economy of Central Banking in Developing Countries*, Princeton University Press, Princeton 1997. A. Posen – 'Declarations are not Enough: Financial Sectors Sources of Central Bank Independence' in B. Bernanke and J. Rotemberg (eds.), *NBER Macroeconomics Annual 1995*, MIT Press, Cambridge, Massachusetts 1995 – noting that there are distributive consequences in the choices of monetary regimes, stated that there is no reason to assume that the adoption of central bank independence is self-enforcing; that choice requires political support, and the financial sector is positioned to provide that support. J. De Haan and G.J. Van't Hag – 'Variation in Central Bank Independence across Countries: Some Provisional Empirical Evidence' (1995) 85 *Public Choice* 235 – raised doubts about Posen's theory. On the relationships between financial sector preferences, low inflation and central bank independence see also G. Miller – 'An Interest Group Theory of Central Bank Independence' (1998) 27 *Journal of Legal Studies* 433 – who provided an interest group theory of CBI. Empirical analyses which faced the CBI endogeneity question are supplied by H.J. Brumm, 'The Effect of Central Bank Independence on Inflation in Developing Countries' (2006) 90 *Economics Letters* 189 and H.J. Brumm, 'Inflation and Central Bank Independence: Two-Way Causality?' (2011) 111 *Economics Letters* 220.

34 P. Moser, 'Checks and Balances, and the Supply of Central Bank Independence' (1999) 43 *European Economic Review* 1569. See also A. Cukierman, 'Central Bank Independence and Monetary Control', supra note 28; however his predictions are tested and rejected by A. Cukierman and S.B. Webb, 'Political Influence on the Central Bank: International Evidence', supra note 28 and by J. De Haan and G.J. Van't Hag, 'Variation in Central Bank Independence across Countries: Some Provisional Empirical Evidence', supra note 33. R. Vaubel – 'The Bureaucratic and Partisan Behaviour of Independent Central Banks' (1997) 13 *European Journal of Political Economy* 214 – suggests that central banks, even if formally independent, can be captured; G. Sieg – 'A Model of Partisan Central Banks and Opportunistic Business Cycles' (1997) 13 *European Journal of Political Economy* 503 – proposes a formal model of a captured independent central bank. W. Bernhard – 'A Political Explanation of Variations in Central Bank Independence' (1998) 92 *American Political Science Review* 311 – claims that information asymmetries of the monetary policy process can create conflicts between government ministers, their backbench legislators and, in multiparty government, their coalition partners; an independent central bank can help overcome these conflicts. J.B. Goodman – 'The Politics of Central Bank Independence' (1991) 23 *Comparative Politics* 329 – argues that conservative governments with expected short tenure will adopt an independent central bank to limit the ability of future governments; see also G.M. Milesi-Ferretti, 'The Disadvantage of Tying Their Hands: on the Political Economy of Policy Commitments' (1995) 105 *Economic Journal* 1381. S. Lohmann – 'Partisan Control of the Money Supply and Decentralized Appointment Powers' (1997) 13 *European Journal of Political Economy* 225 – argued that the federalist nature of a government and the use of coalitions in forming government can increase the CBI likelihood. On the relationship between government partisanship and central bank structure see A. Alesina, 'Politics and Business Cycles in Industrial Democracies' (1989) 4 *Economic Policy* 57, A. Alesina and J.D. Sachs, 'Political Parties and the Business Cycle in the United States: 1948–1984' (1988) 20 *Journal of Money, Credit and Banking* 63. See also F.M. Bagheri and N. Habibi, 'Political Institutions and Central Bank Independence: a Cross-Country Analysis' (1998) 96 *Public Choice* 187. J. De Haan and G.J. Van't Hag – 'Variation in Central Bank Independence across Countries: Some Provisional Empirical Evidence', supra note 33 – test the hypothesis that governments planning to incur higher deficits may wish to increase credibility granting more central bank independence; no supporting evidence is found. P. Moser – 'Checks and Balances, and the Supply of Central Bank Independence', supra this note – analyses the relationship between

Others have stressed the role of culture and a tradition of monetary stability in a country in influencing policy choices[35] (*culture view*). These three views all take into account the role of the preferences of the citizens in determining the degree of CBI. In the constituency view current attitudes against the use of inflation tax are relevant; in the institutional and culture views the past anti-inflationary preferences influence the present policy decisions.

Further it is worth noting that the three views can be intertwined in studying under which economic, institutional and cultural conditions reforms of the CBI do or do not take place. It is also evident that these studies acquire greater

---

the central bank independence and the features – check and balances – of the legislative systems; K. Banaian and W.A. Luksetish – 'Central Bank Independence, Economic Freedom and Inflation Rates' (2001) 39 *Economic Inquiry* 149 – demonstrated the connections between economic and political freedom and CBI attributes. P. Keefer and D. Stasavage – 'The Limits of Delegation: Veto Players, Central Bank Independence, and the Credibility of Monetary Policy' (2003) 97 *American Political Science Review* 407 – introduce a theoretical model and empirical evidence on this issue. J. Wood – *The Meanings and Historical Background of Central Bank Independence*, 2007, mimeo, supra note 27 – used an historical perspective to discuss how the CBI ultimately depends on the government's needs. D. Acemoglu, S. Johnson, P. Querubin and J.A. Robinson – 'When Does Policy Reform Work? The Case of Central Bank Independence' (2008) *NBER Working Paper* No. 14033 – shows the relationship between inflation, CBI and political institutions, where the CBI effectiveness depends on the political distortions. C. Bodea and R. Hicks – *Price Stability and Central Bank Independence: Discipline, Credibility and Democratic Institutions*, IPES 2012 Conference, Charlottesville, 10.11.2012, mimeo – discussed the relationship between inflation, CBI and democratic institutions. C. Bodea – 'Exchange Rate Regimes and Independent Central Banks: A Correlated Choice of Imperfectly Credible Institutions' (2010) 64 *International Organization* 411 – analysed the simultaneous choice of both the level of CBI and the exchange rate regime.

35 H. Berger, 'The Bundesbank's Path to Independence. Evidence from the 1950s' (1997) 93 *Public Choice* 427. B. Hayo – 'Inflation Culture, Central Bank Independence and Price Stability' (1998) 14 *European Journal of Political Economy* 241 – claims that people's preferences with respect to price stability matter in explaining low inflation rates, and that the central bank independence is just one aspect of a stability regime, with two competing interpretations on the role of the institutional design: preference-instrument interpretation versus historical-feedback interpretation. R.J. Franzese – 'Partially Independent Central Banks, Politically Responsive Governments, and Inflation' (1999) 43 *American Journal of Political Science* 691 – claims that the effectiveness of central bank independence depends on every variable in the broader political-economic environment. In G. Eggertsson and E. Le Borgne – 'A Political Agency Theory of Central Bank Independence' (2003) *IMF Working Paper* No. 144 – the society – with all agents having homogeneous preferences – determines the CBI solving a delegation problem with a trade off between costs and benefits. Recently C. Crowe – 'Goal-Independent Central Banks: Why Politicians Decide to Delegate' (2006) *IMF Working Paper* No. 256 – demonstrated that CBI is more likely to occur in societies where preferences over different policy dimensions – one is the monetary policy dimension – are heterogeneous. See also S.C.W. Eijffinger and P. Stadhouder, 'Monetary Policy and the Rule of Law' (2003) *CEPR Discussion Paper* No. 3698, D. Acemoglu, S. Johnson, P. Querubin and J.A. Robinson, 'When Does Policy Reform Work? The Case of Central Bank Independence', supra note 34, S. Gollwitzer and M. Quintyn, 'The Effectiveness of Macroeconomic Commitment in Weak(er) Institutional Environment' (2010) *IMF Working Paper* No. 193, K. Hielscher and G. Markwardt, 'The Role of Political Institutions for the Effectiveness of Central Bank Independence' (2011) *CESifo Working Paper* No. 3396, N. Berggren, S.O. Daunfeldt and J. Hellström, 'Social Trust and Central-Bank Independence' (2012) *Research Institute of Industrial Economics Working Paper* No. 920.

importance in periods – like the present one – when there is a tendency towards reforming, or at least questioning, the design of central bank governance.

All in all, the review of the literature shows that whatever view is adopted view to explain CBI evolution we have to focus our research attention on two crucial elements: on the one hand, social preferences; on the other hand, the incentives and constraints that shape the behaviour of the agent responsible for the monetary setting design, i.e. the incumbent policymaker.

3. CITIZENS, POLITICIANS AND THE DESIGN OF THE CENTRAL BANK INDEPENDENCE: THE THEORETICAL FRAMEWORK

Here we go ahead in studying the design of the central bank governance using a delegation framework,[36] which seems to be an efficient way to take into account the abundant, consolidated and still growing literature on the topic, which we have already mentioned in the previous section.

In doing so we adopt the political economy approach[37] that argues that the policymaker's actual choices related to the central bank governance are conditional on the economic and institutional environment at a given time, which in turn determines the political emphasis put on the pros and cons of CBI.

Our framework is based on two hypotheses. First of all, gains and losses of a given central bank setting are variables computed by the incumbent policymaker, who maintains or reforms the central bank regime following his/her own preferences. Secondly, policymakers are politicians, and as such they are held accountable at elections for how they have managed to please voters. All politicians are career-oriented agents, motivated by the goal of pleasing voters in order to win elections.

---

36 The framework has been introduced in D. Masciandaro, 'Politicians and Financial Supervision outside the Central Bank: Why Do They Do It?' (2009) 5 *Journal of Financial Stability* 124.

37 D. Masciandaro, 'E Pluribus Unum? Authorities Design in Financial Supervision: Trends and Determinants' (2006) 17 *Open Economies Review* 73, D. Masciandaro, 'Divide et Impera: Financial Supervision Unification and the Central Bank Fragmentation Effect' (2007) 23 *European Journal of Political Economy* 285, D. Masciandaro, 'Politicians and Financial Supervision outside the Central Bank: Why Do They Do It?', supra note 36, D. Masciandaro and M. Quintyn, 'Helping Hand or Grabbing Hand? Politicians, Supervisory Regime, Financial Structure and Market View' (2008) 19 *North American Journal of Economics and Finance* 153. The framework has been applied in D. Masciandaro, 'Central Bank Governance and Supervision: Economics and Politics' in A.J. Kammel and F. Weiss (eds.), *The Changing Landscape of Global Financial Governance and the Role of Soft Law*, Brill Martinus Nijhoff Publishers, Leiden 2014, forthcoming, to discuss the political drivers which explain specifically the central bank involvement in supervision.

The main difference between various types of politicians concerns which kinds of voters they wish to please in the first place. Therefore CBI is likely to change over time following political preferences, which do not automatically coincide with social ones.

Consider a closed economy with rational expectations and uncertainty. We suppose that the citizens dislike the monetary settings where the incumbent governments can directly and discretionally manage the monetary policy. The citizens know that the politicians may have an incentive to inflate the economy to address different kind of macroeconomic shocks. In other words the politicians have an incentive to systematically use inflation tax.

The rational citizens fully anticipate the political inflation bias and therefore the monetary policy's risk of producing inflation costs without any real gains. All citizens, or at least the majority of voters, dislike the use of inflation tax and like monetary stability, which means that the government cannot systematically use inflation to change the income and wealth distribution. This is a democracy where citizens dislike the political inflationary biases.

The political biases can be explained in several alternative and at the same time complementary ways:

a) First of all there may be advantages – both for electoral and ideological reasons – brought about by an inflationary policy (*partisan bias*);
b) Secondly the governments may try to increase the employment level (*employment bias*);
c) Thirdly a fiscal temptation may arise: the government may have the incentive to use the monetary policy to make the costs of fiscal policies less onerous in economic or political terms (*fiscal bias*);
d) Fourthly the government may be tempted to bail out banks through monetisation (*banking bias*);
e) Finally the government may have the incentive to use accommodative monetary policy to address balance of payment imbalances (*foreign exchanges bias*).

In all these cases the government gives a higher expected value to the short-term benefits relative to the long-term costs of the inflation tax. But citizens understand the political bias and rationally adjust their expectations: in equilibrium there is inflation above the socially optimal level and no real effects. Therefore if the government is the monetary policy authority, monetary policy is likely to be time-inconsistent: all pre-announced monetary paths are not credible.

Here central bank independence comes in. CBI becomes a possible institutional device to address political bias: the monetary policy is delegated to an unelected bureaucracy – the central bank – which is committed to pursuing the goal of monetary stability (conservativeness) – i.e. to avoid any inflationary bias – and it is both independent from the government and accountable to Parliament. The citizens acknowledge that the definition of the optimal level of CBI means exploiting the trade off between avoiding inflationary bias in normal times and having a stabilisation device in extraordinary times.

In a democracy, citizens assign to the elected policymaker the task of designing the optimal level of CBI, i.e. the setting that guarantees the effectiveness of monetary policy. For the sake of simplicity we suppose that the elected policymaker represents both the legislative and the executive powers, i.e. the interests of the majority of Parliament and of the government in charge are perfectly aligned.

The incumbent policymaker is delegated by society to define and implement the optimal level of CBI. The policymaker's reward is based on how he/she (hereafter she) carries out her job, i.e. defining and implementing the level of CBI.

Our policymaker is a politician. Here we assume that the policymaker wishes to please the citizens; an alternative assumption could be that the policymaker's aim is to please specific constituencies, i.e. the lobbies.[38] We adopt the *helping hand view* of the policymaker, namely that she wishes to please citizens rather than a particular constituency or lobby (*grabbing hand view*).

The political reward is function of the social utility while the political costs are function of the effort in implementing the task. The policymaker evaluates every task taking into account the political rewards and costs of the task. Let us describe the three crucial features of the policymaker:

A) Ability: the ability of the policymaker is a random variable.

B) Political reward: The incumbent policymaker wishes to be re-elected. The government needs to provide enough utility to the majority of voters; then her utility function is the social welfare function.

In general, the policymaker wishes to please voters and her goal is the alignment of her interests and the citizens'. But then each delegated task – i.e. each specific alignment – can be more or less convenient from the policymaker's point of view in terms of political gains.

---

[38] See D. Masciandaro, 'Politicians and Financial Supervision outside the Central Bank: Why Do They Do It?', supra note 36.

The incentives for alignment between the policymaker and citizens are a necessary and sufficient condition to find the optimal behaviour of the policymaker. One more step is necessary to find out the effective political reward. The reward will be useful if the citizens' utility exceeds the minimum threshold of utility that they expect from an incumbent government (political competition condition).

C) Political costs: The policymaker knows that if monetary policy is delegated to an independent bureaucracy committed to a goal of monetary stability, rigidities in implementing accommodative policies (conservative veto player event) may arise: inflation tax cannot be used to finance stabilisation policies.

In other words we assume that from the policymaker's point of view the political costs of implementing a CBI regime will depend on her expectations of facing, during her time in office, at least one of five different situations that call for a lax monetary policy, which cannot be implemented if the central banker is not accomodating: political shocks; unemployment shocks; fiscal shocks; financial shocks; and foreign exchange shocks.

From the citizen's point of view, the government can be a natural scapegoat in a crisis situation, but it is not able to control monetary policy tools to implement the right short-sighted policy. In each case the government is likely to be blamed; political costs will arise.

The political cost of the effort in establishing CBI depends on how the incumbent government is blamed when the shocks occur, i.e. on the size of reputation losses.

When a shock occurs, citizens can be more or less sensitive to the use of accommodative policies. From the government's point of view the likelihood of a crisis is not *per se* relevant, but the political cost of a crisis affects the government's reputation. For the sake of simplicity we assume a) that the negative effect on the government's reputation is the same irrespective of the type of shock; and b) that the shocks are independently distributed.

In this framework the size of the reputational costs can determine the difference between optimal CBI and actual CBI. In conclusion, the political cost for the incumbent policymaker of building up a CBI regime is represented by the likelihood of facing a macroeconomic crisis without the possibility of implementing the desired *ad hoc* short-sighted monetary policy.

4. THE CENTRAL BANK INDEPENDENCE BEFORE AND AFTER THE CRISIS: UPS AND DOWNS

Now we can use the theoretical skeleton to mimic the evolution of the central bank governance in the advanced countries before and after the global financial crisis.

Given the exogenous policymaker's ability, on one hand the level of CBI depends on how politically relevant it is for the government to build up a central bank regime that pleases the majority of voters who dislike inflation tax as an economic policy tool, in other words the policymaker's perception of the relevance of the central bank setting matters. On the other hand the government takes into account the expected costs of facing a conservative veto player in monetary affairs when macroeconomic shocks have to be addressed.

What was the situation before the crisis? In the three decades before the 2008 financial meltdown, safeguarding monetary stability became a primary goal in several advanced, emerging and less developed countries, and CBI was the institutional device used to meet the commitment by avoiding the use of inflation tax.[39] The expected high political gains pushed several governments all around the world[40] to enhance the degree of CBI in their countries, accepting the restriction on their future freedom to use the inflation tax through the presence of a veto player. The monetary policy action was associated with less variance of both inflation and output.[41]

Then the crisis came. Is it possible to identify the possible drivers of CBI reform after the 2008 financial meltdown? In general we assume that the gains and losses of a CBI regime are variables computed by the incumbent policymaker, who maintains or reforms the central bank regime, following her preferences. Therefore any situation that influences the policymaker's gains and losses in changing the monetary regime can produce incentives to modify the level of CBI.

If the incumbent government feels that society's aversion to inflation is increasing, a central bank reform is likely to produce greater political gains. Currently in advanced countries both inflation and inflation expectations seem to be stable

39 A. Cukierman, 'The Economics of Central Banking', supra note 12, S.C.W. Eijffinger and J. De Haan, 'The Political Economy of Central Bank Independence', supra note 12.

40 The increase in the central bank independence all around the world during the 1980s and the 1990s is documented in M. Arnone, B.J. Laurens, J. Segalotto and M. Sommer, 'Central Bank Autonomy: Lessons from Global Trends', supra note 26.

41 B. Bernanke, *The Great Moderation*, Eastern Economic Association 2004 Annual Meeting, Washington D.C. 20.02.2004, mimeo and J.B. Taylor – *The Effectiveness of Central Bank Independence Versus Policy Rule*, supra note 22.

at low but positive levels[42] and the same is true for inflation volatility;[43] there is unlikely to be a demand by the citizens to increase the level of CBI. Furthermore, if deflation becomes a concrete macroeconomic problem, political pressures can arise to reduce the central bank's conservativeness and/or CBI.[44]

At the same time any situation that changes the policymaker's political costs in reforming the monetary regime can produce incentives to modify CBI. The policymaker's incentives to decrease CBI in order to be able to implement monetary accommodation are likely to increase if the incumbent government is facing macroeconomic shocks such as: 1) recession; 2) public deficit financing; or 3) bailout needs.

Currently all three of the above-mentioned drivers might be in action. Therefore if the crisis increases the political costs of facing a veto player, politicians have an incentive to decrease CBI. All in all, changes in either political preferences or citizens' preferences can explain the ups – before the crisis – and downs – after the crisis – in the level of independence.

So far, however, the reforms of the central bank settings were exclusively focused on the bank's involvement in supervision. Are these changes relevant in modifying CBI?

In general the likelihood of CBI changes is higher the greater the impact on the central bank's effectiveness in acting as a veto player against the political inflationary biases will be. In this respect the intended and unintended consequences on independence of a change of the central bank's involvement in supervision are far from obvious and predictable.

Let us consider the two dimensions which are usually considered in evaluating the level of CBI:[45] political independence and economic independence. Political independence refers to the discretion given to the central bank in the design and implementation of a policy that is consistent with the goal of monetary stability. Economic independence is related to the freedom of the central bank to choose the set of instruments consistent with the above-defined monetary policy. Therefore

---

42 Among others see IMF, 'The Dog That Didn't Bark; Has Inflation Been Muzzled or Was Just Sleeping' in IMF, *World Economic Outlook April 2013: Hopes, Realities, Risks*, International Monetary Fund, Washington D.C. 2013 and M. Fleckenstein, F.A. Longstaff and H. Lusting, 'Deflation Risk' (2013) *NBER Working Paper* No. 19238.

43 J.B. Taylor, *The Effectiveness of Central Bank Independence Versus Policy Rule*, supra note 22.

44 On Japan see C.J. Neely, 'Political Pressures on the Bank of Japan: Interference or Accountability?' (2013) 7 *Federal Reserve of St. Louis Economic Synopses* 1.

45 V. Grilli, D. Masciandaro and G. Tabellini, 'Political and Monetary Institutions and Public Financial Policies in the Industrial Countries', supra note 26 and S. Fischer, 'Central Bank Independence Revisited', supra note 17.

the more the central bank's involvement in supervision will weaken the priority of the monetary stability in defining and implementing goals and instruments of the monetary policy action, the lower the CBI will be.

To the best of our knowledge the only comparative analysis of the levels of independence which takes into account where the supervision is located[46] shows that the location matters. The analysis of the *status quo* before the crisis demonstrated that supervisors who are located inside the central bank have been granted the highest degree of independence in supervision. In other words, despite the fact that the central banks enjoy a high level of independence, moving supervision inside the central bank is likely to automatically increase the autonomy of that policy.[47] Furthermore unified supervisors located outside the central bank have the lowest degree of such independence. However, the relevance of these results is limited by the fact that concepts and definitions of independence are different in the two fields of monetary policy and supervision;[48] in general the question of the central bank's involvement can be evaluated from two symmetric points of view: on the one hand the effectiveness of the supervision; on the other hand the efficacy of the monetary policy. This chapter is focused on the monetary policy side of the story.[49]

What happens when things go in the opposite direction, i.e. central banks that are specialised in monetary policy come back to supervision? Is the independence as a monetary authority affected when central banks are responsible for financial stability? It is a matter of fact that in the recent reforms of the central bank settings

---

[46] D. Masciandaro, M. Quintyn and M. Taylor, 'Inside and outside the central bank: Independence and Accountability in Financial Supervision: Trends and Determinants' (2008) 24 *European Journal of Political Economy* 833.

[47] A. Cukierman, 'Regulatory Reforms and the Independence of Central Banks and Financial Supervisors' in M. Balling, E. Gnan and P. Jackson (eds.), *States, Banks and the Financing of the Economy: Monetary Policy and Regulation*, SUERF Study 2013/3, Larcier, Brussels 2013.

[48] D. Masciandaro, M. Quintyn and M. Taylor, 'Inside and outside the central bank: Independence and Accountability in Financial Supervision: Trends and Determinants', supra note 46. On analogies and differences between the roles of independence with respect to the conduct of monetary policy and with respect to supervision see M. Arnone and A. Gambini, 'Architecture of Supervisory Authorities and Banking Supervision' in D. Masciandaro and M. Quintyn (eds.), *Designing Financial Supervision Institutions: Independence, Accountability and Governance*, Edward Elgar, Cheltenham 2007, pp. 262–308 and A. Cukierman, 'Regulatory Reforms and the Independence of Central Banks and Financial Supervisors', supra note 47. On the empirics of the central bank independence as supervisor see C. Gaganis and F. Pasiouras, 'Financial Supervision Regimes and Bank Efficiency: International Evidence' (2013) 37 *Journal of Banking and Finance* 5463.

[49] D. Masciandaro – 'Central Bank Governance and Supervision: Economics and Politics', supra note 37 – addresses the supervisory policy side.

in the United States and Europe the goal of financial stability has been elevated.[50] The implications of CBI are far from being consolidated.

Some scholars[51] have claimed that the central bank's involvement in supervision reduces CBI, given that being in charge as a banking supervisor reduces the central bank's commitment – as well as its credibility – as a veto player against inflation. The first argument against the involvement is the possibility of conflicts of interest in managing the two policies that can reduce the effectiveness of pursuing the goal of monetary stability. Furthermore, the probability of conflicts of interest can be endogenous, if the probability of financial instability increases if the fact that the central bank combines monetary and financial stability increases the moral hazard and then the risks of failures of banking firms. Consequently the second argument against the central bank's involvement in supervision is the reputational risks that arise when a central bank is also a supervisor. Failures in supervision can reduce the central bank's reputation, which is a necessary asset to be a credible monetary agent.

Other scholars[52] have however noted that the effect of the supervision involvement on the capacity of the central bank to be an effective monetary authority does not allow clear-cut conclusions, given that arguments for the involvement can be found in the literature. Basically, the central bank's involvement in supervision is supported by arguments related to the information advantages and economies of scale in the monetary policy conduct that derive from having the supervisory functions under the central bank umbrella.

Occupying the middle ground, more scholars[53] have concluded that the consistency between the central bank's involvement in addressing financial stability and the

50 A. Cukierman, 'Monetary Policy and Institutions before, during and after the Global Financial Crisis', supra note 3, D. Masciandaro and M. Nieto, 'Gouvernance du Mécanisme de Supervision Unique: Quelques Réflexions' (2013) 112 *Revue d'Economie Financière* 51.

51 V. Grilli, D. Masciandaro and G. Tabellini, 'Political and Monetary Institutions and Public Financial Policies in the Industrial Countries', supra note 26, O. Issing, *Central Banks - Paradise Lost*, supra note 3.

52 S.C.W Eijffinger and J. De Haan, 'The Political Economy of Central Bank Independence', supra note 12.

53 C. Goodhart and D. Schoenmaker, 'Should the functions of monetary policy and banking supervision be separated?' (1995) 47 *Oxford Economic Papers* 539, A. Cukierman, 'The Economics of Central Banking', supra note 12, A. Cukierman, 'Monetary Policy and Institutions before, during and after the Global Financial Crisis', supra note 3, R. Franck and M. Krausz, 'Why Separate Monetary Policy from Banking Supervision?' (2008) 36 *Journal of Comparative Economics* 388, A. Crockett, 'Central Bank Governance under New Mandates' (2010) *BIS Papers* No. 55, L. Papademos, 'Central Bank Mandates and Governance Arrangements' (2010) *BIS Papers* No. 55, L. Svensson, *Inflation Targeting after the Financial Crisis, Challenges to Central Banking*, Reserve Bank of India's International Research Conference 'Challenges to Central Banking in the Context of Financial Crisis', Mumbai, 12.02.2010, mimeo, B. Aydin and E. Volkan, 'Incorporating Financial Stability in Inflation Targeting Frameworks' (2011) *IMF Working Paper* No. 224, supra note 3, R. Reis, 'Central

effectiveness of monetary policy in controlling the risk of inflation cannot be excluded *a priori*. Therefore the existing literature on the relationship between the effectiveness of the monetary veto player and its involvement in supervision so far provides no uniform and definitive conclusions.

We can give one more perspective: all other things being equal, the citizens' vote on CBI, taking into account risks other than suffering the consequences of the rate of inflation. In this case the question of the redistributive effects linked to the monetary policy can become relevant.[54] For the sake of simplicity consider a population whose preferences against inflation are homogenous, but where the pros and cons of the banking bailouts are heterogeneously distributed among the citizens. If banking instability occurs, the likelihood of a banking bailout has effects on wealth distribution. If the probability of a banking bailout is linked to central bank independence, the citizens may change their preferences regarding CBI depending on the potential financial effects.[55] In this respect it is interesting to note that the global financial crisis is likely to have a negative effect on the reputation of the central banks,[56] which is linked to the financial instability problems *per se*. The concern for financial stability can have implications for the status of independence through the distributional effects on financial portfolios.

The implications for the analysis of the impact on CBI of concrete reforms of central bank involvement in supervision are straightforward: it is necessary to evaluate rule by rule what the consequences are – if any – for the capacity to at least maintain the effectiveness of the central bank as a monetary veto player.

Bank Design' (2013) *NBER Working Paper* No. 19187, L. Reichlin and R. Baldwin, *Is Inflation Targeting Dead? Central Banking After the Crisis*, CEPR, London 2013. S. Fischer – 'Central Bank Independence Revisited', supra note 17 – claimed that the role of the central banker as supervisor is not of much importance. On the empirical relationship between CBI and involvement in supervision see L. Dalla Pellegrina, D. Masciandaro and R.V. Pansini, 'The Central Banker as Prudential Supervisor: Does Independence Matter?' (2013) 9 *Journal of Financial Stability* 415.

54 On the relationship between monetary policy, inflation and redistributive effects see A. Posen, 'Declarations are not Enough: Financial Sectors Sources of Central Bank Independence', supra note 33, J. Bullard and C.J. Waller, 'Central Bank Design in General Equilibrium' (2004) 36 *Journal of Money, Credit and Banking* 95, M. Doepke and M. Schneider, 'Inflation and the Redistribution of Nominal Wealth' (2006) 114 *Journal of Political Economy* 1069, A. Alesina and G. Tabellini, 'Bureaucrats or Politicians? Part I: A Single Policy Task' (2007) 97 *American Economic Review* 169, T. Berriel, *Nominal Portfolio Choice and the Redistribution Effects of Inflation Surprises,* Princeton University Working Paper 2009, mimeo, O. Coibion, Y. Gorodnichenko, L. Kueng and J. Silvia, 'Innocent Bystanders? Monetary Policy and Inequality in the U.S.' (2012) *NBER Working Paper* No. 18710, and H. Hau and S. Lai, 'Asset Allocation and Monetary Policy: Evidence from the Eurozone' (2013) *CEPR Discussion Paper* No. 9581.

55 D. Masciandaro and F. Passarelli, 'Central Banking, Financial Stability and Distributional Monetary Policy: Voting on Independence' *Bocconi University Paolo Baffi Centre Working Paper Series*, forthcoming.

56 O. Issing, *Central Banks – Paradise Lost*, supra note 3.

In this respect let us note the significant example of the European Central Bank (ECB), which can be considered the benchmark for a modern specialised central bank that will now be more involved in supervision.

It has been claimed[57] that today the ECB enjoys a sufficient level of independence as a bank supervisor to seemingly 'piggy back' on the arrangements ensuring monetary policy independence. However, such independence would be further enhanced by: i) the exercise of self-restraint by the European Parliament in its responsibilities of appointment and dismissal of the Chair and Vice Chair of the Supervisory Board so that political considerations derived from their supervisory decisions do not interfere with their European mandate; and ii) the necessary addition of supervisors' legal immunity when exercising their job in good faith. In other words, the effects on the independence of the ECB in hosting the Single European Supervisor are far from being definitively settled.

5. CONCLUSION

Before the global financial crisis, changes in the central bank landscape were characterised by two intertwined features: independent monetary specialisation and supervisory neglect. The above characteristics are two sides of the same coin: the modern central banker was essentially an independent monetary policy agent, focused on monetary goals, which can be pursued by manipulating interest rates.

These trends become evident upon observing the route that the major central banks have followed. The central banks with full responsibility for monetary stability – the Federal Reserve System (Fed), the European Central Bank (ECB), the Bank of England, the Bank of Japan, and the Swiss National Bank – did not have full responsibility for banking supervision. This does not mean that these central banks were not concerned with banking stability, but they generally dealt with it from a macroeconomic perspective and only in relation to their primary mission, i.e. pursuing monetary action.

The modern central bank mainstream can be summarised using the principal–agent terminology.[58] The citizens, who represent the principal, realised that on average the politicians in charge tend to use monetary policy tools to obtain short-term macro goals. The reason for this is that politicians are naturally short-sighted agents, given that they try to maximise their probability of being and/or remaining in charge. Therefore politicians tend to use monetisation to address

---

57 D. Masciandaro and M. Nieto, 'Gouvernance du Mécanisme de Supervision Unique: Quelques Réflexions', supra note 50.

58 D. Masciandaro, 'Central Banking 2.0: Fitting the Mainstream' (2013) 9 *Journal of Financial Stability* 371.

urgent problems of unemployment, fiscal imbalances and banking bailouts. But the more rational and efficient the markets are, the more it is likely that monetisation policies simply produce more inflation and uncertainty, without any real gains.

The citizens realise the politicians' biases in using monetary policy powers and find it optimal to change the rules of the game: monetary policy has to be delegated to an independent and unelected bureaucracy – the central bank – where the bureaucrats in office are designed as career-concerned agents, i.e. they know that their success depends on how they fulfil the goals of their organisation.

Consequently, for monetary policy effectiveness, it is crucial that the mission of the central bank is well defined and established, using three criteria. First of all, the main goal of the central bank has to be monetary stability, in order to avoid the employment bias, i.e. the temptation to use monetary tools to avoid labour market inefficiency problems. Secondly, the central bank cannot finance public deficits and debts in order to avoid the fiscal bias, i.e. the temptation of fiscal monetisation. Thirdly, central bank involvement in supervision and regulation has to be minimised, in order to avoid the banking bias, i.e. the temptation of bailout monetisation.

Furthermore, the mission of the central bank has to be protected from risks of political capture, defining both its independence from the executive power and its accountability with respect to the legislative power. The independence of central banks became the benchmark for evaluating the effectiveness of monetary institutions, supported by empirical analyses which stressed the association between central bank independence and inflation performance.

But now, after the crisis, the situation is changing. The desire to avoid new cases of systemic banking instability and at the same time to address the deep economic crisis has focused new attention on the architecture of the central bank regimes.

Policymakers in all countries have wondered and are still wondering whether to reshape their central bank settings. New proposals to reform these systems have been enacted or are under discussion, at least in Europe and in the United States. In both cases the common trend seems to be an increasing involvement of the central banks in the supervisory field, also taking into account the new distinction between macro and micro supervision.

It is evident that central banking pillars of monetary specialisation and supervisory neglect must be reconsidered. But how? Is it possible to maintain the benefits of the central bank mainstream and at the same time take into account the importance of financial stability? Consequently, is it possible to reintroduce banking responsibilities into the central bank domain in a way that is consistent with the present institutional setting, i.e. without introducing risks of political and/or banking capture?

On these questions the overall suggestion of this chapter is that reconsidering the central banking benchmark implies a relevant risk assumption, which so far has been underestimated. How to hedge this risk is a fundamental issue that must be considered in order to understand not only the economics – if any – of the present demand for central bank reforms, but also what political economy drivers are motivating this demand.

THE ULTRARATIONAL ILLUSION OF FINANCE

Economics and policymaking

Xosé Carlos Arias and Antón Costas

1. INTRODUCTION

Until the 1970s, the prevailing idea was that finance is inherently unstable and could potentially endanger the rest of the economic system. Consequently, regulatory structures were quite strict, the outcome of which was extraordinarily secure financial systems. In fact, there were rather few financial crises of note. However, since then, a dual phenomenon emerged, one that was increasingly cause- and effect-based. On the one hand, new concepts and arguments arose which emphasised the natural efficiency of the financial markets and the assumption that economic subjects behave in a thoroughly rational manner: the Efficient Market Hypothesis (EMH) and the Rational Expectations Hypothesis (REH) gradually became more mainstream elements of financial theory and macroeconomics reasoning, respectively. On the other, the world of finance was undergoing a radical transformation, both in quantitative terms (by the most conservative estimates, its relative weight in the world economy increased by 350% between 1980 and 2007) as well as qualitative ones, as the notion of financial activity shifted drastically during those years through a complex process of four main vectors: innovation, securitisation, deregulation and generalised capital account liberalisation.

EMH and REH predominance was evident not only in academic spheres but also amongst investors and policymakers (the example of Alan Greenspan here would be paradigmatic). These ideas were the fundamental pillars upon which a shared mentality was built, one we shall call a 'belief system', with two major theoretical components that quickly turned psychological: the blind belief in the efficiency of the market mechanism and in the completely rational responses of market agents.

For a few years, the so-called 'Great Moderation', which brought with it the illusion of having finally achieved a cycle-less economic order, with indefinite long-term stability, appeared to legitimise this set of ideas. However, the 2008 financial crisis changed everything: the evidence that international finance was an overly optimistic reality, one that was completely disproportionate and lacking the possibility of any sort of control, created widespread panic in the face of the eventuality of a system collapse. Under these conditions, many top economists and financial analysts directly attributed the origin of the disaster to the EMH and REH. In 2009, one major investor, J. Grantham, summed it up like this: 'The incredibly inaccurate efficient market theory (caused) a lethally dangerous combination of assets bubbles, lax controls, pernicious incentives and wickedly complicated instruments (that) led to our current plight'.[1] The objective in this chapter is to analyse whether this assessment is appropriate by outlining the history of the EMH intellectual development and its methods of influence on the structures (and failings) of regulation and, in broad terms, on policymaking in developed countries.

2. WHEN A THEORY IS MORE THAN AN ARGUMENT: THE EFFICIENT MARKET HYPOTHESIS

Although the beginnings of the EMH can be traced to some early 20th century theoretical developments,[2] a paper published by Eugene Fama in 1965[3] is generally considered to be the starting point for this hypothesis. This is true at least in its strictest version, as the EMH actually takes on two successive forms that are slightly different from each other. The first, which we might call the 'weak form', incorporates the idea of a 'random walk' in the stock exchange, according to which current stock prices have no connection whatsoever to past prices. Therefore, it is not possible to predict future prices based on past prices. Since the relevant information is open and public (and, by definition, unpredictable, since it may change from one moment to the next), it is distributed equally amongst all of the market agents, such that 1) as it is not possible to make a prediction, the 'technical' or 'fundamental analysis' for that prediction loses all value; and 2) no one, not a single agent, can get ahead of the market itself. Burke Malkiel's 1973 book, *A Random Walk Down Wall Street*,[4] helped spread these ideas.

1. J.J. Siegel, 'Efficient Market Theory and the Crisis' *The Wall Street Journal*, 27.10.2009.
2. A. Kirman, 'The Economy and Economic Theory in Crisis' in D. Coyle (ed.), *What's the Use of Economics. Teaching the Dismal Science after the Crisis*, London Publishing Partnership, London 2012, pp. 61–76 and M. Sewell, 'History of the Efficient Market Hypothesis' (2011) *UCL Research Note* No. 11/04.
3. E. Fama, 'Random Walks in Stock Market Prices' (1965) *University of Chicago Graduate School of Business Selected Paper* No. 16.
4. B.C. Malkiel, *A Random Walk Down Wall Street*, Norton, New York 1973.

The 'strong form' of the EMH is the one that Fama himself developed. In short, it consists of assuming that the prices of financial assets always include all the relevant information ('prices fully reflect all known information'); competition between fully informed participants leads to positions of efficient equilibrium. Therefore, the price coincides with the intrinsic value of the securities. It is important here to define the idea of efficiency: ('A market in which prices always "fully reflect" available information is called "efficient"'[5]): 'In an efficient market, competition among the many intelligent participants leads to a situation where, at any point in time, actual prices of individual securities already reflect the effects of information based both on events that have already occurred and on events which as of now the market expects to take place in the future. In other words, in an efficient market at any point in time the actual price of a security will be a good estimate of its intrinsic value'.[6]

With this version of the EMH, there is no sense in talking about market 'bubbles' or 'herd behaviour', nor about any other anomaly in the response of the agents that we could qualify as 'animal spirit'. Bubbles simply do not exist: the market's self-purification elements eliminate them. For any asset, the palpable existence of a 'bubble' would lead rational market agents to sell it immediately and wait to repurchase it at a lower price. The dynamics of downward purchase trends would ultimately eliminate such a bubble completely. At this point, the approach's platonic nature, which heads only its own internal logic, begins to push its way out of the ground: as we shall later see, during the same decades in which the papers published in the best financial research journals accepted it without any doubts, the world was witnessing the largest bubble in the history of finance.

There are also some differences between the various versions of the theory with regard to the scope of application. Although some of the initial contributions to the EMH, such as that of Paul Samuelson,[7] centred around a micro-approach (that is to say, he believed that his reasoning could explain the evolution of a single stock in a specific market), there was soon a shift toward a more macro vision; in other words, the acceptance of its full validity for an aggregate scale market. In fact, this theory went on to become an indisputable part of the so-called *New Macroeconomic Consensus*, which was considered to have become established during the final years of the bubble.[8] To sum up the essence of this increasingly widespread theoretical approach in one sentence, it was a response to an attempt

---

5 E. Fama, 'Efficient Capital Markets: A Review of Theory and Empirical Work' (1970) 25 *The Journal of Finance* 383, 383.

6 E. Fama, 'Random Walks in Stock Market Prices', supra note 3.

7 P.A. Samuelson, 'Proof that properly anticipated prices fluctuate randomly' (1965) 6 *Industrial Management Review* 41.

8 W. Buiter, 'The unfortunate uselessness of most "state of the art" academic monetary economics', *Financial Times*, 03.03.2009.

to 'apply microeconomic principles to macroeconomics'. From this point on, the confluence with the Rational Expectations Hypothesis began to close off a cycle of complete rationality and efficiency that has constituted the nucleus of economic theory of the past few decades. Nevertheless, it is interesting to note that as far as the EMH is concerned, Samuelson himself was rather critical of this vision, since – as a former Keynesian – he believed in the existence of bubbles and elements of instability in the aggregate dynamics of the economy: 'we have no theory of the putative duration of a bubble. It can always go as long again as it has already gone. You cannot make money on correcting macro inefficiencies in the price level of the stock market'.[9] However, it was the macro version of the EMH that was ultimately spread more widely.

In reality, behind the EMH is a rather simple idea, but its formalisation through sophisticated mathematical formulas gave it a high level of academic respectability. Despite its rather aprioristic nature, in a short period of time the financial perspective of most economists changed radically, particularly once it became engrained in some of the most influential models such as – first and foremost – the Black-Scholes model of pricing options, formalised by Robert Merton.[10] Why was this conception of financial markets so seductive at that time? For three main reasons: first and foremost, on account of doctrine: Keynesianism began to collapse as early as the 1970s. Various branches of macroeconomic reasoning launched serious attempts to legitimate the market mechanism in the face of the 'State's failures', which they attributed to Keynesianism. The REH and EMH are the core of New Classical Macroeconomics, which, in turn, is a main vein of this theoretical revolution that quickly gained power. Secondly, it has already been noted that the financial systems came from a certain attitude – which originated during the Great Depression – of little inclination toward risk, due to the prevalence of public controls of all types that were exercised on financial entities. This made them quite sound, but the existence of those controls also introduced some visible elements of inefficiency. From that point on, banks and the entire financial community began to push for deregulation, pressuring public powers in that direction. What they needed was a formal argument to back them up, and the EMH proved quite useful in that regard.

Lastly, it is possible that all of the above would not have made much progress had there not been a vast technological revolution of information flows, one that affected the financial sector unlike any other. Beginning in 1980, a process of tremendous innovation took place in financial services and products, which

---

9 P.A. Samuelson, 'Summing Up on Business Cycles: Opening Address' in J.C. Fuhrer and S. Schuh, *Beyond Shocks: What Causes Business Cycles, Conference Series 42*, Federal Reserve Bank of Boston, Boston 1998, pp. 33–36.

10 J. Quiggin, *Zombie Economics. How Dead Ideas Still Walk Among Us*, Princeton University Press, Princeton, New Jersey 2010.

ultimately transformed the basic idea of what a financial entity is. If, in 1980, a bank represented – above all – the generation of credit negotiated in a physical, recognisable place that was close in proximity to the borrower, by 2005, finances had essentially become a vast virtual network of business without borders, with thousands of agents interacting amongst themselves in Singapore or Buenos Aires, with extraordinarily sophisticated products whose nature was, in many cases, scarcely understood even by the most advanced professionals.

In this new scenario, regulatory structures were confined to an increasingly limited area. Innovation seeks – and in many cases manages – to evade regulatory controls. If to that you add a booming pro-market ideology into the mix, it is not hard to understand how we arrived at 'light-touch regulation', where the idea of self-regulation by the very market agents themselves reigned supreme.[11] In this vision, the market processes are clearly superior for monitoring, anticipating and measuring risk. Alan Greenspan summarised this idea precisely. As we shall later see, among policymakers, he was one of the most steadfast EMH supporters: 'The market-stabilizing private regulatory forces should gradually displace many cumbersome, increasingly ineffective government structures'.[12]

In particular, more than a few transactions with structured products were kept from any effective possibility of strict control. In the business of finance, the presence of secondary market transactions, CDOs, default insurance, and hedge funds has only continued to grow. The new mainstream line of thought in financial theory became the closing element in the construction of this entire empire. For example, there is no doubt that the Black-Scholes model of option pricing was precisely the intellectual foundation that the derivatives markets needed to multiply their operative volumes, based on the belief that this was the best option for the economy as a whole. In the words of Alan Blinder, '[t]heoretical valuation models based on EMH-type reasoning were used by Wall Street financial engineers to devise and prise all sorts of exotic derivatives'.[13]

Another fundamental characteristic of modern capital markets is the radical shift in their temporal dimension. Increasing acceleration has become an essential requirement by which financial entities maximise their balance sheets, particularly in the last 15 years. This is what Andrew Haldane has called the race

---

11 X.C. Arias and A. Costas, *La torre de la arrogancia. Políticas y mercados después de la tormenta*, 2nd ed., Ariel, Barcelona 2011, X.C. Arias and A. Costas, 'The Great Recession and Economic Policy: Roots and Consequences' in J. Bilbao-Ubillos (ed.), *The Economic Crisis and Governance in the European Union,* Routledge, London 2013, pp. 13–30, E. Engelen et al., *After the Great Complacence. Financial Crisis and the Politics of Reform*, Oxford University Press, Oxford 2011.

12 Financial Crisis Inquiry Commission, *The Financial Crisis Inquiry Report,* U.S. Congress, Washington D.C. 2011, p. 28.

13 A. Blinder, *After the Music Stopped*, Penguin, New York 2013, p. 65.

to zero: 'The average speed of order execution on the US New York Stock Exchange has fallen from around 20 seconds a decade ago to around one second today'.[14] In order for this to happen, *high frequency trading,* which spread from New York to stock exchanges around the world, was key. What began humbly in the derivatives markets of the 1990s had by 2012 already encompassed nearly three quarters of negotiation in those markets. An automatised system that justifies itself in its immediate search for prices and quantities between suppliers and claimants of all types of financial assets. None of this could be done without machines: these days, it is not usually humans who make decisions but, rather, large computers capable of handling complex algorithms. This cyber finance world was propelled forward by the *random walk* concept that Malkiel popularised in 1973, and, in broader terms, it was truly legitimised by the EMH theory.

With the rise of modern global financial capitalism, capital markets began to be seen as a nearly infinite network of antennae that market agents made ready to capture any and all signals sent out by other economic players – be they public or private – in order to make investments (or divestments) in a fraction of the time. Since this process is universally observable, it naturally follows that the markets and agents that make decisions therein are omniscient – a characterisation of an economic subject that fits perfectly with the EMH assumptions (and, of course, with the notion of rational expectations). Following this characterisation is a conclusion that uses this approach to help explain the reality of modern-day macroeconomic policies. Through their ongoing debt market negotiations, the markets are consistently making accurate judgements, without any systematic errors, regarding the quality of these policies. This translates into a major restriction for policymakers: in other words, the 'golden straitjacket' concept that Thomas Friedman made popular in his book *The lexus and the olive tree,*[15] which clearly exhibits the basic lines of EMH reasoning.

All of the foregoing points toward a relevant conclusion: the history of contemporary finance is the result of an extraordinarily expansive process in which theory and reality feed off of each other, each propelling the other forward. That is to say, the line of argument sparked the deregulation of the large-scale markets, but, at the same time, their increasing level of autonomy and (supposed) transparency based on immediate and generalised information strengthened the credibility of this standpoint. It is a remarkable and highly unusual phenomenon, particularly when you consider that the EMH assumptions (just like the idea of rational expectations) are incredibly aprioristic and may, in fact, be considered as the 'toughest', most radical and restrictive in the history of social sciences. And, for many, from Robert Solow to Albert Hirschman, they could not have

[14] A. Haldane, *The race to zero,* IEA Sixteenth World Congress, Beijing 2011.
[15] T.L. Friedman, *The lexus and the olive tree,* Farrar, Straus and Giroux, New York 1999.

been farther from the truth. In any case, there is no doubt that we are facing the most extreme variants of the neoclassical notions of rationality and efficiency as equilibrium.

As previously stated, some of the more moderate versions of the EMH accepted, under certain conditions, the existence of elements of irrationality and bubbles, if as nothing more than an exception to the rule. For example, according to Malkiel: 'as long as markets exists, the collective judgment of investors will sometimes make mistakes. Undoubtedly, some participants are demonstrably less than rational (...). Periods such as 1999 where "bubbles" seem to have existed, at least in certain sectors of the market, are fortunately the exception rather than the rule'.[16]

However, there is no doubt that many of its main promoters expressed the theory in more radical and exclusionary terms for nearly three decades and that it was accepted as dogma by individuals within financial entities and regulatory bodies. In any event, there is no question that it has been at the core of economic and financial studies at top universities, making it an essential aspect of the training of today's economists.[17] Neither an ongoing stream of criticism of this approach[18] nor the evidence that the strict application of some of these models had already caused a number of disasters (which is precisely what happened with the Black-Scholes model in the Long-Term Capital Management collapse in the United States in 1998) managed to reverse the trends.

On another note, it is important to point out that during that same period, there were some notable contributions to financial theory that had nothing to do with the EMH. First and foremost, there was Hyman Minsky's financial instability hypothesis,[19] which radically opposed Fama's argument. A variety of behavioural finance theories began to take root through the work of Robert Shiller[20] and

---

16 B.C. Malkiel, 'The Efficient Market Hypothesis and Its Critics' (2003) 17 *Journal of Economic Perspectives* 59.

17 D. Colander et al., *The Financial Crisis and the Systemic Failure of Academic Economics*, University of Copenhagen Department of Economics Discussion Paper 2009, D. Coyle (ed.), *What's the Use of Economics. Teaching the Dismal Science after the Crisis*, London Publishing Partnership, London 2012.

18 B.C. Malkiel – 'The Efficient Market Hypothesis and Its Critics', supra note 16 – describes the systematic relationship between the criticisms, as do A.W. Lo – 'Efficient Markets Hypothesis' in S.N. Durlauf and L.E. Blume, *The New Palgrave Dictionary of Economics*, 2nd ed., Palgrave Macmillan, New York 2008 – and M. Sewell – 'History of the Efficient Market Hypothesis', supra note 2.

19 H.P. Minsky, *Stabilizing an Unstable Economy*, Yale University Press, New Haven, Connecticut 1986.

20 R.J. Shiller, *Irrational Exuberance*, 2nd ed., Princeton University Press, Princeton, New Jersey 2005 and R.J. Shiller, *Finance and the Good Society*, Princeton University Press, Princeton, New Jersey 2012.

Richard Thaler.[21] Similarly, literature on moral hazard, adverse selection, and, in general, informational asymmetries made tremendous progress by applying itself to specific financial market issues. This, in turn, fuelled the argument in favour of regulation of those markets. In some cases – as in the article by Stiglitz and Weiss[22] – these contributions had a significant academic impact but little practical use. In other cases, they simply remained obscured for decades. One great example is Minsky (considered since 2008 as one of the leading economists), who was scarcely mentioned in major economic magazines between 1990 and 2007.[23] It would appear that something similar happened to the great economic historian Charles Kindleberger, who verified the repeated and systematic presence of bubbles and anomalies of all types in the true history of finance.[24] In any case, most of these theories were scarcely visible for several decades, absent from economic manuals and reports by central banks and multilateral agencies.

Undoubtedly, due to its formal rigour and ample academic support, the EMH was the perfect argument for legitimising capitalism's hyperfinancial development between 1980 and 2007. In that regard, far from being a mere 'contribution' or confined to the sphere of academic debate, this theory went quite a bit further to have a significant impact on several key aspects of contemporary economics.

3. FROM THEORY TO AN ENTIRE BELIEF SYSTEM

After 2008, for the most part, this entire empire came crumbling down. Since then, the dramatic evidence that the vision of *market equilibrium* has become completely disconnected from the reality of the financial markets, where suddenly everyone began to fear a generalised collapse, was compounded by anti-EMH criticism, to such an extent that soon it was considered a 'zombie theory'. Investor Georges Soros summed it up nicely: the 'prevailing paradigm of efficient market hypothesis – rational choice theory – has actually run into bankruptcy, very similar to the bankruptcy of the global financial system after Lehman Brothers'.[25]

After the change in the financial climate due to the crisis, some EMH supporters argued that in reality, this theory suffered from 'over-interpretation' and that its real influence on regulatory entities and policymakers was always relatively minor: it was far less significant than we have been led to believe. (More specifically,

21 R. Thaler (ed.), *Advances in Behavioral Finance II*, Sage, New York 2005.

22 J. Stiglitz and A. Weis, 'Credit Rationing in Markets with Imperpect Information' (1981) 71 *American Economic Review* 393.

23 As noted by G.M. Hodgson, 'The great crash of 2008 and the reform of economics' (2009) 33 *Cambridge Journal of Economics* 1205.

24 C.P. Kindleberger, *Manias, Panics, and Crashes*, Basic Books, New York 1989.

25 G. Soros, *Why We Need to Rethink Economics*, The Institute for New Economic Thinking 2013.

comments of this type could be heard after Eugene Fama won the much-contested Nobel Prize in 2013.) However, there is ample proof that for many years EMH theorists believed that their arguments shaped the reality of the financial world. This is confirmed in an interview with Fama in a journal of the Federal Reserve Bank of Minneapolis: 'Few economists have had greater influence on financial theory, and practice, than Eugene Fama (…) Fama's work soon transformed Wall Street, and later Main Street, by giving rise to a proliferation of low-cost index funds …'.[26] The same issue also includes the opinion of Myron Scholes: 'Eugene Fama has had path breaking insights into the functioning of markets, assets-pricing theory, and corporate finance, insights that have benefited market participants worldwide'.[27]

However, aside from what supporters might say, there is no doubt that the main central banks and regulatory agencies – particularly those of the English-speaking world – devised, starting in 1980, a basic set of theoretical references where the ideas of natural market efficiency and rational expectations prevailed. Since at least 1986, the EMH was the main theory of reference for British deregulation philosophy, based on 'market discipline'.[28] This is how the Financial Services Authority (FSA) came into existence in 1997. No one has expressed this with more clarity than its former chairman, Adair Turner, who, upon being asked about 'the intellectual assumptions on which previous regulatory approaches have largely been built', responded: 'The predominant assumption behind financial market regulation – in the US, the UK and increasingly across the world – has been that financial markets are capable of being both efficient and rational and that a key goal of financial market regulation is to remove the impediments which might produce inefficient and illiquid markets. A large body of theoretical and empirical work has been devoted to proving that share prices in well regulated liquid markets, follow "random walks" (…) with prices instead changing as new information becomes available and is assessed by a wide range of independently acting market participants. And the assumption has been that (…) are in general rational in their assessments and that the overall level of prices as a result has a strong tendency towards a rational equilibrium'.[29]

In more general terms, during the decades that preceded the meltdown, the criteria for defining monetary and fiscal policy, and their basic institutional framework (*rules rather than discretion*, *central banks independence*, etc) became

---

26 D. Clement, 'Interview with Eugene Fama' (2007) December 2007 *The Region: Banking and Policy Issues Magazine*.

27 D. Clement, 'Interview with Eugene Fama', supra note 26.

28 R. Woodward, *New institutions but old ideas: the story of the UK's new regulatory regime for financial services*, Speri Comment 02.07.2012.

29 A. Turner, *The Turner Review. A regulatory response to the global banking crisis*, Financial Services Authority, London 2009.

an integral part of the assumption of ultra-rationality of the agents.[30] As far as monetary policy is concerned, its operative models during those years – the so-called Dynamic Stochastic General Equilibrium models – were built according to EMH and REH theoretical outlines. This would explain two of its main defects, which have repeatedly been noted since the financial collapse but which were scarcely mentioned prior to 2008: the total exclusion of all credit cycles and of any connection between monetary policy and macro-prudential bank regulation.[31]

It may seem a tad exaggerated to attribute such a high level of influence to theories that are so highly complex and abstract. The objection could make sense when applied to each of them individually. Therefore, it is essential to understand the evolving dynamics in their entirety: the different assumptions and arguments fed off each other to build a new, crucial belief system in which ultrarationality and automatic equilibrium left no room whatsoever for questioning the limitless nature of financial innovation, the continuous acceleration of exchanges, and deregulation as an object of desire. That is to say, a new dominant conventional wisdom began to emerge, and it undoubtedly had a profound effect on the line of reflection and action of the main national and supranational regulatory bodies and, in general, economic policymaking. Nevertheless, dominant conventional wisdom tends to combine ideas and interests: in recent decades, both elements experienced intense interactions, which ultimately defined an entire mentality, a consistent, strict ideological system.[32] Once more, in the words of Turner: 'Interests and ideology often interact in ways so subtle that is difficult to disentangle them, the influence of interests achieved through an unconsciously accepted ideology (...) Market efficiency and market completion theories can help reassure the top executives of major financial institutions that they must in some subtle way be doing God's work even when it looks at first sight as if some of their trading is simple speculation. (...) industry experts are almost bound to share the industry's implicit assumptions'.[33]

In the midst of all this, a new narrative aimed at legitimising deregulatory tendencies began to emerge amongst the economic and political elite, be it the radicalisation of the arguments in favour of the market mechanism and the

---

30 V.V. Chari and P.J. Kehoe, 'Modern Macroeconomics in Practice: How Theory Is Shaping Policy' (2006) 20 *Journal of Economic Perspectives* 3.

31 C.A.E. Goodhart and D. Tsomocos, 'Default and DGSE models', *VoxEU,* 26.11.2009 and C. Borio, 'The financial cycle and macroeconomics: What have we learnt?' (2012) *BIS Working Paper* No. 395.

32 J. Bhagwati, 'The Capital Myth. The Difference between Trade in Widgets and Dollars' (1998) 77 *Foreign Affairs,* S. Johnson and J. Kwak, *13 Bankers. The Wall Street Takeover and the Next Financial Meltdown,* Pantheon Books, New York 2010, A. Blinder, *After the Music Stopped,* supra note 13.

33 A. Turner, *Economics, conventional wisdom and public policy,* Institute for New Economic Thinking Inaugural Conference, Cambridge, April 2010.

flagellant value of pure risk or the emphasis upon the social and economic value of finances in terms of overall well being.[34]

After the financial meltdown, some of the foremost policymakers criticised themselves profoundly, if briefly (as we shall see, this trend did not continue), for their course of action prior to the crisis. Overall, this belief system has had a rather negative influence, as it assigned minimal value to the likelihood of a disaster and, consequently, blocked the availability of an effective safety net. Thanks to this, today we have a better understanding of how some rather abstract lines of reasoning became the sole agenda for policy-related decision-making.

In the case of the International Monetary Fund (IMF), the esteemed Evaluation Report 2004–2007 of the Independent Evaluation Office (IEO) bluntly interpreted the problems that led to the agency's failure to identify the major risks financial systems were facing. According to the IEO, the main factor was the analytical weaknesses associated with different cognitive biases (a high degree of group thinking, intellectual capture and confirmation bias). The other problems it notes – and it has studied their relationship to the primary issue – are the organisational impediments, the internal governance problems, and the political constraints.[35] Of particular interest is their reference to the significant role of group thinking, a tendency among cohesive groups to consider issues only within a certain paradigm and not challenge its basic premises: 'The prevailing view among IMF staff – a cohesive group of macroeconomists – was that market discipline and self-regulation would be sufficient to stave off serious problems in financial institutions. They also believed that crises were unlikely to happen in advanced economies, where "sophisticated" financial markets could thrive safely with minimal regulation of a large and growing portion of the financial system'.[36]

Similarly, the report highlights a marked confirmation bias, that is to say, a tendency of IMF staff to record only information that was consistent with their beliefs and expectations and to ignore anything to the contrary. Thus, the models for interpreting reality became self-sustaining and circular. Former IMF Chief Economist Simon Johnson left a significant testimony to this in *The Quiet Coup*.[37]

In the case of central banks and specialised regulatory agencies, this belief system was built in a consistent, strict manner. A 2011 survey of 200 central bankers and

---

34 E. Engelen et al., *After the Great Complacence. Financial Crisis and the Politics of Reform*, supra note 11.

35 International Monetary Fund (Independent Evaluation Office), *Performance in the Run-up to the Financial and Economic Crisis: IMF Surveillance in 2004–07*, IMF, Washington D.C. 2011.

36 International Monetary Fund (Independent Evaluation Office), *Performance in the Run-up to the Financial and Economic Crisis: IMF Surveillance in 2004–07*, supra note 35, p. 17.

37 S. Johnson, 'The Quiet Coup', *The Atlantic*, 01.05.2009.

economists from 16 different countries conducted on behalf of the Prime Minister of France reveals that when asked 'is the economic crisis a crisis of economic theory?' 100% of the bankers surveyed answered 'no'. Meanwhile, to the question 'are DSGE Models fundamentally flawed', 82% responded 'no' (as opposed to the 59% of economists who replied 'yes').[38] These data are quite significant, since at the time these arguments had already become the object of serious scrutiny.

In the United States, the influence of the EMH and REH was decisive for defining Federal Reserve policy during Alan Greenspan's nearly 20 years of leadership. Greenspan's financial perspective was radical: he believed that the very nature of regulation impinges upon market freedom ('too complex for human intervention'). It was understood that the use of sophisticated mathematical models based on the assumptions of ultrarationality, efficiency, and lack of uncertainty guaranteed stability all on their own, in a generalised setting of financial innovation, without any room for bubbles, credit cycles or any other sort of anomaly. As Greenspan himself later acknowledged, the relationship between theory and policy was direct: 'All the new concepts with every theoretical advance was embodied in that model –rational expectations, monetarism, all sorts of sophisticated means of thinking about how the economy worked. The Fed has 250 (economic) PhDs in that division and they are all very smart'.[39]

Thus, deregulation progressed more slowly than in any other developed country, and once it was assumed that financial stability was guaranteed, monetary policy was applied exclusively to control inflation. Undoubtedly, more than anyone else, Greenspan embodies the belief system described thus far. Moreover, the strategy's apparent positive results during the years of expansion turned it into a symbol of the era.

The publication by renowned journalist Bob Woodward of the book *Maestro*,[40] which extols Greenspan's virtues right from the very title, demonstrates just how far this belief system managed to penetrate the mass media culture. In fact, many sectors would not have dreamed of disputing Greenspan's figure. They saw him as a sort of magician with the secret codes to economic knowledge, able to promote indefinite progress without any hiccoughs along the way. Along the same lines, other widely distributed publications include the above-mentioned book by Thomas Friedman,[41] who helped spread the idea that markets cannot fail,

38 E. Carré et al., 'Central Banking after the Crisis: Brave New World or Back to the Future?' (2013) *Centre d'Economie de la Sorbonne Working Paper* No. 73.

39 G. Tett, 'An interview with Alan Greenspan', *Financial Times*, 25.10.2013.

40 B. Woodward, *Maestro. Greenspans Fed and the American Boom*, Touchstone, New York 2000.

41 T.L. Friedman, *The lexus and the olive tree*, supra note 15.

and, above all, *The Wisdom of Crowds*, by James Surowiecki[42] who, from the very title of his book, uses psychological and computational reasoning to highlight the notion of the wisdom of crowds. The basic idea is that the intelligence of a crowd of people can surpass that of any expert when facing problems related to cognition, coordination, and cooperation. That is to say, all signs indicate that policymakers did not trample on the aspiration of ultrarationality; rather, it spread vehemently throughout society. Along with it, the model of macroeconomic policy and light-touch regulation enjoyed a high level of support throughout an array of social sectors. More importantly, as these ideas spread more intensely, many lost the notion of the fear that can accompany financial risk: 'As the enthusiasm for the efficient markets hypothesis after Fama's watershed 1965 paper reached excessive levels, it brought forth an unhealthy degree of credulity in people trusting their money to financial markets'.[43] In that regard, because of their decisive assistance in changing society's attitude toward finances, it can be said that the EMH (and the REH) were highly responsible for the Great Recession.

The independence of central banks and regulatory agencies encouraged the idea of converting light-touch regulation into dogma for these types of entities in many countries. However, its influence also expanded, albeit in a more nuanced way, to governments (particularly to the Ministry of Economy and the Treasury) and some legislative sectors. A singular example would be that of Great Britain, where Gordon Brown, Chancellor of the Exchequer for more than a decade, demonstrated limitless confidence in the notion that all elements of capital market regulation should be 'increasingly risk-based'. To justify the massive use of structured instruments, he relied on lines of reasoning taken directly from EMH logic.[44] In fact, his hypotheses were often similar to those of Greenspan, of whom, on a number of occasions, he has declared himself a great admirer. In his economic policy model, Brown gave absolute priority to developing liberalised finances, such that the boom in growth during those years was based principally on extensive leveraging, which turned the British economy into one of the world's most indebted in 2008: 469% of GDP.[45] Shortly before the crisis he foresaw 'an era that history will record as the beginning of a new golden age for the City of London. (...) a new world order was created',[46] but as we shall later see, its change in direction starting in 2008 was quite marked, nearly 180 degrees.

42 J. Surowiecki, *The Wisdom of Crowds*, Anchor Books, New York 2005.

43 R.J. Shiller, *Finance and the Good Society,* supra note 20, p. 170.

44 G. Brown, Speech by the Chancellor of the Exchequer, Mansion House, London, 2006.

45 C. Roxburgh, S. Lund, T. Daruvala, J. Manyika, R. Dobbs, R. Forn and K. Croxson, *Debt and deleveraging: Uneven progress on the path to growth*, McKinsey Global Institute, Washington D.C. 2012.

46 S. Lee, 'Gordon Brown and the British Way of Risk-Based Modernization' (2011) 10 *Observatoire de la société britannique* 45.

Brown is somewhat exceptional here; in the case of other Heads of State or Parliament, the connection with Fama or Lucas' theories was not as direct. Nevertheless, there is no doubt that in a broader sense, the deregulated market belief system spread rapidly – to a greater or lesser extent, depending on the case – throughout the realm of policymaking in the developed world at large. Under the assumption that debt instruments were developed in an utterly transparent and rational setting, their expansion was considered something of a panacea to resolve all kinds of economic problems. For example, in the case of the United States, Raghu Rajan has provided a convincing explanation that the growth – considered guaranteed – of mortgage lending (and its disproportionate development through secondary markets) was devised by the Clinton and Bush Administrations as a way to counteract the increasing inequality in income and wealth due to the downward salary trend (substitution of wages for debt). Thus, since the beginning of the 1990s, in order to promote social cohesion, one of the primary veins of economic policy permitted vast low-cost credit expansion – 'let them eat credit' – which enabled access to ownership for a wide variety of social sectors. The outcome, clearly, was the emergence of a giant bubble.[47]

In continental Europe, this belief system also arose with vigour, in this case within the context of monetary integration into the euro. One significant case was Spain, where a large financial bubble formed around the vast expansion of the real estate sector. Unlimited access to international capital markets (supported by the alleged credibility granted by eurozone membership) helped finance the boom as the key to economic policy (regarding which there was scarcely any differences whatsoever between political parties) and the process of sustained GDP growth over 14 years. The clear indicators that this process was not sustainable – such as a 10% deficit in the 2007 trade balance – were hardly taken into consideration, since the calculations of the political and economic elite did not contemplate any flow interruptions that could occur as a result of a possible financial crisis. In fact, they barely caused any panic whatsoever. In that context, though the Bank of Spain exercised rather rigorous regulation (through the so-called '*provisiones genéricas*') the risk concentration oversight that banks adopted became increasingly lax, which ultimately led to a major banking crisis.[48] Both Spain and the US (with 295% and 230%, respectively, of private debt to GDP in 2008)[49] are proof that during the decades leading up to the meltdown, the tale spun around the unlimited benefits of globalised finances crossed ideological divides, thus encompassing both left- and right-wing governments.

---

47 R.G. Rajan, *Fault Lines: How Hidden Fractures Still Threaten the World Economy*, Princeton University Press, Princeton, New Jersey 2010.

48 X.C. Arias and A. Costas, *La torre de la arrogancia. Políticas y mercados después de la tormenta*, supra note 11.

49 C. Roxburgh, S. Lund, T. Daruvala, J. Manyika, R. Dobbs, R. Forn and K. Croxson, *Debt and deleveraging: Uneven progress on the path to growth*, supra note 45.

4. THE EMH IN THE WAKE OF THE STORM: A SHIFT IN PARADIGM?

The 2008 collapse belied the fundamental EMH assumptions: the market mechanisms (through, for example, credit rating agencies) failed to operate properly, the intended transparency was utterly lacking (in short, little was known about most of the structured products), and the reaction of many market agents was far from 'rational'. In the midst of the panic and improvised bank bailout operations, it became clear that the financial innovation had created a debt vortex that to all intents and purposes was out of control. In light of this new situation, some regulatory entities criticised themselves harshly, expressing their willingness to abandon the theories that had so inspired them over the past 20 years. Among these, notably, was the British FSA. Many of this agency's documents make clear the intense, ultrarational illusion that defined its behaviour for decades. When, in a 2009 report, the agency asked itself 'what went wrong?' the responses given include the financial market innovation, the structured credit, increasing leverage, self-reinforcing irrational exuberance, and 'misplaced reliance on sophisticated maths': 'the very complexity of the mathematics used to measure and manage risks, moreover, made it increasingly difficult for top management and boards to assess and exercise judgement over the risks being taken'.[50]

The report goes on to specifically highlight EMH as the direct inspiration behind those errors and the following conclusions, which thoroughly question that theory, are drawn: 'market efficiency does not imply market rationality; individual rationality does not ensure collective rationality; individual behaviour is not entirely rational; allocative efficiency benefits have limits; empirical evidence illustrates large scale herd effects and market overshoots'.[51]

Through this review, the FSA left behind its belief system which, until just shortly beforehand, had been quite well established. A process of drastic reform began, culminating in the new Financial Services Act, which entered into effect in April 2013 and expanded the regulatory mechanisms in place so as to avoid past mistakes.

In the case of the United States, the main way to investigate the responsibility of ultrarational illusion of finances in generating the crisis is through the Financial Crisis Inquiry Report issued by Congress in 2011: 'More than 30 years of deregulation and reliance on self-regulation by financial institutions, championed by former Federal Reserve chairman Alan Greenspan and others, supported by

---

50 A. Turner, *The Turner Review. A regulatory response to the global banking crisis*, supra note 29, p. 22.

51 A. Turner, *The Turner Review. A regulatory response to the global banking crisis*, supra note 29, pp. 40–41.

successive administrations and Congresses, and actively pushed by the powerful financial industry at every turn, had stripped away key safeguards, which could have helped avoid catastrophe'.[52]

What is even more revealing is that in the wake of the crisis, the two major policymakers who for so many years had defended an ultrarational financial perspective, Alan Greenspan and Gordon Brown, have distanced themselves dramatically from this line of thinking. In recent years, Greenspan has, in part, harshly criticised himself for his hand in the matter. He has distanced himself from his former belief in the EMH and REH, opting instead to adopt an opposing stance: that is to say, behavioural economics.[53] Interestingly enough, he now emphasises the peculiarity of finances: 'In the non-financial part of the system (rational economic theory) works very well… Finance is wholly different from the rest the economy. More specifically, while markets sometimes behave in ways that models might predict, they can also become "irrational", driven by animal spirits that defy maths'.[54]

In Brown's case, after many years of relying on the arguments of ultrarationality and efficiency to report his policies, at a 2011 Harvard conference he stated: 'none of the (economic) theories we had in 2007 stood to examination because markets did not self-adjust. Markets self-destructed'.[55] Thus, the ultrarational illusion of finances crumbled for those who had done the most to transfer it, without any nuances, to the world of policymaking.

After five years of intense controversy, it became clear that the scientific crisis that affected the entire economy was based primarily on the two theories that have dominated this chapter: EMH and REH. As in other periods of the history of economic analysis, the key to this crisis lay in the utter disparity between the theories' assumptions and predictions and what actually occurred. In a notable essay, Jon Elster used the phrase 'excessive ambitions' to sum up his criticism of the attempts to convert the ultrarational illusion of economic behaviour into 'hard science': a strong deductive reasoning based on fragile or imaginary assumptions but which establishes universal conclusions.[56] This is a sort of *intellectual hubris* that is directly associated with a blind faith in the rigor of the mathematical logic used and the power of calculations. At this point, rational expectations, efficient markets, and DSGE models can be seen as the culmination of the economy's old

---

52 Financial Crisis Inquiry Commission, *The Financial Crisis Inquiry Report*, supra note 12, p. xviii.

53 A. Greenspan, *The Map and the Territory. Risk, Human Nature, and the Future of Forecasting*, The Penguin Press, New York 2013.

54 G. Tett, 'An interview with Alan Greenspan', *Financial Times*, 25.10.2013, supra note 39.

55 S. Lee, 'Gordon Brown and the British Way of Risk-Based Modernization', supra note 46.

56 J. Elster, 'Excessive Ambitions' (2009) 4 *Capitalism and Society* 1.

aspiration to assimilate to the method of physics. A.V. Lo (an EMH inner circle author, though he was highly critical of its most severe forms) and M. Mueller have summed it up like this: 'Warning: Physics Envy May Be Hazardous to Your Wealth!: The quantitative aspirations of economists and financial analysts have for many years been based on the belief that it should be possible to build models of economic systems – and financial markets in particular – that are as predictive as those in physics. While this perspective has led to a number of important breakthroughs in economics, "physics envy" has also created a false sense of mathematical precision in some cases'.[57]

The founding of the Institute for New Economic Thinking (INET) in 2010 was a fundamental aspect of the attempt to part ways with this paradigm. In its basic explanation of purpose ('Why the Institute?'), it states: 'The prevailing thinking, that the economy is an idealized system of perfectly rational, optimizing individuals and institutions, who, by trading in markets, bring the economy to a balanced, efficient equilibrium has been rendered obsolete by developments in recent years'.[58]

However, although the state of dissatisfaction has spread tremendously in recent years in relation to the scientific components of the economy,[59] the break with academic prestige of those theories is far from complete. Some surveys conducted on this matter amongst economists have not so much revealed a drastic change in ideas as a clear division of opinions. The survey mentioned in the previous section that involved economists from 16 different countries has shown that 56% believe in a real economic theory crisis, versus the 44% who believe the opposite to be true.[60] We must remember that during those years, two notable REH and EMH authors (Eugene Fama and Thomas Sargent, respectively) were awarded Nobel Prizes. However, it is also true that Fama and Robert Shiller won at the same time: two polar opposite financial theories received awards in tandem,[61] which helps paint a portrait of the confusing times (or, at the very least, the eclecticism) that economic theory was experiencing, which were quite different from the situation in 2007.

---

57 A.W. Lo and M.T. Mueller, 'Warning: Physics Envy May Be Hazardous to Your Wealth!' (2011) 8 *Journal of Investment Management* 13.

58 See <http://ineteconomics.org/about/why-inet> accessed 09.10.2014.

59 D. Colander et al., *The Financial Crisis and the Systemic Failure of Academic Economics*, supra note 17 and D. Coyle (ed.), *What's the Use of Economics. Teaching the Dismal Science after the Crisis*, supra note 17 – both good summaries.

60 J. Elster, 'Excessive Ambitions', supra note 56; E. Carré et al., 'Central Banking after the Crisis: Brave New World or Back to the Future?', supra note 38, p. 21.

61 B. Guerrien and O. Gun, 'Fama-Shiller, Economic Sciences Prize Committee and the "efficient markets hypothesis"' (2014) 66 *Real-World Economics Review* 58.

There are several explanations for this situation of 'theoretical limbo' in which economic and financial theory currently finds itself. Firstly, it is not all that different from what has happened at other times in the past: while it may be true that all of the major economic crises since 1870 occurred alongside scientific revolutions in the economy, these changes were neither drastic nor sudden. On the contrary, they were the result of complex, lethargic processes plagued with setbacks – something similar could happen now. Secondly, there are academic sociological reasons that favour inertia in scientific beliefs: a) training academic economists in the system of ideas established has been both difficult and expensive (that is to say, there would be a significant sunk cost here, associated with irreversible investment in intellectual capital that could go to waste if one economist were to separate himself from the dominant line of thinking); b) it is clear that any transition toward another way of thinking would be accompanied by a process of social education, which many researchers are unwilling to accept; and c) the system of promoting and seeking professional prestige – particularly in relation to the hierarchy of publications – has not changed and will take quite a bit of time to do so, meaning that there are few incentives for expressing criticism or scepticism.[62]

There is one last reason – perhaps the most important of all – that is related to the absence of a clear alternative theory (such as Keynesianism during the Great Depression or New Liberalism during the 1970s). In the realm of financial theory, the behavioural approach has noticeably gained ground over the last few years, but its more open nature, along with its decreased possibility of making exact calculations and predictions and the lack of understanding of many economists and financial experts of its psychological foundation have limited its ability to become the new dominant paradigm, at least in the short term.

In any case, it seems clear that the EMH and REH have ceased to hog the limelight of macroeconomic and financial theories, and nowadays they are more akin to 'zombie economics' than anything else. More importantly: the direct link between these theories and policymaking has been severed in many countries. Since 2009, regulatory strategies have undergone significant change, as has the definition of monetary policy, since they have become more pragmatic and (perhaps precisely due to the 'theoretical limbo') have minimised their connections to concrete theories: this decreased doctrinarism has translated into a revival of economic policy debate. In the monetary/financial sector, the number of proposals has multiplied: tying monetary policy strictly to macro-prudential regulation; including credit cycles in the models; overcoming inflation-targeting; reducing the influence of credit rating agencies and other market regulation mechanisms;

62 X.C. Arias and A. Costas, *La torre de la arrogancia. Políticas y mercados después de la tormenta,* supra note 11.

and even reintroducing some selective capital controls.[63] As previously noted, some key central banks and regulatory bodies have at least partially adopted these new ideas and debates in their policies.

5. CONCLUSIONS

The Efficient Market Hypothesis was a notable effort to rationalise the financial exuberance that ruled the global economy from around 1980. It was based on this theory that the hyperfinancial nature of modern-day capitalism became evermore acute. The EMH has dominated the academic arena of financial theory in recent decades, just as the Rational Expectations Hypothesis became a major point of reference in macroeconomics. Their confluence in a single current radically changed the mentality of the majority of academic economists, such that more extreme notions of neoclassical rationality and efficiency as equilibrium abounded in the new mainstream.

The impact of these ideas was not limited to academic debates; rather, once they were established as a solid, strict belief system, they had a significant effect on the behaviour of regulatory entities and central banks and, more generally speaking, policymaking. The notable consequence of this was that as the concepts of 'market regulation' and 'light-touch regulation' progressed, there was an alleged reduction in regulatory and safety-net mechanisms. Moreover, this belief system spread with significant force throughout society, helping to increase the overall confidence in the stability of financial markets, which were considered infallible and omniscient. The revolution in the flow of information lent credibility to the EMH and REH, and financial theory and reality began to feed off each other.

For the most part, this world came crumbling down with the 2008 crisis, and the ultrarational illusion of finances was, without a doubt, one of its main causes. Since then, more than a radical change of paradigm, we have experienced a situation of 'theoretical limbo'. In any event, EMH and REH no longer take centre stage as they once did, and behavioural finances are gaining ground instead. Of note is the fact that during this period, regulatory and monetary policies have become more pragmatic and abandoned their direct ties to highly restrictive theoretical arguments.

---

63 C. Borio, 'The financial cycle and macroeconomics: What have we learnt?', supra note 31; O. Blanchard, G. Dell'Ariccia and P. Mauro, 'Rethinking Macroeconomic Policy' (2010) *IMF Staff Position Note* No. 10/03; X.C. Arias and J.F. Teixeira, *Heterodoxy and Boundaries: Monetary Policy after the Great Recession*, 2014, forthcoming.

PART II

POST-CRISIS ARCHITECTURES OF FINANCIAL REGULATION IN THE EUROPEAN UNION, THE UNITED STATES OF AMERICA AND CANADA: ACCOUNTABILITY AND RESPONSIVENESS-AND-RESPONSIBILITY

Part II.1

The European Union

GOVERNING FINANCIAL MARKET REGULATION: A CASCADE FROM INTERGOVERNMENTAL BANK RESOLUTION, TO PRUDENTIAL REGULATION, TO CONDUCT REGULATION

Nicholas Dorn

1. SCOPE AND INTRODUCTION

What forms of governance characterise financial market regulation? This chapter looks mostly at European, particularly Eurozone financial market regulation, with some comparative glances. Bank resolution, prudential regulation and market conduct regulation are discussed. The longest part of the text discusses the new Eurozone 'mechanisms' of banking union, with special attention to the European Stability Mechanism (ESM) and to the relationship between this and prudential and conduct regulation. The chapter aims to construct a perspective on the dynamics of governance between these three aspects of financial market regulation.

The European Stability Mechanism (ESM) has a quite specific governance structure, differing from those of prudential and conduct regulation. The ESM is an intergovernmental mechanism outside (but articulated with) the legal framework of the European Union. The ESM was initially set up to offer conditional assistance to sovereign states, however it has been accorded an important role *vis-à-vis* banks. It is argued here that the ESM is becoming the 'big brother' of prudential regulation, with interesting political and legal consequences. For example, the ECB and its Single Supervisory Mechanism must have regard, when supervising banks and assessing their condition, to whatever view might be taken by the Governors of the ESM, who are finance ministers, regarding the availability and applicability of funding for restructuring or orderly winding up of certain banks. For the foreseeable future it is the ESM, not the EU's Single Resolution Mechanism (SRM), which has funds adequate for such purposes.

The chapter starts with a discussion of market conduct regulation, looking first, in an empirical and comparative manner, at US state Attorney Generals, particularly in New York. Locally elected Attorney Generals provide a contrast with appointed market conduct regulators at national level in both the EU and US. The activism of appointees has been lower, historically. Some aspects of cross-jurisdictional conduct regulation by appointee-led agencies are briefly and critically discussed.

Overall, the new architecture of financial market regulation – with its feet variously in EU and national administrative and criminal legislation, in 'independent' prudential bank regulation, and in intergovernmental decision making – amounts to a novel and complex governance design. *Vis-à-vis* democratic principles, this design could be characterised in several ways; here we mention three. First, the new design could be regarded as *status quo*, in the sense that discussion in EU policy circles of action against financial market misconduct implicitly maintains the assumption that prosecutors should be national appointees. An alternative view would be that the emerging regulatory design is *retrogressive*, in the sense that the ECB's assumption of powers as Single Supervisory Mechanism puts further distance between prudential regulation, parliaments and citizens. Finally, some parts of the new architecture could be regarded as being *ambiguous vis-à-vis* democracy. On the one hand, the legal basis of the ESM distances it from the European Parliament, a situation that the ESM's recruitment of the Court of Justice of the European Union (CJEU) may do little to remedy. On the other hand, national parliaments might be able to exert some oversight and control of their finance ministers, who act as Governors of the ESM. National parliaments are supported in this respect by some national constitutional courts. Thus the implications of the ESM for democracy may be thought in terms of various tendencies: diminution, safeguarding or reconstitution of European democracy.

Whilst this chapter pays special attention to relationships *within* the new European (particularly Eurozone) regulatory structure, it starts with a comparative, externally-facing perspective, in order to provide some critical distance.

2. COMPARATIVE PERSPECTIVES: MARKET CONDUCT REGULATION

Empirically and comparatively, the situation of US Attorney Generals at state level is quite striking, as historically they have taken and continue to take a leading part in criminal prosecution of market misconduct. Of course certain cases may be passed for criminal investigation to the Department of Justice. However, historically, state Attorney Generals have led the charge against market misconduct. This is for good reason: in most US states, Attorney Generals are elected and, as such, are subject to a governance structure and a set of motivations that differ from those of federal regulatory agencies. US state Attorney Generals are structurally distant from federal ministries and closer to popular sentiment. Moreover, in the important case of New York, local legislation (the so-called Martin Act) gives greater leverage to prosecutors than in most other state jurisdictions.[1]

The combination of these factors – electoral selection, specific powers and distance from ministerial restraint – gives market (mis)conduct regulation more 'bite' in New York than elsewhere in the US, and also much more than is typical in European countries. Thus, well before the emergence of the financial crisis, New York State Attorney General Elliot Spitzer spoke as follows.

> "The investment banks are at the vortex of all of this (malfeasance)", he claims, arguing that "the risk-reward calculus is so clearly out of kilter with ethical behavior. Yet no one thought the paradigm needed to change. The solution is not more regulation but more innovative application of existing enforcement strategies."[2]

Interestingly, the investigative powers deployed by Spitzer against financial market misconduct in New York were eventually turned against Spitzer himself, disgracing him and causing his resignation – but not however causing the revocation of the said powers, which continued to be utilised by his successors.[3] Prior to the emergence of the financial crisis, such activism contrasted quite sharply with financial market conduct regulation in Europe. In the UK, for example, insider trading was so widespread as to be effectively normalised. The then Financial Services Authority (FSA) carried out so-called 'market cleanliness' monitoring that suggested at least a fifth of trades were made on the basis of inside information. Yet enforcement was virtually non-existent and criminal prosecution unknown, even though such prosecution was possible. Similarly, conflict of interest was not a matter of concern to European regulators before the crisis.[4] Whereas Spitzer was making himself unpopular in the New York financial community many years before the crisis, European regulators only began to adopt anything like the same tone some time *after* the emergence of the crisis: the FSA made its first-ever criminal prosecution for insider dealing in 2008. In 2009 the FSA's Chief Executive spoke in the following terms.

---

1 J. O'Brien, 'The politics of enforcement: Eliot Spitzer, state-federal relations, and the redesign of financial regulation' (2005) 35 *Publius* 449.

2 E. Spitzer, New York Attorney General, speaking in 2004, cited in O'Brien supra note 1, 459.

3 D. Gross, 'Spitzer Gets Spitzered: how Spitzer was brought down by the same kind of investigation he pioneered', *Slate*, 10.03.2008 <www.slate.com/articles/business/moneybox/2008/03/spitzer_gets_spitzered.html> accessed 20.10.2014.

4 N. Dorn, 'Regulatory conceptions of unacceptable market practices under three policy scenarios' (2010) 12 *Journal of Banking Regulation* 24.

> "There is a view that people are not frightened of the FSA (the then UK Financial Services Authority). I can assure you that this is a view I am determined to correct. People should be very frightened of the FSA ...".[5]

However, it would be wrong to posit inherent differences of diligence and activism between European and US regulators. Rather, jurisdictional specifics, the availability of regulatory powers at any particular time, motivations of individuals and the broader political atmosphere are important drivers of enforcement. Enforcement can be blunted by the abilities of large firms to put selected aspects of their activities beyond scrutiny – or alternatively, if the regulator has the requisite powers but is lackadaisical, to provide excuses for laxity.[6] Witness for example the Lehman Brothers affair, which led to investigation in the US only after the 2008 collapse of that firm. In 2010 a report of the Examiner, appointed by the US court in relation to Lehman's bankruptcy, documented Lehman's use of Repo 105, a method of selling and then repurchasing one's assets, the purpose of which was to give a misleading impression in end-of-quarter financial reports.

> 'The Examiner concludes that there is sufficient evidence to support a colorable (plausible) claim that: (1) certain of Lehman's officers breached their fiduciary duties by exposing Lehman to potential liability for filing materially misleading periodic reports and (2) Ernst & Young, the firm's outside auditor, was professionally negligent in allowing those reports to go unchallenged. The Examiner concludes that colorable claims of breach of fiduciary duty exist against (high executives of the company) Richard Fuld, Chris O'Meara, Erin Callan, and Ian Lowitt, and that a colorable claim of professional malpractice exists against Ernst & Young'.[7]

Since the crisis of 2007 onwards, more evidence of market misconduct has come to light: on insider trading; on conflict of interest such as that involving Goldman Sachs;[8] on manipulation of financial benchmarks (Libor; foreign exchange benchmarks, gold markets, etc). Much of this evidence underlines the importance of jurisdictional specifics that either discourage or empower conduct regulation. In some jurisdictions, such as New York, the combination of factors mentioned

---

5 H. Sants, *Delivering intensive supervision and credible deterrence*, Speech by the chief executive of the FSA, at the Reuters Newsmakers event, Financial Services Authority, London, 12.03.2009 <www.fsa.gov.uk/pages/Library/Communication/Speeches/2009/0312_hs.shtml> accessed 24.02.2014.

6 N. Dorn, *Democracy and Diversity in Financial Market Regulation*, GlassHouse (Routledge), Abingdon 2014, see chapter 2.

7 A. Valukas, *Examiner's Report: Lehman Brothers Holdings Inc Chapter 11 Proceedings*, Volume 3, commissioned for the United States Bankruptcy Court, Southern District of New York, Case No 08–13555 (JMP), 11 March, Jenner & Block LLP, New York, 2010, p. 750 <http://jenner.com/lehman/VOLUME%203.pdf> accessed 24.02.2014.

8 N. Dorn and M. Levi, 'Theorising the Security and Exchange Commission's 2010 Settlement with Goldman Sachs' in G. Antonopoulos et al. (eds), *Usual and Unusual Organising Criminals in Europe*, Maklu, Antwerp 2011, pp. 33–54.

earlier made for quite vigorous investigation and prosecution of misconduct. However, some firms had so arranged their operations (and their auditing) within a certain jurisdiction – or *across several* jurisdictions – that they escaped effective scrutiny. To cite again the Lehman Examiner's report:

> 'The Examiner finds insufficient evidence to support a claim that any Lehman officer breached the fiduciary duty of care in connection with managing the risks associated with the more aggressive business strategy Lehman adopted in 2006 (i.e., just before Lehman's collapse.) Lehman's officers were entitled under Delaware law to pursue this aggressive high risk strategy, and the Examiner does not question their business decision to do so; decisions of this type are at the core of the business judgment rule'.[9]

This limitation remains: some jurisdictions continue to accommodate 'aggressive high risk strategy' and there may be limits to what conduct regulators can do about that.[10] That said, following the outbreak of crisis, regulatory sloth in acting against financial market misconduct has become less acceptable in most financial centres. European conduct regulators, and US conduct regulators acting at federal level, have been obliged to act more *as if* they are politically accountable (i.e., more like elected and recallable prosecutors).

Even so, conduct regulators may sometimes have been somewhat constrained by the relative slowness of some of their colleagues in prudential regulation agencies in shaking off old habits. In London there has been considerable embarrassment over Libor manipulation, especially because of the roles of the British Bankers Association (to whom oversight of Libor had been partially outsourced) and of the Bank of England (which found itself subject to claims that it knew about and possibly gave approval to some of the practices involved).[11]

This brings us to the governance and appointment of prudential regulators. It will later be for consideration whether in the future the European Stability Mechanism (ESM) might shape the thinking and actions of prudential regulators working in the context of the Single Supervisory Mechanism (SSM), and of conduct regulators. A governance cascade will then be hypothesised, in which influence

---

9 A. Valukas, *Examiner's Report: Lehman Brothers Holdings Inc Chapter 11 Proceedings,* Volume 1, commissioned for the United States Bankruptcy Court, Southern District of New York, Case No 08-13555 (JMP), 11 March, Jenner & Block LLP, New York, 2010, pp. 166–167 <http://jenner.com/lehman/VOLUME%201.pdf> accessed 24.02.2014.

10 PARLIAMENTARY COMMISSION ON BANKING STANDARDS, *Changing Banking For Good,* Volume I, Stationary Office, London 2013 <www.publications.parliament.uk/pa/jt201314/jtselect/jtpcbs/27/27.pdf> accessed 24.02.2014.

11 C. Binham and D. Schäfer, 'Bank of England faces forex probe scrutiny', *Financial Times,* 07.02.2014, pp. 8–9.

and motivations might flow from the ESM (ministers), to SSM/prudential regulation (appointees), to conduct regulators.

3. HEADS OF PRUDENTIAL AGENCIES: APPOINTMENT THE NORM

Heads of macroprudential and microprudential regulatory agencies are typically appointees, as distinct from being elected (although their confirmation procedures may involve scrutiny by elected persons and sometimes the possibility of not approving a proposed candidate).[12] Many heads of agencies have previous experience within those agencies and some also have experience in the private sector and/or government.

Recently, a combination of factors – the historical evolution of international networks of regulators (central bankers and others), governments' acceptance of an arms-length relations with regulators, and an increasingly strongly felt need for innovative office-holders – have resulted in some interesting appointments. Consider for example the appointment of Mario Draghi to lead the European Central Bank (previously academia, World Bank, Italian Treasury, Goldman Sachs); Mark Carney to the Bank of England (Goldman Sachs, Canadian Department of Finance, Bank of Canada); Janet Yellen to the US Federal Exchange (Federal Reserve Bank of San Francisco, White House Council of Economic Advisers, academia); and Danièle Nouy to the Eurozone's Single Supervision Mechanism (Basel Committee, *Autorité de Contrôle Prudentiel et de Résolution*). Draghi is a non-German national appointed to the helm of the ECB, Carey is the first non-Brit appointed to lead the BoE, Yellen and Nouy are still-rare examples of women at the top of banking regulation, and Nouy is a political scientist rather an economist or banker (though she is a career banking supervisor). Equally interesting is the appointment of Nemat Shafik (International Monetary Fund, UK Department for International Development, academia but 'little financial markets experience)[13] as Deputy Governor of the BoE with responsibility for markets and banking – so responsible for reforms in response to market-rigging (mentioned below).

---

12 EUROPEAN UNION, *Interinstitutional Agreement between the European Parliament and the European Central Bank on the practical modalities of the exercise of democratic accountability and oversight over the exercise of the tasks conferred on the ECB within the framework of the Single Supervisory Mechanism* (2013/694/EU), OJ 2013 No. L 320/1. <www.europarl.europa.eu/document/activities/cont/201312/20131202ATT75338/20131202ATT75338EN.pdf> accessed 24.02.2014.

13 S. Fleming, 'High-flyer parachuted in to help the Old Lady of Threadneedle St', *Financial Times*, 21.03.2014, p. 9. <www.ft.com/cms/s/0/8430072a-b057-11e3-8efc-00144feab7de.html> accessed 23 March 2014.

A combination of factors in these non-traditional appointments – being brought in from a distance, being strongly networked internationally and being expected to deal in innovative ways with complexities and crises – means that appointees are accorded considerable political freedom. This is enhanced because the aforesaid factors combine to put social, political and legal distance between them and citizens. Citizens are locally and nationally based and do not have a hand in appointment. Internationally networked appointees look to each other as peers, forming an 'epistemic community',[14, 15] which has political autonomy, considerable influence and sometimes becomes a lightening rod for either blame or acclaim. For example, for his hubris in the run-up to the financial crisis beginning 2007, previous US Federal Exchange governor Alan Greenspan was widely criticised. On the other hand, Mario Draghi was named as Man of the Year 2013 by the *Financial Times* for his action in 'saving the Euro'.

Choices made in top-level appointments have to be set in the context of the institutional designs of specific regulatory agencies. By some accounts, even before the financial crisis, the ECB's institutional design accorded it greater independence than that accorded to national central banks, indeed it has been suggested that 'the ECB corresponds less to the situation of the British and French central banks in the twentieth century and more to the situation of these banks in the mainly pre-democratic seventeenth, eighteenth and nineteenth centuries'.[16] Moreover, European elites' responses to the crisis has widened the role of the ECB, as one of the sites for banking union (aspects of which are discussed below). However, the ECB now also has to deal with a possibly equally and arguable more powerful co-actor, the European Stability Mechanism (also discussed below).

To summarise so far in broad terms, for the period following the crisis, one could identify two distinct and quite different types of 'sheriff' in financial market regulation. One type, the conduct regulator – generally appointed in the European context but in the US at state level directly and locally elected – has a legal background and strives to root out misconduct. One level up, the second type, the prudential regulator, is a national/regional appointee, typically has an economics and/or market background, and is obliged to innovate, in order to save finance capital from its follies. As the crisis developed and deepened, both regulatory types were obliged to show greater activism. However, from 2012 onwards, both those types, and their specific modes of governance, began to be

[14] P. Haas, 'Introduction: epistemic communities and international policy coordination' (1992) 46 *International Organization* 1.

[15] M. King, 'Epistemic Communities and the Diffusion of Ideas: Central Bank Reform in the United Kingdom' (2005) 28 *West European Politics* 94.

[16] R. Elgie, 'Democratic accountability and central bank independence: historical and contemporary, national and European perspectives' (1998) 21 *West European Politics* 53, 63.

accompanied and possibly overshadowed by others. Centre stage in the Eurozone is the European Stability Mechanism (ESM).

4. INTERGOVERNMENTALITY: NEW LYNCHPIN FOR BANKING REGULATION

The European Stability Mechanism (ESM) is one of three Eurozone 'mechanisms' of banking union, the other two being the Single Supervisory Mechanism (SSM) for Eurozone banks and the Single Resolution Mechanism (SRM).

The SSM[17] is the prudential supervisor for Eurozone banks. In relation to banks that are 'significant on a consolidated basis' (in terms of their size, economic importance and significance of cross-border activities), the ECB takes the lead, whilst banks that are 'less significant' in those terms are attended to by national authorities.[18] The SSM is constituted within the ECB: draft decisions are prepared by a Supervisory Board, consisting of national supervisors and ECB representatives, then passed to ECB's Governing Council. The SSM does not apply to banks in EU member states that are not in the Eurozone, though such countries can choose to 'opt in'.

The SRM has been very slow to evolve and from 2012–2014 became something of a political football. The German banking sector, government and lawyers were initially wary that the SRM might constitute a backdoor form of 'transfer union'. The European Parliament for a while withheld legislative consent, trying to use this as leverage to achieve changes in the third of the mechanisms, the ESM. In any case the SRM has considerable practical limitations (see below), which limit its practical relevance during its initial years.

The ESM, which is the main focus for our interest here, represents a novel form of governance for Eurozone member states and banks.

> 'The purpose of the ESM shall be to mobilise funding and provide stability support under strict conditionality, appropriate to the financial assistance instrument chosen, to the benefit of ESM Members which are experiencing, or are threatened by, severe financing problems, if indispensable to safeguard the financial stability of the euro area as a whole and of its Member States. For this purpose, the ESM shall be entitled to raise funds by issuing financial instruments or by entering

17 Council Regulation (EU) No. 1024/2013 of 15 October 2013 conferring specific tasks on the European Central Bank concerning policies relating to the prudential supervision of credit institutions, OJ 2013 No. L 287/63, summarising the SSM at Article 2(9).

18 Council Regulation (EU) No 1024/2013, supra note 17, Article 6(4).

into financial or other agreements or arrangements with ESM Members, financial institutions or other third parties'.[19]

The ESM was originally conceived as a means of providing conditional assistance to Eurozone member states finding themselves in financial difficulty due to any mixture of banking failures and fiscal imprudence. Conditionality is designed to avoid moral hazard and to help sovereigns to get back on track (there is considerable controversy here, which however is not the focus of this chapter). During the course of 2010–13 there was widespread concern over linkage between sovereigns and 'their' banks – the damaging effects of which could be intensified when sovereigns came under pressure to socialise bank losses, as in the case notably of Ireland. Eventually it became recognised that leaving individual Eurozone states to deal with 'their' banks increases financial stress upon the states concerned, as Greece and later Spain also showed: maintaining the connectedness between stressed banks and stressed sovereigns dragged the latter down.

Therefore a more collective solution was sought. In June 2012, as the Euro Area Summit Statement put it, 'the ESM could … have the possibility to recapitalize banks directly'.[20] The sense of flexibility in the Eurozone was enhanced in the autumn of that year by the qualified success of the ECB's promise of Outright Monetary Transactions (OMT), bringing calm if not health to the Eurozone systems of banking.[21] In short, it became appreciated that, insofar as the crisis was partly a banking crisis, it could be addressed as such (leaving aside for present purposes its continuing potential *vis-à-vis* Eurozone sovereign states). This was given further momentum by the realisation in 2013 that arrangements foreseen for recapitalising banks by the Single Resolution Mechanism (under the EU treaty) could be significantly under-funded for as much as a decade after its eventual launch (and possibly for much longer). That limitation follows from the

---

19 ESM TREATY, *Treaty Establishing the European Stability Mechanism Between the Kingdom of Belgium, the Federal Republic of Germany, the Republic of Estonia (et al)*, European Council, Brussels, 2013, Article 3, 10 <www.european-council.europa.eu/media/582311/05-tesm2.en12.pdf> accessed 24.02.2014.

20 HEADS OF STATE OF EURO AREA, *Euro Area Summit Statement*, The Council, Brussels, 29.06.2012, p. 1 <www.consilium.europa.eu/uedocs/cms_data/docs/pressdata/en/ec/131359.pdf> accessed 24.02.2014.

21 In one sense, the OMT was spectacularly successful, being an example of a form of guarantee or insurance that is sufficiently credible not to be tested. In some other senses, it was less positively regarded, some neoliberal critics seeing it as a backdoor method for supporting Eurozone states (by bolstering banks whose weakening position might otherwise have drawn upon funds from equally ailing sovereigns). Other commentators, including the present author, have observed a contrast between, on the one hand, the ECB's uplifting of banks and, on the other hand, its advocacy of austerity measures falling upon other sectors of the economy and upon citizens: N. Dorn, 'Connectedness, Crisis and the Challenge to European Democracy: from rapture, through fear, to banalisation of financial markets' in J. Cruz, C. Cardoso, A. Leite and R. Faria (eds.), *Infrações Económicas e Fiisnanceiras: estudos de criminologia e de direito*, Coimbra Editora, Coimbra 2013.

SRM's reliance on funding by the banking industry, as a form of self-insurance, which of course takes time to build up a reserve. By contrast the ESM is front-end funded by participating states and international investors. The ESM first successfully tapped the market for funds in late 2013.[22]

As a result, the ESM became viewed as providing the *financial means* for restructuring or resolution of Eurozone banks (although precautionary recapitalisation as such is supposed to be achieved through the market, where possible).[23] The ESM uses funding raised initially from Eurozone Member States, this being augmented by issuance of bonds on the international markets (see the references above to '*mobilise* funding (...) by issuing financial instruments or by entering into financial or other agreements or arrangements with ESM Members, *financial institutions* or other third parties'.[24] Initially the ESM recapitalised Spanish and Cypriot banks (Spain exited ESM funding in late 2013).

The ESM has proved controversial, in ways that are very relevant for financial market regulation. The European Council gave the green light for Eurozone EU member states to agree the ESM treaty on an intergovernmental basis, by means of an amendment to the Treaty on Functioning of the European Union (TFEU). Quite separate from that, the ESM treaty itself gives jurisdiction to the Court of Justice of the European Union (CJEU). The first test of the legality of the ESM came to the CJEU in the form of the Pringle case – in which the CJEU found that the TFEU amendment merely 'confirms' a pre-existing ability of member states to make intergovernmental agreements.[25] Thus the ESM is held not to rest upon the EU treaties in any way. On the other hand, in coming to its judgement, the CJEU affirmed that the Court can be given jurisdiction by an intergovernmental treaty, thus keeping the door open to further such arrangements in future.[26] Thus the ESM is confirmed to be an intergovernmental organisation, outside the legal order of the EU: even so, the CJEU has been drafted in and the ESM 'borrows' the European Commission for its conditionality assessments. Yet the European Parliament plays no formal part in setting up or monitoring the ESM. So, accountability zero, from the Parliament's point of view; however as things stand there is not much that the Parliament can do about that.

---

22 R. Wigglesworth, 'EU's bailout fund enjoys high demand in maiden €7bn bond issue', *Financial Times*, 08.10.2013 <www.ft.com/intl/cms/s/0/47d2dee0-2ffd-11e3-80a4-00144feab7de.html> accessed 24.02.2014.

23 ESM, *FAQ on the main features of the future ESM direct bank recapitalisation instrument*, (no date), pp. 1–4 <www.esm.europa.eu/pdf/FAQ%20Direct%20Bank%20Recapitalisation%20280620131.pdf> accessed 24.02.2014.

24 HEADS OF STATE OF EURO AREA, *Euro Area Summit Statement*, supra note 20, p. 1, emphasis added.

25 E. De Lhoneux and C. Vassilopoulos, *The European Stability Mechanism Before the Court of Justice of the European Union*, Springer, New York/Heidelberg 2014.

26 E. De Lhoneux. AND C. Vassilopoulos, *The European Stability Mechanism Before the Court of Justice of the European Union*, supra note 25.

The Constitutional Courts of some Eurozone member states have channelled other challenges, cases being brought *inter alia* on grounds of constitutionality.[27] The issues around the ESM are further complicated by being related to the ECB's promise of OMT (Outright Monetary Transactions), in the sense that both initiatives have attracted legal challenges in the same period of time. In February 2014, the German Federal Constitutional Court partially separated the issues[28] and in March 2014 it rejected the various challenges (the basis for doing so will be returned to in the next section of the chapter).[29]

What is of primary concern for present purposes is not the legal detail but the governance outturn as it comes into sight. The question is, how are decisions made under the ESM, by whom and under what conditions? The ESM's form of governance is quite distinct from of the SSM; in the latter, macroprudential supervision is mapped onto the model of central bank independence. The ESM's governance is also distinct from that of the SRM, which falls *in part* under the SSM.[30] And the governance of the ESM is of course quite different from that appertaining to financial market conduct supervision. Within the ESM, there are three layers: a Board of Governors, who are typically Ministers of Finance; a Board of Directors, typically finance ministry officials; and of course an ESM Director and staff.[31] Direct representation of governments (as distinct from appointment of extra-governmental persons) is, of course, normal in intergovernmental

27 GERMAN LAW JOURNAL 2013 14(1), 1–338 (Special Section – The ESM Before the Courts, whole issue).

28 FEDERAL CONSTITUTIONAL COURT, Press release no. 9/2014, Bundesverfassungsgerichts, Karlsruhe, 07.02.2014. <www.bundesverfassungsgericht.de/pressemitteilungen/bvg14-009en.html> accessed 24.02.2014.

29 FEDERAL CONSTITUTIONAL COURT, *Decision, Zitierung: BVerfG, 2 BvR 1390/12 vom 18.3.2014, Absatz-Nr (1–245)*, Bundesverfassungsgerichts, Karlsruhe, 18.03.2014 <www.bverfg.de/entscheidungen/rs20140318_2bvr139012en.htm> accessed 19.03.2014.

30 Proposals for the SRM and its associated Fund resulted in inter-institutional horse-trading, in which the European Parliament in March 2014 declared victory, see: EUROPEAN PARLIAMENT COMMITTEE ON ECONOMIC AND MONETARY AFFAIRS, *Parliament negotiators rescue seriously damaged bank resolution system*, Press Release, 20.03.2014 <www.europarl.europa.eu/news/en/news-room/content/20140319IPR39310/html/Parliament-negotiators-rescue-seriously-damaged-bank-resolution-system> accessed 24.02.2014. The original proposal for SRM was as follows: EUROPEAN COMMISSION, *Proposal for a Regulation of the European Parliament and of the Council establishing uniform rules and a uniform procedure for the resolution of credit institutions and certain investment firms in the framework of a Single Resolution Mechanism and a Single Bank Resolution Fund and amending Regulation (EU) No. 1093/2010 of the European Parliament and of the Council*, COM(2013) 520 final <http://eur-lex.europa.eu/LexUriServ/LexUriServ.do?uri=COM:2013:0520:FIN:EN:PDF> accessed 24.02.2014. For the regulation as finally agreed, see Regulation of the European Parliament and of the Council establishing uniform rules and a uniform procedure for the resolution of credit institutions and certain investment firms in the framework of a Single Resolution Mechanism and a Single Bank Resolution Fund and amending Regulation (EU) No. 1093/2010 of the European Parliament and of the Council, OJ 2014 No. L 225/1. The consequence is that the SRM is a half-way house between the SSM and the ESM.

31 ESM, *Corporate Governance*, 2014 <www.esm.europa.eu/about/governance/index.htm> accessed 24.02.2014.

organisations. It is all the more clearly required in the case of the ESM which, in the manner of an IMF for the Eurozone, acts as a forum for bargaining over deployment of resources. Those resources have been raised from ESM states and then augmented by bond offerings to the market, fulfilment of which the ESM is responsible for.

How then can the position of the ESM Board of Governors (the top layer of its governance) be characterised, *vis-à-vis* the member states from which the Governors are drawn? In considering this, let us take of note of a particular view, that the ESM is not only extra-EU but also post-national.

> 'In a certain number of the challenges to the ESM, sovereignty was considered through the "legitimacy link" ostensibly mediated between National Parliaments and the ESM by Member States' representatives in the ESM Board of Governors. However, this link varied substantially between the Member States, given that it depended upon the architecture of the legislative and executive branches and political control thereof, as well as the innate difference between debtor and creditor States of the ESM. More importantly, unanimity in decision-making in the ESM Board of Governors is subject to exceptions and Member States may find themselves *de facto* and de *jure* excluded from decision-making in certain circumstances, such as if they are outvoted. Overall, one can say that every possible step and device to construct "postnational" arrangements, conventional or otherwise, has been availed of in this process. The esoteric character of these arrangements is thus further reinforced by its operational impact upon the Member States'.[32]

The present author goes along with that analysis to a limited extent. Under non-emergency condition, unanimity is required for decisions of the ESM Board; however under emergencies, Governors can arrive at a decision by qualified majority voting (85%).[33] Thus *to some extent* the hurdles for decision-making in the ESM Board mimic those at EU Council meetings (which is subject under some conditions to unanimity and under other conditions to qualified majority voting). However, whereas under qualified majority voting in the Council, voting weights are related to population numbers, voting weights in the ESM (as in the ECB) are determined by shareholdings of member states. Consider also that the persons involved are broadly the same as those in a meeting of Eurogroup finance ministers: the ESM's governing Board is indeed akin to Eurogroup finance ministers under different arrangements. Although the quote just above refers to

---

32 E. Fahey and S. Bardutzky, *Adjudication of Postnational Norms in the EU Courts, Plural – A Case Study of the European Stability Mechanism*, 2013 Inaugural symposium of the MJIL Emerging Scholarship Project, University of Michigan Law School, Michigan, 2013, pp. 104–105 <www.mjilonline.org/wordpress/wp-content/uploads/2013/07/FaheyBardutzky.pdf> accessed 24.02.2014.

33 ESM Treaty, supra note 19, Article 4(4).

these arrangements as being "postnational", the contrary view could be held: that the ESM is *more* national (in the sense of being intergovernmental) than the EU. Alternatively, others might see here a federalist advance guard or inner ring. The difference perhaps is whether one prefers to see things as they are now or as a step to some possible future, albeit hypothetical integration.

To fine-tune and deepen the analysis, we can observe that the design of the ESM rules out any possibility that an ESM Governor might be called to account by his or her corresponding Finance Minister; they are generally the same person. Moreover, what has been disposed of for purposes of the ESM is the European Parliament, at least for the foreseeable future. As for the longer term, one could not absolutely rule out the integration of the ESM into the community architecture, *à la* Schengen (which the Amsterdam Treaty incorporated into the EU, with opt-outs). However, there seems to be a greater legal and financial distance between the ESM and the EU legal order than between Schengen and the EU (Schengen being a play on what used to be called first and third pillar matters, which the ESM goes way beyond). Thus, although the situation may change in time, as things stand the ESM is extra-EU *but not* post-national. Some of the wider implications of this will be taken up briefly at the end of this chapter, after a consideration of some issues *vis-à-vis* national parliaments.

5. NATIONAL PARLIAMENTS: DEMOCRACY OR DISPERSAL

With the entry of finance ministers into what we have suggested is the apex of the regulatory pyramid, the ESM, the relationships between those ministers and their national parliaments might reintroduce some elements of democracy. That at least is the presumption of the German Federal Constitutional Court which, as noted above, has been repeatedly called upon to assess the legitimacy of new EU, Eurozone and international agreements. The 18 March 2014 Decision of the Court is worth close study, not only for the conclusions arrived at, but also for its clear articulation of complainants' arguments – from which the Court decisively distances itself through its rather *black letter* reading of the ESM treaty. Here there is space only to briefly illustrate this distancing. One complainant had argued a hypothetical but nevertheless quite credible scenario of expediency overcoming democratic decision making, which the Court summarised as follows.

> 'The overall budgetary responsibility of the Bundestag is in particular violated by the fact that the ESM Treaty establishes an obligation under international law for the Contracting Parties to consent to possible capital increases and re-capitalisations, if they are necessary to preserve or restore the functioning of the European Stability Mechanism. If the authorised capital stock of EUR 700 billion were not

(or no longer) sufficient to fulfil the tasks of the European Stability Mechanism – because, for instance, a large state like Italy has difficulties in meeting payments, or because the capital stock is used up – a systematic and teleological interpretation of the ESM Treaty would sustain a capital increase or a re-capitalisation, so that the European Stability Mechanism could continue to fulfil the tasks assigned to it by its Contracting Parties, especially, as emphasised in the preamble to the Treaty, the commitment to ensuring the financial stability of the euro area. In such a situation, the Bundestag would be bound by international law and, regardless of its formal participation rights, no longer be able to autonomously decide on the capital increase or re-capitalisation'.[34]

In response, the Court observed that 'no provision of the Treaty may be interpreted as leading to payment obligations higher than the portion of the authorised capital stock corresponding to each ESM Member, as specified in Annex II of the Treaty, without prior agreement of each Member's representative and due regard to national procedures'.[35] Moreover, 'the necessary legitimation is ensured by the fact that these decisions cannot be taken against the vote of the German representative'.[36] It was found to be important by the Court that the German representative on the ESM board possesses a 'blocking minority for decisions adopted by a qualified majority (Art. 4 sec. 5 TESM)' which, according to that treaty, could not be diluted through future accession of other states to the ESM.[37]

For the present author, three observations seem to be in order. First, a reading of the 18 March 2014 Decision of the Court suggests that considerable *epistemic distance* exists between at least some of the complainants and the Court, the basis of which is as follows. In their arguments, some of the complaints seem implicitly to adopt a *socio-legal* perspective, pointing to what might occur in practice – e.g., that ESM Board members might form a common culture, 'going native' in the sense of agreeing crisis-management measures between themselves, then pleading *force majeure* and putting pressure on the national governments and parliaments to agree, post-hoc. The Decision of the Court, on the other hand, seems to arise more from a *black latter law* perspective, on the basis of a strict reading of the text of the ESM treaty. The latter is indeed crafted so as to give the necessary guarantees that are due to national parliaments (or at least to the Bundestag).

Second, if one follows the logic of the Decision of the Federal Constitutional Court, and then uses it to assess the situation of other ESM member states, it is notable that only the German ESM Board member has a blocking minority (85% of shareholdings is the hurdle, Germany having 20%). Any other ESM Board

[34] FEDERAL CONSTITUTIONAL COURT, *Decision, Zitierung: BVerfG, 2 BvR 1390/12 vom 18.3.2014, Absatz-Nr (1–245)*, supra note 29, Section III, line 37.

[35] Ibid, line 188.

[36] Ibid, line 191.

[37] Ibid, line 192.

member (and hence country) can be outvoted, regardless of reservations and parliamentary votes: a case of democracy in one country, it would seem. It is in retrospect quite remarkable that all Eurozone states signed up to this, yet it is in Germany that the ensuing debate has been so fierce.

Third, all is not lost, in terms of the prospects for democracy. The arrangements which the Governors/finance ministers have *vis-à-vis* their national parliaments vary considerably. Also, that relationship is a 'work in progress' as far as the EU is concerned – and all the more so in relation to the ESM. This is something for the parliaments themselves to address, however we can identify some starting points. A study commissioned for the European Parliament, carried out by the Trans European Policy Studies Association and Notre Europe-Jacques Delors Institute, finds seven models of parliamentary activities related to European Council meetings. These are: a traditional model, i.e. limited involvement (e.g. Hungary); a 'Europe as usual' model, following the system established for ordinary legislation (e.g. Italy); an expert model (e.g. Finland); a 'public forum' model, based on plenary sessions (e.g. Ireland); a 'government accountability' model, based on plenary sessions after the summits in order to question the government policy (e.g. UK); a 'policy maker' model with emphasis put on ex-ante control (e.g. Germany); and a 'full parliamentarization' model (e.g. Denmark).[38]

It would be a short step for the national parliaments to extend to the ESM their practices developed in relation to European Council meetings.

Within the structurally differing models, a quite familiar spectrum of political positions can be identified. Broadly speaking, debates over the ESM follow the lines of debates over its temporary forerunner, the European Financial Stability Facility (EFSF). Council Regulation 407/2010 allowed for establishment of the EFSF via an intergovernmental agreement outside the EU treaties. Debates in national parliaments covered the ratification of the EFSF and an increase in its funds. On the basis of an analysis of those debates, Closa and Maatsch find two groups for the EFSF and two against.[39] The proponents consist of 'pragmatists' (who saw economic advantages or necessity) and 'idealists' (in the sense of being pro-integration). Opponents also consist of two groups, which Closa and Maatsch call 'nationalistic' on the right and 'anti-austerian' on the left.

---

[38] W. Wessels, O. Rozenberg, M. Van Den Berge, C. Hefftler, V. Kreilinger and L. Ventura, *Democratic Control in the Member States of the European Council and the Euro zone summits, Study*, European Parliament Directorate General for Internal Policies, Brussels, 2013, p. 49 <www.europarl.europa.eu/RegData/etudes/etudes/join/2013/474392/IPOL-AFCO_ET(2013)474392_EN.pdf> accessed 24.02.2014.

[39] C. Closa and A. Maatsch, 'In a Spirit of Solidarity? Justifying the European Financial Stability Facility (EFSF) in National Parliamentary Debates' (2014) 52 *Journal of Common Market Studies* 826.

> 'The nationalistic subgroup, composed of Eurosceptic opposition parties representing the economic right, rejected the EFSF out of economic considerations (predominantly national) and because it implied a loss of sovereignty and would signify a breach of the SGP (Stability and Growth Pact). In principle, anti-solidarity frames (of discussion) dominated the discourse of that group and parliamentarians voiced arguments such as 'there is no bail-out envisaged in EU law' and 'each state has to be responsible for its own debt'. The second subgroup of opponents, the 'anti-austerians', was composed of Eurosceptic opposition parties representing the economic left. In their view, the EFSF would neither help states that received a bail-out nor benefit the overall economy of the eurozone. This attitude responded to measures outlined for the EFSF that gave priority to the interests of banks and stipulated strong austerity measures, which this group believed would eventually lead to an economic recession'.[40]

Amongst Closa and Maatsch's idealists (federalists), one might imagine a certain sense of *schadenfreude*: regret that the task could not (for now) be achieved within the legal order of the EU, yet gladness that the boundary of action has been widened, in the tradition of the advance guard (which in this particular case consists of the great majority of EU member states). This group, the Eurosceptical parties and the anti-austerians may all be expected to seek accountability by finance ministers/ESM Governors and may to some extent seek to tie their hands (a procedure that for Germany has been reinforced by judgements of the Federal Constitutional Court, mentioned above). It is possible that Closa and Maatsch's pragmatists may be less interested in scrutiny, or may use it to widen the discretion of finance ministers, given pragmatists' tendency to side with the banking industry and with 'whatever it takes' arguments. One balance, there would seem to be a quite high level of political interest in ESM-related matters, which bodes well for the introduction of democratic debate, cutting across the norms of intergovernmental agreement. Clearly, there is much work to be done here, as national parliaments address the issue raised by the ESM. It will be interesting to see whether and how inter-parliamentary co-working on this issue might be possible or – to view things from a more pluralistic perspective (which might be relevant in the emerging partly post-EU legal and political space) – whether and how political differences can be brought into dialogue, populating the slowly emerging inter-parliamentary space.[41]

---

40 C. Closa and A. Maatsch, 'In a Spirit of Solidarity? Justifying the European Financial Stability Facility (EFSF) in National Parliamentary Debates', supra note 39, 9.

41 C. Mouffe, 'Democracy in a multipolar world' (2009) 37 *Millennium: Journal of International Studies* 549. A shorter and more accessible text is: C. Mouffe, *Five Minutes with Chantal Mouffe: "Most countries in Europe are in a post-political situation"*, Thinkers on Europe series (blog), London School of Economics, London, September 2013 <http://bit.ly/18midhv> accessed 24.02.2014.

To some extent, the issues discussed in this chapter can be illuminated by being put into a longer-term historical context. Speaking in 2014, Marco Buti, Director-General for Economic and Financial Affairs at the European Commission, recalled two contrasting views expressed in the early years of European Monetary Union, concerning relationships between the ECB and the fiscal authorities of member states (i.e., finance ministries).[42] One view (which Mr Buti felt has been shown to be correct) was that, in times of stress within EMU, member states would tend to cooperate together and with the ECB. A factor in this was that EMU would 'cement' the position of the banking sector, so counteracting any residual tendencies towards divergence by member states. An alternative and somewhat harsher view at the time of the birth of EMU was that 'the strength of the ECB was based in the *dispersal* of the fiscal authorities', the latter having to be 'beaten' in order for the ECB to do its job.[43] One can ask to what extent this historical reflection is of continuing relevance today, in relation to questions of power and leadership between finance ministries and the Eurozone mechanisms discussed in this chapter. The immediate aftermath of the Eurozone crisis might indeed indicate that Eurozone member states' fiscal/finance authorities have been agenda-takers, rather than being agenda-makers. However, with the advent of the ESM, that relationship may be changing. Moreover, the position of the banking sector today is more vulnerable than hitherto, both economically and politically, possibly reducing the extent to which the sector can act as a vector for centralised, technocratic influence upon member states.

None of this should be taken to imply that whatever the ESM determines in relation to banking will necessarily be either normatively desirable or functionally effective. Rather, the point is an analytical one: times change. It is necessary again to stress that outcomes can be re-shaped by parliamentary activism and influence, in an economic context and a political atmosphere differing from preceding decades.

6. CONUNDRUMS OF THE NEW POLITICAL ARCHITECTURE

In the course of this chapter, we have introduced the idea that the new European arrangements for governance of financial markets might be seen as a governance

42 M. Buti, *Discussant's remarks*, Conference for the 20th anniversary of the establishment of the European Monetary Institute, at the National Bank of Belgium, Brussels, 12.02.2014.

43 M. Buti, *Discussant's remarks*, supra note 42, cited from the present author's contemporaneous notes; emphasis added. On dispersal, see also M. Buti and P. Van Den Noord, 'Fiscal policy in EMU: rules, discretion and political incentives' (2004) *European Commission Directorate-General for Economic and Financial Affairs Economic Paper* No. 206, p. 11. <http://ideas.repec.org/p/euf/ecopap/0206.html> accessed 24.02.2014.

cascade – so, introducing new dynamics into the relations between regulators, and also into the relations between regulators and the political realm (relations between technocrats and representatives of democracy, in other words). This can be summarised as a three-step process. Influence might flow:

(1) from the European Stability Mechanism, the Governors of which are finance ministers, whose voting weights accord with the shareholdings of the states that they represent;
(2) to and through the Single Supervisory Mechanism, acting as the Eurozone prudential regulator, the SSM being led by ECB staff and national regulators, generally central banks;
(3) with implications for regulators of market conduct, which either might be given a green light for vigorous enforcement (as is currently the case) or might be subtly discouraged, depending on how ESM and SSM actors see things at particular times.

Going forward, these considerations become central to European financial market regulation. As funding master, the ESM is potentially very powerful. For example the SSM/ECB, in coming to findings about whether particular Eurozone banks require restructuring or dissolution,[44] must have an eye to how the ESM see the issues and whether it would be willing and able to act. As a variation on standard commentaries that stress the increasing power of the ECB, we might consider whether, as a consequence of the SSM coming into being in what we have portrayed here as a context financially dominated by the intergovernmental ESM, the high tide of ECB independence has been reached and is already passing. Finance ministers meeting in the context of the ESM constitute the new power centre.[45]

For their part, conduct regulators may feel constrained from vigorously investigating and prosecuting market misconduct, if the consequences include large fines and further reputational damage for banks, distressing them sufficiently to bring them uncomfortably close to insolvency in the eyes of the market and/or the SSM. Unless the ESM Board and prudential regulators favour that result,

[44] D. Nouy, *Financial Times Interview with Danièle Nouy*, Chair of the Supervisory Board of the Single Supervisory Mechanism, European Central Bank, Frankfurt, 10.02.2014 <www.ecb.europa.eu/press/key/date/2014/html/sp140210.en.html> accessed 24.02.2014.

[45] In coming to this view, one does not rule out countervailing possibilities – such that influence flows from the ECB, and/or from the European Commission, to the ESM. The ECB President may attend meetings of ESM Board and so could influence its thinking, particularly in an atmosphere of crisis management; nevertheless the financial levers are beyond the ECB's grasp, being in the hands of finance ministers. It should be noted that the Commission constructs the terms of conditionality for countries requiring ESM support, so Commission influence is stronger upon those support-seekers than upon the support-givers. On these grounds, one could acknowledge ECB and Commission influences, whilst still anticipating ESM/finance minister steering (and, hopefully, the growth of an inter-parliamentary form of governance).

conduct regulators may be constrained. To put it the other way around, in the evolving cascade structure, a necessary condition for a generalised high level of investigation and aggressive prosecution by conduct regulators would be that the Governors of the ESM have in mind to resolve some big banks. The situation is made more complicated by some paradoxes at the heart of the ESM and other mechanisms, which Kern Alexander has summarised.

> 'Regarding the European Stability Mechanism (ESM), the newly developed direct bank recapitalisation programme requiring euro area national governments to contribute 10/20% of the total ESM contribution unless justified by exceptional circumstances (as well as inject capital should the bank not fulfil the 4.5% Tier 1 equity ratio requirement) has been criticised by some as defeating the tool's very purpose of breaking the link between failing banks and sovereigns'.[46]

That paradox concerning the immediate future builds upon a paradox about the recent past: that the ECB's Long-term Refinancing Operations (LTRO) has already tightened the connection between sovereigns and 'their' banks. This is because the LTRO 'led governments to turn to their banks as buyers-of-last-resort', using 'ECB funding to invest in sovereign bonds (the so-called "Sarkozy Trade")'.[47] We are concerned here with these ironies only to point up how complex they make the situation facing the regulatory community (ESM, SSM, SRM and conduct regulators). Essentially, both the ESM and the SRM are insurance schemes, initiated when the patients who are already sick and have difficulty in contributing to the funds from which they and others may shortly be obliged to draw. Under the ESM, sovereigns subscribe to an insurance scheme for sovereigns and/or banks; under the SRM, banks collectively subscribe for the benefit of some (and also to benefit some sovereigns, to follow the logic of the "Sarkozy Trade", noted a few lines above). Such subscriptions imply that, in the near term, weakness may be increased for banks. Only if such schemes raise considerable sums in the market (as the ESM has begun to do) can the burden on the insured be made bearable. Continuing to raise funds is only possible if the market remains confident of pleasant outcomes: that is to say, maybe some recapitalisations plus a few restructurings or even collapses would be ok, as long such actions do not impact severely on major market participants (those regarded as having a large national 'footprint' and/or as being Euro-systemically significant). One implication must

---

46 K. Alexander, Written Evidence in House of Lords EU Economic and Financial Affairs Sub-committee 'Genuine Economic and Monetary Union, Evidence', 14.02.2014, p. 4 <www.parliament.uk/business/committees/committees-a-z/lords-select/eu-economic-and-financial-affairs-and-international-trade-sub-committee-a/news/gemureportpublished> accessed 14.02.2013.

47 K. Alexander, Written Evidence in House of Lords EU Economic and Financial Affairs Sub-committee 'Genuine Economic and Monetary Union, Evidence', supra note 46, p. 4.

be that policy makers and regulators will continue to have sensitivity to bad news on any front, including misconduct.

Thus, in times of crisis and reconstruction (post-2008), just as in times of Ponzi-exuberance (pre-2008), conduct regulators may receive mixed messages from regulatory colleagues.

There are however some important qualifications to the hypothesised relationships and pressures concerning conduct regulators. First, their current activism *vis-à-vis* market manipulation is being driven partly by injured parties' suspicions and the latters' desire for redress via civil actions; also by law firms' and consultants' interest in generating business.[48] This may place limits upon the ability of the ESM Governing Board and on the SSM to define the frame within which misconduct is identified, investigated and prosecuted: it would hardly be acceptable for conduct regulators to get too far behind private actors and the specialised media.

A second qualification is that conduct regulators outside the Eurozone concern themselves with banks acting internationally. US conduct regulation clearly impacts European banks; all the more since the emergence of the crisis. It seems unlikely (though not impossible) that US state prosecutors – or authorities in countries such as China – would be very open to signals of concern from the ESM or the SSM. Moreover, if foreign conduct regulators act, then their European counterparts may find it hard not to do similarly. That is one clear limitation to the extent to which European conduct regulation may be tied to the objectives of the SSM and ESM.

Thirdly, in addressing these issues, one should not forget or discount investigations by the competition authorities. These do not form part of the cascade that we have described: their forms of governance differ from those of financial market regulators, at least in formal terms. Were competition authorities to be autonomous not only in theory but also in practice, that could be significant in relation to their administrative investigations, determinations, fines and conditions of settlement in matters such as Libor and forex manipulation.[49] Nevertheless, senior staff in competition authorities may feel that they live in 'the real world' – that is to say, within the same broad policy climate and in similar epistemologic waters as do finance ministers and prudential regulators. Given this, they would not wish to rock the boat too much, meaning that they may seek ways of reconciling their specific responsibilities with those of the ESM and SSM. Going forward, there are

48 FTFM, 'Fear over gold price rigging put investors on alert', *Financial Times Fund Management Supplement*, 24.02.2014, p. 1.

49 FINANCIAL TIMES REPORTERS, 'Forex in the Spotlight', *Financial Times*, 16.02.2014, p. 5. <www.ft.com/intl/cms/s/0/a296da48-9579-11e3-8371-00144feab7de.html> accessed 24.02.2014.

some interesting hypotheses for research across disciplinary boundaries, as well as some important normative issues.

In circumstances of political sensitivity and systemic uncertainty, the continuing and indeed mounting flow of revelations (as of 2012–2014) about market manipulation raises many questions, spreading from conduct regulation to prudential regulation and potentially to the ESM. Historically, some prudential and conduct regulators exhibited a tendency to blame politicians for favouring markets to the extent of reigning in regulators.[50] Regulators' *apologias* also illustrate not only behind-closed-doors political capture but also regulators' retreat from their own, previous 'regulatory rapture' – a state in which regulators, as well as politicians, acted as cheer-leaders for 'their' firms.[51] Since the emergence of the crisis and its persistence in the banking sector in the Eurozone, prudential regulators have become less tolerant of market malfeasance, which is ironic insofar as many banks in the Eurozone, weakened by their past excesses, are less able to absorb reputational damage and large fines than they would have been pre-2007. On that basis, the ESM and prudential regulators might signal to conduct regulators that they should proceed carefully. On the other hand, the weakened condition of banks means that conduct regulation may have more leverage against them than pre-2007. On that basis, the ESM and prudential regulators might see conduct regulation as a lubricant for much broader reform.

These are empirical and contingent questions. In the present atmosphere of strong political support for reform of financial markets, conduct regulation is facilitated. As a consequence, all manner of market manipulations, conflicts of interests, insider trading and other malfeasance comes to our attention. If in the future the broader atmosphere changes – due to ESM ambivalence or for other reasons – then conduct regulation might again lose impetus. One way to cut that *Gordian knot* would be to move to a situation in which heads of financial market conduct regulatory agencies are elected, reorienting their governance away from the regulatory cascade, and towards citizens. What might be the prospects of changes in governance along such lines in Europe? In 2010 Spain called for EU-level prosecution of those speculating against the Euro,[52] trying to hitch that proposal to European Commission proposals for a European Public Prosecutor's

---

50 R. Winnett, 'Gordon Brown helped fuel banking crisis – FSA head', *The Telegraph*, 25.02.2009 <www.telegraph.co.uk/finance/financialcrisis/4808373/Gordon-Brown-helped-fuel-banking-crisis-FSA-head.html> accessed 19.10.2014.

51 J. Anderson, 'The Public Utility Commission of Texas: A Case of Capture or Rapture?' (1982) 1 *Review of Policy Research* 417.

52 J. Pawlak, 'Spain calls for EU prosecutor to protect euro', *Reuters news agency*, 03.03.2010. <http://in.reuters.com/article/2010/03/03/eu-euro-prosecutor-idINLDE6222G620100303> accessed 24.02.2014.

Office on matters of EU fraud.[53] Hence the Spanish proposal questioned the level at which prosecution is organised but not the assumption that chief prosecutors are 'naturally' appointees rather than elected officers. No such reform that is currently on the table in the EU/Eurozone debate; which is not to rule out the possibility that it might in future come into political debate, the latter looking rather unpredictable.

That being the case in Europe, conduct regulators remain invigorated – or constrained – by the broader epistemic community of which they are a part. For the Eurozone, that community is defined as banking union and its three mechanisms; for the wider EU, the still-important but somewhat politically decentred European Supervisory Authorities (ESAs). The latter cover securities trading and insurance, whilst the Eurozone mechanisms cover only banking (formally speaking, yet consider again the impact on securities of the ECB's promise of Outright Monetary Transactions). There remains the question of the evolution of relations between Eurozone banking union mechanisms – where we have drawn particular attention to the ESM as a new pivotal and possibly paramount arena – and the 'outs'. The latter retain their own, national arrangements for prudential regulation, precautionary intervention and resolution, although a *Modus Vivendi* has to be found.

From a perspective sensitive to the EU's democratic deficit, it is possible that the complexity and inward-facing nature of the expanding community of European financial regulation has deepened and *institutionalised* that deficit. And yet any such conclusion may be premature, as national parliaments have yet to find their feet in the new, complex and cascading regulatory structure (see above). The clear losers appear to be the European Parliament and with it any prospect of a *pan-EU* demos. The Parliament extracted from the ECB certain duties concerning the latter's post-hoc accountability in respect of the SSM,[54] yet the Parliament appears to have been decisively sidelined by the ESM. To position the Parliament in relation to the regulatory cascade, one might see it (regretfully) as a downstream pool, in which endangered species roll their eyes as they try to digest what has been washed down to them. Is that too pessimistic an image of the place of the European Parliament in relation to these matters? Possibly not, insofar as national parliaments may have greater potential to develop political leverage *vis-à-vis* finance ministers and hence *vis-à-vis* the ESM at the top of the regulatory cascade. To summarise, contingency might be introduced into the cascade 'from above' by activism by national parliaments, and 'from below' by

---

53 EUROPEAN COMMISSION, *Proposal for a Council Regulation on the establishment of the European Public Prosecutor's Office*, COM(2013) 534 final, pp. 19–20.

54 EUROPEAN UNION, *Interinstitutional Agreement between the European Parliament and the European Central Bank on the practical modalities of the exercise of democratic accountability and oversight over the exercise of the tasks conferred on the ECB within the framework of the Single Supervisory Mechanism*, supra note 12.

activism by conduct regulators, as well as from foreign regulators and from the financial markets themselves, and possibly from the European Parliament.

Undoubtedly, developments in banking union, resolution, prudential regulation and conduct regulation present a series of wake-up calls, not only to finance and regulatory specialists, but also to scholars of European integration and democracy.[55] Recent commentaries suggest that the three classic analytical frameworks for analysis of European integration – neofunctionalism, liberal intergovernmentalism and the EU as a *sui generis* organisation, with features of both – all receive some empirical support from recent events.[56] In neofunctionalist terms, the flurry of policy making in response to the crisis might be regarded as evidence of spillover effects, thinking in particular about the ECB, the SSM and conduct regulation in the immediate aftermath of the crisis. Liberal intergovernmentalism might also seem to have been partially revived by the crisis, witness the ESM, even if the latter might better be understood in terms of neoliberal intergovernmentalism.[57] As for the EU being a *sui generis* organisation, the increasingly complexity of its relationships with various 'add-ons' and/or 'opt-outs' could favour such an analysis. Bruno de Witte has argued that in legal terms the EU is more intergovernmental than *sui generis*;[58] all the more so, we might add, with the ESM being added to the mix. It would be beyond the scope of this chapter (and indeed of the book) to attempt to engage further with these questions, nevertheless we are justified in putting down the following marker. The intergovernmental ESM and its relations with other aspects of financial market prudential and conduct regulation are more than ripples on the surface of the EU: they are signs of its re-making.

7. ACKNOWLEDGEMENTS

The author thanks past colleagues and students in the Erasmus School of Law (ESL), notably masters students taking the global governance course in 2012, who discussed some of the issues discussed here. Also to Anna Sting and Arien van 't Hof, PhD candidates in economic governance at ESL, who offered comments on a draft in early 2014. Thanks are also due to Simone White, for commenting on early drafts and to the editor of this book, for helping to shape the chapter. Needless to say, the usual disclaimer applies.

55 M. Cappelletti, M. Seccombe and J. Weiler, *Integration Through Law*, Walter de Gruyter, Berlin 1986.

56 R. Vilpišauskas, 'Eurozone Crisis and European integration: functional spillover, political spillback?' (2013) 35 *Journal of European Integration* 361.

57 C. Crouch, *The Strange Non-death of Neo-liberalism*, Polity, Chichester 2011.

58 B. De Witte, 'The European Union as an International Legal Experiment' in G De Búrca and J. Weiler (eds.), *The Worlds of European Constitutionalism*, Cambridge University Press, Cambridge 2012, pp 105–149.

THE EUROPEAN SECURITIES AND MARKETS AUTHORITY: ACCOUNTABILITY TOWARDS EU INSTITUTIONS AND STAKEHOLDERS

Carmine Di Noia and Matteo Gargantini

The paper highlights how the traditional concepts of independence and accountability towards stakeholders apply to the European Securities and Markets Authority (ESMA). ESMA's relationships with national competent authorities, which retain direct supervisory powers with limited exceptions, and the EU Institutions, which are competent for the adoption of legislative and non-legislative regulatory measures, are also considered. ESMA organization and operations are strongly influenced by the position of the new Authority within the EU institutional framework. The European Court of Justice confirmed the legitimacy of the legal basis of ESMA itself and of its powers. ESMA governance still displays some features of a network among national supervisors because its quasi-regulatory functions and supervisory tasks are constrained by limitations directly or indirectly dictated by the Treaties. The analysis shows that tasks conferred to ESMA fall short to match its relatively high accountability, which is on the contrary aligned with international best practices. We suggest therefore some reform proposals that could help streamline regulatory and supervisory functions at EU level, thus allowing ESMA to better exploit its potential while avoiding the risk of excessive centralization of supervisory powers.

Opinions of the authors are personal and do not necessarily coincide with those of their respective organizations or of the ESMA Securities and Markets Stakeholder Group whose working group on ESAs' review was chaired by Carmine Di Noia. Although the essay is the result of common reflections, paragraphs 1, 2, 4.1, and 4.2.1.3 shall be attributed to Carmine Di Noia (corresponding author) and paragraphs 3, 4.2.1.1, 4.2.1.2, 4.2.2, and 5 to Matteo Gargantini. The law in this chapter is up to date to mid-2014.

1. INTRODUCTION

This chapter addresses the structure, functions, and powers of the European Securities and Markets Authority (ESMA), one of the three supervisory agencies created in 2010 by the European Union in reaction to the financial crisis. ESMA is certainly a more powerful institution than the Committee of European Securities Regulators (CESR) was in its capacity as a Lamfalussy Level 3 committee, although institutional obstacles and the cautiousness of many Member States, national competent authorities and market players stopped a stronger centralization of regulatory and supervisory powers. Moreover, the governance of the new body still relies on representation of national competent authorities, so that ESMA can also be regarded as a reinforced network among regulators, as well as an instrument for further Europeanization of supervisory functions. Central features of ESMA are its stronger accountability and, more generally, its enhanced relationships with other key players in financial regulation, such as the European Commission, the European Parliament, EU and national authorities, and stakeholders in general. As is the case for any supervisor, the regulatory framework that sets the stage for these relationships is paramount in striking the balance between agency independence, on the one hand, and accountability, on the other.

After an overview of the process by which the European Supervisory Authorities (ESAs) were created, the paper provides a general introduction to the theoretical rationale for independence and accountability of financial supervisors, showing the importance of the two principles and explaining to what extent they may result in a trade-off (par. 2–3).

In light of this theoretical analysis, par. 4.1.1 describes the main features of ESMA organisation. After sketching out the characteristics of the internal governance structure, the paper specifically focuses on the devices the founding Regulation deploys to ensure that the Authority is also accountable *vis-à-vis* the EU institutions and the public in general, including the interested stakeholders.

A distinctive feature of ESMA internal organisation is the presence, mandated by the founding Regulation, of a stakeholder group which performs relevant advisory tasks and closely interacts with the other bodies of the Authority. In par. 4.1.2, we focus on the features of the ESMA Securities and Markets Stakeholder Group and analyse its governance as well as its activity in the first period of its life.

Par. 4.2.1–2 address ESMA governance from a procedural standpoint, and show how the organizational structure dynamically operates when quasi-regulatory functions are carried out within the post-Lisbon institutional balance. Par. 4.2.3 performs a similar analysis for supervisory powers.

Finally, par. 5 evaluates the efficiency of the current legislative framework in light of the EU institutional balance as interpreted in the case-law of the Court of Justice of the European Union (including case C-270/12), and provides some suggestions for further improvement of the existing equilibrium.

2. THE CREATION OF ESMA

In November 2008, the European Commission created a High Level Group chaired by Mr Jacques de Larosière to devise possible solutions to strengthen the European supervisory arrangements, to better protect citizens, and to rebuild trust in the financial system. The final report presented in February 2009 suggested the creation of an integrated European system of financial supervision.[1] Building on the Report, in September 2009 the Commission proposed the creation of a European Systemic Risk Board (ESRB) to deal with macro-stability issues,[2] and the replacement of the existing supervisory architecture, based on the Level 3 Committees, with a European system of financial supervisors (ESFS), consisting of the ESRB itself and of three European Supervisory Authorities (ESAs): a European Banking Authority (EBA), a European Securities and Markets Authority (ESMA), and a European Insurance and Occupational Pensions Authority (EIOPA). On 22 September 2010, the European Parliament – following agreement by all Member States – voted through the new supervisory framework proposed by the Commission. This framework was confirmed by the ECOFIN Council on 17 November 2010. The new bodies were established as from January 2011.[3]

In the ESFS, macro-prudential supervision is entrusted to the ESRB,[4] which is responsible for identifying and analysing systemic developments and operates

1 The High-Level Group on Financial Supervision in the EU, *Report of the High-Level Group on Financial Supervision in the EU*, Brussels, 25.02.2009 (*de Larosière* Report), pp. 48–58.

2 The proposal was anticipated by the Commission Communication on European Financial Supervision (COM(2009) 252 final), 27 May 2009, which set out the structure of the new financial supervisory architecture.

3 ESRB is located in Frankfurt, as its secretariat is provided by the European Central Bank. ESMA is in Paris, EIOPA in Frankfurt and EBA in London: the ESAs headquarters replicate those of their predecessors. Besides an obvious explanation in terms of path-dependence, the location of the ESAs outside Brussels reflects, from a geographical standpoint, the decentralised organization of the Authorities, which contributed to the political viability of the new architecture (see e.g. P. Craig, *EU Administrative Law*, Oxford University Press, Oxford 2012, p. 143).

4 The follow-up of the ESRB's analysis are recommendations and warnings to the supervisors (Art. 3(2)(c) and (d) Regulation (EU) No 1092/2010). Notwithstanding their non-binding nature, such acts have a significant political weight (E. Wymeersch, 'Europe's New Financial Regulatory Bodies' (2011) 11 *Journal of Corporate Law Studies* 443, 450). ESMA has committed

as a network among the three ESAs,[5] the European Commission, and the European and National Central Banks. National financial supervisors and the Chairperson of the Economic and Financial Committee are also represented at the ESRB without voting rights.[6] Micro-prudential supervision (*rectius* regulation) is the responsibility of the ESAs, including their Joint Committee, and national supervisors. The legal basis of the ESAs is Article 114 of the Treaty on the Functioning of the European Union (TFEU), which allows the adoption of "measures" aimed at the approximation of national law and administrative action whenever this is required for the establishment and the functioning of the internal market according to Article 26 TFEU.[7] According to the European Court of Justice (ECJ), besides underpinning measures directly addressed to Member States, this flexible provision may also extend to the creation of administrative European bodies.[8] The ESAs' founding Regulations mention this case-law and specify that, in line with ECJ reasoning, the establishment of the Authority facilitates the uniform application and consistent interpretation of EU law, and

to address such recommendations on a "comply or explain" basis (ESMA, *Frequently Asked Questions. A Guide to Understanding ESMA* (ESMA/2011/009), p. 8).

5 See, respectively, Regulation (EU) No 1093/2010 for the European Banking Authority; Regulation (EU) No 1094/2010 for the European Insurance and Occupational Pensions Authority; Regulation (EU) No 1095/2010 for the European Securities and Markets Authority.

6 Regulation (EU) No 1092/2010 on European Union macro-prudential oversight of the financial system and establishing a European Systemic Risk Board. The secretariat of ESRB was attributed to the ECB with Council Regulation (EU) No 1096/2010 "conferring specific tasks upon the European Central Bank concerning the functioning of the European Systemic Risk Board": the Regulation has not been issued under art. 114 TFEU but under art. 127(6) after a proposal from the European Commission, the opinion of the European Parliament and the opinion of the European Central Bank itself. This has paved the way to the establishment of the Single Supervisory Mechanism over banks, which attributes supervisory competences to the ECB using the same tool.

7 A. Neergaard, 'European Supervisory Authorities. A New Model for the Exercise of Power in the European Union?' (2009) 11 *Euredia* 603, 617 *et seq.*

8 See ECJ, Case C-217/04, *United Kingdom v. Parliament and Council,* 02.05.2006 (ENISA ruling), para 44; T. Tridimas, 'Financial Supervision and Agency Power: Reflections on ESMA' in N. Shuibhne and L.W. Gormley (eds.), *From Single Market to Economic Union. Essays in Memory of John A. Usher*, Oxford University Press, Oxford 2012, p. 66. The ruling is regarded – together with the "smoke flavouring" decision: see ECJ, Case C-66/04, *United Kingdom v. Parliament and Council,* 06.12.2005, para 45 – as a symptom of a general loose approach by the ECJ when it comes to policing the compliance of EU agencies with general principles such as conferral and subsidiarity (Art. 5 TEU; P. Shammo, 'The European Securities and Markets Authority: Lifting the Veil on the Allocation of Powers' (2011) 48 *Common Market Law Review* 1879, 1906, 1909 *et seq.*), which might challenge, if widely interpreted, the delegation of certain tasks to the ESAs. See the Advocate General's opinion in ECJ, Case C-270/12, *United Kingdom of Great Britain and Northern Ireland v. European Parliament and Council of the European Union*, 22.01.2014, which reiterates that Art. 114 represents an appropriate legal basis for the creation of the ESMA (para 34), but not for the conferral of powers resulting in a replacement of national decision making (para 52). The Court final decision adopts a broader interpretation of Art. 114 that allows for such a substitution under certain conditions.

therefore contributes to financial stability (see e.g. Recital 17 Regulation No 1095/2010).[9]

Within this institutional design, the ESMA is responsible for the integrity, transparency, efficiency and orderly functioning of financial markets, and contributes to ensuring that the taking of investment and other risks is appropriately regulated and supervised and that investors are sufficiently protected (Articles 1(5) and 8).

3. INDEPENDENCE AND ACCOUNTABILITY OF FINANCIAL REGULATORS: AN OVERVIEW

The importance of independence in the management of financial regulation and supervision is recognised by the mainstream legal and economic literature. Although no uniform opinion exists on the reasons for outsourcing to external bodies some of the functions which would originally belong to the central government, one of the most common explanations refers to the problem of time inconsistency in policy choices regarding the financial sector.[10] While politicians may be inclined to favour short-term policies with the aim of being re-elected at the end of their term, regulators should be less easily influenced by such incentives and might therefore be in a better position to adopt welfare-increasing decisions in the long run, to the extent that the nomination procedure and other strategies such as cooling-off periods sufficiently insulate them from pressures by voters at large or by specific vested interests.[11]

Another traditional explanation refers to delegation as a tool for reducing decision costs in matters where specific skills are needed, as the creation of agencies may

[9] While the Recital offers a formal justification for the establishment of the ESAs, substantial critiques have been raised of the ability of a centralized regulatory and supervisory system to adequately address financial risks, which might even be worsened by the increased possibility of systemic errors (N. Moloney, 'The European Securities and Markets Authority and Institutional Design for the EU Financial Market – A Tale of Two Competences: Part (1) Rule-Making' (2011) 12 *European Business Organization Law Review* 41, 70 *et seq.*).

[10] The time-inconsistency explanation is typically developed for monetary policy by central banks. It reasons that absent independence from politics, central banks would be tempted to systematically inflate prices to lower unemployment and increase nominal gross output (see e.g. K. Rogoff, 'The optimal degree of commitment to an intermediate monetary target' (1985) 100 *Quarterly Journal of Economics* 1169, 1173 and 1180).

[11] A. Alesina and G. Tabellini, 'Bureaucrats or politicians? Part II: Multiple policy tasks' (2008) 92 *Journal of Public Economics* 426, 440 and 444 *et seq.* While this model is widely applied for – monetary policy (supra note 10) and – prudential regulation, some authors believe that lawmakers could directly take care of information regulation (M. Quintyn and M.W. Taylor, 'Regulatory and Supervisory Independence and Financial Stability' (2003) 49 *CESifo Economic Studies* 259, 269). However, time inconsistency affecting law-making and supervision in financial markets can also discourage investments.

help gather expertise in bodies characterized by detailed institutional objectives. Agencies may also facilitate the adoption of decisions on controversial and intractable problems where the majority mechanism could not produce efficient results.[12] Furthermore, independent bodies detached from the central government may ease the implementation of public participation, e.g. through open consultations or stakeholder representation, so as to convey more information to the administrative process.[13] Finally, the creation of agencies in the EU context, besides facilitating the pooling of knowledge, may also help reduce coordination problems among Member States[14] through centralisation of powers, because States are more willing to accept delegation to agencies,[15] in whose governing bodies they are typically represented, rather than to the Commission.[16]

One might of course disagree that certain decisions, which are inherently political, should be left to bureaucrats who lack democratic legitimacy.[17] However, once the case is made for outsourcing certain functions to bodies outside the scope of democratic representation, it is widely acknowledged that good performance of institutional tasks by those bodies requires some degree of independence from both politicians and the regulated entities.[18] When a function has been carved out of the State's central body, a lack of independence from either politicians or regulated entities would create perverse incentives in the exercise of the

12 K.J. Arrow, 'A Difficulty in the Concept of Social Welfare' (1950) 58 *The Journal of Political Economy* 328; D.B. Spence, 'Administrative Law and Agency Policy-Making: Rethinking the Positive Theory of Political Control' (1997) 14 *Yale Journal on Regulation* 407, 443.

13 On the informative benefits of participation see D.B. Spence and F. Cross, 'A Public Choice Case for the Administrative State' (2000) 89 *Georgetown Law Journal* 97, 124 *et seq.*

14 P. Magnette, 'The Politics of Regulation in the European Union' in D. Geradin et al. (eds.), *Regulation through Agencies in the EU. A New Paradigm of European Governance*, Edward Elgar, Cheltenham 2005, p. 7 *et seq.*

15 Commission Communication COM(2008) 135 final, 2 and 5; T. Tridimas, 'Financial Supervision and Agency Power: Reflections on ESMA', supra note 8, p. 63.

16 For further analysis see M. Egeberg et al., 'Building executive power at the European level: on the role of European Union Agencies' in M. Busuioc et al. (eds.), *The agency phenomenon in the European Union*, Manchester University Press, Manchester, 2012, p. 29 *et seq.*

17 Strong political implications are typical of central banking (on the optimal allocation of monetary policy decisions between politicians and central banks see S.C.W. Eijffinger and M.M. Hoeberichts, 'Central Bank Accountability and Transparency: Theory and Some Evidence' (2002) 5 *International Finance* 73) while the same critique is less appealing for other non-majoritarian institutions (especially in the EU: G. Majone, 'Delegation of Regulatory Powers in a Mixed Polity' (2002) 8 *European Law Journal* 319, 327), including securities supervisors, although technical decisions in the area of financial markets law may have redistributive effects as well (see M. Shapiro, 'The Problems of Independent Agencies in the United States and the European Union' (1997) 4 *Journal of European Public Policy* 276, 280 and 284 *et seq.*). See also OECD, *Principles for the Governance of Regulators – Public Consultation Draft*, OECD, Paris 2013, p. 34 *et seq.*

18 See G. Majone, 'Strategy and Structure: the Political Economy of Agency Independence and Accountability' in OECD Working Party on Regulatory Management and Reform (ed.), *Designing Independent and Accountable Regulatory Authorities for High Quality Regulation*, OECD, Paris 2005, p. 130 *et seq.* See also OECD, *Principles for the Governance of Regulators – Public Consultation Draft*, supra note 17, p. 32 *et seq.*

regulatory and supervisory functions. For example, the members of a supervisory body that is independent only in a formal sense might be tempted to follow political or lobbying pressure while easily becoming scapegoats should a scandal or a systemic turmoil emerge: this would decrease the overall quality of financial regulation and supervision, as those having substantial control over the agency – in this case, politicians – would not bear responsibility for their choices.[19]

At the same time, the rise of independent regulators creates an agency problem because, as in any other delegation of functions, bureaucrats may satisfy their own interests instead of pursuing the institutional objectives of their mandate.[20] Supervisors' employees may be driven by career concerns, for instance. These may provide incentives to pass window-dressing measures instead of more effective remedies which are less perceivable by the public.[21] In financial regulation, this is all the more true because the objectives of supervisors are harder to define,[22] and therefore to measure,[23] if compared to those of other independent entities such as

---

19 Shifting responsibility in order to avoid the risk of being blamed is another explanation for the delegation of regulatory and supervisory functions (E. Kane, 'Principal-Agent Problems in S&L Salvage' (1990) 45 *Journal of Finance* 755, 756), at least where the actual net benefits of regulatory measures are not immediately perceived, so that no counterbalancing incentive exists to retain regulatory powers in order to enjoy full credit (M.P. Fiorina, 'Legislative Choice of Regulatory Forms: Legal Process or Administrative Process?' (1982) 39 *Public Choice* 33, 46 *et seq.*). In this respect, it should come as no surprise that the preferences of politicians tilt towards attributing responsibility for some sensitive and potentially unpopular choices to an agency (A. Alesina and G. Tabellini, 'Why Do Politicians Delegate?' (2005) *NBER Working Paper* No. 11531, 17 *et seq.*), while covertly trying to influence the latter at the same time (for an insightful description see e.g. J.A. Allison, *The Financial Crisis and the free Market Cure*, McGraw Hill, New York 2013, p. 21 *et seq.*). Of course, a symmetric reasoning can apply: once delegation is made and independence is ensured, the accountability of the delegating body shall not go beyond its effective influence over the agency (see the EU Commission's concerns in the Commission Communication COM(2008) 135 final, 8).

20 For an example in the field of deposit insurance and bank resolution see E. Kane, 'Principal-Agent Problems in S&L Salvage', supra note 19, 760.

21 See L. Enriques, "Regulators' Response to the Current Crisis and the Upcoming Reregulation of Financial Markets: One Reluctant Regulator's View' (2009) 30 *University of Pennsylvania Journal of International Law* 1147, 1153 *et seq.*, for further thoughts on the way regulators can also tackle concerns about public opinion by adopting purportedly ineffective measures with a view to showing that some effort is made in a context where taking no action would be more rational.

22 See P. Craig, *EU Administrative Law*, supra note 3, p. 161 (precise definition of agency objectives greatly enhances accountability).

23 For instance, as pointed out by C. Goodhart – 'Regulating the regulator – An Economist's Perspective on Accountability and Control' in E. Ferran, and C. Goodhart (eds.), *Regulating Financial Services and Markets in the 21st Century*, Hart Publishing, Oxford 2001, p. 151 – progress toward the statutory objective to reduce financial crime is very difficult to ascertain. Think about prevention of financial fraud: once a company is discovered having cooked the books, supervisors are often blamed for not having done their job. However, it is impossible to say how many other scams have been prevented from the outset because of regulation or early detection, since events not occurring are no news. Moreover, even when the supervisor uncovers a fraud, it is usually blamed for not having detected it earlier, before any damage occurred. Both cognitive biases skew the perception and the measurement of supervisors' effectiveness and, still worse, may foster overregulation (see text accompanying infra note 304).

central banks.[24] Statutory duties are inevitably vaguely defined, that vagueness being exacerbated by the long-term nature of the relationship between supervisors and stakeholders. Funding statuses cannot contemplate all possible future states of the world, and therefore cannot always effectively constrain regulators' behaviour. On the contrary, the incompleteness of the statutes requires that administrative discretion steps in to fill the gaps.[25] Moreover, the presence of multiple direct and indirect stakeholders increases the risk that the agents deviate from their duties towards the principals,[26] as any measure which would not satisfy one group of interests might well be justified on the basis that it is aimed at protecting another group. Accountability tools are devised to tackle these shortcomings.

According to the traditional view, in democratic systems the power to make discretionary choices can only be conferred upon unelected bodies to the extent that such bodies are legitimized by accountability. In a similar vein, accountability compensates for independence, adding a strengthened control by the principal to the benefits of agency specialization. However, in a context where stakeholders are not represented by a single homogeneous constituency, accountability to a group of interests also increases independence from other stakeholders:[27] it has therefore been stressed that independence and accountability do not necessarily represent a trade-off, since the former cannot properly operate without the latter.[28] This analytical framework contributes to explaining why the three ESAs,

24 An example are the potentially conflicting objectives of transparency and orderly functioning of financial markets (as illustrated by the rule that broadens the scope for delaying the publication of inside information where doing so would threaten financial stability: Art. 17(5) Regulation (EU) No 596/2014 of the European Parliament and of the Council on insider dealing and market manipulation (market abuse) (MAR). Of course, similar trade-offs also affect prudential regulation and monetary policy, as may be the case for short and long-term stability of the financial system (see respectively M. Quintyn and M.W. Taylor, 'Regulatory and Supervisory Independence and Financial Stability', supra note 11, 284; J.A. Allison, *The Financial Crisis and the free Market Cure,* supra note 19, p. 18 *et seq.*), but financial supervision is especially susceptible to the consequences of multiple statutory functions (E. Hüpkes et al., 'The Accountability of Financial Sector Supervisors: Principles and Practices' (2005) 16 *European Business Law Review* 1575, 1582).

25 See D. Masciandaro et al., 'The Economic Crisis: A Story of Supervisory Failure and Ideas for the Way Forward' in M. Balling et al. (eds.), *New Paradigms in Banking, Financial Markets and Regulation?,* Larcier, Brussels 2012, pp. 21 and 33.

26 D. Masciandaro et al., 'Inside and Outside the Central Bank: Independence and Accountability in Financial Supervision. Trends and Determinants' (2008) 24 *European Journal of Political Economy* 833, 834; T. Conzelmann et al., *Regulatory overhaul in the EU and the US following the financial crisis – what role for accountability?,* Paper prepared for the ECPR Standing Group on International Relations Conference, Stockholm 09–11.09.2010, p. 4.

27 G. Majone, 'Independence vs Accountability? Non-Majoritarian Institutions and Democratic Government in Europe' (1994) *European University Institute Working Paper* No. 94/3, p. 26 (independence and accountability should be regarded as mutually reinforcing rather than mutually exclusive).

28 E. Hüpkes et al., 'The Accountability of Financial Sector Supervisors: Principles and Practices', supra note 24, 1577.

as well as other supervisors across the globe and other EU agencies,[29] deploy administrative law tools, such as consultations and consultative panels, which enable multiple stakeholders to have voice in the regulatory process. Not only do these devices convey fresh knowledge to administrative processes,[30] but the early involvement of those affected by the impending rules also makes spontaneous compliance more likely:[31] in both cases, accountability increases the (actual or perceived) legitimacy of regulatory action.[32]

4. ESMA ACCOUNTABILITY: GOVERNANCE AND PROCEDURES

In every jurisdiction, legislators adopt various strategies to constrain regulators' discretion as prescribed by relevant statutes and to ensure that bureaucrats employed by agencies strive to fulfil statutory objectives.[33] For the sake of exposition, we roughly divide these strategies in two sets, with the caveat that this taxonomy inevitably includes some overlapping areas.[34]

The first set refers to the governance of agencies,[35] and encompasses the rules that in a static perspective set the organization of the regulator, the composition of its internal bodies, and the power to appoint its members. These structural features may increase or decrease the voice of coalitions having a stake in regulatory action, including the legislator.[36] Nonetheless, no matter how effective *ex ante* arrangements can be, they will never ensure that regulators and supervisors

---

29 E. Vos, 'Independence, Accountability and Transparency of European Regulatory Agencies' in D. Geradin et al. (eds.), *Regulation through Agencies in the EU. A New Paradigm of European Governance*, Edward Elgar, Cheltenham 2005. p. 128 *et seq.*

30 See infra note 84 and accompanying text.

31 E. Hüpkes et al., 'The Accountability of Financial Sector Supervisors: Principles and Practices', supra note 24, 1579 *et seq.* and 1587 *et seq.*

32 Therefore, input-oriented legitimacy contributes to increasing output-oriented legitimacy (see the classification by F. Scharpf, *Governing in Europe: Effective and Democratic?*, Oxford University Press, Oxford 1999, p. 6 *et seq.*).

33 See M. Bovens, 'Analysing and Assessing Accountability: A Conceptual Framework' (2007) 13 *European Law Journal* 447, 455 *et seq.* In many respects, the strategies adopted in administrative law resemble those enacted to address agency problems in company law. For a taxonomy and an overview see J. Armour et al., *The Anatomy of Corporate Law. A Comparative and Functional Approach*, Oxford University Press, Oxford 2009, p. 37 *et seq.*

34 J.R. Macey, 'Organizational Design and Political Control of Administrative Agencies' (1992) 8 *Journal of Law Economics and Organization* 93. 95.

35 In this paper, the term "governance" refers to ESMA internal (or corporate) governance (see e.g. M. Quintyn, *Governance of Financial Supervisors and its Effects – A Stocktaking Exercise*, SUERF, Vienna 2007, p. 7).

36 M. McCubbins et al., 'Structure and Process, Politics and Policy: Administrative Arrangements and the Political Control of Agencies' (1989) 75 *Virginia Law Review* 431, 440 *et seq.* See also J.R. Macey, 'Organizational Design and Political Control of Administrative Agencies', supra note 34, 100 (the ability to structure the initial design of an agency is the most powerful device available to politicians).

always comply with their duties – or, stated more cynically, that they do not break the leash the legislator may be willing to maintain.[37] Procedures are therefore needed that dynamically involve the principals (or their representatives) during the regulatory process and allow for *ex post* reactions in case the regulators do not fulfil their obligations. The second set of legislative devices comprises mechanisms aimed at ensuring ongoing accountability.

4.1. THE GOVERNANCE OF ESMA

4.1.1. The governing bodies of the authority

The founding Regulation has granted ESMA legal personality, as well as administrative and financial autonomy.[38] Although ESMA is formally referred to as a "Union body" (Article 5), rather than as an agency,[39] its status eased the attribution of wider responsibilities and streamlined the interaction with other EU bodies, thus facilitating the establishment of a clear framework for accountability. ESMA – as well as the other ESAs and the ESRB – "shall be accountable to the European Parliament and the Council" (Article 3 Regulation (EU) No 1095/2010). Beside this general principle, a number of specific provisions hold ESMA accountable to the EU institutions, including the Commission, although this is not formally listed among the entities enjoying accountability.[40] Some ensure accountability on how ESMA performs its tasks and on the way it is globally managed, while others require that the institutions be informed on the rulemaking and supervisory processes. We first analyse ESMA accountability from the standpoint of its organisation.

The governance of ESMA is composed of a Board of Supervisors, a Management Board, a Chairperson, an Executive Director, and a Board of Appeal, which constitute the core of the organisation (Article 6),[41] and comprises other internal

37 D.T. Hornstein, 'Complexity, Adaptation, and Administrative Law' (2005) 54 *Duke Law Journal* 913. 931.

38 This ensures that ESMA retains not only a regulatory and supervisory independence, but also an institutional and budgetary one (M. Quintyn and M.W. Taylor, 'Regulatory and Supervisory Independence and Financial Stability', supra note 11, 275 *et seq.*).

39 After the creation of the ESAs, the EU institutions have agreed to adopt the term "agency" when establishing new authorities in the future. The common approach should avoid any confusion as for the qualification of these EU bodies (see the Joint Statement of the European Parliament, the Council of the EU and the European Commission on decentralised agencies, 12 June 2012, 3 (hereinafter: 2012 Interinstitutional Joint Statement)).

40 See DG Internal Policies (European Parliament), *Review of the New European System of Financial Supervision (ESFS). Part 1* (2013) www.europarl.europa.eu accessed 09.10.2014, p. 42.

41 The two-tier governance system adopted by the ESAs founding Regulations, albeit not isolated, does not follow the traditional pattern for EU agencies, which are more often organized on the basis of a monistic (one-tier) system (Commission Communication COM(2008) 135 final,

bodies with ancillary functions, such as the Securities and Markets Stakeholder Group. The Board of Supervisors is the highest-ranking body of the hierarchical structure; it has the power to direct the activity of the Authority as a whole and bears responsibility for the final adoption of supervisory decisions (Article 43), including draft regulatory and implementing technical standards under Articles 10 and 15 of the founding Regulation.

The Board of Supervisors is chaired by the Chairperson (who has no voting right) and is composed of the (voting) "head"[42] of one competent authority for each EU Member State. The Board also comprises four non-voting members from the Commission, the ESRB and the other two ESAs respectively. While attendance by the ESRB's and ESAs' representatives fosters coordination among the European constituencies of the ESFS, the presence of a member appointed by the Commission facilitates the maintenance of the unity and integrity of EU policy in the field of financial regulation.[43] The Executive Director attends the Board meetings, without voting power (Article 1(6)).[44] Decisions are taken by simple majority, with the exception of those regarding the exercise of quasi-rulemaking powers and other sensitive measures, which require a qualified majority (Article 44). Decisions concerning the draft statements anticipating estimated revenues and expenditures for the incoming year fall into the latter category,[45] but final approval of the budget is remitted to the Council and the Parliament, as it is part of the General Budget of the EU (Article 63).[46] ESMA general costs are financed in part (about 60 per cent[47]) by the national authorities, depending on their respective weight in voting power, and in part by the General

5). Dualistic (two-tier) governance is allowed, when required by efficiency reasons, by the 2012 Interinstitutional Joint Statement, at 5.

42 However, the rule is applied in a flexible manner so as to allow high-level representatives other than chairperson to join the Board of Supervisors (e.g., the Danish FSA is represented in the Board of Supervisors, as well as in the Management Board, by one of its Deputy Director General). Furthermore, each competent authority must appoint a high-level alternate, who may replace the acting member in the Board of Supervisors when the latter cannot attend. In Member States where more than one authority is responsible for supervision according to ESMA Regulation, those authorities shall agree on a common representative; nevertheless, when an item to be discussed by the Board of Supervisors does not fall within the competence of the national authority represented in the Board, a representative from the relevant national authority, who shall be non-voting, may also join the Board.

43 See Commission Communication, The operating framework for the European Regulatory Agencies, COM(2002) 718 final, 2.

44 There are no explicit exceptions to the Executive Director's right and obligation to attend the Board of Supervisors, but attendance should be excluded for meetings convened to decide the possible renewal of the mandate. The same applies to the Chairperson in case of a new mandate.

45 Another example are decisions taken upon recourse against a provisional ban on a financial activity (Art. 9(5)); see para 4.2.3.1.

46 See also Regulation (EU) No 1268/2012 enacting Art. 208 Regulation (EU, Euratom) No 966/2012.

47 DG Internal Policies (European Parliament), *Review of the New European System of Financial Supervision (ESFS). Part 1*, supra note 40, p. 52.

Budget (Article 62), within the section of the European Commission; however, ESMA may also collect fees from some regulated entities, such as credit rating agencies.[48] The budget approval represents one of the main accountability tools in the hands of the institutions,[49] but its inclusion in the European Commission's section may reduce the available resources and hinder ESMA's independence. For this reason, the three ESAs advocate a distinct budgetary linc.[50]

The Chairperson is also a member of the Management Board, where she has voting power as opposed to what happens when she is sitting in the Board of Supervisors. The Management Board comprises also six other members "elected by and from" the heads of national competent authorities for a two-and-a-half year term, renewable once. These members' mandates are overlapping – a staggered composition being *de facto* implemented – and subject to a rotating arrangement (Article 45(1)). In order to extend accountability to functions other than high-level decisions allocated to the Board of Supervisors, a representative of the Commission and the Executive Director attend, without voting power, the meetings of the Management Board. Direct access to information regarding the Board's discussion should improve coordination when executing the decisions taken at the outcome of the Board debate.[51]

The interaction between the decision-making and monitoring functions of the Board of Supervisors, on the one hand, and the steering and executive role of the Management Board, on the other hand, is well represented by the process for the adoption of the annual and the multi-annual work programmes of the Authority. Both documents are proposed by the Management Board and approved by the Supervisory Board (Articles 43 and 47) and are subsequently transmitted for information to the European Parliament, the Council, and the Commission,[52] and made available to the public at large. Therefore, besides

---

48 Direct collection of funds enhances agency independence, in light of the risks embedded in budget approval by political bodies (J. Seligman, 'Self-Funding for the Securities and Exchange Commission' (2004) 28 *Nova Law Review* 233).

49 See e.g. M. Shapiro, 'The Problems of Independent Agencies in the United States and the European Union', supra note 17, 288; D.S. Rubenstein, '"Relative Checks": Towards Optimal Control of Administrative Power' (2010) 51 *William and Mary Law Review* 2169, 2207 (harnessing the purse strings is crucial, as "an unfunded agency is a powerless one").

50 DG Internal Policies (European Parliament), *Review of the New European System of Financial Supervision (ESFS). Part 1*, supra note 40, pp. 53–55.

51 See also M. Busuioc and M. Groenleer, 'Wielders of supranational power? The administrative behavior of the heads of European Union Agencies' in M. Busuioc et al. (eds.), *The agency phenomenon in the European Union*, Manchester University Press, Manchester 2012, p. 141 *et seq*.

52 According to the 2012 Interinstitutional Joint Statement, p. 9, the Commission should issue a formal advice on the annual and multi-annual work programmes.

being an internal governance tool in the hands of the two Boards,[53] the work programmes also enhance ESMA accountability to the other EU institutions and its stakeholders. This happens for various reasons. First, early disclosure of the regulatory and supervisory priorities allows a review of the policy that ESMA is concretely willing to pursue within the inevitably wide statutory objectives set by the founding Regulation (Articles 1(5) and 8),[54] as institutional tasks alone may hardly operate as an effective benchmarks against which performance can be measured.[55] Second, the ESMA agenda allows all interested stakeholders to know that a consultation will be launched in the future on one or more specific topics they may be interested in, so that they can more effectively participate in the administrative process.[56] Third, the work programmes facilitate measuring ESMA performances *ex post*, with respect to the targets that the Authority itself has deemed appropriate for its management.[57]

Strong accountability to the EU Parliament is foreseen in the nomination process of the Chairperson and the Executive Director. The Chairperson (a full-time independent professional selected "on the basis of merit" and "following an open selection procedure"[58]) is appointed by the Board of Supervisors, but the European Parliament, which also hears the selected candidate, has one month to object the designation.[59] An even stronger role for the EU Parliament is foreseen for the nomination of the Executive Director, as the appointment of the latter by the Board of Supervisors[60] requires the preliminary confirmation by the Parliament (Article 51).

---

53 Not only does the drafting of a working plan help prioritise the action of ESMA, thus rendering its supervision more focused and effective, but it allows the Board of Supervisors to internally control employee performance in light of the programme.

54 The dissemination of a business plan makes it easier to identify flawed analysis of market developments and misguided regulatory responses (see L. Enriques and G. Hertig, 'Improving the Governance of Financial Supervisors' (2011) 12 *European Business Organization Law Review* 357, 375; see also OECD, *Principles for the Governance of Regulators – Public Consultation Draft*, supra note 17, p. 51).

55 E. Ferran, 'Examining the United Kingdom's Experience in Adopting the Single Financial Regulator Model' (2003) 28 *Brooklyn Journal of International Law* 257, 296 *et seq.*

56 ESMA, *Public Statement on Consultation Practices* (ESMA/2011/11), p. 2.

57 All the more so since the ESMA annual report (see below) sheds light on the performance of supervision (L. Enriques and G. Hertig, 'Improving the Governance of Financial Supervisors', supra note 55, 375; 2012 Interinstitutional Joint Statement, 11). Key performance indicators may also facilitate *ex post* evaluation (see *ibid.*, 9; OECD, *Principles for the Governance of Regulators – Public Consultation Draft*, supra note 17, p. 63 *et seq.*).

58 As opposed to what happened for CESR's selection procedure, the Chairperson is not appointed among the representatives of national competent authorities (ESMA (2011/009), supra note 4, p. 9).

59 European Parliament, Green light from Parliament for financial watchdog chiefs, press release 3 March 2011.

60 "On the basis of merit" and "following an open selection procedure" as is the case for the Chairperson. See also the 2012 Interinstitutional Joint Statement, at 6.

At the end of the five-year term, the Chairperson undergoes an evaluation performed by the Board of Supervisors, which assesses the results achieved during the Chairperson's tenure and compares them against the duties and the requirements of the Authority for the coming years. On the basis of this exercise, the Board of Supervisors evaluates whether the first term of office should be extended (Article 48(3)).[61] Moreover, the Chairperson is held accountable during the tenure through a section of the annual report which reports on his performance during the year (Articles 43(5) and 47(6)).

The annual report is also a key tool for the accountability of ESMA as a whole,[62] because it provides information on ESMA regulatory and supervisory activities, as well as on administrative and financial matters (Article 53(7)). It is formally proposed by the Management Board for approval by the Board of Supervisors, but it rests upon a report prepared by the Executive Director. The report, besides being transmitted to the European institutions, is also made public to allow scrutiny by stakeholders that can check the actual performance described in the report against the policy envisioned by the previously issued work programmes.

While the annual report enhances ESMA accountability by shedding light on its regular activity, the founding Regulation provides for a more structural triennial review of ESMA (and ESAs') organization and achievements.[63] According to Article 81, the Commission shall examine[64] whether the ESAs' architecture remains the preferable solution, as opposed to more integrated supervisory models such as the "twin peaks" – also envisaged by the *de Larosière* Group as a possible long-term arrangement[65] – or a single regulator.[66] Finally, accountability

---

61 Although the norm is not crystal-clear, the assessment seems to be required only at the end of the first five years of tenure (Art. 48(4)). However, nothing seems to prevent a similar exercise from being performed at the end of the extended terms of office, possibly in the annual report according to Art. 43(5). Even though this would not be a device as effective as the evaluation of the first term, it would represent a mechanism for the accountability of the Chairperson, if only from a reputational standpoint.

62 As well as of national authorities for infringement of Commission's opinions or ESMA decisions issued in case of breach of EU law (Art. 18(8) Reg. 1095/2010).

63 See also the 2012 Interinstitutional Joint Statement, at 13 (suggesting overall evaluation every five years). Review under Art. 81 also presents the opportunity to assess whether one or more recommendations of the Joint Statement shall be implemented in the ESAs' governance (see the Roadmap accompanying the Joint Statement, at 3).

64 See EU Commission, Public consultation ESFS review. Background document (2013), 2.

65 See the de Larosière Report, supra note 1, p. 58.

66 See G. Di Giorgio and C. Di Noia, 'Designing a Regulatory and Supervisory Framework for Integrated Financial Markets' in P. Alessandrini et al. (eds.), *The Changing Geography of Banking and Finance*, Springer, London 2009, p. 215 *et seq*, p. 215; C. Di Noia and M.C. Furlò, 'The New Structure of Financial Supervision in Europe: What's Next?' in E. Wymeersch et al. (eds.), *Financial Regulation and Supervision. A Post-Crisis Analysis*, Oxford University Press, Oxford 2012 p. 172 *et seq*, p. 186 *et seq*. (suggesting a four-peaks model based on differentiation of institutional objective along the following criteria: macro-stability; prudential regulation; investor protection; competition). For a review of the literature, E. Wymeersch, 'The Structure

towards the EU institutions is ensured on *ad hoc* basis by the power of the European Parliament and the Council to solicit opinions from ESMA (Article 34) or to ask the Chairperson to make statements and deliver written reports on specific topics (Article 50).

The Board of Appeal, comprising six members and six alternates who step in whenever there is suspicion that a member is not acting independently (or if a member resigns), is a joint body of the three ESAs in charge of reviewing decisions taken by ESMA according to its supervisory powers (Article 60).[67] Each of the ESAs appoints two members and two alternates from a list of candidates proposed by the Commission on the basis of their expertise in finance and supervision (Article 58),[68] but the requirement that Board of Appeal members must be independent when ruling reduces the risk that the Commission itself may *de facto* second-guess ESMA decisions (Articles 59(1) and (2)). Independent scrutiny is all the more important since, according to some scholars,[69] the scope of the review goes beyond questions of legality.[70] For decisions taken by the Board of Appeal or, where conditions set forth by Art 60(1) Reg. 1095/2010 are not met, by ESMA itself, review by the Court of Justice of the European Union (CJEU) under Article 263 TFEU[71] ensures also judicial accountability (Article 61) of administrative action.[72] In such circumstances, preliminary scrutiny by the Board performs a filtering function against specious appeals.[73]

of Financial Supervision in Europe: About Single, Twin Peaks and Multiple Financial Supervisors' (2007) 8 *European Business Organization Law Review* 239, 239 *et seq.*

67 See infra para 4.2.3. Decisions that can be appealed include requests for information or investigations as well as supervisory measures addressed to credit rating agencies and trade repositories (see Art. 61(3)(g) and 73(3) Reg. 648/2012; Art. 23b and 24 Reg. No. 1060/2009). For an overview see W. Blair, 'Board of Appeal of the European Supervisory Authorities' (2013) 24 *European Business Law Review* 165.

68 Although the relevance of supervisory experience may foster like-mindedness thus making controls more indulgent (Partsch (2011), 48 *et seq.*), the risk of self-reference is reduced by the Commission's previous selection of candidates.

69 E. Wymeersch, 'The European Financial Supervisory Authorities or ESAs' in E. Wymeersch et al. (eds.), *Financial Regulation and Supervision. A Post-Crisis Analysis*, Oxford University Press, Oxford 2012, p. 295.

70 In its decision taken on the case Global Private Rating Company "Standard Rating" Ltd v. ESMA (10 January 2014), the Board of Appeal, deciding on a case concerning ESMA's refusal to register an applicant rating agency, stated that, having regard to the European jurisprudence, it "has to consider whether the respondent correctly applied the applicable Regulations and other applicable instruments, whether the respondent was entitled to reach the refusal decision, or was wrong to refuse registration, and whether the decision was vitiated by procedural irregularity or unfairness" (par. 44).

71 Or according to Art. 265 in case of failure to act.

72 A thorny issue for the incentives of supervisors is their liability regime. According to the founding Regulation, ESMA is responsible for damages caused by it or its staff when performing statutory duties (Art. 69), jurisdiction being granted to the CJEU (the reproduction of Art. 340 TFEU is frequent in regulations setting up new EU agencies; P. Craig, *EU Administrative Law*, supra note 3, p. 157).

73 D. Geradin, 'The Development of European Regulatory Agencies: What the EU Should Learn from American Experience' (2005) 11 *Columbia Journal of European Law* 1, 33.

Besides "vertical" accountability *vis-à-vis* the Parliament and the Council, and judicial accountability, "horizontal" accountability[74] within the ESFS is also facilitated by the Joint Committee,[75] which operates both as a common forum among the three ESAs on topics where their respective competences overlap and as a platform for exchanging information with the ESRB.[76] Although the primary function of the Committee is to ensure coordination among the authorities, it may also produce wider benefits in terms of accountability on some sensitive issues that might be particularly prone to regulatory capture, such as accounting principles, since deeper confrontation among peers may prevent the passage of misguided decisions by one (reputedly captured) authority. The mechanism is strengthened when the three ESAs have to reach an agreement before adopting measures on areas of common competence (Article 56(2)), and horizontal accountability may also be provided by peer review exercises or other forms of cooperation with extra-EU regulators.[77] Although Reg. No. 1095/2010 contains no explicit provision, as opposed to peer reviews promoted by ESMA itself among national competent authorities (Article 30), a similar result can be reached through ESMA membership in international organizations or networks of supervisors.[78]

4.1.2. The Securities and Markets Stakeholder Group

Next to the Joint Committee, the most straightforward form of horizontal accountability in the governance of ESMA is the Securities and Markets Stake-

[74] See also T. Schillemans, 'Accountability in the Shadow of Hierarchy: The Horizontal Accountability of Agencies' (2008) 8 *Public Organization Review* 175, 190 *et seq.* (horizontal accountability involves control by either peers or stakeholders, and better performs its functions if accompanied by vertical accountability).

[75] The Joint Committee is composed of Members and Observers. Members are the Chairpersons of EBA, EIOPA and ESMA (who rotate as Chairperson of the Joint Committee on a yearly basis, in the following order: EBA, ESMA, and EIOPA), and the Chairperson of each sub-committee (including especially the chairman of the most important one, on financial conglomerates). Observers are the Executive Directors of EBA, EIOPA and ESMA, a representative of the European Commission and a representative of the European Systemic Risk Board.

[76] Arts. 54 and 56 Reg. No. 1095/2010 provide a list of such areas (financial conglomerates; accounting; auditing; cross-sectoral developments and risks; retail investment products; money laundering) but also refer, more generally, to the application of any other legislative act falling within the area of competence of more than one authority. See also Art. 32(4), which fosters coordination among the ESAs in the performance of stress-tests (that includes the development of common methodologies and the communication of the results).

[77] Peer review is increasingly adopted to ensure horizontal accountability among participants to supervisory networks. It relies on soft enforcement mechanisms such as peer pressure and the threat of exclusion of peers from the network (G. Dimitropoulos, 'Holding National Administrative Bodies Accountable through Peer Reviews: the FATF Case' in S. Cassese et al. (eds.), *Global Administrative Law. Cases, Materials, Issues,* 3rd ed., IRPA–IILJ 2012, p. 12 *et seq.*).

[78] E.g. ESMA is an associate member of IOSCO, which encourages consistent implementation of its principles concerning disparate issues of financial markets regulation (see IOSCO Technical Committee, *Mitigating Systemic Risk. A Role for Securities Regulators* (OR01/11), 2001).

holder Group.[79] Direct representation of stakeholders within the organisation of regulators has gained momentum during the last decade as an accountability tool and a device to render rulemaking more effective.[80] Many European regulators have set up boards representing consumers and the regulated industry to improve the effectiveness of their regulations and strengthen their legitimacy.[81] From the standpoint of accountability, engagement of multiple stakeholders in the agency governance enhances regulators' responsiveness to the relevant constituencies, since these latter will have a say in the regulatory process, and may reduce the risk of capture by other, possibly conflicting, stakeholders. From the perspective of legitimacy, early involvement of groups that will be affected by new regulation increases the likelihood of spontaneous compliance, thus enhancing the effectiveness of resulting rules by providing incentives which go beyond the traditional command-and-control approach based on the deterrence of sanctions.[82] Finally, from the point of view of effective rulemaking, stakeholder engagement embeds wider expertise in the regulatory process,[83] thus increasing the quality of information available to the authority, and enhances the debate over proposed rules even in circumstances where some constituencies would otherwise be excluded because of the technical nature of the issues at stake.[84] Concerns for legitimacy, accountability, and effectiveness explain why authorities often ensure stakeholder participation on a self-regulatory basis, in the absence of a provision mandating their creation. This was the case before the creation of ESMA, with CESR's Market Participants Consultative Panel, which along with other expert groups set up on specific matters assisted CESR in the performance of its tasks.[85] Although other instruments, such as public consultations, may provide a reliable

---

79 Following T. Schillemans, 'Accountability in the Shadow of Hierarchy: The Horizontal Accountability of Agencies', supra note 75, 179, we consider accountability towards stakeholders as horizontal accountability (other possible classifications being downward, citizen, or societal accountability).

80 E. Ferran, *Building an EU Securities Market*, Cambridge University Press, Cambridge 2004, p. 96.

81 E. Hüpkes et al., 'The Accountability of Financial Sector Supervisors: Principles and Practices', supra note 24, 1600 *et seq.*

82 See the compliance pyramid outlined by I. Ayres and J. Braithwaite, *Responsive Regulation: Transcending the Deregulation Debate*, Oxford University Press, Oxford 1992, p. 35. See also D.T. Hornstein, 'Complexity, Adaptation, and Administrative Law', supra note 37, 959; P. Iglesias-Rodriguez, 'The role of interests groups in EU financial regulation after the European Supervision Authorities in the Financial Field: the case of the Stakeholder Groups' (2011) *ESIL Conference Paper* No. 10/2011, pp. 4 and 15 (also highlighting the risk of capture); OECD, *Principles for the Governance of Regulators – Public Consultation Draft*, supra note 17, p. 56.

83 Past experience in EU financial regulation shows that involvement of private actors has often helped define appropriate policy responses (E. Ferran, *Building an EU Securities Market*, supra note 81, p. 59 *et seq.* and 82 *et seq.*).

84 Labelling a subject matter as "technical" may shield the debate on the relevant draft measures from the public at large (N. Dorn, 'Render Unto Caesar: EU Financial Market Regulation Meets Political Accountability' (2012) 34 *Journal of European Integration* 205).

85 J. Mendes, *Participation in EU-Rulemaking: A Rights-Based Approach*, Oxford University Press, Oxford 2011, p. 285 *et seq.*; P. Iglesias-Rodriguez, 'The role of interests groups in EU

source of expertise and enhance stakeholders' engagement, our experience as former securities regulators shows that they are not sufficient.[86] Early involvement of the private sector is pivotal to adequate regulation,[87] as gathering information only after an initial opinion is already crystallised in a draft position exposes the regulatory process to confirmation biases and framing effects.[88] At the same time, confirmation biases on the appropriateness of regulatory measures already in force may also be reduced by continuous shareholder engagement, which can shed light on the need to review existing rules that have become obsolete over time.[89]

However, stakeholder participation is a double-edged sword. It can increase independence by allowing a cross-check among the interested constituencies, but it can also facilitate regulatory capture.[90] Moreover, as in any other delegation of tasks, an agency problem arises between stakeholder representatives and the represented stakeholders themselves. Some devices deployed to foster accountability of the regulator may therefore be replicated, at a lower level, for stakeholder panels, to ensure that the latter are responsible towards both the delegating authority and the represented constituencies; the same applies where subgroups are created within a representative panel. Stakeholder representation within ESMA operates accordingly, so that accountability may be framed, in this respect, as a system where the smaller internal body replicates (some features of) the larger in a Matryoshka-like structure.

In broad terms, direct representation may follow different patterns. For instance, it can be extended to academics or not, and stakeholder engagement may by

financial regulation after the European Supervision Authorities in the Financial Field: the case of the Stakeholder Groups', supra note 83, p. 7.

86 For a different view see E. Chiti, 'An important part of the EU's institutional machinery: features, problems and perspectives of European agencies' (2009) 46 *Common Market Law Review* 1395, 1402.

87 In the US system, confrontation with interested stakeholders prior to the initiation of the notice-and-comment procedure is provided by the Negotiated Rulemaking Act (5 USC § 561 ff.), which codifies a pre-existing informal practice (D. Zaring, 'Informal Procedure, Hard and Soft, in International Administration' (2005) 5 *Chicago Journal of International Law* 547, 579).

88 S.J. Choi and A.C. Pritchard, 'Behavioral Economics and the SEC' (2003) 56 *Stanford Law Review* 1, 27 *et seq.* ("feedback on the proposal may get less weight than it would have if the information had been solicited before the SEC fixated upon a specific proposal").

89 *Ibid.*, 30 and 45.

90 Any reform involves redistribution of wealth, so that stakeholder participation is likely to drift into rent-seeking (G. Hertig, 'Trading and Clearing Reforms in the EU: A Story of Interest Groups with Magnified Voice' (2011) 23 *Zeitschrift für Bankrecht und Bankwirtschaft* 329, 329; E. Ferran, *Building an EU Securities Market*, supra note 81, p. 104 *et seq.*). However, capture is a weak analytical tool, as one cannot easily tell regulatory measures which are grounded solely on the basis of a "public interest" (whatever it is) from those adopted under the pressure of other incentives (L.G. Baxter, '"Capture" in Financial Regulation: Can We Channel It Toward the Common Good?' (2011) 21 *Cornell Journal of Law and Public Policy* 175, 175).

ensured by establishing practitioner, consumer and academic panels either as separated bodies or as a single board.[91] CESR's Market Participants Consultative Panel mainly comprised industry representatives, but its composition was flexible, due to the absence of a mandating statutory provision. The Panel was grounded on the CESR Charter, which referred to "market participants, consumers and other end users of financial services", and thus did not make the engagement of academics mandatory.

Nowadays, the ESMA founding Regulation[92] ensures representation to investors, the industry and academia within the Securities and Markets Stakeholder Group (SMSG) (Article 37).[93] The concurrent participation of different constituencies in a multilateral context, as opposed to one-to-one meetings, is likely to enhance the quality of the dialogue by virtue of direct confrontation among potentially divergent positions,[94] although recourse to a stakeholder panel does not of course shift the governance of the Authority into a pure collaborative model.[95] In order to make representation more effective, the Regulation sets numerical and qualitative limits for membership of the SMSG, either directly or indirectly through binding guidelines to the ESMA Board of Supervisors. The SMSG comprises 30 members representing in "balanced"[96] proportions financial market participants operating in the Union (at least ten members), their employees' representatives, consumers,

[91] According to the 2012 Interinstitutional Joint Statement, at 5 and 14, a separate group should be created when stakeholder representation is appropriate but representatives are not included in the highest body of the agencies, the latter being the default solution. An opposite – and wiser – position is followed by the OECD, which suggests creating *ad hoc* bodies for stakeholder representation, in order to avoid conflicts of interests (OECD, *Principles for the Governance of Regulators – Public Consultation Draft*, supra note 17, p. 46). See also EU Commission, Transparency/Relations with stakeholders (Analytical fiche No 30; 2010), 4 (board representation of stakeholders may reach excessive size).

[92] The same applies to the other ESAs. Overall, there are currently four stakeholder groups because EIOPA has two such bodies: one related to insurance and the other to pension funds (Art. 37 Regulation (EU) No 1094/2010).

[93] No similar function is performed by other groups, such as the Committee on Financial Innovation (Art. 9(4) Reg. 1095/2010), where only the competent national authorities are represented.

[94] Involvement of investors may in particular reduce the risk of capture by providing the regulatory process with an alternative perspective, to be added to those of regulators and the industry: I. Ayres and J. Braithwaite, 'Tripartism: Regulatory Capture and Empowerment' (1991) 16 *Law & Social Inquiry* 435, 435.

[95] Collaborative governance entails direct engagement of participants in the decision making process, rather than mere consultation (C. Ansell and A. Gash, 'Collaborative Governance in Theory and Practice' (2007) 18 *Journal of Public Administration Research and Theory* 543, 544 *et seq.*).

[96] ESMA seems to have applied "balance" as a selective criterion within the group of financial market participants rather than extending it to the equilibrium among the different constituencies, which would have been difficult to achieve because the overall number of members representing market participants is set by the Regulation itself.

users of financial services, and representatives of SMEs. At least five of its members shall be independent top-ranking academics.[97]

The appointment procedure must ensure, "to the extent possible", that the SMSG has a balanced composition as regards the constituencies, the nationality, and the gender of its members in order to enhance its representativeness. It starts with a public call for applications and ends, after a two-step selection by ESMA staff and the Management Board, with a decision by the Board of Supervisors. Both the Management Board and the Board of Supervisors are informed on all the candidacies, and are not bound by previous selections.[98] The clarification of the selection procedure and its criteria bestows greater transparency on the final decision by the Board of Supervisors; in the past, members of the Market Participants Consultative Panel within CESR were appointed without a public notice and according to undefined requisites.[99]

In practice, in order to first appoint the SMSG, the Authority (at that time still operating as CESR) launched a public announcement looking for potential candidates wishing to apply for either the office or a list of alternates from which they could be selected if a panel member had to be replaced. The candidates were asked to classify themselves into different – while sometimes overlapping – categories, depending on the interests they represented.[100] For some categories, ESMA also required the candidates to have at least either four years of experience in the financial service field or, for those representing financial institutions, four years of professional experience. ESMA then appointed the first SMSG members (and alternates):[101] 10 (6) members represent financial markets participants, 7 (5) represent users of financial services, 2 represent financial services employee, 5 (2) represent consumers, 1 represents SMEs, and 5 (2) represent the academia. Members of the SMSG serve for two and a half years. After their term, a new

97 CESR's Consultative Panel also set a minimum number (5) for representatives of retail investors (CESR, *Call for expressions of interest regarding the setting up of ESMA Securities and Markets Stakeholder Group* (CESR/10-1466), 26 November 2010, p. 1).

98 ESMA, *Stakeholder Group Renewal Procedure 2013* (ESMA/2013/703), p. 8.

99 See J. Mendes, *Participation in EU-Rulemaking: A Rights-Based Approach*, supra note 86, p. 285 *et seq*.

100 The relevant categories of stakeholders give an idea of the range of the represented interests: financial services intermediaries; market infrastructure providers (regulated markets, MTFs, CCPs, CSDs and trade repositories); issuers (potentially including SME's); institutional investors (insurance, pension funds or asset management firms); representatives of shareholders; users and distributors of financial information (auditors, accountants, information providers, rating agencies or analysts); IT developers for financial service firms; alternatives investment fund managers; representatives of financial service employees (employees' representatives from a firm/company or trade unions); representatives of retail investors or individual retail investors; individuals representing the interests of small and medium-sized enterprises (SMEs); top ranking academics.

101 See ESMA decision No. 123 of 12 April 2011.

selection process takes place,[102] but existing panellists may apply for a second term (Article 37(4)). The SMSG Rules of Procedure foster individual accountability of members by providing that records of attendance and participation should be considered when deciding whether to extend the first tenure (Article 11(4)).

The appointment procedure limits ESMA discretion in the selection of its counterparties in the regulatory dialogue and has the advantage of having already been tested, as it closely resembles the procedure adopted by the European Securities Markets Expert Group (ESME), a stakeholder group which the EU Commission set up in 2005 and which led to the publication of a number of documents on the application of the financial services directives.[103]

The ESMA founding Regulation ensures that the SMSG has a self-regulatory power to adopt the rules concerning its organization ad operation (Article 37(6)).[104] In October 2011, the SMSG approved its own rules of procedure[105] (RoP), which further specify its governance. For example, the RoP provide for a chairperson, to be elected by consensus or by majority voting when this proves impossible, and a vice-chairperson (or two in case of a tie at the moment of the election) (Article 2). While the RoP encourage decision-making by consensus, a quorum of two-thirds of the members – which can also be reached by a written procedure (Article 8) – is in any case required both for convening the Group and passing decisions, including the adoption and amendments to the RoP; dissenting opinions supported by at least three members may also be included in the final statement (Articles 3(3) and 7).[106] Early circulation of information among members ensures that there is sufficient time to assess documents submitted to the SMSG, the notice periods being three weeks in advance for the agenda and at least one week for the working documents (Articles 4(2) and 5(2)). Furthermore, information sharing is also facilitated by direct contacts, as the SMSG regularly meets, at least twice a year, with the Board of Supervisors (Article 40(2) Reg. 1095/2010), and the

102 ESMA (2013/703), supra note 99.

103 A list of relevant documents was available on the ESME webpage in the Internal Market Directorate website which has been cancelled recently.

104 Those rules, where they go beyond what is stated by the Regulation, are only binding for the SMSG in charge, while future groups are free to change them if they so wish. The first SMSG has however recommended continuity (SMSG (Securities and Markets Stakeholder Group), *Contribution to ESFS consultation. An SMSG review of the ESA's including a self-assessment* (SMSG/2013/013), p. 12).

105 See SMSG (Securities and Markets Stakeholder Group), *Decision of the Securities and Markets Stakeholder Group* (ESMA/2011/SMSG/1 final).

106 Supermajority quorums and disclosure of dissenting opinions ensure that representatives of the financial industry are not in substantial control of the SMSG (P. Iglesias-Rodriguez, 'The role of interests groups in EU financial regulation after the European Supervision Authorities in the Financial Field: the case of the Stakeholder Groups', supra note 83, pp. 12–13).

ESMA Chairperson,[107] as well as a representative of the Commission, are invited to attend all the SMSG's meetings (Article 11 RoP).

In addition to the ESMA as a whole, the SMSG also prepares an annual work programme and an annual report, to be included in the ESMA report (Article 16 RoP).[108] Its ability to set part of its own agenda and its direct accountability to the public at large, as well as to the Authority, increases the SMSG's independence from the Authority itself. A further analogy with the ESMA Regulation lies in the fact that, just as the Authority may revert to the SMSG for advice on a technical issue, the SMSG can invite external guests for the same reason (Article 13 RoP).

In its self-regulatory capacity, the SMSG may establish working groups on technical issues in agreement with the Authority (Article 37(4) Reg. 1095/2010; Article 10(1) RoP). Working groups are interim committees set up to deal with specific issues and dissolved once their mandate is performed. The operating rules of working groups closely mirror those of the SMSG, as does their composition, which should where possible ensure representation of the same stakeholders as the SMSG. The Regulation and RoP does not provide for delegation of SMSG functions to working groups, so the latter operate only as advisory committees, the final decision being left to the Group as a whole (Article 10 RoP). In 2011 and 2012, twelve working groups – each chaired by an independent *rapporteur* – have been established on various issues.[109]

The founding Regulation requires ESMA to provide adequate secretarial support to the SMSG. Furthermore, "adequate compensation" is granted to members representing non-profit organizations or academia, while industry representatives are expressly excluded from the benefit. Although "compensation" can be, and actually is, interpreted as extending to remuneration, it would appear more sensible to limit its scope to reimbursement of travel expenses, as is also suggested by Article 5(4) RoP. On the contrary, repayment is ruled out for members other than academics and representatives of non-profit organizations.[110] These are funded by the stakeholders they belong to with no participation by ESMA. The underlying idea is that positive discrimination can establish a level playing field among participants, thus ensuring equal representation to all stakeholders irrespective of

[107] ESMA Chairperson can ask the Vice-Chairperson and/or members of the Authority's Management Board and/or the Chairpersons of the relevant Standing Committees and working groups of the Authority and/or members of the Authority's staff to join specific meetings. In practice, the Chairperson and the Executive Director attend all meetings.

[108] Actually, up to 2013 the SMSG report has not been enclosed in the ESMA report, which only mentioned it.

[109] SMSG (Securities and Markets Stakeholder Group), *SMSG Annual Activity Report 2011–2012* (ESMA/2012/SMSG/53), p. 9.

[110] ESMA, *Call for expressions of interest regarding ESMA Securities and Markets Stakeholder Group* (ESMA/2013/702 Rev 1), p. 3.

their available financial resources,[111] and reflects historical underrepresentation of retail investors – usually represented by non-profit institutions – in the EU regulatory process.[112] Nonetheless, excluding any reimbursement of travel expenses for industry representatives may lead to capture, because as long as industry is bearing the costs of participation, it is more likely to expect specific results from members' participation in the SMSG work.

This raises the issue of potential conflicts of interest of the SMSG members as a consequence of their relationship with the relevant constituencies. Although no provision directly addresses this issue, the Regulation clearly states that SMSG members are "representing" the different stakeholders, while only academics are expressly referred to as "independent" members (Article 37(2)). This statement is reinforced by the fact that the Board of Supervisors appoints the SMSG members "following proposals from the relevant stakeholders" (Article 37(3)). Although applications are in practice sent by individuals who qualify themselves as representatives of a constituency,[113] and there is therefore no certainty that all the members are supported by the stakeholders they should represent, a direct link between a candidate and a specific subset of stakeholders is made clear from the outset. These rules, together with the principles for the funding of members, show that the SMSG is composed of stakeholder representatives facing no limitation in promoting the interests of a specific constituency. In the same vein, the SMSG RoP require that members disclose, before deliberations are taken, any conflict of interest other than that of belonging to their organisation (Article 12), thus assuming that bringing forward the interests of these entities does not result in any breach of members' duties. The regulatory approach to representation realistically accepts the idea[114] that providing a forum where interests can be expressed and consequently discussed within a transparent confrontation can improve the quality of regulation and reduce the incentives – both for the Authority and the stakeholders – to indulge in concealed lobbying activity. At the same time, the SMSG rules of procedure state that all members serve in a personal capacity (Article 1(2) RoP), so that they cannot be compelled to support any specific position, nor can they be substituted by the organisations they belong to. Any evaluation of the opportunity to promote a proposal which may affect an organisation is therefore left to its representative members. Neither the relevant constituency nor the ESMA may object to the member's decision.

---

111 According to Recital 49 of Reg. No. 1095/2010, adequate compensation should be granted to those representing academia and non-profit organisations in order to "allow persons that are neither well-funded nor industry representatives to take part fully in the debate on financial regulation". It is thus assumed that non-profit organisations, to the extent that they represent consumers or retail users, necessarily lack financial resources.

112 E. Ferran, *Building an EU Securities Market*, supra note 81, p. 105.

113 See the Application Form attached to ESMA (2013/702 Rev 1), supra note 111.

114 See infra note124 and accompanying text.

Finally – and, once more, as with the ESMA itself – accountability of the SMSG is also ensured horizontally. The Stakeholder Group directly liaises with other user groups established in the area of financial services by the Commission or by Union legislation (Recital 48 Reg. 1095/2010; Article 20 RoP).[115] Although the primary function of these interactions is to ensure coordination with similar committees set either within or outside other ESAs, direct confrontation among different stakeholder groups should reduce the risk of regulatory capture; in a multilateral context, flawed positions pursued by a captured committee are more likely to emerge and, in any case, less likely to affect the final regulatory outcome.

4.2. THE PERFORMANCE OF REGULATORY AND SUPERVISORY FUNCTIONS

ESMA has tasks related to both regulation and supervision. The distinction between the two functions is theoretically clear, and the legislative framework relies upon it, too.[116] While regulation refers to the drafting of rules (i.e. normative acts), supervision concerns application of those rules in individual cases,[117] which encompasses administrative monitoring and enforcement. In practice, distinguishing the two may not be easy,[118] for instance because supervisory acts concerning multiple market participants may not always be distinguished from rules having general effects towards an identified set of addressees.

The blurred boundaries between regulation and supervision have fundamental implications under the Treaties and the CJEU case-law. While the former can only be delegated to the Commission – or exceptionally, for implementing measures only, to the Council (Article 291 TFEU) – the latter may be entrusted to other EU bodies, although the Commission and Member States maintain the primary responsibility for the application of EU law. Therefore, any measure which empowers ESMA to adopt decisions formally classified as supervisory may be questioned, either directly under Article 263 or, once the relevant deadline

115 Although the groups may share one or more members, multiple applications by candidates are not recommended (ESMA (2013/703), supra note 99, p. 7).

116 See E. Wymeersch, 'Europe's New Financial Regulatory Bodies', supra note 4, 446.

117 E.g. E. Wymeersch, 'The Future of Financial Regulation and Supervision in Europe' (2005) 42 *Common Market Law Review* 987, 988.

118 J-P. Schneider, 'A Common Framework for Decentralized EU Agencies and the *Meroni* Doctrine' (2009) 61 *Administrative Law Review* 29, 30 (rulemaking can no longer be strictly separated from administrative action concerning individual an concrete cases); E. Wymeersch, 'The Structure of Financial Supervision in Europe: About Single, Twin Peaks and Multiple Financial Supervisors', supra note 67, 242 (supervision often implies regulation and vice-versa). See also E. Ferran, 'Understanding the New Institutional Architecture of EU Financial Market Supervision' in E. Wymeersch et al. (eds.), *Financial Regulation and Supervision. A Post-Crisis Analysis*, Oxford University Press, Oxford 2012, p. 140 (increasingly detailed regulatory measures reduce the room for subsequent discretion in supervision).

expires, under Article 267 TFEU, where the measure substantially confers on the Authority the power to pass non-legislative acts having "force of law" (i.e.: a normative nature).[119]

The distinction between normative acts – which can only be adopted by the Commission – and supervisory measures is also relevant from the perspective of (quasi-)judicial accountability. Judicial oversight of normative measures is sometimes more lenient if compared to the assessment of individual measures, mainly because the traditional criteria of judicial review do not fit well with acts that, besides lacking immediate consequences for individuals, usually entail some degree of administrative discretion.[120] From a procedural standpoint, judicial review of ESMA supervisory acts requires previous appeal of the contested decision before the Board of Appeal (Article 263(5) TFEU). As is the case for non-privileged applicants before the CJEU, the Board of Appeal can be seized only for measures directly addressed to the claimant or which are of direct and individual concern to her (Article 60(1) Reg. 1095/2010).[121] On the contrary, draft technical standards issued by ESMA can be challenged neither at the CJEU nor at the Board of Appeal because they are only preparatory measures,[122] while full review is possible for the final standards as endorsed by the Commission.

In the following sections, we will rely on the traditional taxonomy when focussing on the procedural mechanisms through which ESMA operates, first in the regulatory and then in the supervisory activity. Attention will be paid in our analysis to the role performed by the EU institutions and by stakeholders in the administrative procedure, which will be regarded as a stage where multiple actors interplay. As demonstrated by the "enrolment analysis" of administration,[123] the dynamic interaction among those engaged in the regulatory and supervisory process helps elucidate the determinants of the administrative acts which are eventually adopted. From this standpoint, the effects produced by the direct or indirect participation of the relevant actors to the process enrich the traditional – and rather static – concept of accountability.

---

119 See also infra, para 5.1.

120 A.H. Türk, 'Oversight of Administrative Rulemaking: Judicial Review' (2013) 19 European Law Journal 126, 126 and 136.

121 See ECJ, Case C-25/62, *Plaumann & Co. v. Commission of the European Economic Community*, 15.07.1963; H.C.H. HOFMANN, G.C. ROWE and A.H. TÜRK, *Administrative Law and Policy of the European Union*, Oxford University Press, Oxford 2011, p. 826 *et seq*. According to T. Tridimas, 'Financial Supervision and Agency Power: Reflections on ESMA' supra note 8, p. 81, the Board of Appeal is not bound by the ECJ interpretation of the standing to sue and can therefore adopt a more expansive interpretation.

122 ECJ, Case C-60/81, *International Business Machine Corporation (IBM) v. Commission*, 11.11.1981, para 10.

123 J. Black, 'Mapping the Contours of Contemporary Financial Services Regulation' (2002) 2 *Journal of Corporate Law Studies* 253, 261 *et seq*.

4.2.1. *The regulatory powers of ESMA*

4.2.1.1. The reformed regulatory architecture

The regulatory architecture enacted in the wake of the recent financial turmoil has not abolished the four-level structure of the financial services regulation which was adopted under the auspices of the Lamfalussy committee.[124] However, the weaknesses of this process in the establishment of a truly harmonised financial regulation across Europe were made evident even before the financial crisis, so much so that the Lamfalussy Review supported, already in 2007, reinforcing the legal status of the Level 3 committees and strengthening the Level 3 coordination, with a view to achieving further integration in the internal market for financial services.[125]

In order to take advantage of the benefits delivered by the existing multi-layered governance while improving on the past experience, Regulation (EU) No 1095/2010 has enriched the Lamfalussy process by extending the applicability of Article 290 and 291 TFEU to part of the Level 3 measures.[126] The reformed system therefore combines the nuanced Lamfalussy approach with the post-Lisbon Treaty rules on delegated and implementing acts in order to bestow more effectiveness on the regulatory and supervisory tools available to ESMA and the EU institutions at each layer of the procedure. This evolution seeks to ensure a consistent application of the European rules and to upgrade the quality of national – and, increasingly, cross-border – regulation and supervision, taking advantage of a European single rule-book applicable to all financial market participants in the internal market.[127]

In this new framework, Level 1 legislation is meant to set delegated and implementing powers to be enacted not only in the context of Level 2 initiatives,

---

124 Final Report of the Committee of Wise Men on the Regulation of European Securities Markets, Brussels, 15 February 2001. The Report was endorsed by the Stockholm Council of Economics and Finance Ministers on 23 March 2001 (see the Results of the Council of Economics and Finance Ministers, 22 March 2001) and then agreed upon by the European Parliament on 5 February 2002 (European Parliament Resolution on the Implementation of Financial Services Legislation (2001/2247(INI)), 2002).

125 EU Commission, Review of the Lamfalussy Process. Strengthening Supervisory Convergence, 2007, (COM(2007) 727).

126 ESMA therefore follows the growing model of the European agencies rulemaking power which combines: (i) participation in the legislative rulemaking by way of an advisory role, (ii) adoption or drafting of technical rules, and (iii) adoption of soft law instruments (E. Chiti, 'European Agencies' Rulemaking: Powers, Procedures and Assessment' (2013) 19 *European Law Journal* 93, 99).

127 Recital 5, Regulation (EU) No 1095/2010.

but also by a subset of Level 3[128] measures referred to as "technical standards".[129] As far as regulation is concerned, enhanced harmonization is indeed mainly pursued by way of strengthened Level 3 instruments, part of which now fall into the scope of the TFEU non-legislative (or quasi-regulatory) delegated and implementing acts,[130] and are therefore remitted to the Commission for formal adoption, while others still retain their soft-regulatory nature, albeit tightened by virtue of a newly-framed "comply or explain" principle,[131] and fall into ESMA competence. But Level 2 measures, which have hitherto represented the bulk of delegated non-legislative acts, are still part of the architecture,[132] and are adopted according to the specific process set by the delegating rule under Article 290 TFEU for delegated acts[133] or under the new comitology procedure under Regulation (EU) No 182/2011 for implementing acts to be adopted under Article 291 TFEU.[134]

---

128 Categorisation of technical standards as Level 3 measures, albeit not unanimous, is followed by the majority of commentators (see e.g. E. Wymeersch, 'The European Financial Supervisory Authorities or ESAs', supra note 70, p. 251; M. Lamandini, 'I regolamenti europei istitutivi del comitato per il rischio sistemico e delle autorità europea di vigilanza su assicurazioni, banche, strumenti finanziari mercati' (2012) 35 *Nuove Leggi Civili Commentate* 211, 219; J.L. Raptis, 'European Financial Regulation: ESMA and the Lamfalussy process, the Renewed European Legislative Process in the field of Securities Regulation' (2012) 18 *Columbia Journal of European Law Online* 61, 64). We base our classification on the fact that, according to the Omnibus Directive, these measures are made conditional on traditional Level 2 provisions, if any. Another taxonomy would classify the said measures, based on their quasi-regulatory nature, within the Level 2 (FSA, *A Brief Guide to the European Union and its Legislative Processes,* 2011, <www.fca.org.uk/your-fca/documents/european-union-and-its-legislative-processes> accessed 11.10.2014, p. 27) or a new "Level 2+" layer (D. Weber-Rey, *Lisbon Treaty: impact on EU decision-making,* Presentation to EIOPA Stakeholder Groups – joint meeting, 19.10.2011, p. 22 <https://eiopa.europa.eu> accessed 25.10.2014.

129 N. Moloney, 'The European Securities and Markets Authority and Institutional Design for the EU Financial Market – A Tale of Two Competences: Part (1) Rule-Making' supra note 9, 66.

130 See supra note 129 for the classification of these measures under Level 3.

131 See text accompanying infra note 187.

132 Level 2 measures are likely to maintain their dominant position in the future (N. Moloney, 'The European Securities and Markets Authority: a perspective from one year on' (2013) 68 *Zeitschrift für öffentliches Recht (Austrian Journal of Public and International Law)* 59, 71).

133 The basic default features of the quasi-legislative process are outlined in EU Commission, Communication on Implementation of Article 290 of the Treaty on the Functioning of the European Union (COM(2009) 673 final), which also foresees the systematic consultation of experts (*ibid.*, 4), although these will not be organised in a comitology committee. The Communication was subsequently endorsed and further detailed by a Common Understanding among the Commission, the Council and the Parliament.

134 The comitology procedure only applies under Art. 291 TFEU, as implementing measures should in principle be left to Member States; therefore, only in this case does the need arise to ensure that Member States may control the Commission's exercise of its powers. The comitology procedure adds further complexity to the relationships among the actors actually or potentially involved in the regulatory process (see supra note 124). However, although Art. 291(3) TFEU provides that the rules and general principles concerning mechanisms for control by Member States of the Commission's exercise of implementing powers be set in advance by way of regulations, Art. 1 and Recital 6 Regulation (EU) No 182/2011 implicitly allow for the granting of implementing power without the need to follow the comitology procedure.

Non-legislative acts can therefore take a variable form, depending on their position (Level 2 or 3)[135] within the Lamfalussy process, on the adopted instrument (directive or regulation), and on whether they are meant to either supplement or implement the Level 1 basic principles under the scope of Article 290 and Article 291 TFEU respectively. In the regulatory cascade from Level 1 to Level 3, the Level 2 layer can be skipped when the legislation delegates the Commission to directly adopt technical standards; when Level 3 measures are instead contemplated in order to develop or specify Level 2 acts, the hierarchical predominance of the latter shall be respected.[136] After the enactment of the new architecture, Directive 2010/78/EU (Omnibus Directive) revised the existing Level 1 instruments in order to reshape the coordination among the legislative and regulatory measures.[137] In some areas, the new Level 3 instruments have been simply added to Level 2 acts previously in force,[138] while the intermediate regulatory layer is no longer foreseen in other fields.[139]

On the contrary, no enabling rule delegating the power to adopt guidelines or recommendations is *ex ante* needed, although the Level 1 legislation exerts some influence. First, reference is sometimes made at Level 1 to recommendations and guidelines in order to signal that further harmonisation through non-binding measures in a specific field would be beneficial, and therefore desirable.[140] Second, the power to adopt standards and recommendations is in principle ruled out in areas covered by regulatory or implementing technical standards (Recital 26 Regulation (EU) No 1095/2010).

135 Hierarchical levels also determine the regulatory procedure, as the comitology procedure under Regulation (EU) No 182/2011, by default, applies neither to regulatory nor to implementing technical standards, unless otherwise established by the delegating act: see FSA, *A Brief Guide to the European Union and its Legislative Processes*, supra note 129, p. 28; S. Kerjean, *Towards a Union Financial Sector RuleBook. The case of the banking sector*, p. 10 <https://www.ecb.europa.eu/events/conferences/shared/pdf/reg_fs/session3_topic2_kerjean.pdf??ae2677d118bd81a35d68be5b98484666> accessed 24.10.2014. But see N. Moloney, 'The European Securities and Markets Authority and Institutional Design for the EU Financial Market – A Tale of Two Competences: Part (1) Rule-Making' supra note 9, 75 (the European Securities Committee is involved in the adoption of implementing technical standard by way of a "comitology-style oversight").

136 See Recital 13 Directive 2010/78/EU.

137 For a review of the affected rules see D. Fischer-Appelt, 'The European Securities and Markets Authority: the beginning of a powerful European securities authority?' (2009) 3 *Law and Financial Markets Review* 21, 22 *et seq.*

138 See e.g. Art. 1(5) Directive 2003/6/EC (on uniform conditions for the exemptions from market abuse prohibitions in case accepted market practices are carried out).

139 See e.g. Art. 4(3) Directive 2003/71/EC (on specification of exemptions from the duty to publish a prospectus).

140 See e.g. Art. 16(2) Directive 2004/39/EC (ESMA may develop guidelines regarding the methods competent authorities should adopt when monitoring the ongoing compliance by investment firms with the conditions for the initial authorisation). See also N. Moloney, 'The European Securities and Markets Authority: a perspective from one year on', supra note 133, 71.

Within this framework, ESMA can be approximately considered the successor of CESR as a Level 3 authority, as it has inherited the tasks previously attributed to the latter. At Level 2, ESMA has retained the regulatory functions of CESR, as it is still charged with an advisory role *vis-à-vis* the EU Commission in drafting measures implementing the Level 1 directives or (increasingly) regulations (Article 8),[141] when the legislative instrument so provides. At Level 3, ESMA is entrusted, as CESR was, with promoting convergence among national competent authorities through non-binding measures, but also contributes to the creation of a single rule-book through quasi-regulatory instruments.

Neither technical standards nor recommendations (or guidelines) may exceed the purview of the matters set by the legislative acts specifically referred to by Article 1(2) of the founding Regulation.[142] The list of the EU directives set forth by Article 1(2) therefore circumscribes the ESMA scope of regulatory (as well as supervisory) activity. To be sure, no direct constraint is provided, as reference is also made to "any (...) legally binding Union act (further to those listed in the provision) which confers tasks on the Authority", but the rule nonetheless curbs the powers of ESMA in that it clarifies that no action is allowed beyond what is prescribed by specific legislative measures.[143] Moreover, one of the merits of the provision also lies in its status as a single source of information which fosters the accountability of the Authority, as it makes it easier for all the interested stakeholders to know which fields of regulation and supervision ESMA is responsible for.[144]

---

141 N. Moloney, 'The European Securities and Markets Authority and Institutional Design for the EU Financial Market – A Tale of Two Competences: Part (1) Rule-Making' supra note 9, 65.

142 Such areas are those within the scope of directives concerning investor compensation schemes, settlement finality, admission to listing, financial collaterals, market abuse, prospectuses, investment services, transparency requirements for listed companies, collective investment undertakings, banks (but without any prejudice to the competence of EBA on prudential supervision, alternative investment funds, credit rating agencies. Directives on financial conglomerates, money laundering and distance marketing of consumer financial services are also included to the extent that they apply to investment services or collective investment. ESMA powers also include "all directives, regulations, and decisions based on those acts".

143 Among these rules, three are worth mentioning. First, a general provision requires ESMA to prepare, if necessary, guidelines and recommendations additional to those adopted under Art. 1(2) in order to address systemic risk posed by key financial markets participants (Art. 22(3)), i.e. market participants that can affect the stability, integrity or efficiency of EU financial markets (Art. 4(1)(2)). Second, ESMA has the power to adopt guidelines and recommendations in the context of its wider efforts to ensure that national Investor Compensation Schemes under Directive 97/9/EC are adequately funded by financial markets participants (the importance of the principle requiring funding by market participants – rather than by taxpayers – is demonstrated, in the more sensitive field of depositors compensation schemes, by the decision rendered by EFTA Court, Case E-16/11, *EFTA Surveillance Authority and European Commission v Iceland*, 28.01.2013, para 138 *et seq.*). Third, ESMA may adopt guidelines and recommendations at the outcome of peer reviews of national competent authorities (Art. 30(3)).

144 The EU legislator has seemingly taken on the task of keeping the provision up to date: see Dir. 2011/61/EU (amending Art. 1(2) Regulation (EU) No 1095/2010 in order to replace, within the list of relevant sources of ESMA powers, the previous generic mention of future legislation on alternative investment fund managers with a specific reference to the relevant directive).

However, Article 1(3) Regulation 1095/2010 empowers the Authority to "act in the field of activities of market participants" also on issues not directly covered in the acts referred to in Article 1(2) – clearly, through measures that do not require specific delegation of powers.[145] Such issues include matters of corporate governance, auditing and financial reporting, to the extent that "actions by the Authority are necessary to ensure the effective and consistent application" of the acts listed by Article 1(2).[146] While this expansion of authority is applicable, *mutatis mutandis*, to the other ESAs, ESMA is also granted exclusive competence to take "appropriate action in the context of take-over bids, clearing and settlement and derivative issues". As this enlarged competence may overlap with those of the other ESAs,[147] enhanced coordination is needed among the three Authorities to avoid conflicting measures. This is remarkably the only rule in the Regulation where the term "market participants" is used, while in the rest of the act the term "financial market participants" is instead used to refer to "any person in relation to whom a requirement in the legislation referred to in Article 1(2) or a national law implementing such legislation applies". Absent a specific definition of "market participants", the letter of the law may further enlarge the ESMA scope of activity to include entities not addressed by specific Level 1 or Level 2[148] instruments (as is the case, e.g., for proxy agents[149]).

4.2.1.2. Strengthening regulatory harmonisation. The new quasi-rulemaking powers

Depending on the Level 1 mandate to the Commission, which retains the power to adopt the regulatory measures, ESMA may be entrusted to elaborate two kinds of technical standards – in the form of either regulation or decision[150] – to be submitted to the Commission for endorsement: regulatory technical standards (Article 10), representing "delegated" non-legislative acts under Article 290 TFEU, or implementing technical standards (Article 15), which fall into the purview of

145 For a critique of this limitation of the purview of technical standards see C. Di Noia and M.C. Furlò, 'The New Structure of Financial Supervision in Europe: What's Next?', supra note 67, p. 185.

146 Reference to corporate governance is meaningful if one considers the US debate over the SEC indirect regulatory powers in this field in the presence of a State competence on company law (see M.J. Roe, 'Delaware and Washington as Corporate Lawmakers' (2009) 34 *Delaware Journal of Corporate Law* 1, 12).

147 E. Wymeersch, 'The European Financial Supervisory Authorities or ESAs', supra note 70, p. 248.

148 *Ibid.*

149 ESMA, *Final Report. Feedback statement on the consultation regarding the role of the proxy advisory industry* (ESMA/2013/84). See also N. Moloney, 'The European Securities and Markets Authority: a perspective from one year on', supra note 133, 73 *et seq.*

150 Technical standards in form of decision may fit the adoption of waivers from general obligations (see E. Wymeersch, 'The European Financial Supervisory Authorities or ESAs', supra note 70, p. 252).

Article 291 TFEU. Whether the former or the latter shall be adopted is up to the Level 1 measures to define.[151]

The reference to either regulatory or implementing technical standards affects the scope of ESMA and Commission discretion in the preparation (and amendment) of the measures, as well as the quasi-rule making procedure that shall be followed at Level 3. In cases where the European Parliament and the Council grant the Commission the power to adopt non-legislative measures by means of delegated acts under Article 290 TFEU, ESMA may develop draft regulatory technical standards aimed at supplementing or amending non-essential elements[152] of the legislative act, in order to ensure consistent harmonisation in the regulated matters.[153] On the contrary, when reference is made to implementing technical standards, only measures strictly implementing the Level 1 legislation are allowed (Article 291 TFEU).[154]

Characterising the ontological differences between regulatory or implementing technical standards is, however, far from easy.[155] According to their nature, both measures shall not go beyond the scope set by the legislative act they are based on, and shall not in any case "imply strategic decisions or policy choices" (Articles 10(1) and 15(1)).[156] Moreover, if a measure amending the Level 1 act can

151 For the legislative acts in force as at the date ESMA was established, an *ad hoc* review performed by the Omnibus Directive has determined the areas where ESMA is called to prepare one or the other draft technical standard. At the time we are writing, the proposal for a second Omnibus Directive aimed, *inter alia*, at widening the areas covered by the ESMA technical standard in the field of prospectus regulation is pending (see Commission Proposal for a Directive amending Directives 2003/71/EC and 2009/138/EC (COM(2011) 8 final), 19 January 2011).

152 See ECJ decision on case C-240/90, *Germany v. Commission*, I-05383 European Court reports (1992), § 36–7 (rules establishing "essential elements" are rules "essentials to the subject-matter envisaged" and "which are intended to give concrete shape to the fundamental guidelines of Community policy").

153 For instance, the power to develop draft regulatory technical standards is envisaged for the definition of the requirements – namely reputation and expertise – that prospective managers must satisfy in order for their investment firm to obtain authorisation to perform investment services on a professional basis (art. 7(4) Directive 2004/39/EC).

154 See e.g. Art. 9(6) Reg. (EU) No 648/2012 (EMIR) (ESMA shall draft implementing technical standards in order to establish the format and frequency of reports to be filed by counterparties of derivative contracts with trade repositories).

155 D. Fischer-Appelt, 'The European Securities and Markets Authority: the beginning of a powerful European securities authority?', supra note 138, 25.

156 See also Recital 22, Regulation (EU) No 1095/2010. On the other hand, one may easily argue that both regulatory and implementing technical standards cannot but entail political consequences (N. Moloney, 'The European Securities and Markets Authority and Institutional Design for the EU Financial Market – A Tale of Two Competences: Part (1) Rule-Making' supra note 9, 68); once again, distinguishing between the two may therefore prove difficult, while institutional control by the European Parliament and the Council of the compliance by ESMA and the Commission on their technical – as opposed to political – mandate only addresses regulatory technical standards (see text accompanying infra note 168). See also infra note 284.

be easily recognised as such, the boundary between a measure supplementing and another implementing a legislative act is admittedly a blurred one, as every enacting rule adds some further prescriptions to the enacted provision,[157] thereby slightly changing the framework of a legislative basic act the rules of which do not provide, in that respect, full and comprehensive regulation.[158] Some help could possibly be provided by a distinction grounded on the idea that delegated acts should be used when the Commission is empowered to determine what the concerned entities should do, while implementing acts would be confined to cases where the non-legislative measure is aimed at pinpointing how the said entities shall carry out an obligation set within the basic act, as might be the case for a provision setting out a standard communication format.[159] However, such a provision may also be regarded as a way to add other obligations,[160] and the distinction would turn out to be quite subjective.

Concerns about the procedure to be followed, and in particular about the role of the institutions, are thus likely to influence the Level 1 choice between the two subsets of technical standards.[161] To the extent that ESMA is called, in its capacity as a Level 3 body, to develop draft regulatory technical standards, the European Parliament and the Council retain a veto power on the measures adopted by the Commission,[162] while this is not the case when implementing technical standards are at stake. The ability to prevent the entry into force of the technical standards is noteworthy from the perspective of (increased) accountability by ESMA, but may raise some doubts about the possibly reduced independence of the quasi-regulatory procedure as a whole.[163] How independent the rulemaking activity will be is indeed up to the institutions to decide, as the real scope of the scrutiny by the

[157] P. Craig, 'Delegated Acts, Implementing Acts and the New Comitology Regulation' (2011) 36 *European Law Review* 671, 673. See also the Advocate General's opinion in case C-270/12, supra note 8, paras 78 and 80.

[158] An attempt to draw a distinction between the scope of Art. 290 and 291 based on discretion left to the delegated institution – and therefore on its ability to change the framework of the legislative act – is carried out by the EU Commission (see COM(2009) 673 final, 4).

[159] Such as the one provided for by Art. 12(9) Directive 2004/109/EC, which enables the Commission to adopt standard forms, templates and procedures to be used when notifying major holdings in listed companies.

[160] *I.e.* using a specified format or a particular means of communication.

[161] See in general H.C.H. Hofmann, G.C. Rowe and A.H. Türk, *Administrative Law and Policy of the European Union*, supra note 122, pp. 238 and 532 *et seq.*

[162] Art. 290(2)(b) TFEU. If the Commission adopts the technical standards endorsing the ESMA proposal, the period during which the other institutions may object is reduced from three months to one, with the possibility to extend the time span by one further month. See also Art. 12 Regulation (EU) No 1095/2010, which enables the European Parliament and the Council to revoke at any time the delegation of quasi-rulemaking power (Art. 290(2)(a) TFEU): however, opposition rather than revocation is the ordinary means of control over delegated acts (Commission Communication COM(2009) 673 final, 7). In order to exercise the veto power or to revoke the delegation, the European Parliament shall act by a simple majority, and the Council by a qualified one (Art. 290(2) TFEU).

[163] Independence of ESMA from the Commission is an even more sensitive issue: see below.

Parliament and the Council is crucial in this respect.[164] In particular, a relatively higher level of independence may be expected if objections are raised not so much to second-guess the merit of the technical standards, although the institutions encounter no limit in this respect,[165] but rather to assess whether such standards involve, as a matter of fact, policy issues.[166]

Along these lines, ESMA (and the Commission) are held accountable for their technical mandate more strictly when drafting regulatory technical standards than when developing implementing technical standards, as these latter quasi-regulatory measures are not subject to a formal veto.[167] The distinction between regulatory and implementing technical standards is therefore remarkable from the standpoint of accountability and independence, although the practical intensity of the scrutiny by institutions and interested stakeholders may be less divergent than it might appear at first sight. Veto power aside, the quasi-rulemaking procedures for the adoption of technical standards, whichever their nature, are in fact substantially the same.[168] Within such procedures, an array of devices ensures accountability to the institutions and the interested stakeholders. ESMA may submit the standards only upon public consultation and after requesting the opinion of the SMSG. Consultation may only be avoided when it is "disproportionate" in relation to either the scope and impact of the technical standard concerned or the particular urgency of the matter (Article 10(1) and 15 (1)).[169]

The European Parliament and the Council are also constantly involved in the cumbersome quasi-rulemaking procedures that lead to the adoption of technical standards. They receive the draft standards from the Commission as soon as the ESMA submits them for endorsement. As the responsibility for adopting final measures lies with the Commission, the latter is by no way compelled to endorse the draft standards in full. On the contrary, the draft measures may "in

164 At the same time, the exercise of veto power by collective decision-makers, such as the Council and the Parliament, face structural limitations that may reduce its effectiveness (D.B. Spence, 'Administrative Law and Agency Policy-Making: Rethinking the Positive Theory of Political Control', supra note 12, 436).

165 Commission Communication COM(2009) 673 final, 9.

166 N. Dorn, 'Render Unto Caesar: EU Financial Market Regulation Meets Political Accountability', supra note 85.

167 Judicial accountability, mainly under the form of legality review triggered by Member States (Art. 263 TFEU), may in any case provide a rigorous scrutiny for implementing technical standards too.

168 J.L. Raptis, 'European Financial Regulation: ESMA and the Lamfalussy process, the Renewed European Legislative Process in the field of Securities Regulation', supra note 129, 66.

169 The same applies in exceptional circumstances where ESMA does not deliver the draft measures within the expected deadline. This being the case, the Commission regains its original power to adopt the technical standards, but it has to comply with the same default procedure concerning consultation of the Stakeholder Group and interested parties (Art. 10(3) and 15(3)).

very restricted and extraordinary circumstances"[170] be endorsed in part, with amendments, or not be endorsed at all; however, in no case may the Commission change the content of the draft regulatory technical standards prepared by ESMA without triggering a special coordination procedure whereby ESMA may amend the standards and resubmit them in the form of an opinion.[171] Whenever the Commission does not endorse a draft regulatory technical standard, it shall immediately inform the Parliament and the Council (Article 14(1)).[172] Both are also informed of the opinion which ESMA is subsequently required to deliver (with no distinction in this case between regulatory and implementing technical standards).[173]

Restrictions in the Commission's ability to reject the draft standards reflect, at the normative level, the underlying and substantial equilibrium in which ESMA enjoys an inherent strength in the preparation of the drafts as a consequence of both the specialized skills of its staff and the legitimacy bestowed by stakeholder engagement.[174] This is made explicit by Recitals 23 and 24 of Regulation (EU) No 1095/2010, according to which the Commission should refuse full endorsement of the ESMA draft measures only by way of exception, "since the Authority is the actor in close contact with and knowing best the daily functioning of financial markets" and "given the technical expertise of the Authority in the areas where regulatory technical standards should be developed, note should be taken of the

---

170 See also Recital 23 of the founding Regulation, stating that "draft regulatory technical standards would be subject to amendment if they were incompatible with EU law, did not respect the principle of proportionality or ran counter to the fundamental principles of the internal market for financial services as reflected in the *acquis* of Union financial services legislation." See H. Hofmann and A. Morini, 'Constitutional aspects of the pluralisation of the EU executive through "agencification"' (2012) 37 *European Law Review* 419. 430 (this limitations will guide the Court in interpretation of the Commission's capacity to amend the draft standards). See also infra note 176.

171 E. Ferran, 'Understanding the New Institutional Architecture of EU Financial Market Supervision', supra note 119, p. 143. Limitations on the possibility to have a say in the preparation of draft regulatory measures are all the more important because the Commission loses its power to adopt quasi-regulatory measures when the Level 1 delegations confers the initiative upon ESMA (see M. Busuioc, 'Rule-Making by the European Supervisory Authorities: Walking a Tight Rope' (2013) 19 *European Law Journal* 111, 115).

172 Communication to the other two EU institutions of Commission's dissenting opinions which refuse full endorsement is surprisingly not foreseen when implementing technical standards are at stake. Informal communication channels aside, the Council and the Parliament may therefore know that the procedure is in a deadlock only at the time they receive the subsequent ESMA opinion. Another – this time motivated – distinction between the two procedures lies in the fact that a forma; mediation procedure is envisaged for dissents on regulatory technical standards only (Art. 14(2)).

173 Once again, this information is also provided when the Commission adopts the technical standards without a draft from ESMA according to Art. 10(3) and 15(3) (infra note 193).

174 See L. Schrefler, 'The Usage of Scientific Knowledge by Independent Regulatory Agencies' (2010) 23 *Governance: An International Journal of Policy, Administration, and Institutions* 309, 315 (scientific knowledge may also serve the purpose of increasing the agencies' standing in the political arena).

Commission's stated intention to rely, as a rule, on the draft regulatory technical standards submitted to it by the Authority."[175] In case of disagreement, both the statements strongly shift the burden of proof to the Commission; according to ESMA, the Commission should restrict itself to checking that the draft measures are in the Union interest and are compatible with EU law,[176] but this wish is slightly in tension with the fact that the Commission has historically not restrained from amending CESR's Level 2 technical advices when it deemed it appropriate.[177] Indeed, notwithstanding these limitations, the Commission has hitherto interpreted its powers quite broadly. To date, endorsement has been refused in three instances, where Commission's criticism focused either on the technical standards' compatibility with EU legislation[178] or on the fact that the proposed measures could imply policy choices or strategic decisions.[179]

When the Parliament and the Council are engaged in communication concerning ESMA draft measures, whichever their formal role under either Article 290 or 291 TFEU, they are likely to step in and influence the process if they are not satisfied that the draft measures comply with the Commission and ESMA mandate. Furthermore, if a disagreement exists between the Commission and ESMA, the Parliament and the Council may also back one of the two against the other. In a similar scenario, ESMA has been regarded as more likely to receive support,[180]

---

175 This equilibrium underpins the theoretical framework that highlights how formal and informal elements affect the interaction among the actors in the process.

176 ESMA (2011/009), supra note 4, p. 4 *et seq.*

177 See E. Ferran, *Building an EU Securities Market*, supra note 81, p. 88.

178 The first case where endorsement was refused regarded the participation of national competent authorities to colleges set up for the authorisation of central counterparties (Art. 18 Reg. (EU) No 648/2012 (EMIR)); ESMA, *Guidelines and Recommendations regarding written agreements between members of CCP colleges* (ESMA/2013/661) p. 4). The second case was connected to the possibility to exclude from the category of open-ended alternative investment funds those schemes which redeem shares or units less frequently than on a yearly basis (Art. 4(4), 16(1) and 19(3) Dir. 2011/61/EU (AIFMD); see EU Commission, Letter to ESMA, 4 July 2013). In this latter circumstance, ESMA disagreed with the Commission's statement and recalled the exceptional nature of the refusal to endorse draft standards. However, it aligned with the Commission position to ensure timely implementation of EU legislation (ESMA, *Opinion on draft regulatory technical standards on types of AIFMs under Article 4(4) of Directive 2011/61/EU* (2013/ESMA/1119)).

179 In the third relevant case, the Commission refused to endorse ESMA's draft implementing technical standards amending Regulation (EU) No 1247/2012, which contains measures implementing the EMIR Regulation, including reporting duties on exchange traded derivatives. ESMA proposed to delay the entry into force of the new technical standards so as to be able to issue guidelines and recommendations on certain technical aspects before the interested firms were required to comply. However, according to the Commission, the regulatory framework was not uncertain even in the absence of such guidelines, and "postponing the starting date of the reporting obligation for exchange traded derivatives would (have hindered) the achievement of a key objective of EMIR, that is, the identification, monitoring, assessment and mitigation of systemic risk arising from derivative contracts by almost one year" (Commission Communication, 7 November 2013). See supra note 155 and accompanying text.

180 N. Moloney, 'The European Securities and Markets Authority and Institutional Design for the EU Financial Market – A Tale of Two Competences: Part (1) Rule-Making' supra note 9, 77.

as the Commission has the upper hand in any instance by virtue of its ability to block the draft technical standards on an autonomous basis.[181] In any event, the equilibrium of the regulatory procedure is affected by the combination of the information and expertise of the supported disputant (be it ESMA or the Commission), on the one hand, with the authority and legitimacy of the Council or the Parliament, which are very likely to orient the final outcome of the process, on the other hand.[182] All the more so, of course, when either the Council or the Parliament may act as vetoing institutions.[183]

With a view to promoting the safety and soundness of markets and convergence of regulatory practice (Article 16), ESMA can also resort to the soft law tools that constituted the typical Level 3 measures under the CESR founding documents:[184] guidelines and recommendations.[185] The entry into force of guidelines and recommendations does not require *ex post* endorsement by the Commission, nor do the Parliament and the Council enjoy any formal power to step into the drafting process. Once again, ESMA position has been strengthened if compared to that of CESR.[186] First, ESMA is entitled to receive information by both national competent authorities and financial markets participants whether they comply with a guideline or a recommendation; competent authorities that do not comply are named (and shamed) by way of an *ad hoc* publication and in the ESMA annual report. Second, national supervisors may also be asked to state the reasons for the lack of compliance, which may also be made public if ESMA so decides. Third, the annual report must outline how ESMA intends to ensure that its guidelines or recommendations are complied with in the future (Article 16(4)), which makes the regulatory model less flexible than a pure "comply or explain" system. At the same time, accountability has also been reinforced,[187] in order to ensure

181 According to a commentator, should the Commission be willing to retain as far as possible its regulatory capacity, it could decide to make broad use of its powers to refuse full endorsement of technical standards (M. Busuioc, 'Rule-Making by the European Supervisory Authorities: Walking a Tight Rope', supra note 172, 122 *et seq.*).

182 See also para 4.1.2.

183 In assessing the reciprocal interactions among the constituents of the process, potential regulatory capacity is almost as important as the actual involvement (J. Black, 'Mapping the Contours of Contemporary Financial Services Regulation', supra note 124, 264).

184 Non-binding instruments will supposedly maintain a central role in the European financial regulation whenever regulators are not able to reliably assess the possible effects of a proposed measure (E. Wymeersch, 'Europe's New Financial Regulatory Bodies', supra note 4, 449).

185 Standards are no longer included in the lists of non-binding measures (see Art. 3 of Commission decision 2009/77/EC establishing the Committee of European Securities Regulators, now repealed). According to the new taxonomy, standards now fall into the scope of the measures adopted under Art. 290 or 291 TFEU.

186 Moreover, "national courts are bound to take recommendations into consideration in order to decide disputes submitted to them, in particular where they cast light on the interpretation of national measures adopted in order to implement them or where they are designed to supplement binding (Union) provisions" (ECJ, Case C-322/88, *Salvatore Grimaldi v Fonds des maladies professionnelles*, 13 December 1989, para 18).

187 However, judicial accountability is still limited: see infra note 383.

that the whole architecture is balanced, as ESMA is required to perform open consultations and the Securities and Markets Stakeholder Group must release its opinion or advice before guidelines and recommendations are adopted, where ESMA deems it appropriate.[188]

In its quasi-regulatory capacity, ESMA has also used more flexible instruments, even in the absence of an express enabling provision. An example is the publication of Q&A documents, which are updated on a continuous basis in order to solve regulatory uncertainties in specific matters.[189] In a similar vein, soft guidance can also be issued within feedback statements, in order to foster self-regulation by anticipating that ESMA is willing to adopt more formal measures, including formal recommendations, in case market participants do not deliver satisfactory results.[190] Another example are public statements representing the views of working groups, often gathering representatives of national competent authorities, operating within ESMA.[191]

4.2.1.3. The role of the Securities and Markets Stakeholder Group

A key accountability device for the exercise of regulatory powers is the SMSG. When performing its tasks, the SMSG carries out both compulsory and optional activities. While the latter are conducted on the SMSG's own initiative, the former are typically fulfilled in reaction to an input by ESMA, especially in connection with consultations.

The SMSG is consulted on initiatives concerning the adoption of technical standards, guidelines and recommendations. The opinion of the SMSG is always compulsory before draft technical standards can be adopted. The SMSG significantly retains its power and duty to deliver an opinion even in the exceptional circumstances where public consultation by ESMA does not take place, because it

---

188 ESMA therefore retains a significant discretion on the procedure to be followed when issuing soft regulatory measures, as opposed to draft technical standards, since consultation and advice for recommendations and guidelines are only needed insofar as they are deemed appropriate, while draft technical standards may not be released without stakeholder involvement unless this would be disproportionate. Such a diverging approach has raised concerns about the ability to ensure that all the relevant information is provided and all the engaged stakeholders are represented in the process for the adoption of soft law (E. Chiti, 'European Agencies' Rulemaking: Powers, Procedures and Assessment', supra note 127, 105 *et seq.*).

189 See e.g. ESMA, *Questions and Answers – Prospectuses* (ESMA/2013/594); *Id.*, ESMA, *Questions and Answers – Implementation of the Regulation (EU) No 648/2012 on OTC derivatives, central counterparties and trade repositories (EMIR)* (ESMA/2013/1527).

190 ESMA (2013/84), supra note 150, p. 27 (on proxy advisors). This approach fosters cooperation by market participants to the preparation of soft-law measures (P. Iglesias-Rodriguez, 'The role of interests groups in EU financial regulation after the European Supervision Authorities in the Financial Field: the case of the Stakeholder Groups', supra note 83, p. 6).

191 See e.g. ESMA, *Information on shareholder cooperation and acting in concert under the Takeover Bids Directive* (ESMA/2013/1642).

would be disproportionate in light of the scope and impact of the draft technical standards. Of course, this is not the case when public consultation is avoided because actions by ESMA must be taken urgently; in such circumstances, the SMSG must be informed as soon as possible. The SMSG must also be consulted in the exceptional cases where the European Commission can adopt technical standards without a draft from ESMA (Article 10(3) and 15(3)).[192]

ESMA would seem to have wider discretion concerning guidelines and recommendations, as it will request SMSG's opinion or advice only "where appropriate" (Article 16(2)). However, Article 37 states that the SMSG "shall" be consulted on actions taken in accordance with Article 16, to the extent that these do not concern individual financial market participants; it would seem therefore that ESMA should in any case receive the SMSG's advice irrespective of the legal measure to be adopted.[193] Similarly, no discretion is granted when guidelines and recommendations concern individual financial markets participants, as in this case no SMSG opinion is required, in order to avoid both the emergence of possible conflicts of interests and the communication of individual news among other stakeholders, who might be competitors.

The aim of the SMSG is to "help facilitate consultation with stakeholders in areas relevant to the tasks of the Authority" (Article 37). The rule is not interpreted as meaning that the SMSG has an obligation to answer to public consultations. Although replying to public consultations is an option,[194] especially when preliminary advice is given without formality and requires some documentation, this might sometimes be problematic given the wide stakeholder representation within the Group, which can easily lead either to empty answers, in order to find a floor consensus among the members, or to collections of minority opinions of no use. Furthermore, replies by the SMSG are likely to overlap with individual responses by the SMSG constituencies directly addressed to ESMA. On the contrary, reference to facilitation of consultations suggests that the SMSG's preferential role should be to have a dialogue with ESMA before a consultation document is issued. While performing this task, the Group should be aided by access to "all the necessary information", if not covered by professional secrecy, at ESMA disposal (Article 37(4)). The SMSG may thus step in at a very early stage (before the document is discussed by the Board) or afterwards, by delivering an opinion on a draft consultation document before it is finally approved.[195]

192 See supra notes 170 and 174.

193 As we show below, rules applicable to technical standards also stress the importance of the SMSG's opinions, as these may be required even where consultations are not performed because disproportionate.

194 See e.g. ESMA, *Final Report. Guidelines and Recommendations on the Scope of the CRA Regulation* (ESMA/2013/720), Annex I.

195 This is also the opinion of the SMSG currently in place: "Such facilitation of consultation implies the Group being asked to give its advice in advance of the issue of any such consultation

This is also made clear by Recital 48 of the founding Regulation, which requires that the SMSG be involved in the impact assessment that must support the technical standards; contextual development of the proposals and their respective cost-benefit analyses represents a best practice.[196] Impact assessment exercises are among the most effective accountability tools,[197] and delegated and implementing measures are no exception.[198] The SMSG can play a key role in making these mechanisms effective. Its ability to enter the process at an early stage, before a consultation document crystallises the initial ESMA position, greatly enhances its influence on the final decision, because minor variations in the initial conditions of the regulatory work may significantly affect the outcomes.[199]

The second area of intervention of the SMSG relates to the activities performed on its own initiative. Although no specific act is mandated in this area (the SMSG "may" submit), the Regulation suggests that the overall advisory role of the Group represents a duty. An implicit indication is the compulsory number of meetings ("at least four times a year") which the SMSG has to hold, irrespective of ESMA requests to intervene into the consultation process. This is also an area where the Group may fully deploy the expertise ensured by its diverse composition and build upon the different experiences it gathers, because of the freedom to analyse relevant topics in advance of ESMA official initiatives and of the possibility to trigger the supervisory process as a first mover, rather than focusing on specific aspects of draft technical standards.[200]

Among the activities performed by the SMSG on its own initiative is the power to point out possible violations of EU law by national competent authorities so that ESMA may decide to launch a procedure under Article 17.[201] This function allows the SMSG to enhance vertical accountability of national competent authorities *vis-à-vis* the European Union, and may also possibly help monitor compliance by

by the Authority" (see RoP, Recital 2). See also SMSG (2013/013), supra note 105, pp. 4, 13 and 38.

196 A. Alemanno and A. Meuwese, 'Impact Assessment of EU Non-Legislative Rulemaking: The Missing Link in 'New Comitology'' (2013) 19 *European Law Journal* 76, 85.

197 Regulatory impact assessment is commonly regarded as an effective accountability mechanism, which provides justification to the regulatory action by allowing a comparison between divergent hypothetical rules. See in general OECD, *Introductory Handbook for Undertaking Regulatory Impact Analysis* (RIA), OECD, Paris 2008; S. Rose-Ackerman, *Public Choice, Public Law and Public Policy*, Keynote address, First World Meeting of the Public Choice Society, Amsterdam, 31.03.2007, p. 12.

198 See A. Alemanno and A. Meuwese, 'Impact Assessment of EU Non-Legislative Rulemaking: The Missing Link in 'New Comitology'', supra note 197, 86 *et seq* – on the relationship between legislative and non-legislative impact assessments.

199 D.T. Hornstein, 'Complexity, Adaptation, and Administrative Law', supra note 37, 926.

200 Also in favour of a greater SMSG's role in identifying priorities for the ESAs, DG Internal Policies (European Parliament), *Review of the New European System of Financial Supervision (ESFS). Part 1*, supra note 40, p. 15.

201 See text accompanying infra note 208.

Member States themselves. Indeed, although the power of ESMA (and therefore of the SMSG) does not directly refer to non-compliance by Member States, insofar as national supervisors are violating EU law because they are properly performing their duties under national provisions, enforcement against competent authorities may put violation by national jurisdictions in the spotlight.[202]

In delivering its positions, the SMSG may submit "opinions" or "advice": the former relate to specific topics already at the ESMA agenda, while the latter permits the SMSG to provide reasoned positions on more general matters. The SMSG may address opinions and advices to ESMA "on any issue related to the tasks of the Authority", and in particular when the Authority exercises its quasi-rulemaking powers (Articles 10–6) or is involved in the harmonisation of divergent supervisory approaches (Article 29), in peer reviews of competent authorities (Article 30), and in the assessment of market developments (Article 32), namely in high-level analysis of the financial market industry. This may also confirm the opportunity for ESMA to consult the SMSG on its own initiative before adopting any position relating to such matters, including acts which are formally drafted as public statements,[203] let alone the fact that before the administrative procedure is over, it might not be clear which final legal instrument will be chosen.

However, the width of the formula also seems to allow the SMSG to comment on procedural aspects, such as Level 1 measures setting the timing for the adoption of quasi-regulatory acts, in case the proposed timing is inadequate for ESMA to properly perform its quasi-regulatory functions, or to intervene more generally, such as on ESMA organization; for instance, the SMSG has expressed its position on the ESA's review in an autonomous reply to the consultation performed by the EU Commission under Article 81 Regulation 1095/2010.[204]

4.2.2. *The supervisory powers of ESMA*

4.2.2.1. Cross-sectoral supervisory powers: addressing national competent authorities and market participants

ESMA also plays a crucial role in supervision. In some instances, in line with previous CERS' experience as a network of supervisors,[205] ESMA is entrusted with

---

202 E. Wymeersch, 'Europe's New Financial Regulatory Bodies', supra note 4, 458 *et seq.*

203 One of the improvements achieved by the new regulatory framework for EU financial supervision is that involvement of stakeholders representatives is no longer subject to discretionary decisions by the Authority: see P. Iglesias-Rodriguez, 'The role of interests groups in EU financial regulation after the European Supervision Authorities in the Financial Field: the case of the Stakeholder Groups', supra note 83, p. 9.

204 See SMSG (SMSG/2013/013), supra note 105.

205 See in general: G. Majone, 'Delegation of Regulatory Powers in a Mixed Polity', supra note 17, 336; W. Weiss, 'Agencies Versus Networks: From Divide to Convergence in the

the task of coordinating national competent authorities, so that its supervisory role is indirect and is mainly connected to the ability to influence local supervisors. Among the tools that help harmonization are peer reviews (Article 30), colleges aimed at coordinating multiple competent authorities (Article 21), opinions directed to national supervisors, personnel exchanges, and training programmes (Article 29). ESMA discretion in this filed is widened by the possibility to resort to instruments not envisaged by the founding Regulation, when needed (Article 29(2)).

However, ESMA (as well as the other ESAs) has also been entrusted with more intrusive powers permitting it to address financial market participants, either through the national competent authorities or, in case of local inertia, directly. These supervisory powers are cross-sectional and can therefore be exercised irrespective of the field of regulation involved within the general limits set forth by Article 1(2) and (3) of the founding Regulation, though sometimes an express enabling provision is needed. ESMA power to take individual decisions directly addressed to financial market participants in some specific cases is of particular relevance because it can easily result in the performance of direct enforcement *vis-à-vis* private entities, which might create some legislative tensions in the absence of a conferral of powers to EU bodies within the Treaties.[206] We describe the relevant provisions below with a focus on the role performed by the EU institutions. The analysis will show how accountability towards those institutions easily turns into direct participation by the latter to the administrative process.

The most relevant power of ESMA towards national competent authorities and market participants relates to the breach of EU law, including the regulatory and implementing technical standards (Article 17). In particular, ESMA has the power to investigate, after giving notice, whether a competent authority[207] has failed to apply the relevant EU acts (referred to in Article 1(2)[208]), or has applied them in a way which appears to ESMA as breaching EU law, "in particular by failing to ensure that a financial market participant satisfies the requirements laid down in those acts". Investigations may be initiated spontaneously or upon request by one

Administrative Governance in the EU' (2009) 61 *Administrative Law Review* 45, 47 *et seq.* and 59 *et seq.*; M. Shapiro, 'Independent agencies' in P. Craig and G. de Búrca (eds.), *The Evolution of EU Law*, Oxford University Press, Oxford 2011, p. 119. See also text accompanying supra note 42 and infra note 348.

206 P. Shammo, *EU Prospectus Law*, Cambridge University Press, Cambridge 2011, p. 238.

207 The authority under investigation must provide ESMA with all the required information (Art. 17(2)(2)).

208 No reference is made to Art. 1(3). This limited reference curtails ESMA ability to enforce EU law, such as takeover law, which is referred to only in Art. 1(3), so that enforcement should be left to the Commission under Art. 258 TFEU (see Art. 1(4)). The same seems to apply for ESMA decision which, although necessary to ensure the effective and consistent application of directives mentioned by Art. 1(2), are not expressly envisaged by the same directives (see Art. 1(3)).

or more national competent authorities, the European Parliament, the Council, the Commission or, notably, the Securities and Markets Stakeholder Group. In all instances, ESMA has no strict duty to perform an inquiry, so any evaluation of the plausibility of the accusation is up to the Authority itself, in keeping with the well-known principle of independence with accountability, even though the willingness to conduct thorough inquiries may be curbed by the governance of the Authority.[209] According to its internal procedure, ESMA will first perform a preliminary evaluation of the admissibility and, if it takes a positive decision, will then carry out a second assessment to establish whether the request deserves further investigation (both steps are delegated to the Chairperson and her deputy).[210]

The SMSG's ability to file a request against a national competent authority for inadequate application of EU law may represent a powerful tool in the hand of investors and the financial industry. This may prove particularly attractive whenever, as is often the case, petitioning a national court would create an adversarial relationship with the local supervisor; on the contrary, the governance of the SMSG, and the independence of its members, can shield the constituency that initiated the request from being identified as an antagonist of the local authority. Submissions by individuals or private entities are not explicitly contemplated but also are not ruled out,[211] and can therefore be taken into account.[212]

Investigation may have different outcomes, depending on the ground of allegations, the reaction by the national competent authority, and the nature of the rule whose violation is claimed: the remedies are hierarchically coordinated, so that resorting to the more coercive act – addressing market participants – is possible only when the lighter touch of the previous intervention has proven insufficient, in conformity with the principle of proportionality. As a first step, if the inquiry has demonstrated to the satisfaction of ESMA that a violation has occurred,[213] ESMA itself may address a recommendation to the competent authority, setting out the action necessary to comply with EU law.[214] However, if the (alleged) non-compliance persists, enforcement is passed to the Commission, which within one month (and, in any case, no later than three months after

209 See infra text accompanying infra note 347.

210 See ESMA, *Decision on Breach of Union Law Investigations* (ESMA/2012/BS/87), Art. 2 and 3.

211 ESMA (2012/BS/87), supra note 211, Art. 2(2); E. Wymeersch, 'Europe's New Financial Regulatory Bodies', supra note 4, 458.

212 See the case addressed by the first Board of Appeal's decision (*SV Capital OÜ v. EBA*, 24.06.2013). The decision also shows that Art. 17 may represent an instrument for ESMA second-guessing of interpretation of EU law by national competent authorities.

213 In order to avoid permanent investigations, the inquiry cannot last for more than two months (Art. 17(3)).

214 The competent authority shall, within ten working days of receipt of the recommendation, inform ESMA of the steps it has taken or intends to take to ensure compliance with EU law.

adoption of the ESMA recommendation) may issue a formal opinion requiring the competent authority to align with EU law (Article 17(4)).[215]

The relationship between ESMA and the Commission under Article 17(4) is telling. It shows that, when the going gets tough and a pure recommendation is not able to achieve significant results, the tough get going by threatening a possible recourse to the mechanisms provided for by Article 258 TFEU.[216] Indeed, the Commission maintains wide discretion in many respects. First, it delivers a formal opinion on its own initiative, so that the enforcement action may proceed in circumstances where ESMA would agree that the competent authority has eventually complied with the law.[217] Second, the reverse is also true, so that the same procedure is interrupted if the Commission deems that the breach of the law, if ever existed, has come to an end. Furthermore, between these two extremes, the Commission also enjoys discretion concerning the action required from the competent authority because it can depart from ESMA recommendations,[218] which only have to be taken into account.[219]

The third step of the procedure, which once more may be resorted to insofar as the previous phase is performed unsuccessfully, is back again under ESMA control. If the national competent authority does not comply with the formal opinion of the Commission, and the necessity arises to remedy "in a timely manner such non-compliance in order to maintain or restore neutral conditions of competition in the market or ensure the orderly functioning and integrity of the financial system", ESMA may by-pass the national supervisor by adopting an individual decision directly addressed to a financial market participant, thereby requiring the necessary action to comply with EU law (Article 17(6)).[220]

---

215 As is the case for the ESMA recommendation, the competent authority has ten working days to provide information on its future compliance with the EU law.

216 Art. 258 is also wider in scope, because it applies to violations of EU law by Member States, including their respective legislators, and may therefore be triggered in cases where national authorities cannot be faulted (E. Wymeersch, 'The European Financial Supervisory Authorities or ESAs', supra note 70, p. 256). See also supra text accompanying note 203.

217 A similar enforcement by the Commission is more likely to concern major and crystal clear infringements (E. Wymeersch, 'Europe's New Financial Regulatory Bodies', supra note 4, 455).

218 For a different opinion see T. Tridimas, 'Financial Supervision and Agency Power: Reflections on ESMA' supra note 8, p. 73 (the Commission is in principle bound by ESMA recommendation).

219 A different wording is remarkably used, as shown below, regarding the content of the third act of the enforcement process, namely the ESMA decision directly addressing a financial market participant, which "shall be in conformity with the formal opinion issued by the Commission" (Art. 17(6)(2)).

220 The injunction may also require the cessation of one or more specific practices (see infra note 242 and accompanying text).

Of course, ESMA does not have exclusive control of the enforcement mechanisms; since under the TFEU the primary function of detecting and prosecuting breaches of EU law lies with the Commission, the latter retains the power to bring the matter before the CJEU (Article 258 TFEU). The boundaries of ESMA powers therefore determine to what extent the action of the Authority and the Commission can overlap. In this respect, according to Article 17(6), ESMA may address financial market participants only if the (allegedly) violated law sets requirements which are directly applicable to them. The expression is used in the TFEU in a narrow sense so as to cover only EU law instruments which do not require implementation in national jurisdictions, namely Regulations (Article 288 TFEU), but it is sometimes mentioned by the CJEU case-law to describe measures having direct effects.[221] An interpretation aligned with Article 288 TFEU would provide safer legal basis for ESMA action[222] and is therefore preferable.[223] That conclusion is also confirmed by Recital 29 of Regulation 1095/2010, but it would also curb supervisory powers when the relevant piece of EU legislation is a Directive having direct (vertical) effects.[224] In such instances, enforcement would be entrusted to the Commission according to Article 258 TFEU and would therefore address Member States rather than market participants, thus preventing access to the swift and prompt remedy devised by Article 17(6).[225]

Along with enforcement of EU law under Article 17, the second case where ESMA has direct supervisory powers on a general basis relates to action in emergency situations (Article 18). Whenever "adverse developments" may undermine the orderly functioning and the integrity of financial markets or the stability of the EU financial system, ESMA may foster actions by national competent authorities (if more than a supervisor is involved, ESMA must also facilitate a coordinated effort). If the emergency situation is certified by the Council – whose decision

221 See K. Lenaerts and P. Van Nuffel, *European Union Law*, Sweet & Maxwell, London 2011, pp. 812 *et seq.* and 895.

222 Note that this first interpretation would not be unproblematic for regulations lacking direct effects (as is the case whenever a margin of discretion is left to Member States: see ECJ, Case C-403/98, *Azienda Agricola Monte Arcosu v. Regione Autonoma della Sardegna*, 11.01.2001, para 26 *et seq.*; K. Lenaerts and P. Van Nuffel, *European Union Law*, supra note 222, p. 895; P. Craig and G. De Búrca, *EU Law. Text, Cases, and Materials*, Oxford University Press, Oxford 2011, p. 190). In those circumstances, the question arises whether ESMA should override national legislators or – more likely – confine itself to enforcing EU legislation which has both direct applicability and direct effects.

223 T. Tridimas, 'Financial Supervision and Agency Power: Reflections on ESMA' supra note 8, p. 73.

224 See ECJ, Case C-41/74, *Van Duyn v. Home Office*, 04.12.1974, para 12 *et seq.*; ECJ, Case C-148/78, *Pubblico Ministero (Public Prosecutor) v. Tullio Ratti*, 05.04.1979, para 21 *et seq.* Also covered by Art. 17 are EU primary law provision with direct effects (E. Wymeersch, 'The European Financial Supervisory Authorities or ESAs', supra note 70, p. 257; ECJ Case C-26/62, *Van Gend en Loos v. Nederlandse Administratie der Belastingen*, 05.02.1963).

225 E. Ferran, 'Understanding the New Institutional Architecture of EU Financial Market Supervision', supra note 119, p. 147.

may be triggered by the Commission, the ESRB or ESMA itself – the Authority may in the same circumstances also address individual decisions to national supervisors and, if the latter do not comply, to financial market participants, thereby requiring the action or inaction which is deemed necessary to comply with their obligations under that legislation (Article 18(2–4)). As is the case for enforcement of EU law, ESMA market participants may be addressed only when the applicable legislative or quasi-legislative measure sets requirements which are directly applicable to them. Although this limitation may be substantial, the main hurdle to the enactment of Article 18 seems to be the lengthy process required for ESMA to be enabled to directly intervene, which is obviously incompatible with the timing of emergency situations seriously affecting one or more key market participants.[226]

The third situation in which ESMA can directly address market participants on the basis of a general capacity relates to the power to settle disagreements between competent authorities in cross-border situations,[227] where a Level 1 provision so provides[228] (Article 19). In comparison with the other examples of direct intervention, the EU institutions do not play a decisive role when ESMA performs this facilitating function, in spite of the fact that the decision may involve the use of wide discretion,[229] and divergent views will often reveal a breach of EU law by a disputant. In the first step of the procedure, which can be activated either *ex officio* or upon request, ESMA operates as a mediator for the settlement of the disagreement (Article 19(2)). If the concerned competent authorities fail to reach an agreement within the conciliation phase, ESMA may deliver a decision requiring them to take specific action, or to refrain from action, with binding effects for the competent authorities. If the decision of ESMA is not observed, the Authority may adopt an individual decision addressed to a financial market participant ordering the action necessary to comply with its obligations under EU law, including the cessation of any practice (Article 19(4); the usual limitation to directly applicable rules applies).

ESMA is required to ensure that its decisions in emergency situation or settlement of disagreements do not impinge fiscal responsibilities of member states (Article 38).[230] This limitation to ESMA powers draws an important

226 SMSG (2013/013), supra note 105, p. 7.

227 On the contrary, the joint committee may settle disagreements between competent authorities across sectors (banks, securities and insurance): Art. 20; ESMA (2011/009), supra note 4, p. 6.

228 See e.g. Art. 35 Dir. 2011/61/EU (on disagreements concerning the conditions for marketing units or shares of third countries alternative investment funds in the EU).

229 P. Shammo, *EU Prospectus Law*, supra note 207, p. 235 *et seq.*

230 This limitation, which was added following pressure by the Council (T. Conzelmann et al., *Regulatory overhaul in the EU and the US following the financial crisis – what role for accountability?*, supra note 26, p. 12), is subject to criticisms because of its vagueness (SMSG (2013/013), supra note 105, p. 7).

boundary between national and supranational competences, as it shows that the final responsibility for supervision rests with the Member States in any case where a decision could have an impact on state budgets.[231] Where a Member State considers that an action taken under Article 18 and 19 impinges on its fiscal responsibilities, it may notify ESMA and the Commission[232] that such decision will not be implemented. The decision is then suspended, and it is up to ESMA to decide on further actions: when the decision is upheld, the Council has the final say. One can clearly see that the suspension itself may deprive European intervention of any effectiveness; in order to avoid an instrumental use of the right of notification, certain measures which are clearly unable to have "a significant or material fiscal impact" (Article 38(5)), such as short selling restrictions or trading halts, should be excluded from Article 38 by way of explicit provision.

Of course, in fields where decisions involve budgetary consequences for Member States, externalities may *ex ante* distort the incentives of supervisors and allocate fiscal burdens unevenly *ex post*, as the recent financial turmoil has demonstrated. In similar circumstances, while a fully-fledged centralised supervision is not viable (and perhaps not even desirable), a strengthened cooperation is nonetheless required whenever the subsidiarity test is met (Article 5 TEU).[233] This is particularly true for supervision of transnational groups, as a consequence of the spill-over effects that are likely to stem from inadequate supervisory practices in one or more Member States. In similar circumstances, the preferential regulatory tool adopted by EU legislation is the creation of a college of supervisors for every market participant or conglomerate of market participants involved in the supervision.[234] ESMA must ensure the streamlined functioning of every college as

---

[231] See EU Commission Communication, European financial supervision (COM(2009) 252 final), 27 May 2009, 9. Fiscal responsibility is the most important driver for decisions concerning where to allocate supervisory powers on EU financial markets, so that Member States maintain their powers whenever they would bear the costs of a possible insolvency of market participants. On the contrary, conferral and subsidiarity (Art. 5 TEU) are not that crucial (P. Shammo, 'EU Day-to-Day Supervision or Intervention-based Supervision: Which Way Forward for the European System of Financial Supervision?' (2012) 32 *Oxford Journal of Legal Studies* 1, 10). However, experience has already demonstrated that the home country control principle already violates the link between power and risk whenever systematically relevant branches fail (M. Lamandini, 'When More is Needed: The European Financial Supervisory Reform and Its Legal Basis' (2009) 6 *European Company Law* 197, 201).

[232] Notification shall be performed, for urgent matters or for settlements of disagreements respectively, within three days or two weeks after notification of ESMA decision to the national competent authority.

[233] See also Art. 4(3) TEU and Art. 6 and 197 TFEU.

[234] After the transfer of supervision on credit rating agencies to ESMA (see para 4.2.3.2 below), the main example is that of central counterparties (CCPs), which are supervised by the national competent authority with the involvement of a college comprising both ESMA and other national authorities supervising the entities that are most likely to be affected by the operations of the CCPs (Art. 18 Regulation (EU) No 648/2012). The college releases an opinion on the authorisation of the CCP, which rests with the national competent authority (Art. 19). The opinion's effects depend on its direction (if positive, a denial of the authorisation is subject

well as a consistent supervisory approach by different colleges,[235] to reduce the risks of inconsistent actions that will inevitably arise until this baroque mechanism[236] is superseded by full centralization.[237] With a view to exploiting all the potential of cross-border coordinated supervision, the founding Regulation also defines a set of tasks ESMA may perform along with those specifically established by the legislative acts referred to by Article 1(2). In particular, ESMA may initiate Europe-wide stress tests taking into account the systemic risk posed by financial market participants referred in Article 23[238] and oversee the activities carried out by national competent authorities (Article 21 Reg. 1095/2010).

Finally, ESMA has a competence representing a mix of regulation and supervision in consumer protection and financial activities.[239] Some of the relevant tasks are drafted in general terms (Article 9(1)). In particular, the Authority is to take a leading role in promoting transparency, simplicity and fairness in the market for consumer financial products or services across the internal market, including by: collecting, analysing and reporting on consumer trends; reviewing and coordinating financial literacy and education initiatives by the competent authorities; developing training standards for the industry; and contributing to the development of common disclosure rules. ESMA will also monitor new and existing financial activities and may issue warnings in the event that a financial activity poses a serious threat to its statutory objectives as laid down in Article 1(5).[240]

Other more detailed powers enable ESMA direct intervention in the market. For example, the Authority may temporarily prohibit or restrict certain financial activities (apparently including the selling or the acquisition of

to a "comply or explain" rule; if negative, the authorisation cannot be released) and on the approving majority (in case of qualified majorities rebutting the request for authorisation, a referral to ESMA is possible under Art. 19 Regulation 1095/2010).

235 In order to achieve these aims, ESMA may perform its mediating functions according to Art. 19.

236 See critically M. Lamandini, 'When More is Needed: The European Financial Supervisory Reform and Its Legal Basis', supra note 232, 202.

237 E. Avgouleas, *Governance of Global Financial Markets. The Law, the Economics, the Politics*, Cambridge University Press, Cambridge 2012, p. 320 *et seq.*

238 Art. 23 Regulation No 1095/2010 deals with the identification and the measurement of systemic risk, and provides that the Authority shall, in consultation with ESRB, develop supervisory criteria for these two matters and an adequate stress-testing regime which includes an evaluation of the possibility that systemic risks posed by financial market participants increase in situation of stress. Financial market participants that may pose systemic risks shall be subject to strengthened supervision and, where necessary, to the recovery and resolution procedures referred to in Art. 25.

239 These tasks were not inserted in the original Commission proposal and were added by the European Parliament.

240 See para 2.

financial products[241]) that "threaten the orderly functioning and integrity of financial markets or the stability of the whole or part of the financial system in the Union", in the cases specified and under the conditions laid down in the relevant legislative acts or if so required in the case of an emergency situation according to Article 18 (Article 9(5)). The provisional effects of these decisions, which require that a review be performed at least every three months, may prove particularly efficient when the issue addressed is affected by uncertainty because of the absence of a scientific *communis opinio*:[242] since the effects of short selling restrictions are highly controversial,[243] it is not by chance that Article 28 Regulation (EU) No 236/2012 is among the rules allowing direct intervention on the basis of Article 9(5), thus enabling ESMA to prohibit – or to impose conditions (including notification duties) on – the acquisition of net short positions on certain financial instruments.[244] Temporary restrictions may in any case be adopted only on a subsidiary basis, i.e. in the absence of effective measures taken by national competent authorities; if adopted, ESMA measures replace any national measure possibly in force.[245] The narrow requirements[246] for the prohibition of certain activities have been questioned by the SMSG, whose review of the ESA's functioning suggests including consumer protections among the goals contemplated by Article 9(5).[247] Far from simply enlarging the scope of application of the bans, such an amendment would also increase supervisory attention to products. The ensuing powers – although formally conferred in the field of supervision – should therefore be carefully exercised in order to avoid the risk usually connected to products regulation, such retail overreliance by investors on regulators' (implicit) label on non-banned financial products.[248]

More in general, the adoption of legislative measures giving effect to Article 9(5) does not require unanimity as long as it is based on Article 114 TFEU. As made

241 Similar powers are foreseen by Art. 31–3 of the Commission Proposal for a Market in Financial Instrument Regulation (COM(2011) 652 final), 20 October 2011 (see N. Moloney, 'The European Securities and Markets Authority: a perspective from one year on', supra note 133, 76 *et seq.*). See also, implicitly, E. Wymeersch, 'The European Financial Supervisory Authorities or ESAs', supra note 70, p. 274.

242 See S.J. Choi and A.C. Pritchard, 'Behavioral Economics and the SEC', supra note 89, 43. Periodical review of regulations in place is recommended by OECD, *Principles for the Governance of Regulators – Public Consultation Draft*, supra note 17, p. 21, and represents a best practice in supranational financial regulation (D. Zaring, 'Informal Procedure, Hard and Soft, in International Administration', supra note 88, 578).

243 See infra note 288.

244 O. Juurikkala, 'Credit Default Swaps and the EU Short Selling Regulation: A Critical Analysis' (2012) 9 *European Company and Financial Law Review* 307, 322 and 334 *et seq.*

245 See Advocate General's opinion C-270/12, supra note 8, para 24. For further comment on Art. 28 and its relevance under the *Meroni* doctrine see para 5.1.

246 DG Internal Policies (European Parliament), *Review of the New European System of Financial Supervision (ESFS). Part 1*, supra note 40, pp. 16, 105–106.

247 SMSG (2013/013), supra note 105, p. 6.

248 On the effects of (positive) labeling see N. Moloney, *How to Protect Investors. Lessons from the EC and the UK*, Oxford University Press, Oxford 2010, pp. 142–145.

clear by the ECJ in case C-270/12[249] measures for the approximation of jurisdictions can also concern individuals or specific products (para 106).[250] Absent enabling rules such as Article 28 Reg. (EU) 236/2012, the Authority may also assess the need to prohibit or restrict certain types of financial activity and, when this is the case, inform the Commission in order to facilitate the adoption of any such measures. Prohibitions or restrictions so adopted do not face time constraints and can be drafted as normative acts, in contrast to the limits imposed on *ad hoc* measures (Article 9(5)).[251]

4.2.2.2. ESMA as a single EU supervisor: the case of credit rating agencies

It is however in the field of credit rating agencies (CRAs) that ESMA supervisory powers are closer to those of a truly independent pan-European watchdog, as in this area supervision, including enforcement,[252] requires no intermediation by national competent authorities.[253] The direct day-to-day supervision is currently confined to areas where the cross-border implications of the regulated activity is high and, at the same time, the resolution of the interested market participants would have limited financial implications (particularly in the case of bail-outs by Member States).[254] Therefore, although the Commission proposal was more ambitious – as it tried to centralize supervision on entities with Europe-wide reach, including clearing houses[255] – ESMA has been granted direct supervision over a small set of market participants.[256] The CRA Regulation (Reg. No 1060/2009, as amended) entrusts ESMA with the responsibility of the initial registration and the ongoing supervision of CRAs – while national supervisors maintain their competences on the use of ratings[257] – and provides the Authority

[249] For a more complete analysis of the decision and its implications see C. Di Noia and M. Gargantini, 'Unleashing the European Securities and Markets Authority: Governance and Accountability After the ECJ Decision on the Short Selling Regulation (Case C-270/12)' (2014) 15 *European Business Organization Law Review* 1.

[250] See the opposite opinion of the Advocate General, *ibid.*, para 54 *et seq.*

[251] On the relevance of the scope of this power and the discretion it entails see infra, text accompanying note 269.

[252] In other matters, direct enforcement outside the circumstances analysed in para 4.2.3.1 is allowed only upon delegation by national competent authorities (Art. 28(3)).

[253] Among the three ESAs, only ESMA has been granted with direct and exclusive supervisory powers.

[254] See supra note 234. See also N. Moloney, 'The European Securities and Markets Authority and Institutional Design for the EU Financial Market – A Tale of Two Competences: Part (2) Rules in Action' (2011) 12 *European Business Organization Law Review* 177, 211.

[255] Commission Communication COM(2009) 252 final, 11.

[256] See e.g. Art. 55–74 Reg. EMIR, entrusting ESMA with the supervision of trade repositories. Trade repositories do not pose significant risks in case of bankruptcy, since they operate as collectors and storage mechanisms of data concerning derivative transactions (either over-the-counter or cleared through a CCP) and provide aggregate data to the public and detailed information to qualified entities (such as ESMA itself and other regulators).

[257] N. Moloney, 'Reform or revolution? The Financial Crisis, EU Financial Markets Law, and The European Securities and Markets Authority' (2011) 60 *International and Comparative Law*

with a wide range of supervisory tools including requests for information and the power to conduct investigations and on-site inspections (Article 23b, 23c and 23d).[258] ESMA supervisory powers in the field of credit rating are accompanied by enhanced accountability towards the EU institutions, since an *ad hoc* annual report is prepared on the supervisory measures[259] adopted under CRA Regulation, including fines and periodic payments (Article 36a and 36b) imposed for violations of the applicable rules (Article 21(6)).[260]

In analysing of ESMA relationship with the Commission, it is worth highlighting the regulatory framework for the application of such measures, as the mechanism is likely to represent a model if similar powers are conferred on ESMA in the future – an analogous set of rules applies for the supervision of trade repositories (Article 64 Reg. EMIR). While according to the initial regulation proposal the Commission would have maintained the power to apply penalties, the final Regulation entrusts ESMA with this task. However, in order to comply with the restrictions imposed by the *Meroni* doctrine,[261] the Regulation provides a complete list of the possible infringements (Annex III) and the criteria to be followed to select the supervisory measure and to set the Level of the pecuniary sanction (including a catalogue of aggravating and mitigating factors – Annex IV).[262] As a result, a very narrow – albeit not negligible – discretion is left to ESMA, whose main task therefore consists in the ascertainment of the relevant facts, rather than in the calibration of the applicable sanction.

Quarterly 521, 528.

258 According to Regulation (EU) No 513/2011, all powers and responsibilities concerning supervision and enforcement with respect to CRAs have moved to ESMA from 1 July 2011.

259 Supervisory measures for infringements include, e.g., temporary prohibitions from issuing a rating, suspensions of the use of credit ratings for regulatory purposes throughout the EU, and withdrawal of registration (Art. 24).

260 See ESMA, *Credit Rating Agencies Annual Report 2012* (ESMA/2013/308). A thematic work plan is also prepared (ESMA, *2013 CRA Supervision and Policy Work Plan* (ESMA/2013/87)).

261 See para 5.1 below.

262 See R.G. Alcubilla and J.R. Del Pozo, *Credit rating Agencies on the Watch List*, Oxford University Press, Oxford 2012 111 *et seq.* and 119 *et seq.*

5. EVALUATING THE REGULATORY AND SUPERVISORY ARCHITECTURE: SOME REFORM PROPOSALS

5.1. IN THE SHADOW – OR IN THE LIGHT? – OF MERONI AND ROMANO. THE INSTITUTIONAL TENSIONS FRAMING THE POWERS OF ESMA

Thus far, the analysis has shown how ESMA is held accountable towards the EU institutions and other stakeholders through a wide array of techniques, which operate both on a structural (governance) and on a functional (procedural) basis. However, in other instances, the normative tools do not fit into the category of accountability, that necessarily refers to control over the exercise of delegated powers, but rather show limitations in the delegation itself that are imposed by the EU Treaties, as interpreted by the CJEU.[263] Overall, the emerging picture is that of an Authority which enjoys a multitude of significant powers – in particular if compared with CESR's – but has limited autonomy in some key areas, especially in the regulatory sphere.[264]

The CJEU jurisprudence has indeed played a crucial role in shaping the relationship between ESMA and the Commission. The *Meroni* decision[265] has *inter alia*[266] established that powers may be delegated from the Commission to other EU bodies only if this does not entail any conferral of discretion amounting to actual policymaking. In the Court's wording, delegation of powers "can only relate to clearly defined executive powers". If, on the contrary, the delegated entity enjoyed a wide margin of discretion entailing the "execution of actual economic

---

263 For ESMA, as well as for the ESAs in general, the high level of accountability is not matched by an equal independence. For a quantitative analysis see D. Masciandaro et al., 'Exploring the Governance of the New European Banking Authority – A Case for Harmonization?' (2011) 7 *Journal of Financial Stability* 204, 210 ("the score for accountability (…) seems excessively high given the modest level of the Authority's independence"). See also DG Internal Policies (European Parliament), *Review of the New European System of Financial Supervision (ESFS). Part 1*, supra note 40, p. 47.

264 For a similar assessment of EU agencies in general see C. Scott, 'Agencies for European Regulatory Governance: A Regimes Approach' in D. Geradin et al. (eds.), *Regulation through Agencies in the EU. A New Paradigm of European Governance*, Edward Elgar, Cheltenham 2005, p. 79. On ESMA, see C. Di Noia and M. Gargantini, 'Unleashing the European Securities and Markets Authority: Governance and Accountability After the ECJ Decision on the Short Selling Regulation (Case C-270/12)', supra note 250.

265 ECJ, Case C-9/56, *Meroni & Co., Industrie Metallurgiche, SpA v. High Authority of the European Coal and Steel Community*, 13.06.1958 (Meroni Decision), 152.

266 Other important principles set by the decision are that "a delegation of power cannot be presumed" (*Meroni* decision, supra note 267, 151), but must be explicitly stated, and that the delegated entity cannot be entrusted with "powers different from those which the delegating authority itself received under the treaty". Hence, the need arises to ensure that the accountability tools to which the delegating institution is subject still apply to the delegated entity (*ibid.*, 149 *et seq.*).

policy", then the institutional equilibrium of powers enshrined into the Treaties would be breached, as no legislative or discretional executive power is granted to bodies other than the EU institutions.[267] Furthermore, according to the ECJ decision rendered in *Romano*,[268] these bodies may not be empowered to adopt acts "having the force of law".[269] Both decisions, and *Meroni* in particular, are still considered "good law" by the majority of scholars and, most important, by the Commission[270] and the other EU institutions.

When weighing the actual relevance of *Meroni*, some consideration shall be given to the main concern that apparently drove the judges at the time the decision was rendered, i.e. the need to ensure that no substantial exercise of power could escape the judicial review of the CJEU. Before the Lisbon Treaty was adopted, no review of legality was explicitly[271] envisaged for acts passed by bodies other than the EU institutions, so that any substantial transfer of powers would have deprived the persons concerned of the standing to sue with regard to delegated acts.[272] However, new Article 263 and 267 TFEU now cover acts of bodies, offices, and agencies of the Union, too, and the rationale for ensuring legal protection to natural and legal persons within the EU appears much less of a concern. Therefore, the relevance of *Meroni* nowadays mainly depends on the fact that it reflects the perspective that agencies are executive or quasi-regulatory bodies detached from the Commission, the central EU administrative body, and that delegated policymaking faces the limitations set by the Treaties, as made clear by Article

267 T. Tridimas, 'Financial Supervision and Agency Power: Reflections on ESMA' supra note 8, p. 61.

268 ECJ, Case C-98/80, *Giuseppe Romano v Institut national d'assurance maladie-invalidité*, 14.05.1981, para 20.

269 In other languages, the decision rather refers to acts having a normative nature (P. Shammo, 'The European Securities and Markets Authority: Lifting the Veil on the Allocation of Powers', supra note 8, 1892 *et seq.*; M. Chamon, 'EU agencies between *Meroni* and *Romano* or the devil and the deep blue sea' (2011) 48 *Common Market Law Review* 1055, 1064). As opposed to *Meroni*, *Romano* involved delegation of powers by the Council and the European Parliament. For the continuing relevance of Romano see Advocate General's opinion in case C-270/12, supra note 8, para 84.

270 E. Chiti, 'An important part of the EU's institutional machinery: features, problems and perspectives of European agencies', supra note 87, 1421 *et seq.*; T. Tridimas, 'Financial Supervision and Agency Power: Reflections on ESMA' supra note 8, p. 63. See also e.g. the Impact Assessment accompanying the proposal for Regulation (EU) No 513/2011 (SEC(2010) 678), 2 June 2010, 13 and 30.

271 Judicial review of administrative acts adopted by non-institutional bodies was deemed admissible under the case-law of the CJEU (Case T-411/06, *Sogelma v. European Agency for Reconstruction (EAR)*, 08.10.2008, para 36 *et seq.*), but the Lisbon Treaty has removed residual doubts (H.C.H. Hofmann, G.C. Rowe and A.H. Türk, *Administrative Law and Policy of the European Union*, supra note 122, p. 801; L. Coutron, 'L'infiltration des garanties du procès équitable dans le procédures non juridictionnelles' in C. Picheral (ed.), *Le droit à un procès équitable au sens de droit de l'Union européenne*, Anthemis, Limal 2012, p. 181 *et seq*).

272 See *Meroni* decision, supra note 267, 152. On the importance of judicial review as a rationale of *Meroni* see M. Chamon, 'EU Agencies: Does the *Meroni* Doctrine Make Sense' (2010) 17 *Maastricht Journal of European And Comparative Law* 281, 297.

290 and 291 TFEU.[273] This perspective hinges upon the nature of EU institutions as entities entrusted with powers assigned by Member States under the Treaties,[274] so that sub-delegation should be allowed within the limits set by the same treaties. Some scholars have stressed that, in the case of the ESAs, *Meroni* is not pertinent because delegation is actually made by (authorities within) Member States, rather than by the Commission,[275] a process which makes the Europeanization of competences easier because of the involvement of national supervisors within the agencies, or because delegated powers are not always clearly conferred on the Commission by the Treaties.[276] Notwithstanding this line of reasoning, the rationale of the decision is still generally deemed applicable on a basis we deem convincing, as according to the Treaties the said powers would be in principle granted to one of the EU institutions,[277] and only in a subsequent logical – albeit not chronological – moment, can they be conferred on the agencies.[278] On the contrary, conferral of executive powers entailing wide discretion on bodies other than the EU institutions – or, one might even argue, other than the Commission[279] – would surreptitiously amend the Treaties by way of secondary legislation.[280]

Similarly, it has also been stressed that *Meroni* is already repeatedly violated by the founding Regulations of many EU agencies, which are entrusted with tasks

---

273 See P. Craig, *EU Administrative Law*, supra note 3, p. 154 *et seq.*; H. Hofmann and A. Morini, 'Constitutional aspects of the pluralisation of the EU executive through "agencification"', supra note 171, 442.

274 See also, for a more flexible stance, G. Majone, 'Delegation of Regulatory Powers in a Mixed Polity', supra note 17, 328.

275 See e.g. D. Geradin, 'The Development of European Regulatory Agencies: What the EU Should Learn from American Experience', supra note 74, 10; for a review P. Shammo, 'The European Securities and Markets Authority: Lifting the Veil on the Allocation of Powers', supra note 8, 1893. The point is also raised by the Advocate General's opinion in C-270/12, supra note 8, (para 6 and 90–1), which however concludes that *Meroni* still applies, with a view to protecting the EU institutional equilibrium (see infra text accompanying note 328).

276 See e.g. E. Chiti, 'An important part of the EU's institutional machinery: features, problems and perspectives of European agencies', supra note 87, 1422.

277 The greater flexibility that the ECJ has adopted when assessing the EU institutional balance (see E. Chiti, 'An important part of the EU's institutional machinery: features, problems and perspectives of European agencies', supra note 87, 1423 *et seq.*; for further references see also P. Shammo, 'The European Securities and Markets Authority: Lifting the Veil on the Allocation of Powers', supra note 8, 1894), although well-grounded in the lack of a sharp separation of powers within the EU (G. Majone, 'Delegation of Regulatory Powers in a Mixed Polity', supra note 17, 323 *et seq.*), cannot therefore be easily invoked in order to restrict *Meroni*, because the issue at stake is, rather than the position of an institution *vis-à-vis* the others, the conferral of powers to one institution in particular, namely the Commission, under the Treaties (Art. 17(1) TEU).

278 Convincingly, J-P. Schneider, 'A Common Framework for Decentralized EU Agencies and the *Meroni* Doctrine', supra note 119, 37 *et seq.*; P. Shammo, 'The European Securities and Markets Authority: Lifting the Veil on the Allocation of Powers', supra note 8, 1894.

279 In line with the principle of the unity and integrity of the executive functions: see supra note 43. For a convincing critique see E. Chiti, 'An important part of the EU's institutional machinery: features, problems and perspectives of European agencies', supra note 87, 1441.

280 See also A. Neergaard, 'European Supervisory Authorities. A New Model for the Exercise of Power in the European Union?', supra note 7, 609 *et seq.*

going well beyond a pure executive function;[281] the same line of reasoning also highlights that the Court of First Instance (now General Court) has already recognised, without deeming it unlawful, the attribution of similar powers to EU agencies.[282] However, although the evolution of administrative governance inevitably pushes towards the enlargement of independent agencies' powers, it should also be stressed that the new trends do not entail the conferral of any discretion with regard to economic policy, as no balance of rival interests is performed by the EU agency,[283] at least formally, or is explicitly or implicitly allowed by the CJEU decisions.[284]

The continuing relevance of the traditional CJEU case-law,[285] not only for executive agencies,[286] has been at stake in the action brought on June 2012 by the United Kingdom against the EU Parliament and the Council questioning the legality of Article 28 Reg. (EU) No 236/2012 on short selling, which allows ESMA to take *ad hoc* measures limiting short selling and other equivalent practices when required

---

281 M. Chamon, 'EU Agencies: Does the *Meroni* Doctrine Make Sense', supra note 274, 293; D. Curtin and R. Dehousse, 'European Union agencies: tipping the balance?' in M. Busuioc et al. (eds.), *The agency phenomenon in the European Union*, Manchester University Press, Manchester 2012, p. 198 *et seq.*

282 M. Chamon, 'EU Agencies: Does the *Meroni* Doctrine Make Sense', supra note 274, 294, and M. Chamon, 'EU agencies between *Meroni* and *Romano* or the devil and the deep blue sea', supra note 271, 1059, referring to the decision rendered in the Case T-187/06, *Schräder v. Community Plant Variety Office (CPVO)*, 2008. The decision is also noteworthy because it clearly sets the limit of judicial review of administrative decisions involving technical appreciations. See also H.C.H. Hofmann, G.C. Rowe and A.H. Türk, *Administrative Law and Policy of the European Union*, supra note 122, p. 244.

283 For a different opinion see T. Tridimas, 'Financial Supervision and Agency Power: Reflections on ESMA' supra note 8, p. 65 (ESMA arbitrates between conflicting public interests because it arbitrates conflicting interests of national supervisory authorities).

284 The *Schräder* decision was rendered in a case involving the refusal by the Community Plant Variety Office (CPVO) to acknowledge the existence of a new plant variety for which a right was sought; although the evaluation performed by the CPVO on similar applications may result in wide technical appreciation, it does not amount to any sort of policy discretion. For a similar distinction see P. Shammo, *EU Prospectus Law*, supra note 207, p. 33 *et seq.*; P. Craig, *EU Administrative Law*, supra note 3, p. 174. On conflicting objectives in regulators' activity see OECD, *Principles for the Governance of Regulators – Public Consultation Draft*, supra note 17, p. 25.

285 See E. Chiti, 'An important part of the EU's institutional machinery: features, problems and perspectives of European agencies', supra note 87, 1421; S. Griller and A. Orator, 'Everything under control? The "way forward" for European agencies in the footsteps of the Meroni doctrine' (2010) 35 *European Law Review* 3, 20; P. Craig, *EU Administrative Law*, supra note 3, p. 155, all referring *inter alia* to C-301/02, *Tralli v. ECB*, 26.05.2005, and T-369/94 and 85/85, *DIR International Film and others v. Commission*, 19.02.1998, as case-law confirming the validity of *Meroni*.

286 See Art. 6(1) Council Regulation (EC) No 58/2003. Executive agencies are entrusted with tasks relating to the mere implementation of EU programs, with the exclusion of discretionary powers. These latter may instead be conferred upon regulatory (or decentralised) agencies, to which the ESAs belong. While "executive agencies are directly dependent on the Commission, and exclusively accountable to it", regulatory agencies "operate under a management or supervisory board composed by Member States' representatives and some representatives of the Commission" (Advocate General's opinion C-270/12, supra note 8, para 21).

by the need to safeguard the financial stability of the Union.[287] The UK's plea was mainly grounded on alleged violation of the *Meroni* and *Romano* decisions. As for the former, it argued that ESMA enjoys excessive discretion with respect to the evaluation of the triggering events,[288] the selection of the measures to adopt, and the scope of application. As for *Romano*, the UK challenged the nature of the measures arguing that the conditions set by ESMA to limit the acquisition of net short positions may have the force of law to the extent that they are addressed to a wide set of market participants and concern an equally wide array of financial instruments.

As we mentioned, the ECJ has dismissed the action in its entirety.

The Court has clearly established that Meroni is still good law. Therefore even though nowadays the framework for challenging EU bodies' decisions is clear, as opposed to what happened at the time Meroni was released (para 43), *Meroni's dictum* still applies (para 45–53).

The Court has stated that the powers available to ESMA are precisely identified in the Level 1 and Level 2 Regulations and subject to judicial review in the light of the objectives established by the three EU institutions which delegated those powers to ESMA (Para 53–54).

For example, ESMA measures are subject to the condition that no competent national authority has taken effective measures to address the threat. ESMA must also ensure that such measures do not not have a detrimental effect on the efficiency of financial markets, including by reducing liquidity in those markets or creating uncertainty for market participants. Furthermore, ESMA must respect some procedures like consultation with the ESRB and notification to national competent authorities.

---

287 Case C-270/12, supra note 8. See also supra text accompanying note 246.

288 But see the Level 2 measures further detailing the circumstances where a threat is posed to the orderly functioning and integrity of financial market (Art. 24(3) Regulation (EU) No 918/2012). It is also worth stressing that, although ESMA technical discretion is undoubtedly wide, the objective of the measures to be adopted is only the safeguarding of the financial stability, so ESMA' decisions do not seem to entail any policymaking (in general, W. Weiss, 'Agencies Versus Networks: From Divide to Convergence in the Administrative Governance in the EU', supra note 206, 58; see also the Advocate General's opinion, para 94 *et seq.*). The discretion amounts only to deciding whether short selling bans may or may not, in specific market conditions, have net positive outcomes, in light of the highly debatable global effects of such measures on liquidity and volatility (see e.g. M. Clifton and M. Snape, *The Effect of Short-Selling Restrictions on Liquidity: Evidence from the London Stock Exchange* (2008) <www.londonstockexchange.com> accessed 09.10.2014; A. Beber and M. Pagano, 'Short-Selling Bans around the World: Evidence from the 2007–09 Crisis' (2013) 68 *Journal of Finance* 343; E. Avgouleas, 'A New Framework for the Global Regulation of Short Sales, Why Prohibition is Inefficient and Disclosure Insufficient' (2010) 15 *Stanford Journal of Law* 376).

Moreover, the Court, interpreting *Romano*, states that, as the TFEU expressly permits EU bodies, offices and agencies to adopt acts of general application, ESMA is also entitled to adopt such acts provided that the conditions set out in *Meroni* are complied with (para 66). In reviewing both *Meroni* and *Romano*, the ECJ seems to adopt a single standard when evaluating the latitude of ESMA powers – including discretion under *Meroni* and general applicability under Romano.

5.2. EVALUATION OF EFFICIENCY. RULEMAKING

As the previous analysis shows, the ESAs are, within the plethora of EU agencies, among those which have been granted the most extensive powers. However, commentators tend to consider that the existing architecture, while improving the previous system, is far from perfect.[289] According to this view, European authorities should enjoy wider autonomy in their rulemaking activity[290] and greater discretion in the application of penalties.[291] A similar evolution would indeed render ESMA more similar to the traditional model followed by national independent authorities,[292] and it appears that the accountability mechanisms in place under Reg. 1095/2010 are adequate to support an increased level of autonomy.[293] We evaluate in this par. whether the ESFS should be improved in its rulemaking functions and suggest in par. 5.2.2 some reform proposals, which in our opinion could fit EU primary law as interpreted by the ECJ (par. 5.2.3). Parr. 5.3.1–2 provide a similar analysis for supervisory powers.

---

289 According to E. Wymeersch, 'The European Financial Supervisory Authorities or ESAs', supra note 70, p. 238, the current system is "untenable" in the long run.

290 See in general G. Majone, 'Delegation of Regulatory Powers in a Mixed Polity', supra note 17, 332; D. Geradin, 'The Development of European Regulatory Agencies: What the EU Should Learn from American Experience', supra note 74, 16. For a more positive view with reference to the ESAs see C. Di Noia and M.C. Furlò, 'The New Structure of Financial Supervision in Europe: What's Next?', p. 184.

291 E.g. E. Ferran, 'Understanding the New Institutional Architecture of EU Financial Market Supervision', supra note 119, p. 142; N. Moloney, 'The European Securities and Markets Authority and Institutional Design for the EU Financial Market – A Tale of Two Competences: Part (1) Rule-Making' supra note 9, 78; N. Moloney, 'The European Securities and Markets Authority and Institutional Design for the EU Financial Market – A Tale of Two Competences: Part (2) Rules in Action', supra note 256, 222, who however also cautions against the risks of an excessive centralisation of financial supervision.

292 European Agencies cannot be equated to national independent authorities because they lack independence from the Commission (E. Chiti, 'An important part of the EU's institutional machinery: features, problems and perspectives of European agencies', supra note 87, 1399). As opposed to what Chiti stresses (*ibid.*, 1400 *et seq.*), we believe that stakeholder involvement – which is widely resorted to by independent authorities at national level: see e.g. Financial Conduct Authority (FCA), Corporate governance of the Financial Conduct Authority, April 2013, 4 and 37; Sec. 9 and 10 UK Financial Services and Markets Act 2000, as amended – does not compromise independence (see also supra text accompanying note 28), instead.

293 See supra note 263.

Opinions supporting increased discretionary powers for ESMA and the other ESAs in their rulemaking functions have merits. Enhanced autonomy would avoid duplication of work and, therefore, would facilitate concentration of the available skilled resources within a single entity.[294] In contrast, the existing division of roles between ESMA and the Commission in the adoption of technical standards prevents any direct judicial accountability for ESMA, which formally only finalises a preparatory act,[295] and focuses judicial review only on the Commission. That is problematic given that the Commission might simply rubber-stamp draft technical standards whose substance has been determined by ESMA, a separate entity endowed with better technical expertise on the topic. In order to avoid formal and automatic endorsement – the same opinion goes on – the Commission should hire further skilled staff, thus calling into question the basis for outsourcing some administrative functions to external entities.[296] Moreover, a simplified architecture for the adoption of quasi-regulatory measures and for the exercise of direct supervisory powers against market participants could streamline the administrative process, making it quicker and less prone to political bargaining – and, possibly, to turf wars – involving the three EU institutions.

The complex procedure established by Article 17(4) Reg. 1095/2010 and the regulation of quasi-regulatory functions well illustrate these points. In both cases there is a duplication of tasks for ESMA, which is directly involved with the interested parties and, when applicable, with the stakeholders, and for the Commission, which in order to substantially fulfil its role must repeat, at least in part, the evaluations already made by ESMA. The transition towards a new supervisory architecture therefore still looks incomplete. The current framework is indeed increasingly vertically centralized, as a consequence of transfers of powers from Member States to ESMA, but horizontally decentralised at its highest level, as a result of the significant powers retained by the EU institutions. This amplifies the costs of the administrative machinery and reduces the advantages of regulatory autonomy. As long as these arrangements are maintained, some of the benefits arising from the long-term credibility of independent authorities are lost,

294 See supra text accompanying note 12. However, it would be naïve to expect staff reductions by national competent authorities as a consequence of the increased centralization of regulatory and supervisory functions.

295 As a consequence, draft technical standards may be challenged neither under Art. 263 TFEU nor under Art. 60(1) Reg. 1095/2010 (supra note 123).

296 M. Chamon, 'EU Agencies: Does the *Meroni* Doctrine Make Sense', supra note 274, 292.

since the Commission, which is more prone to political pressure[297] and, reportedly, to lobbying activity,[298] may be exposed to problems of time inconsistency.[299]

On the other hand, the risk should not be neglected that an increased delegation of powers to ESMA could also have some side effects. Although regulatory competition is no panacea,[300] an agency having monopolistic access to quasi-normative instruments may pursue self-interested policies,[301] disregard innovation,[302] or indulge in excessive regulation,[303] either by establishing excessively restrictive measures when a delegation of powers is needed under Article 290 and 291 TFEU, or by adopting non-binding standards, thus charging national supervisors and market participants with a "comply or explain" obligation.[304] Moreover, the disappearance of any regulatory competition among national authorities – and between these latter and ESMA – as a consequence of the single EU-wide rulebook would further exacerbate this risk.[305] Most importantly ESMA's possible perverse incentives would not be counterbalanced,

---

297 Especially in the wake of financial crises, independent authorities may also suffer, although to a lesser extent, from impulsive reactions that can break previous supervisory or regulatory patterns (L. Enriques, "Regulators' Response to the Current Crisis and the Upcoming Reregulation of Financial Markets: One Reluctant Regulator's View', supra note 21).

298 See E. Ferran, *Building an EU Securities Market*, supra note 81, p. 104.

299 Although particularly dangerous for monetary policy (see supra note 10), sudden variations in regulatory policy are also unwelcome by investors. For an example, compare C. McCreevy, *The future of regulation*, Reform Scotland's Spring Lecture, Edinburgh, 13.05.2009 <http://europa.eu/rapid/press-release_SPEECH-09-242_en.htm> accessed 13.11.2013 (policymakers should not swing the pendulum of re-regulation too far, nor should they fall prey to populist tendencies; the Commission will not adopt regulation that may encourage risk aversion) with M. Barnier – *Speech at the European Parliament* – ECON Committee, 31.01.2010 – ("no market, no financial player, no product, no territory should be able to escape anymore relevant regulation"). See also E. Ferran, 'Crisis-driven regulatory reform: where in the world is the EU going?' in E. Ferran et al. (eds.), *The Regulatory Aftermath of the Global Financial Crisis*, Cambridge University Press, Cambridge 2012, p. 81.

300 E. Chiti, 'An important part of the EU's institutional machinery: features, problems and perspectives of European agencies', supra note 87, 1426 ("it is not demonstrated that administrative competition among national authorities induces the latter to modify their practice in relation to the mobility of the regulatees").

301 E. Ferran, *Building an EU Securities Market*, supra note 81, p. 91.

302 J.R. Macey, 'Administrative Agency Obsolescence and Interest Group Formation: A Case Study of the SEC at Sixty' (1994) 15 *Cardozo Law Review* 909, 934.

303 Excessive regulation may also serve self-interested strategies to the extent that it responds to the misplaced desire to exclude frauds regardless of the costs, as a consequence of the skewed public perception of the agencies' performance (G. Gil, 'Independent Financial Regulators' (2007) Quarter III /2007 *CNMV Bulletin* 35, 47 *et seq.*). See also supra note 23.

304 See e.g. S.J. Choi and A.C. Pritchard, 'Behavioral Economics and the SEC', supra note 89, 45; L. Enriques and T.H. Tröger, 'Issuer Choice in Europe' (2008) 67 *Cambridge Law Journal* 521, 550. In the US, where a single regulator with weak competition constraints is in place, the issue of regulatory costs, and of the accountability mechanisms that could curb overregulation, is still an open one: see the proposal for a SEC Regulatory Accountability Act (H.R. 1062) adopted by the House of Representatives on 17 May 2013 (enhancing the impact assessment procedure to be followed by the SEC before passing new rules and imposing a review of the regulations in force every five years according to a specific assessment plan).

305 L. Enriques and T.H. Tröger, 'Issuer Choice in Europe', supra note 306, 539.

at the EU level, by the most straightforward accountability mechanism, namely the designation (and renewal) of office holders in top-level positions within the Authority.[306] That is because the Commission has no say in the appointment of the members of the Board of Supervisors, which in this respect remain accountable to their national governments.[307] Although the head of a local regulator could not be deemed responsible at Member State level for having pursued the ESMA institutional objectives to the detriment of national interests,[308] she would encounter no risk of being removed – or not being renewed – should she choose to satisfy local demands, since Member States would have no incentives to substitute those who are performing well from a national perspective at the expense of full compliance with Article 42 Reg. (EU) 1095/2010.[309]

5.2.1. *Reform proposals for rulemaking functions: centralization vs. monopolization*

The side effects of having a single regulator in place may be partially avoided by retaining slight competition between ESMA and the Commission. A potential challenge to ESMA monopolistic power could in fact be beneficial to the extent that it limits the side effects of having a single regulator in place, such as reduced incentives to reach a higher level of efficiency; after all, the Commission can already reject or amend technical standards "in very restricted and extraordinary circumstances", so the departure of ESMA model from the pattern of traditional independent authorities is not very pronounced in this respect.[310]

A more effective system could be one based on tacit approval – rather than express endorsement – by the Commission, which would retain the ability

306 Proposals for a new appointment mechanism applicable to all the EU agencies, which would give equal space to Council and Commission appointees within the authorities and which would not ensure Member States representation, have been abandoned (compare the Commission's Draft Interinstitutional Agreement on the operating framework for the European regulatory agencies (COM(2005) 59 final), 25 February 2005, at 7, with the 2012 Interinstitutional Joint Statement, at 5).

307 P. Craig, *EU Administrative Law*, supra note 3, p. 162 and 173; M. Chamon, 'EU Agencies: Does the *Meroni* Doctrine Make Sense', supra note 274, 301 *et seq*.

308 ESMA (2011/009), supra note 4, p. 11; E. Wymeersch, 'The European Financial Supervisory Authorities or ESAs', supra note 70, p. 241 *et seq*.

309 See P. Shammo, *EU Prospectus Law*, supra note 207, p. 39 *et seq*. See also D. Geradin, 'The Development of European Regulatory Agencies: What the EU Should Learn from American Experience', supra note 74, 29 *et seq*.; M. Shapiro, 'Independent agencies', supra note 206, p. 117; IMF (International Monetary Fund), 'European Union: Publication of Financial Sector Assessment Program Documentation -- Technical Note on Issues in Transparency and Accountability' (2013) *IMF Country Report* No. 13/65, p. 11.

310 During ESMA existence so far, the Commission has refused to endorse draft technical standards in some circumstances (see supra note 178-9). Moreover, although departure from Level 2 technical advices and/or draft implementing measures is not unknown (*ibid*., 76), it remains an exception (E. Ferran, 'Crisis-driven regulatory reform: where in the world is the EU going?', supra note 301, p. 73 *et seq*.).

to veto and/or modify draft technical standards, and possibly non-binding measures, prepared by ESMA.[311] In other words, the Commission would enjoy a power comparable to a call option on the final step of the (quasi-regulatory or supervisory) administrative process,[312] substantially in line with its current position. At the same time, the process would be streamlined whenever – as the case will ordinarily be – no need for intervention arises, because the option would be exercised only when "in the money", namely when there is room for improving the quality of regulation. The promptness of the review could also take advantage of a system of enhanced monitoring by means of one or more signalling devices ("fire alarms")[313] that could flag regulatory or supervisory measures that may be problematic, thus facilitating the Commission's role as a "police patrol".[314] Within this context, the SMSG might enjoy a special status if it were entrusted with the power to manifest its scepticism about new developments. One or more individual members of the Group can also play a similar albeit informal role, with a view to voice opposition by a dissatisfied constituency.[315]

The mechanism would partially[316] resemble the system envisaged by the Congressional Review Act, which mandates (executive and) independent authorities to submit the rules they have adopted, before they can take effect, to

[311] Commission's approval of technical standards by "non-opposition" was originally suggested in the Communication on European Financial Supervision (COM(2009) 252 final), 9.

[312] For a general theory see I. Ayres, *Optional Law. The Structure of Legal Entitlements*, Chicago University Press, Chicago 2005, p. 2 *et seq.* According to another classification, the Commission's option could be a "switcher", i.e. a system adopted to shift the regulatory power from an entity to another (P. Shammo, *EU Prospectus Law*, supra note 207, p. 41 *et seq.*).

[313] M. McCubbins and T. Schwartz, 'Congressional Oversight Overlooked: Police Patrols Versus Fire Alarms' (1984) 28 *American Journal of Political Science* 165. See also D.B. Spence, 'Administrative Law and Agency Policy-Making: Rethinking the Positive Theory of Political Control', supra note 12, 415; S. Rose-Ackerman, *Public Choice, Public Law and Public Policy*, supra note 198, p. 7 *et seq.*; D.S. Rubenstein, '"Relative Checks": Towards Optimal Control of Administrative Power', supra note 50, 2209 *et seq.*; K. Datla and R. Revesz, 'Deconstructing Independent Agencies (And Executive Agencies)' (2012) *NYU School of Law, Public Law Research Paper* No. 12–44, p. 42 *et seq.*

[314] Adoption of *ex post* measures of accountability (see D.B. Spence, 'Administrative Law and Agency Policy-Making: Rethinking the Positive Theory of Political Control', supra note 12, 415 *et seq.*; P. Shammo, 'The European Securities and Markets Authority: Lifting the Veil on the Allocation of Powers', supra note 8, 1903), as opposed to *ex ante* controls, would provide more flexibility to the system, avoiding Commission enrolment when this would only delay the adoption of normative measures.

[315] D.S. Rubenstein, '"Relative Checks": Towards Optimal Control of Administrative Power', supra note 50, 2209.

[316] While the Congress power increases the democratic legitimacy of the administrative act, a similar role conferred upon the EU Commission would ensure legitimacy of ESMA acts under the institutional equilibrium envisaged by the Treaties.

the US Congress.[317] Where the relevant provision qualifies as "major rule",[318] a sixty-day period is granted before the entry into force.[319] The US Congress is then enabled to adopt a disapproval resolution, invalidating the said rule, the President in turn being able to veto the disapproval unless it is passed with a supermajority quorum.[320] If compared with the US system, the mechanism we conjecture might reach a higher level of effectiveness, as the veto power granted to the Commission would not face the limitations that affect *ex post* controls such as those performed by the US Congress, namely collective action problems[321] and filibustering by interested minorities.[322] For the same reason, the existing European Parliament's and Council's power to revoke the delegated power to adopt regulatory technical standards could not work as a perfect substitute of the Commission's role in counter-weighting a hypothetical monopolistic regulatory power of the ESMA. At the same time, unlike the US system where the President may step in only once the Congress has adopted a disapproval resolution, under the mechanism we suggest the veto power of the Council and the Parliament would not depend on an intervention by the Commission, and the legitimacy of the regulatory procedure *vis-à-vis* the TFEU would thus be preserved. In this context, the regulatory impact assessment under Articles 10(1) and 15(1) of the founding Regulation would enhance accountability towards the Commission, which has the skills required to evaluate the quality of the economic justifications submitted by ESMA.[323] Once more, this equilibrium may build upon the US experience – in which the Office of Information and Regulatory Affairs (OIRA) reviews the cost-benefit analysis of the federal executive agencies – while partially improving on it, since the absence of OIRA review for independent agencies, including the Securities and Exchange Commission, is regarded as a drawback of the US regulatory process.[324]

---

317 5 U.S.C., § 801 (a)(1)(A). Before the enactment of the Congressional Review Act, review of individual acts by the Congress had been judged unconstitutional in *Immigration and Naturalization Service v. Chadha*, 462 U.S. 919 (1983) (see 'The Mysteries of the Congressional Review Act' (2009) 122 *Harvard Law Review* 2162, 2164–5).

318 A "major rule" is, with some simplifications, a rule that according to the Office of Management and Budget may significantly affect the economy (5 U.S.C. 804(2)).

319 5 U.S.C., § 801 (a)(3)(A).

320 See 'The Mysteries of the Congressional Review Act', supra note 319, 2166.

321 D.B. Spence, 'Administrative Law and Agency Policy-Making: Rethinking the Positive Theory of Political Control', supra note 12, 436; see also supra note 12.

322 See D.S. Rubenstein, '"Relative Checks": Towards Optimal Control of Administrative Power', supra note 50, 2209.

323 The Impact Assessment Board may provide useful expertise. See also the EU Commission Communication on Impact Assessment (COM(2002) 276 final).

324 R.W. Hahn and C.R. Sunstein, 'A New Executive Order for Improving Federal Regulation? Deeper and Wider Cost-Benefit Analysis' (2002) 150 *University of Pennsylvania Law Review* 1489, 1496 and 1531 *et seq.*; D. Geradin, 'The Development of European Regulatory Agencies: What the EU Should Learn from American Experience', supra note 74, 44; K. Datla and R. Revesz, 'Deconstructing Independent Agencies (And Executive Agencies)', supra note 315, p. 5. For possible relevant developments in the US securities regulation see supra note 304.

5.2.2. *Feasibility according to the Meroni doctrine and the EU Treaties*

The solution we propose in par. 5.2.2 would inevitably push against the boundaries of the *Meroni* limitations, as it might marginalize the Commission – thus widening ESMA powers – by allowing the entry into force of technical standards in the absence of an explicit endorsement. However, we believe that granting a veto power to the Commission would still fit the institutional architecture set by the Treaties as interpreted by the CJEU jurisprudence.[325]

No problem arises if one adopts the view that the *Meroni* doctrine can now be relaxed because review by the CJEU is ensured for acts adopted by EU bodies as well as institutions, or because protection of the EU institutional equilibrium should be more flexibly interpreted.[326] However, as we have already highlighted, *Meroni* is still widely regarded as good law by the EU institutions, and the distinction between discretion in economic policy and technical appreciation still represents a guiding criterion for European jurisprudence when assessing the tasks of EU agencies.[327] According to the ECJ Advocate General, the new Articles 290 and 291 TFEU, while allowing direct attribution of powers by the legislature to an agency, do not remove the need to preserve the institutional balance within the EU. Therefore, the delegated power must be sufficiently specific and must not include policy decisions or value judgements.[328]

It is nonetheless true that the new institutional context, together with the presence of the Board of Appeal for the three ESAs,[329] lessens some of the concerns that were addressed in *Meroni*,[330] and therefore permits a flexible interpretation of its dictum. In particular, it has been convincingly posited that a power to veto the decisions taken by the delegated authority, or to refer the matter to the legislator, would preserve the Commission's prerogatives under the Treaties, as

325 See also E. Wymeersch, 'The European Financial Supervisory Authorities or ESAs', supra note 70, p. 238 (the Lisbon instruments, such as revoking the delegation, could also apply to the relationship between the Commission and the financial authorities).

326 See supra notes 272 and 276.

327 See supra note 270.

328 Advocate General's opinion C-250/12, paras 88 and 92 *et seq.*

329 On the relevance of internal review mechanisms in light of *Meroni* see ; S. Griller and A. Orator, 'Everything under control? The "way forward" for European agencies in the footsteps of the Meroni doctrine', supra note 287, 29.

330 D. Geradin, 'The Development of European Regulatory Agencies: What the EU Should Learn from American Experience', supra note 74, 15; J-P. Schneider, 'A Common Framework for Decentralized EU Agencies and the *Meroni* Doctrine', supra note 119, 40 and 43; E. Chiti, 'An important part of the EU's institutional machinery: features, problems and perspectives of European agencies', supra note 87, 1422 *et seq.*; S. Griller and A. Orator, 'Everything under control? The "way forward" for European agencies in the footsteps of the Meroni doctrine', supra note 287, 29; P. Craig, *EU Administrative Law*, supra note 3, p. 176. See also the Advocate General's opinion C-250/12, para 72.

interpreted by the CJEU.[331] In the field of securities regulation, not only would this equilibrium be a legitimate solution, but, as our previous analysis shows, it might also represent an efficient device for providing ESMA with appropriate incentives.

If what has been argued thus far is correct, possible limitations to our suggestions could rather stem, on a general basis, from the interpretation of Articles 290 and 291 TFEU, which the Commission invoked during the preparation of the ESAs Regulations to question the delegation of quasi-regulatory powers.[332] One might in fact justifiably consider that mere "non-opposition" could bring sub-delegation too far, as it would deprive the Commission of the powers conferred by the Treaties.[333] In this case, an amendment to the EU treaties would be needed. At the same time, a much larger tension with the EU constitutional framework already descends form the constraints that the ESAs Regulations set for the Commission's intervention in the non-legislative rulemaking process. The bargaining mechanism set by Articles 10 and 15 in case full endorsement is refused and, more important, the possibility to question the draft measures only in exceptional circumstances and for limited reasons[334] substantially reduce the Commission's prerogatives. Therefore, however grounded this objection to a veto power mechanism may be,[335] it should in the first place deal with the legitimacy of the current system, rather than with the one we propose.

---

331 S. Griller and A. Orator, 'Everything under control? The "way forward" for European agencies in the footsteps of the Meroni doctrine', supra note 287, 27 *et seq*. See also supra note 311. For some critiques see however M. Chamon, 'EU Agencies: Does the *Meroni* Doctrine Make Sense', supra note 274, 292.

332 M. Busuioc, 'Rule-Making by the European Supervisory Authorities: Walking a Tight Rope', supra note 172, 117. After the enactment of the three ESAs, the statement is repeatedly reported in many Commission's legislative proposals (*ibid.*).

333 See e.g. A. Neergaard, 'European Supervisory Authorities. A New Model for the Exercise of Power in the European Union?', supra note 7, 627 ("a tacit endorsement does not seem sufficient to lead to that the act is adopted by the Commission").

334 Namely, incompatibility with EU law, breach of the proportionality principle and of the fundamental principles of the internal market (see supra note 171). This equilibrium between the Commission and the ESAs reflects the tension between the constitutional architecture and the institutional practice, which may sometime enlarge the powers conferred to the EU agency (H. Hofmann and A. Morini, 'Constitutional aspects of the pluralisation of the EU executive through "agencification"', supra note 171, 420 and 426).

335 See e.g. M. Chamon, 'EU agencies between *Meroni* and *Romano* or the devil and the deep blue sea', supra note 271, 1067 *et seq*; contra P. Shammo, 'The European Securities and Markets Authority: Lifting the Veil on the Allocation of Powers', supra note 8, 1884.

5.3. EVALUATION OF EFFICIENCY. SUPERVISION

A monopolistic exercise of powers may also negatively affect supervisory and non-mandatory normative measures such as guidelines and recommendations.[336] While some scholars have long advocated the creation of a single EU securities and exchange commission,[337] the risk has also been stressed that an excessive centralization of supervisory powers may have significant adverse consequences,[338] such as the loss of expertise developed through the years by adaptation to local peculiarities and the increase of systemic risk if the standardised supervisory approach proves flawed.[339]

Overall, ESMA role in financial supervision will mostly depend on its ability and willingness to adopt a proactive stance *vis-à-vis* the national regulators so as to either push towards a higher level of coordination, which would facilitate cross-border activities, or to allow for more flexibility in the practice of supervision, which would ensure some degree of competition and experimentation. Even though the architecture of the ESFS follows a hub-and-spoke model that centralizes rulemaking but remits supervision and implementation to the periphery,[340] ESMA ability to promote a common supervisory culture and to foster shared supervisory practices may bring in the long run a stricter alignment of the approaches adopted by competent authorities. In this respect, the precision of the opinions provided under Article 29 and the stringency of peer reviews according to Article 30 – whose results are however made public only if the relevant national authority so agrees[341] – will be key to set an appropriate level of coordination,[342]

---

336 We address guidelines and recommendations here because they fall outside the purview of Art. 290 and 291 TFEU and because they are important drivers of national supervision.

337 For a complete review see E. Wymeersch, 'The Structure of Financial Supervision in Europe: About Single, Twin Peaks and Multiple Financial Supervisors', supra note 67, 239 *et seq.*

338 A model explaining divergent implementation and justifying a flexible and decentralized approach to harmonized enforcement is developed by P. Nicolaides, 'The Political Economy of Multi-Tiered Regulation in Europe' (2004) 42 *Journal of Common Market Studies* 599.

339 N. Moloney, 'The European Securities and Markets Authority and Institutional Design for the EU Financial Market – A Tale of Two Competences: Part (2) Rules in Action', supra note 256, 186 *et seq*; P. Shammo, 'EU Day-to-Day Supervision or Intervention-based Supervision: Which Way Forward for the European System of Financial Supervision?', supra note 232, *passim*. See also, in general, R. Romano, 'Regulating in the Dark' (2012) *Yale Law & Economics Research Paper* No. 442.

340 Commission Communication COM(2009) 252 final, 9; E. Wymeersch, 'The European Financial Supervisory Authorities or ESAs', supra note 70, p. 235 *et seq.*

341 This limitation is playing a role in making peer reviews less effective, while a switch to independent reviews performed by ESMA itself was suggested (first by SMSG (2013/013), supra note 105, p. 6, and then by DG Internal Policies (European Parliament), *Review of the New European System of Financial Supervision (ESFS). Part 1*, supra note 40, pp. 100–101).

342 On the role of peer review processes see Búrca et al. (2013) (in the most advanced forms of transnational governance, peer reviews are not merely a platform for exchanging views among participants. Rather, they are an instrument for learning from diverse experiences and for determining whether solutions adopted by one or more participants are defensible).

depending on the concerned matter.[343] For instance, anecdotal and statistical[344] evidence shows that prospectus approval can be either a quick formality or a lengthy process, depending on the jurisdiction involved. Peer review, being a soft accountability tool,[345] has therefore been hitherto unable to curb divergences in some sensitive matters where the general approach to supervision is at stake.[346]

As far as supervision is concerned, the main difference between ESMA and a traditional authority lies in the fact that the intensity of the scrutiny relies on the inclination of the majority of the scrutinized entities,[347] whose representatives sit on the Board of Supervisors.[348] Therefore, the functions of ESMA can be exercised with variable intensity depending on the willingness of national authorities to either enter a game where they can export their supervisory practices,[349] with the risk of being also forced to import those of the others, or to maintain a leeway of discretion at national level.[350] By analogy with the unstable patterns characterising cartelists' conflicting incentives,[351] national authorities may be willing to endorse anticompetitive agreements while regaining autonomy when possible. A crucial factor in setting an equilibrium between these two extremes is the majority required for the adoption of decisions by the Board of Supervisors,[352] because the

343 The scope of review is wide, as it is not limited to supervisory practices but also involves the governance of supervisors (Art. 30) and their independence (Recital 41). See Partsch (2011), 46.

344 CESR, Report on the Supervisory Functioning of the Prospectus Directive and Regulation (CESR/07–225) (2007), 31.

345 A stricter approach might however be adopted in the future: N. Moloney, 'The European Securities and Markets Authority: a perspective from one year on', supra note 133, 80.

346 N. Moloney, 'The European Securities and Markets Authority and Institutional Design for the EU Financial Market – A Tale of Two Competences: Part (2) Rules in Action', supra note 256, 184.

347 Although the three ESAs cannot be properly defined as a supervisor of the supervisors (E. Wymeersch, 'The European Financial Supervisory Authorities or ESAs', supra note 70, p. 236), their statutory powers inevitably entail a scrutiny of national practices.

348 The ESAs maintain the strong intergovernmental feature of the pre-existing 3L3 committees (Partsch (2011), 48; in general, W. Weiss, 'Agencies Versus Networks: From Divide to Convergence in the Administrative Governance in the EU', supra note 206, 63).

349 See P. Shammo, 'EU Day-to-Day Supervision or Intervention-based Supervision: Which Way Forward for the European System of Financial Supervision?', supra note 232, 26 (the ESFS is likely to work effectively if national authorities challenge each other when necessary). See also N. Moloney, 'The European Securities and Markets Authority and Institutional Design for the EU Financial Market – A Tale of Two Competences: Part (1) Rule-Making' supra note 9, 71 *et seq.* (institutional consensus within ESMA is a fragile one, as authorities may want to break the equilibrium in order to establish their influence in the EU).

350 See N. Moloney, 'The European Securities and Markets Authority and Institutional Design for the EU Financial Market – A Tale of Two Competences: Part (2) Rules in Action', supra note 256, 214 *et seq.* Different equilibria may also be reflected in the latitude of delegation of tasks by the competent authorities to ESMA according to Art. 28 of the founding Regulation.

351 K.N. Hylton, *Antitrust Law. Economic Theory & Common Law Evolution*, Cambridge University Press, Cambridge 2003, p. 68 *et seq.*

352 P. Shammo, *EU Prospectus Law*, supra note 207, p. 40; P. Shammo, 'EU Day-to-Day Supervision or Intervention-based Supervision: Which Way Forward for the European System of Financial Supervision?', supra note 232, 12 *et seq.*

possibility to decide by qualified majority – e.g. for Level 3 acts[353] – or even by simple majority, as opposed to the consensus mechanism followed by CESR,[354] may increase the incidence of the authorities that are more willing to back up ESMA interventionism. This analytical framework might also work, at least in part, when supervision is centralized, as is the case for CRAs,[355] with regard to delegation of specific tasks to local authorities (Recital 15 and Article 30 Reg. (EU) No 1060/2009),[356] which allows slight decentralisation of direct supervision. Overall, although the position of competent authorities from major EU countries was reportedly overcome in some instances,[357] a first assessment of ESMA's work shows that the composition of the Board of Supervisors has chilled the exercise of supervisory functions, apparently because of the inherent conflict of interest affecting national supervisors' ole in ESMA's governance.[358]

In comparison with its role in the exercise of regulatory powers, here the Commission seems less at the centre of the stage, so that the relationship between ESMA independence and its accountability resembles more closely that of a traditional supervisor, in spite of the limitations imposed by the EU treaties as interpreted by the CJEU.[359] To be sure, the Commission's enforcement under Article 258 TFEU is more incisive, and direct intervention under Article 17, 18 and 19 is a last resort device,[360] but the mere possibility that ESMA initiative may result in a formal infringement procedure confers effectiveness to its recommendations.[361] At the same time, efficiency may take advantage of the fast track ensured by ESMA procedures. Moreover, ESMA enjoys greater autonomy in its coordinating functions under Article 29 and 30, as well as in some specific areas such as CRAs and short selling supervision,[362] where it is free to set the preferred intensity of restrictions to local authorities. Even taking into account the possibility of granting the Commission the power to raise concerns before

353 D. Fischer-Appelt, 'The European Securities and Markets Authority: the beginning of a powerful European securities authority?', supra note 138, 24.

354 However, the possibility to pass resolutions with the opposition of one or two members and, in case of disagreement, to resort to qualified majorities reduced hold-up problems (Art. 6 Charter of the Committee of European Securities Regulators (CESR/08–375d), September 2008).

355 See para 4.2.3.2. For some effects of the *Meroni* doctrine on supervision see supra text accompanying note 262.

356 R.G. Alcubilla and J.R. Del Pozo, *Credit rating Agencies on the Watch List*, supra note 264, p. 56.

357 DG Internal Policies (European Parliament), *Review of the New European System of Financial Supervision (ESFS). Part 1*, supra note 40, p. 34.

358 SMSG (2013/013), supra note 105, p. 7; DG Internal Policies (European Parliament), *Review of the New European System of Financial Supervision (ESFS). Part 1*, supra note 40, pp. 14–5.

359 See para 5.1.

360 N. Moloney, 'The European Securities and Markets Authority and Institutional Design for the EU Financial Market – A Tale of Two Competences: Part (2) Rules in Action', supra note 256, 202 and 212.

361 ESMA (2011/009), supra note 4, p. 5.

362 See supra text accompanying note 287.

the European Parliament and the Council if a decision is likely to violate EU law or contradict EU policy objectives,[363] reliance on the Commission as an effective counterbalancing force for ESMA excessive interventionism would be misplaced, considering the Commission's limited expertise in supervision and its natural tendency to foster Europeanization of local powers.

5.3.1. *Reform proposals for supervisory functions: integration vs. uniformity*

To the extent that the desired legislative outcome is a more integrated European supervision,[364] the most effective lever in the hand of the legislators would seem to be either a further centralization of supervisory functions or a revision of ESMA governance.[365] Conferral of wider direct supervisory powers might not be politically viable in the light of the consequences this might have on Member States' fiscal responsibility and would most likely require a Treaty amendment.[366] The governance revision would represent a feasible alternative leaving room for more flexibility and adaptation to local specificities. It should be aimed at reducing the influence of national regulators in the management, while leaving to the Board of Supervisors a monitoring role over the Authority's general conduct. Such equilibrium could be reached by shifting the barycentre of the governance to the Management Board,[367] which should also be reshaped as a body comprising independent members appointed by the EU institutions – e.g. by the Council upon non-binding opinion of the Parliament.[368] This would partly overcome the existing conflict of interests in the management of the Authority by national supervisors.

---

[363] As envisaged by the Roadmap agreed upon by the European institutions as a follow-up to their common approach on EU decentralized agencies (2012 Interinstitutional Joint Statement).

[364] Claims for further integration of EU supervision were first voiced at EU level by CESR, *Which supervisory tools for the EU securities markets? Preliminary Progress Report* (CESR/04-333f) ("Himalaya Report"), p. 10 *et seq.*

[365] See supra note 36.

[366] See supra note 234.

[367] This would also enhance the distinction between monitoring and managing functions (see L. Enriques and G. Hertig, 'Improving the Governance of Financial Supervisors', supra note 55, 367 *et seq.*).

[368] M. Lamandini, 'I regolamenti europei istitutivi del comitato per il rischio sistemico e delle autorità europea di vigilanza su assicurazioni, banche, strumenti finanziari mercati', supra note 129, 221; C. Di Noia and M.C. Furlò, 'The New Structure of Financial Supervision in Europe: What's Next?', p. 186 (both referring to the ECB model). For further examples see H. Hofmann and A. Morini, 'Constitutional aspects of the pluralisation of the EU executive through "agencification"', supra note 171, 437. See also SMSG (2013/013), supra note 105, p. 8; DG Internal Policies (European Parliament), *Review of the New European System of Financial Supervision (ESFS). Part 1*, supra note 40, pp. 14–15, 117; IMF (International Monetary Fund), 'European Union: Publication of Financial Sector Assessment Program Documentation – Technical Note on Issues in Transparency and Accountability', supra note 311, p. 11 (where publication of detailed minutes is also suggested in order to stress different views among Board members, thus reducing the incentives to be prone to national influence).

Either in the new governance we propose or as a consequence of the interplay among national authorities within the existing organization, greater interventionism in national supervision is likely to arise[369] at least in specific circumstances, such as in the aftermath of a financial turmoil or a serious default,[370] while the Commission is not likely to curb this tendency. Bearing this in mind, a possible way to improve the current architecture would be to ensure that ESMA has a duty to evaluate whether the supervisory practices it promotes (either by way of guidelines and recommendations or otherwise) should be regarded as the only admissible ones or, on the contrary, whether divergent approaches may reasonably be adopted upon request. When the latter is the case, deviations from the standard behaviour should be allowed under continuous monitoring by ESMA itself, in order to ensure that deviations do not result in any outright failure to fulfil the objectives set forth by Article 1(5) Regulation 1095/2010.[371] The entity of the minority opposing the adoption of guidelines within the Board of Supervisors and the position adopted by the SMSG or its constituencies might be proxies for the admissibility of deviations, thus fostering a system that would always ensure a more integrated supervision, but a more uniform one only when needed.[372]

This outcome would admittedly not be easy to reach, as it would entail a self-analysis by the competent authorities of the inherent limits of the supervisory tools they usually employ.[373] However, one of the most important lessons from the current financial crisis is the confirmation that supervisors, as well as market participants, face rationality constraints. A wise approach to regulation would be one that acknowledges that the wisdom of financial authorities is limited, because there are causal relationships in financial markets phenomena whose mechanisms are not yet understood, and are therefore unknown, as well as events which have not yet even been identified as possible future outcomes, thus

---

369 E. Ferran, 'Crisis-driven regulatory reform: where in the world is the EU going?', supra note 301, p. 48 *et seq.*

370 Interventionism may represent the biggest problem also at horizontal level (L. Enriques, "Regulators' Response to the Current Crisis and the Upcoming Reregulation of Financial Markets: One Reluctant Regulator's View', supra note 21), although in similar circumstances a slightly political-oriented body such as the Commission is unlikely to take a restrictive stance.

371 For a similar, albeit more articulated, proposal in the field of transnational banking regulation see R. Romano, 'Regulating in the Dark', supra note 341. Note that experimentation and diversity can also be beneficial outside prudential regulation, as a consequence of the need to adapt surveillance to the specificity of the local context and of the systemic consequences of financial market supervision (Arts. 21(2)(b) and 22–4 Reg. No 1095/2010).

372 See also E. Ferran, 'Crisis-driven regulatory reform: where in the world is the EU going?', supra note 301, p. 51 *et seq.* (warning against the risk that supervisory judgment by local authorities within the EU may be displaced in the future).

373 For some suggestions on how to address these new supervisory challenges see J. Black, 'Restructuring Global and EU Financial Regulation: Character, Capacities, and Learning' in E. Wymeersch et al. (eds.), *Financial Regulation and Supervision. A Post-Crisis Analysis*, Oxford University Press, Oxford 2012, p. 43 *et seq.* See also E. Wymeersch, 'Europe's New Financial Regulatory Bodies', supra note 4, 449 (guidance and recommendations may prove particularly useful in fields where formal rulemaking would create unpredictable externalities).

being unknowable.[374] Moreover, even undisputed causal correlations may turn out to be mistaken when exceptional occurrences, such as fat tails, emerge.[375] This awareness suggests avoiding any boldness when selecting the supervisory strategy to be adopted in certain fields, because major flaws that go unnoticed may magnify the consequences of future financial turmoil to the extent that they are unanimously adopted in all the relevant jurisdictions, thus increasing systemic risk.[376] On the contrary, a more flexible strategy could allow for monitored experimentalism[377] and would ensure that the specificities related to each single market and jurisdiction are taken into account.[378] A stricter approach[379] should on the contrary be adopted in fields where no such epistemological uncertainties exist and the adoption of a single rulebook requires consistent implementation across the Union. For instance, once a policy decision is taken by Level 1 legislation substantially ruling out issuer choice on where to file an application for prospectus approval[380] and choosing maximum harmonization, there is no reason not to ensure that each national authority strictly complies, when performing supervision, with the applicable rules on the timing and intensity of the process for approval, as well as on the information that issuers may be requested to disclose.

The adoption of a nuanced approach like the one we suggest is only occasionally reflected by the applicable rules.[381] For instance, the duty to adopt temporary

---

374 F.X. Diebold et al., 'Introduction' in F.X. Diebold et al. (eds.), *The Known, the Unknown, and the Unknowable in Financial Risk Management: Measurement and Theory Advancing Practice*, Princeton University Press, Princeton, New Jersey 2010, p. 1 *et seq.*

375 R.J. Herring, 'The Known, the Unknown, and the Unknowable in Financial Policy: An Application to the Subprime Crisis' (2009) 26 *Yale Journal on Regulation* 101, 102.

376 For instance, supervisors may have divergent preferences as regards the viability of a risk-based approach (which concentrates supervision on areas where the risk is higher that one or more statutory objectives are not met: see UK Financial Conduct Authority (FCA), Journey to the FCA, October 2012, 42). But even if a risk-based approach were recommended as the only strategy able to maximize the expected benefits of supervision in a context of limited resources (for the continuing appeal of this technique under the new trend of "intensive supervision" in the UK see J. Black, 'Charting the fortunes of Principles Based Regulation' in V. De Luca et al. (eds.), *Capitalismo prossimo venturo. Etica, regole, prassi*, Università Bocconi Editore, Milano 2010, p. 276), different techniques would still be applicable to risk-analysis and, most important, to the translation of the analysis into actual surveillance.

377 On "experimentalist governance" and the role of peer review process see G. De Búrca et al., 'New Modes of Pluralist Global Governance' (2013) 45 *New York University Journal of International Law and Politics* 723.

378 See N. Moloney, 'The European Securities and Markets Authority and Institutional Design for the EU Financial Market – A Tale of Two Competences: Part (2) Rules in Action', supra note 256, 203 *et seq.*; P. Shammo, 'EU Day-to-Day Supervision or Intervention-based Supervision: Which Way Forward for the European System of Financial Supervision?', supra note 232, 22 *et seq.*

379 See E. Wymeersch, 'Europe's New Financial Regulatory Bodies', supra note 4, 454 *et seq.*

380 See Art. 2(1)(m) and 13 Directive 2003/71/EC. See also L. Enriques and T.H. Tröger, 'Issuer Choice in Europe', supra note 306, 530 *et seq.*

381 For a theoretical framework see D.T. Hornstein, 'Complexity, Adaptation, and Administrative Law', supra note 37, 944 *et seq.*

measures and to reconsider them periodically or upon request of a Member State, according to Article 9(5) Reg. No 1095/2010, is a step in the direction of experimentation and shows that the legislators were conscious of the inevitably limited rationality of supervisors.[382] However, the regulatory framework for guidelines and recommendations seems to push in the opposite direction. First, it suggests that ESMA should manage supervisory diversity in an adversarial manner, through a mechanism which closely resembles a "name and shame" system, rather than according to a traditional "comply or explain" approach where noncompliance, if exhaustively motivated, does not entail reputational damage and could even be appreciated to the extent that it allows a coherent adaptation of general principles. Second, although guidelines and recommendations are not binding, the provision in Article 16(4) that the annual reports should outline how the Authority intends to ensure compliance by dissenting competent authorities clearly shows that divergent supervisory practices can be *de facto* allowed for limited periods of time only.

A less pretentious approach to supervision, as the one we suggest, would require that the founding regulation be amended. *De lege lata*, a similar result could be achieved by framing guidelines and recommendations so as to explicitly provide for some margins of monitored variance in specific contentious issues and by calibrating supervisory measures in a flexible manner. However, absent a rule whereby ESMA would be requested to consider the feasibility of deviations from its standards and to motivate denials, this would be a second best solution. In the first place, ESMA evaluations would not easily be subject to judicial scrutiny where they are adopted through non-binding measures,[383] in spite of their actual effectiveness in limiting discretion by local supervisors.[384] Second, for individually binding measures, judicial review of proportionality and subsidiarity (Article 5 TEU), which are weakly policed by the EU judiciary,[385] would not be likely to effectively prevent excessive intrusion.

382 See supra, text accompanying note 89.

383 A. Kaczorowska, *European Union Law*, Routledge, London and New York 2013, p. 417 (only acts with binding legal effects fall under Art. 263 TFEU). However, some openness has been shown by the CJEU to possible review, under Art. 263 and 277 TFEU, for guidelines capable of producing external effects (see H.C.H. HOFMANN, G.C. ROWE and A.H. TÜRK, *Administrative Law and Policy of the European Union*, supra note 122, p. 807 *et seq.*).

384 T. Tridimas, 'Financial Supervision and Agency Power: Reflections on ESMA' supra note 8, p. 71.

385 N. Moloney, 'The European Securities and Markets Authority and Institutional Design for the EU Financial Market – A Tale of Two Competences: Part (2) Rules in Action', supra note 256, 219. See also, for the ECJ jurisprudence, supra note 8.

THE ROLE OF CIVIL SOCIETY IN EU FINANCIAL REGULATION

Guillaume PRACHE

'The interests of European investors, consumers and SMEs, must be at the centre of the reform'.
(European Commission, 4 March 2009)

1. INTRODUCTION: A CRUCIAL AND OUTSTANDING ISSUE FOR THE EUROPEAN ECONOMY AND DEMOCRACY

In March 2009, the European Commission (EC) recognized the need to put 'the interests of European investors, consumers and SMEs at the centre of the financial markets reform'. The Commission therefore announced it will 'ensure that the voice of European investors is much more strongly heard on all financial issues'.

However, three years later, the European Economic and Social Committee still reported that 'one of the reasons for the financial crisis was *inadequate and ineffective regulation and supervision of the financial markets.*

One of the difficulties in financial regulation is how to ensure that *differing and contradictory positions are given a balanced hearing.*

There is no effective counterweight to the legitimate representation of the financial sector's interests.

Political debate primarily plays out between the legislator on one side and the financial sector concerned on the other'.[1]

Despite the creation and the development of BETTER FINANCE for all (formerly 'EuroFinUse', in short 'Better Finance') in 2009 and of Finance Watch in 2011 (section 2), and despite the build-up of independent competence (section 3),

The author wrote this chapter in his own personal capacity.

[1] EUROPEAN ECONOMIC AND SOCIAL COMMITTEE, Opinion of the European Economic and Social Committee on how to involve civil society in financial regulation CESE 472/2012 – ECO/298.

organised civil society still faces two major hurdles to become an 'effective counterweight' to the financial sector in the European political debate:

- resources (section 4); and
- equal access (section 5) to the public authorities.

2. THE CURRENT REPRESENTATION OF FINANCIAL SERVICES USERS AND OF THE CIVIL SOCIETY AT LARGE

2.1. THE CREATION OF BETTER FINANCE (THE EUROPEAN FEDERATION OF FINANCIAL SERVICES USERS) IN 2009

Before 2009, there was no civil society organisation dedicated to representing the 'civil society' interests in financial services at the European level, except for the specific case of individual shareholders who created 'Euroshareholders' as an Association Internationale Sans But Lucratif (non-profit international association) under Belgian law in 1992. It was very representative of European individual shareholder interests as it gathered about thirty national shareholder and other investor and saver organisations from around Europe. But – in addition to its limited scope – its resources were very small, barely allowing it to rent an office in Brussels and to organise one or two meetings per year. It had no paid staff and did not even have the resources to actively take part in the public consultation processes put in place by the European Commission.

From 2007, I became a user-side financial expert to the European Commission as a member of the FIN-USE expert group.[2] And when the 2008 financial crisis happened, I realised that the Commission had become fully and publicly aware that the lack of an 'effective counterweight' to the financial industry lobbies was one of the reasons for the regulators and supervisors having failed to prevent the crisis or at least to minimise its devastating economic and social impact.

I was one of the people stressing to them that one of the key reasons for this problem was the dire lack of resources of the financial services user-side.

In September 2008, the European Parliament's Committee on Economic and Monetary Affairs (ECON) – through the voice of MEP Rapporteur Pervenche Berès (then Chair of ECON) – stressed 'the need for funding to support consumer and SME organisations in better representing their interests by enabling them to

[2] See infra note 24.

hire experts to advise them on the various Commission initiatives and comitology (Lamfalussy level 3 committees) consultations in the area of financial services'.[3]

The Commission also fully recognised this factor, hence its public Communication of 4 March 2009 on 'Driving European Recovery': 'The Commission therefore proposes to provide direct funding to facilitate the capacity-building of investor stakeholders to represent their interests in financial services policies at EU level … A proposal will be presented by the end of 2009'.[4]

This public and strong commitment certainly helped me to convince Euroshareholders and several other individual investor, saver and other financial services user associations from several European countries to regroup and create Better Finance (the European Federation of Financial Services Users).[5] The scope of Better Finance is much larger than that of Euroshareholders: Better Finance represents the interests of all individual financial services users: savers, investors, shareholders, bond holders, fund investors, pension fund participants, bank savers, life insurance policy holders, mortgage borrowers, etc. The Founding Members are Euroshareholders, ADICAE of Spain, FAIDER of France, DSW of Germany, the VEB from the Netherlands, and VZMD from Slovenia. Better Finance registered as an 'Association Sans But Lucratif' under Belgian law on 28 September 2009. In order to save costs, Euroshareholders and Better Finance have been managed together from the start: same premises, same staff, and I became both Managing Director of Better Finance and Secretary General of Euroshareholders, replacing Jean-Pierre Paelinck in that role, as he was retiring from this responsibility. The president of Better Finance – Jella Benner-Heinacher from the German Member Organisation DSW[6] – also became president of Euroshareholders, succeeding Peter Paul de Vries from the Netherlands.

At the same time, the Dutch investor association, the VEB, a member of both Euroshareholders and of Better Finance, was also fully convinced of the need to reinforce the defence of individual investor interest, and to do that at the EU level given the growing importance and dominance of EU financial law over Member States' legislation. The VEB and its Managing Director Jan Maarten Slagter decided to make a special contribution to the European Federation, enabling us for the first time to hire two people. Most unfortunately, the above-mentioned commitment from the European Commission failed to materialise for three years

3 European Parliament, Opinion of the Committee on Economic and Monetary Affairs for the Committee on Budgets on the draft general budget of the European Union for the financial year 2009, 2008/2026(BUD).

4 European Commission, *Communication for the Spring European Council, Driving European Recovery, Volume 1,* COM(2009) 114 final, Annex 1, p. 4.

5 Formerly known as 'EuroFinUse' and as 'EuroInvestors' initially.

6 In March 2013, she was replaced by Jean Berthon, the president of the French federation FAIDER.

(2009–2011): in 2009, Better Finance was denied funding from the DG Health and Consumers (in charge of consumers and running a yearly grant programme 'Funding for European consumer organisations'). And the DG Internal Markets and Services (in charge of financial services) did not put out a call for grants before December 2011, following the creation of Finance Watch on the initiative of more than 20 members of the European Parliament – see below sections 2.2 and 4.

In 2012, Euroshareholders merged into Better Finance, making the latter the only dedicated expert and advocate for all financial services users at the European level. Today (2014) it gathers more than 50 organisations of financial services users throughout Europe. In turn, those member associations have more than 4.5 million individual members (natural persons). The complete list of Better Finance member associations can be found on its website.[7] The European Federation now has five full-time employees.

2.2. THE CREATION OF FINANCE WATCH[8] IN 2011

In 2011, several MEPs joined forces to create Finance Watch.

In the summer of 2010, some Members of the European Parliament noticed that they had become inundated with requests to meet representatives of the financial industry. At the same time, they were dealing with ever more technical financial legislation coming through Brussels in the aftermath of the financial crisis of 2008.

This group of MEPs became concerned that an asymmetry of lobbying could lead to undemocratic outcomes as reform proposals were altered by the industry lobby on their way to becoming law. They therefore launched a cross-party call for action in July 2010, which became known as the 'Initial Call for a Finance Watch'.

In December 2010, the MEPs funded a six-month position to investigate whether a new, independent body could be created to improve the way civil society's voices were represented in the legislature on matters of financial reform. This led to more than 120 meetings with representatives of civil society, including Better Finance, and other organisations, and eventually to a set of concrete proposals for Finance Watch.

Finance Watch was registered on 28 April 2011 as an Association Internationale Sans But Lucratif (non-profit international association) under Belgian law. Better

---

7 <http://betterfinance.eu/> accessed 19.10.2014.

8 <www.finance-watch.org/> accessed 19.10.2014.

Finance was one of the Founding Members and a Member of the Board. At the end of 2011, though, Better Finance had to withdraw from the Board and from the organisation itself in order to be able to apply for the grant call issued by the European Commission for a 'Pilot Project – Capacity building of end-users and non-industry stakeholders in Union policy making in the area of financial services'. Indeed, Finance Watch wanted to apply by itself. It was not possible for Better Finance – which had been fighting for three years to get badly needed public European support (see below section 4 – resources) – to also apply as a member of another grant applicant. Nevertheless, the two organisations remain very close in terms of purpose and objectives.

Today (2014), Finance Watch comprises about 40 member organisations from 'civil society', including more than 10 trade unions or federations of trade unions. The six Member Organisations represented on its Board are the European Trade Union Confederation (ETUC),[9] Friends of the Earth Europe (FOEE),[10] Transparency International EU Office,[11] UNI Europa,[12] CECODHAS Housing Europe[13] and the European Consumer Organisation (BEUC).[14] Finance Watch membership does not include dedicated investor, saver or other financial services users' organisations. Finance Watch and Better Finance are therefore quite complementary: the latter dedicated to the representation of financial services users, the former representing mostly other segments of 'civil society'.

3. COMPETENCIES ARE NOT THE MAIN ISSUE FOR A BALANCED ROLE BETWEEN THE FINANCIAL SECTOR AND CIVIL SOCIETY

The Panel discussion at the 28 November 2011 Hearing held by the European Economic and Social Committee on *the requirements for organised civil society to articulate their interests regarding financial regulation* identified three major ones: *competence*, *resources* and *access*.

The experience of Better Finance since 2009 shows that competence is indeed an issue, but not the major one: independent competence does exist. The problem is the resources to hire it. Despite an acute imbalance with the financial sector in terms of resources, Better Finance has indeed managed to develop a network of recognised experts who are independent from the financial industry, and

9 <www.etuc.org/> accessed 19.10.2014.
10 <www.foeeurope.org/> accessed 19.10.2014.
11 <www.transparencyinternational.eu/> accessed 19.10.2014.
12 <www.uniglobalunion.org/fr/contact/uni-europa> accessed 19.10.2014.
13 <www.housingeurope.eu/> accessed 19.10.2014.
14 <www.beuc.org/> accessed 19.10.2014.

increasingly recognised by the EU authorities. More recently, so has Finance Watch.

Today Better Finance provides by far the largest part of individual user experts of the financial advisory expert groups of the European Authorities that allow them on board.

3.1. 'LEVEL ONE' EU AUTHORITIES

European Commission:

- Financial Services User Group (FSUG)[15]

Established by the European Commission in 2010, it comprises 20 members. Currently:

- Three of them are independent academics;
- Two represent SMEs;
- Six of the 10 experts representing user organisations are from Better Finance itself or from Better Finance member organisations (Germany, The Netherlands, Romania, Slovakia, and Spain). The FSUG vice chair is the author of this chapter.

- EU Expert Group on taxation of savings

This expert group advises the EC DG Taxation and Customs Union (TAXUD) on the taxation of income from savings and investments following the release of the EU Savings Directive on the taxation of interest income in the EU. In 2011, realising that this group did not include any representatives of savers and investors, Better Finance asked and obtained the right to designate one representative. We designated a tax lawyer who agreed to do this for us pro bono.

- Still several consultative groups run or funded by the EU do not allow for the representation of users per se. In particular, the European Economic and Social Committee (EESC), EFRAG (European Financial reporting Advisory Group), and the 'Pensions Forum'[16] do not include any representative of financial services users although they are one of the most relevant and important stakeholders, in particular in the areas of pensions and of financial reporting.

---

[15] See below, section 3.2.

[16] See European Commission, Commission Decision of 9 July 2001 on the setting-up of a committee in the area of supplementary pensions (2001/548/EC), OJ 2001 No. L 196/26.

3.2. 'LEVEL TWO' EU AUTHORITIES

The 'European System of Financial Supervision' was established in 2011 following the 2008 financial crisis and the proposals of the De Larosière Report of 2009. It replaced the European Committees known as CESR (Committee of European Securities Regulators), CEBS (Committee of European Banking Supervisors) and CEIOPS (Committee of European Insurance and Occupational Pensions Supervisors). It comprises four institutions:

- the ESRB (European Systemic Risk Board);[17]
- and three European Supervision Authorities (ESAs):
  - ESMA (European Securities and Markets Authority);
  - EBA (European Banking Authority);
  - EIOPA (European Insurance and Occupational Pensions Authority).

By law, each Authority is equipped with one (or two, in the case of EIOPA) consultative 'Stakeholder Group(s)' (article 37 of the ESAs Regulations). The Stakeholder Groups each have 30 members and are supposed to incorporate all stakeholder categories (industry, users, others), which is a different approach from the Commission and from many national financial supervisors who have established different consultative bodies for each main category of stakeholders. We refer for example to the UK's FCA's Financial Services Consumer Panel[18] or to the EC FSUG (see above section 3.1 and below, section 4.2). As for the ESAs, individual user representatives are included in these 'all-in-one' 'stakeholder groups'.

17 <www.esrb.europa.eu> accessed 19.10.2014.

18 <www.fca.org.uk/about/governance/who/statutory-panels/consumer-panel> accessed 19.10.2014.

Table 1. 'Consumer/Retail User' representation in the EU financial advisory groups
(Number of memberships as of March 2014)

	BETTER FINANCE[19]	FINANCE WATCH	BEUC	Total 'consumer'/ 'retail user' members	Annual compensation per member
EC FSUG (Financial Services User Group)	6	0	4	15/20[20]	€10,000
ESAs (four SGs)	**14**	**0**	**5**	25/120	€1,650[21]
Securities and Markets Stakeholder Group ESMA	5	0	1	9/30	
Banking Stakeholder Group EBA[22]	4	0	3	8/30	
Insurance and Reinsurance Stakeholder Group EIOPA	1	0	1	4/30	
Occupational Pensions Stakeholder Group EIOPA	4	0	0	4/30[23]	
Funding from the EU (2013)[24] - € million	**0.287**	**1.213**	**2.236[25]**		

Source: Better Finance research, 2014.

[19] Memberships held by persons affiliated to BETTER FINANCE or to one of its Member Organisations.
[20] Out of the 20 member FSUG, three are academics and two represent SMEs.
[21] Maximum amount assuming members claim maximum amount of preparatory work for all meetings.
[22] Six 'consumers' and four 'users of banking services', but two of those are not retail users.
[23] Despite Recital 47 of the EIOPA Regulation – Regulation (EU) No 1094/2010 of the European Parliament and of the Council of 24 November 2010 establishing a European Supervisory Authority (European Insurance and Occupational Pensions Authority), amending Decision No. 716/2009/EC and repealing Commission Decision 2009/79/EC, OJ 2010 No. L 331/48 – there is no 'consumer'/'retail user' category, only a 'representative of beneficiaries' (which includes one trade union representative). One 'academic' is a member of Better Finance.
[24] Transparency Register of the European Commission.
[25] 2012, not comparable: BEUC's mandate covers many other consumer goods and services than financial services.

When the representation of financial services users is possible and to the extent that it is *actually* allowed, Better Finance plays a very active role in the ESAs Stakeholder Groups:

- ESMA (European Securities and Markets Authority): the Securities and Markets Stakeholder Group (SMSG)[26]
  Five of the SMSG members categorised by ESMA as 'consumers' or as retail users as of March 2014 are from Better Finance or from Better Finance member organisations (Lithuania, the Netherlands, Poland and Spain). The elected first chair (the author of this chapter) is also from Better Finance: he was the only European financial stakeholder group chair coming from the user-side.[27]

- EBA (European Banking Authority): the Banking Stakeholder Group (BSG)[28]
  Of the eight BSG members categorised by EBA as 'consumers'/'retail users' as of January 2014, four are from Better Finance (its president) or from a Better Finance member organisation (Spain, Romania, Italy).

- EIOPA has two stakeholder groups:
  - The Occupational Pensions Stakeholder Group (OPSG)[29]
    Three of the five OPSG members categorised by EIOPA as 'pension beneficiaries' as of January 2014 are from a Better Finance (the author of this chapter) or from a Better Finance member organisation (Denmark and Romania); and one independent academic is also a member of Better Finance (Slovakia). However, another so-called 'pension beneficiary' is presented as working for a European trade union organisation, so certainly this representative should be considered as an 'employee representative' rather than a 'consumer'/'retail user' representative as per the EIOPA Regulation (recital 47).
  - The Insurance and Reinsurance Stakeholder Group (IRSG)[30]
    Of the six IRSG members categorised by EIOPA as 'consumers' as of January 2014, one is from Better Finance. Another is from the Polish Ombudsman office, so should not really be considered a consumer representative. Another comes from an insurance promotion organisation for which we found no evidence that it represents consumers. There is also one 'user representative' but he is the French insurance ombudsman who

[26] <www.esma.europa.eu/SMSG> accessed 19.10.2014.

[27] He had to renounce to apply again for chairmanship in 2014 due to the failure of ESMA to provide the legally required adequate compensation and support; see below section 3.3.

[28] <www.eba.europa.eu/about-us/organisation/banking-stakeholder-group> accessed 19.10.2014.

[29] <https://eiopa.europa.eu/about-eiopa/organisation/stakeholder-groups/occupational-pensions-stakeholder- group/index.html> accessed 19.10.2014.

[30] <https://eiopa.europa.eu/about-eiopa/organisation/stakeholder-groups/insurance-reinsurance-stakeholder-group/index.html> accessed 19.10.2014.

is paid by the insurance industry. That leaves only four true consumer/ retail user representatives, and only one dedicated representative of life insurance policy holders, although life insurance is one of the most popular retail investment products in Europe.

- The ESRB[31] has no representative of financial services users in its only consultative groups. However, the former chair of Finance Watch is a member of the Advisory Scientific Committee (ASC).

4. RESOURCES: ONE OF THE KEY UNFULFILLED REQUIREMENTS IDENTIFIED BY THE EC SINCE 2009

There are currently two ways for the European Authorities to provide financial support for civil society's involvement in the design of EU financial policies:

- support to civil society organisations;
- support to individual civil society experts.

4.1. EMERGING SUPPORT FOR EUROPEAN CIVIL SOCIETY ORGANISATIONS INVOLVED IN FINANCIAL SERVICES POLICY

The European Commission's March 2009 public commitment to fund investors' representation did not materialize before 2012.

European Commission, March 2009:

> 'The interests of European investors, consumers and SMEs, must be at the centre of the reform ... The Commission will ... ensure that the voice of European investors is much more strongly heard on all financial issues.
>
> The Commission therefore proposes to provide direct funding to facilitate the capacity-building of investor stakeholders to represent their interests in financial services policies at EU level ... A proposal will be presented by the end of 2009'.[32]

---

[31] European Systemic Risk Board.

[32] European Commission, *Communication for the Spring European Council, Driving European Recovery, Volume 1* COM(2009) 114 final, supra note 4.

European Commission, November 2011:

> 'a major obstacle remains that hinders adequate end users and non-industry stakeholders' participation in Union policy making particularly in the area of financial services, namely the scarcity of resources and specialised expertise. Consumer bodies as well as civil society organisations do not have adequate resources to properly cover a wide range of often highly technical topics and develop the expertise to take a more proactive role in Union financial services policy making'.[33]

European Economic and Social Committee, February 2012:

> 'It may in certain cases be appropriate to provide civil society organisations with financial support from EU funds in order to rectify deficiencies in the representation of key interests.
> In such cases, it must be ensured that:
>
> - the financial contributions are fully transparent;
> - that the independence of the organisations is guaranteed;
> - and that they are not given preferential treatment in their dealings with the Commission over organisations that have not received such support'.[34]

Actually the European Commission never presented a proposal to fund 'the capacity-building of investor stakeholders to represent their interests in financial services policies at EU level'. But, following the creation of Finance Watch by Members of the European Parliament in 2011 (see above section 2.2), the Commission eventually published a call to fund a 'Pilot Project – Capacity building of end-users and non-industry stakeholders in Union policy making in the area of financial services'[35] on 16 December 2011:

> 'This call for proposals aims at providing a financial contribution (operating grant) for the year 2012 for the operating and functioning of an European expertise centre in the financial services area to the direct benefit of European end-users and non-industry stakeholders. ... The aim of the pilot project is, through the support provided by an expertise centre to the benefit of European end-users and non-industry associations, to enhance the latter's capacity to participate in Union policymaking in the area of financial services, with the objective of

---

33 European Commission, *Pilot Project – Capacity building of end-users and non-industry stakeholders in Union policy making in the area of financial services*, MARKT/A2/PS/fm (2011) 1355903.

34 European Economic and Social Committee, Opinion of the European Economic and Social Committee on How to involve civil society in financial regulation, supra note 1.

35 <ec.europa.eu/dgs/internal_market/docs/grants/call-for-proposals-2011-175-h_en.pdf> accessed 19.10.2014.

> providing policymakers with other views than those expressed by the financial sector industry and of informing the wider public of the issues at stake in the regulation of financial markets for consumers, end-users, retail investors and other nonindustry stakeholders.'

In May 2012, this €1.25 million grant was awarded to two applicants: Finance Watch was awarded €1,025,000 and EuroFinUse €225,000. It is the very first time the EU has recognised the public interest nature of the representation of retail investors and other users of financial services by providing financial support to the European representative organisation.

In April 2013, the European Commission awarded a total of €1.5 million under the same 'Pilot Project', €1,212,000 to Finance Watch and €287,000 to Better Finance. That year marked the end of the two-year 'Pilot Project'. The European Parliament voted a total 2014 grant budget of €1.75 million under a new 'Preparatory Action' bearing the same label as the former 'Pilot Project': 'Capacity building of end-users and non-industry stakeholders in Union policy making in the area of financial services'. The European Commission then issued a call for proposals in December 2013, which closed on 31 January 2014. The Commission's decision is expected in spring 2014.

Table 2. EC funding of European civil society organizations involved[36] in financial policy

	2010	2012
European Trade Union Confederation (ETUC)	€1,722,937	€4,225,352
UNI Europa	€1,378,327	€1,477,054
European Consumer Organization (BEUC)	€2,567,585	€2,014,973
Friends of the Earth Europe	€947,983	€733,162
Transparency International	€1,633,454	€11,814,238
Finance Watch	not applicable	€881,566
Better Finance (EuroFinUse)	0	€210,680

Source: EC Financial Transparency System, 2010, 2012.

As the tables 2 (above) and 3 (below) show, this financial support is still quite modest compared to that already provided to other civil society stakeholders, and is also very modest compared to the lobbying power of the financial industry

[36] Directly or indirectly: the first five European civil society organisations are not focused on financial services, but are all members of Finance Watch.

lobbies. Indeed the biggest trade lobby organisation of all by far is that of the European financial markets companies. In addition, BIPAR (insurers) is sixth and the European Banking Federation is twelfth. However, it is still a historical move four years after the beginning of the worst financial crisis in Europe since 1929.

Table 3. Business organisations declaring EU lobbying spending
Estimated costs to the organisations directly related to representing interests to EU institutions in latest year (in €)

I	**Association for Financial Markets in Europe**	Above €10,000,000
II	Enel Ingegneria e Ricerca S.p.A.	Above €10,000,000
III	Ericsson	€8,750,000–9,000,000
IV	Accenture International SARL	€8,250,000–8,500,000
V	European Seed Association	€8,250,000–8,500,000
VI	**BIPAR – European Federation of Insurance Intermediaries**	€6,000,000–6,250,000
VII	European Chemical Industry Council	€6,000,000
VIII	Union Européenne du Commerce du Bétail et des Métiers de la Viande	€4,750,000–5,000,000
IX	ExxonMobil Petroleum & Chemical	€4,750,000– 5,000,000
X	Siemens AG	€4,729,533
XI	Microsoft Corporation	€4,500,000–4,750,000
XII	**European Banking Federation**	€4,250,000–4,500,000

Source: Greenwood and Dreger. *Transparency Register data as of 5 January 2013. Records from subcategory 'Trade, business & professional associations'.* Organisations decide whether to report their costs as a range or an absolute figure.

Of course, as of today (2014), the future and sustainability of such support to the financial services user representation remains unknown. The 2014 'Preparatory Action' can be renewed for a maximum of two years, depending on the approval by the European Parliament on a yearly basis. It is up to the Commission to propose the conversion of this 'Preparatory Action' into a more sustainable multi-year support. Any support from 2015 on will in any case depend on the European Parliament and Council decisions on the EU 2015 Budget and beyond.

Regarding support to independent user-side organisations, another behaviour by European authorities is quite detrimental to independent user-side not-for-profit organisations: in most cases, research and consulting tenders from the EU (which represent millions of euros every year) are awarded to commercial consultants or to think tanks partially or totally funded by the industry, and sometimes to academics. Typically, those commercial consultants, once hired, get a support letter from the EU authority to ask for the help, input, feedback and sometimes surveys from investor and user organisations ... for free. To ensure more independence of consulting and research in the area of financial services, and to end the discrimination against user organisations in the awarding of research and consulting contracts, EU authorities should strongly encourage their commercial consulting provider firms to partner with independent user organisations where relevant, instead of asking them to serve as pro bono sub-contractors.

4.2. IMPROVED SUPPORT TO INDIVIDUAL USER EXPERTS IN 'LEVEL ONE' EUROPEAN AUTHORITIES

FIN-USE (2004–2010)[37]

In 2004, the European Commission established a forum of financial services users (FIN-USE) in order to secure expert input on the user-side into internal market financial services initiatives so that a more active and informed involvement of users could be achieved. It comprised 15 members.

From day one, the Commission acknowledged the need to provide adequate compensation to user-side financial experts. Following the 2008 financial crisis, the Commission increased its support to the user experts of FIN-USE by increasing their yearly gross compensation from €7,000 to €10,000. This is a fixed amount and the same for all members including the chair and vice chair.

FSUG (since 2010)

In 2010, the Commission decided to revamp its user-side consultative bodies, replacing FIN-USE with the FSUG (Financial Services User Group). In the 'Communication for the European Council – Driving European Recovery',[38] the Commission put the interests of European investors, consumers and SMEs at the centre of the financial market reform. As a measure to achieve these targets, the Commission set up the Financial Services User Group (FSUG).[39] The group's task is to:

- advise the Commission in the preparation of legislation or policy initiatives which affect the users of financial services;

[37] <http://ec.europa.eu/internal_market/finservices-retail/finuse_en.htm> accessed 19.10.2014.

[38] European Commission, *Communication for the Spring European Council, Driving European Recovery, Volume 1*, COM(2009) 114 final, supra note 4.

[39] European Commission, Commission Decision of 20 July 2010 setting up a Financial Services User Group (2010/C 199/02), OJ 2010 No. C 199/12.

- provide insight, opinion and advice concerning the practical implementation of such policies;
- proactively seek to identify key financial services issues which affect users of financial services; and
- liaise with and provide information to financial services user representatives and representative bodies at the European Union and national level.

FSUG has 20 members, who are individuals appointed to represent the interests of consumers, retail investors or micro-enterprises, and individual experts with expertise in financial services from the perspective of the financial services user. FSUG meets eight times a year in Brussels and its Chair is elected from amongst the group members. The Commission (jointly DG Internal Market and Services and DG Health and Consumers) provides secretarial services for the group.

The financial support for FSUG members remains the same as for FIN-USE members.[40] In addition, the Commission provides an annual research budget to the FSUG, recognising the need for independently commissioned research in the area of financial services.

4.3. INADEQUATE SUPPORT TO USER EXPERTS IN 'LEVEL TWO' EUROPEAN AUTHORITIES

The 2010 European Regulations establishing a new European system of Financial Supervision (ESFS) created three European financial authorities, as detailed in section 3.2 above. They are much more challenging for individual user-side experts as:

- the four 'stakeholder groups' are much more technical and specialized than the 'Level 1' consultative body (at the European Commission level); and
- user-side experts are not alone, but grouped with industry experts who have infinitely deeper expert and administrative resources to support them.

Nonetheless, the legal requirements to provide adequate compensation to not-for-profit non-industry expert members of the groups, and to provide adequate administrative support, are in our view not being met, creating a very serious issue for the representation of the user-side interests in European financial regulation and supervision. This issue is magnified by the lack of legally required balance of representation between the various stakeholders, and, in particular, between

[40] Besides the €10,000 gross compensation, travel and lodging expenses are reimbursed following the relevant policies of the Commission.

the industry and industry provider members on the one hand, and the retail user members on the other (see below, section 5.1).

- There is no *'adequate compensation'* as required by article 37.4 and recital 49[41] of the Regulations: 'Members of the (Securities and Markets) Stakeholder Group representing non-profit organisations or academics should receive *adequate compensation* in order to allow persons that are neither well-funded nor industry representatives to take part fully in the debate on financial regulation.'

  Indeed, despite complaints from user-side organisations to the ESAs, this compensation is set by the ESAs at €18.75 gross per hour, i.e. €150 per day. This compares to typically €2,750 per day (18 times more) paid by the EU to senior commercial consultants. It would mean that for the European authorities the 'adequate' value of user-side international financial experts is much closer to that of a babysitter than that of a commercial consultant. This perception shows the level of respect for international 'level two' authorities for user expert representatives, and highlights the huge gap between their actual decisions and their talk about 'reaching out to consumers'.

  Even more shockingly, this user expert compensation set by the ESAs is *six to more than 10 times lower than the compensation received by financial user experts of the European Commission*[42] – although those deal with far less technical 'level one' issues, and in a less challenging mode (the EC expert group does not mix user and industry experts together).

  This actually very often prevents user-side experts from getting more involved in financial policy design, because of their very limited resources, as publicly recognised by the European authorities since the 2008 financial crisis. This is all the more disappointing as – at the same time – ESA executives often stress how challenging it is to find user-side experts! Besides, the ESAs' policies in this respect are also unfortunately quite confusing and mix 'compensation' on the one hand with travel reimbursements and lodging costs on the other hand.[43]

  Better Finance – which is making an exceptional effort to provide user-side experts to these highly technical advisory groups (see table 1 above) –

---

41 Same provisions for the EBA and for the EIOPA stakeholder groups (recital 48 for the latter) – see infra note 53.

42 The European Commission's user-side experts of the FSUG (Financial Services User Group) receive a fee of €10,000 per year (plus reimbursement of travel expenses). If one counts only meetings, annual compensation of not-for-profit members of the more technical ESA SGs is €900, i.e. 91% lower. If one adds the maximum time to take preparatory work into account (maximum eight hours per meeting as allowed by the ESAs), not-for-profit members of ESA SGs are still paid only €1,650, i.e. 83% less than FSUG members.

43 For example, the ESAs 'policy' set an overall cap of €10,000 per annum on compensation and travel expenses together, making no distinction between the two: so there could be situations where the compensation of non-industry representatives might be even lower than €18.75 per hour, if they have to incur high travel expenses.

publicly asked for an actual implementation of the law and for ESAs to comply with the adequate compensation requirement in its public response to the European Commission Public Consultation on the Review of the European System of Financial Supervision that closed on 31 July 2013.[44] The *Financial Times* echoed this response in its 26 August 2013 edition.[45] The ESMA Securities and Markets Stakeholder Group also publicly criticised this inadequate compensation in its public position paper on the Review of the ESFS.[46]

Finally, the October 2013 report on the Review of the new European System of Financial Supervision requested by the European Parliament's Committee on Economic and Monetary Affairs stressed that '*improving the compensation of not-for-profit associations of consumers* could make a marked difference for all of the ESA Stakeholder Groups'.[47]

Despite these calls for fulfilling the adequate compensation requirement of European law, the ESAs did not change their compensation policy for not-for-profit independent experts one bit, forcing the Better Finance MD to renounce applying for the renewal of his chairmanship of the ESMA Securities and Markets Stakeholder Group in January 2014.[48]

- *Secretarial support* is often not adequate as required by article 37.4 of the Regulations, at least at ESMA: the former chair of the SMSG (belonging to a under-resourced retail user organisation with no secretarial support to assign to his SMSG work) had to dedicate more than 20% of his total working time to the management of the SMSG.

  Few plain English documents or presentations on the more technical issues (like MiFIR for example) are provided by the ESAs despite requests, making it very difficult for the retail user representatives who do not have expert resources on hand to effectively participate and influence such working groups (plus they are far too few as mentioned below). The Securities and

44 <www.eurofinuse.org/fileadmin/user_upload/documents/Position_Papers/Financial_Supervision/EuroFinUse_Respon se_ESFS_Review-31-07-13.pdf> accessed 19.10.2014.

45 J. Kenchington, 'EU 'snubs investors' on reform's', *Financial Times*, 26.08.2013.

46 ESMA Securities and Markets Stakeholder Group, *SMSG contribution to the ESFS Consultation. An SMSG review of the ESA's including a self-assessment*, SMSG/2013/013, p. 18.

47 European Parliament, Directorate General for Internal Policies Policy Department A: Economic and Scientific Policy, *Review of the New European System of Financial Supervision (ESFS). Part 1: The Work of the European Supervisory Authorities (EBA, EIOPA and ESMA) – The ESFS's Micro-Prudential Pillar* IP/A/ECON/ST/2012-23, PE 507.446, 2013.

48 His public statement made at the 29.01.2014 SMSG meeting, detailing the reasons, has been published on Better Finance's website www.betterfinance.eu/fileadmin/user_upload/documents/Images_News___Events/BF_Communication_SMSG_Chair.pdf accessed 19.10.2014.

Markets Stakeholder Group[49] also points to its lack of adequate support as a problem to fix.
The above-mentioned October 2013 Report requested by the European Parliament's Committee on Economic and Monetary Affairs also pointed out that 'there is a *recognised shortage* of resources provided by the ESAs to their Stakeholder Groups, limiting their ability to challenge the ESAs. While the ESAs have provided resources and support to its Stakeholder Groups to the best of their ability, a modest increase in administrative and research resources, as well as the allocation of more senior ESA staff time to Stakeholder Group issues would enhance their effectiveness'.

5. NO EQUAL ACCESS TO THE EUROPEAN AUTHORITIES

Financial services users' experts and advocates do not have equal access to the European authorities compared to those of the financial industry.

5.1. NO OR UNBALANCED REPRESENTATION IN EU CONSULTATIVE BODIES

Despite recent efforts from the European Commission to better balance the composition of its various advisory bodies between the industry on the one hand, and users on the other hand, individual investors and other financial services users are not represented as such in many EU bodies or EU-supported bodies such as the EESC,[50] the ESRB consultative bodies, the Pensions Forum,[51] EFRAG,[52] etc.

There is no '*balanced representation' of retail users* in the stakeholder groups of the European Supervisory Authorities, although such a balance is required by law. Article 37.2 of the ESAs Regulations[53] and recital 48 of the ESAs Regulations

[49] ESMA Securities and Markets Stakeholder Group, *SMSG contribution to the ESFS Consultation. An SMSG review of the ESA's including a self-assessment,* supra note 46.

[50] EESC <www.eesc.europa.eu/?i=portal.en.home> accessed 19.10.2014.

[51] This body set up by the EC does not include any representative of pension fund participants despite its claim to represent all stakeholders.

[52] EFRAG. This organisation receives support for half of its budget (€3 million in 2012) from the EC to promote the European financial reporting standards; it does not include any representatives of individual investors among its members or governing bodies.

[53] Regulation (EU) No. 1095/2010 of the European Parliament and of the Council of 24 November 2010 establishing a European Supervisory Authority (European Securities and Markets Authority), amending Decision No. 716/2009/EC and repealing Commission Decision 2009/77/EC, OJ 2010 No. L 331/84 (ESMA Regulation), Regulation (EU) No. 1093/2010 of the European Parliament and of the Council of 24 November 2010 establishing a European Supervisory Authority (European Banking Authority), amending Decision No. 716/2009/

indeed provide that 'a Securities and Markets Stakeholder Group ... should represent, *in balanced proportions*, financial market participants, small and medium-sized enterprises (SMEs), academics *and consumers and other* retail users of financial services'.[54]

Retail user representatives amount to at most four in the 30-member-strong stakeholder groups, where industry representatives and their providers (auditors, lawyers, etc.) make up 15 or more of the 30 members.

The composition of the first 30-member Stakeholder Groups designated in 2011 by the ESAs for two-and-a-half-year mandates is as follows, as identified by Better Finance:

- three user representatives versus at least 15 for the industry and its suppliers in the Banking one;
- four user representatives versus 18 for the industry and its suppliers in the Insurance and Reinsurance one;
- three pension fund participants in the Pensions one versus at least 16 for the industry and its suppliers;
- four user representatives versus at least 14 for the industry and its suppliers in the Securities and Markets Group.

One reason for this striking imbalance is, among other things, that ESAs labelled service providers to the financial industry (such as accountants, lawyers, etc.) as 'users', thus violating the Regulations (the recitals clearly specify users as being 'retail' 'users' exclusively – see above). The worst case is the Occupational Pensions Group where we could identify only two representatives of retail users (labelled as 'beneficiaries') out of a total of 30 group members. This is all the more concerning given the extraordinary magnitude of the pensions issue in Europe.

Better Finance sent protest letters to the three ESAs, and subsequently filed three complaints to the European Ombudsman against EBA (Banking Group) and against EIOPA (Insurance Group and Pensions Group) in September 2011. BEUC (the European Consumer Organisation) filed two similar complaints at the same time regarding the Banking and Insurance Groups. The complaints addressed the absence of the required balanced representation between the financial industry

EC and repealing Commission Decision 2009/78/EC, OJ 2010 No. L 331/12 (EBA Regulation) and Regulation (EU) No. 1094/2010 of the European Parliament and of the Council of 24 November 2010 establishing a European Supervisory Authority (European Insurance and Occupational Pensions Authority), amending Decision No. 716/2009/EC and repealing Commission Decision 2009/79/EC, OJ 2010 No. L 331/48 (EIOPA Regulation) – establishing respectively ESMA, EBA and EIOPA.

54 Recital 48 as well for the banking SG, and recital 47 for the insurance and pensions SGs.

and its providers on the one hand and the consumers and other retail users on the other. In particular, the ESAs had classified providers of the financial industries as 'users' of financial services, whereas the recitals of the relevant European law clearly specify that 'users' mean 'retail' users.

By the time of the first renewal of the four Stakeholder Groups in 2013, the Ombudsman had unfortunately still not published any decision on these complaints. But informal contacts between the Ombudsman and the ESAs[55] led the ESAs to introduce changes in the application process for the renewal of the first stakeholder groups in May–July 2013, in particular by specifying that the 'users' category of stakeholders are 'retail' users of financial services – with the exception of the Pensions Group (where no such category exists anymore but has been more or less replaced by a 'professional associations' one).

As shown by table 1 above, the ESAs did react to the comments of the European Ombudsman, as the number of 'consumers'/'users'/'beneficiaries' members increased in all but one of the ESA Stakeholder Groups (from four to nine in ESMA, three to eight in EBA and two to four in EIOPA Pensions). In addition, the 'users' category – when used by the ESAs – no longer includes providers to the industry but rather only retail users, in compliance with the law.

On 19 December 2013 (EBA) and on 26 February 2014 (EIOPA), the European Ombudsman issued a decision on our complaints of September 2011 against EBA's and EIOPA's previous and first selections of their respective Stakeholder Group members. The Ombudsman decided that EBA and EIOPA had committed – among other things – an instance of maladministration 'by including in the "users" category of the Stakeholders Groups applications from representatives of entities which are clearly not retail users of the services provided by the financial sector, but rather providers of remunerated services to the latter'. Thus the Ombudsman agreed with one of our main complaints. But she did not find any 'maladministration' in the remaining acute lack of balance between consumers/ retail users on the one hand and industry/industry providers on the other. Thus, in our view, the Ombudsman did not address the 'balanced' representation requirement of the European laws governing the ESAs.

This striking imbalance of representation to the detriment of the retail user-side in the consultative bodies of the European Financial Supervisors makes it very challenging for the largely outnumbered user experts to make their voice heard. The too few retail user experts also suffer from 'inadequate' and – in our view, as explained above – illegal levels of compensation and support. For these reasons,

[55] For instance, ESMA acknowledged getting input form the Ombudsman in its 2013 Call for SMSG members.

the ESAs may well face a shortage of quality user-side expert applications in the near future. They will then bear the responsibility for the acute imbalance of influence between the industry representatives and those of retail users; that same imbalance that was rightly identified by the European Union as one of the causes of the regulators and supervisors' failure to prevent the 2008 financial crisis.

5.2. THE GOVERNANCE OF EU AUTHORITIES

The governance of the new ESAs is not favourable to retail users' protection:

- User protection is only sixth and last of the ESAs objectives (see article 1(5) of the ESAs Regulations) and is mixed with financial stability and solvency of financial institutions, objectives that up to now have been privileged by the ESAs.
  ESMA's overall objective is to protect the public interest. The wording of paragraph (5) focuses primarily on stability and effectiveness of the financial system. Article 1(5) subsequently lists ESMA's overall objectives. The ESMA SMSG suggests to change the order of these objectives in order to give better visibility to ESMA's role in enhancing consumer and investor protection'.[56]
  Better Finance publicly supported this recommendation from the ESMA SMSG. In addition, the ESAs suffer from a potential conflict of objectives between 'stability' and user protection to the detriment of the latter. Several EU Member States have separated the supervision of these areas by creating different supervision agencies. This is the so-called 'twin peaks' model of supervision. For example financial supervision in the UK is now split between the FCA (Financial Conduct Authority) – which focuses on client protection – and the PRA (Prudential Regulation Authority) which is under the umbrella of the Bank of England. The ESAs Regulations provide that the 2013 ESFS Review must address this issue (article 81(2)(b)). Better Finance supports the ESMA SMSG's recommendation to move to a twin peaks model. 'We think that the appropriate solution for EU financial system governance is the "twin-peaks model" which was also envisaged by de Larosière Report, according to which the regulatory framework should evolve "towards a system which would rely on only two Authorities: The first would be responsible for banking and insurance issues, as well as any other issue which is relevant for financial stability (e.g. systemically important hedge funds, systemically important financial infrastructures). The second Authority would be responsible for conduct of business and market issues, across the three main financial sectors.'

[56] ESMA Securities and Markets Stakeholder Group, *SMSG contribution to the ESFS Consultation. An SMSG review of the ESA's including a self-assessment,* supra note 46.

This lack of priority given to user protection may also contribute to other deficiencies of the ESAs in user protection: the ESAs have no real powers to ban products or to prevent their distribution to retail customers, and their duty to 'report on consumers trends' (article 9(1) of the ESAs Regulations) is only fulfilled in a very limited way.[57] In particular, none of the ESAs actually measures the real performance of the savings products offered to EU citizens.

- The Boards of Supervisors of the ESAs are composed only of national supervisors. However, the national supervisors are the very bodies that the ESAS are supposed to control. Like the ESMA SMSG, Better Finance asks the ESAs' boards to be opened up to independent experts, like what has been decided for the European Central Bank's Board. This issue is compounded by the fact that several national financial regulators have weak governance themselves, with their governing bodies including people from the industry and none from the retail user-side. The International Monetary Fund criticised in particular the governance of the French securities and markets regulator for that reason: 'In addition, the participation of industry representatives – some on active duty – in the Boards of AMF and H3C has the potential to create conflict with commercial interests. While arrangements are in place to address conflicts of interest, alternative mechanisms should be established to ensure that market expertise is brought into the decision-making process. Finally, given the current governance model whereby different interests are represented at the level of the Board *the limited direct representation of retail investors at that level should also be addressed*'.[58]

  The ESMA Securities and Markets Stakeholder Group also publicly advocated for the boards of the European Supervisory Authorities to be more independent, and recommended introducing independent board members like in the European Central Bank's Board.[59] Better Finance published the same position in its response to the Public Consultation on the Review of the European System of Financial Supervision in 2013.

  In turn, the boards of the national supervisors often do not include people with a user background, and too often only include people with a financial industry background. This inadequate governance of EU Member State financial supervisors has been well documented by FIN-USE.[60]
- The distribution of retail investment products is not properly supervised, since the ESAs have a 'silo' organisation by legal product category, although all these products are often sold by the same financial intermediaries. This

57 See both the ESMA SMSG and the EuroFinUse published papers on the Review of the ESFS, supra notes 46 and 44 respectively.

58 IMF, 'France: Financial System Stability Assessment' (2012) *IMF Country Report* No. 12/341, para. 48 <www.imf.org/external/pubs/ft/scr/2012/cr12341.pdf> accessed 19.10.2014.

59 See ESMA Securities and Markets Stakeholder Group, *SMSG contribution to the ESFS Consultation. An SMSG review of the ESA's including a self-assessment,* supra note 46.

60 See FIN-USE, *Position Paper on Consumer Voice in Financial Services*, 2009 <http://ec.europa.eu/internal_market/fin-use_forum/docs/consumer_voice_en.pdf> accessed 19.10.2014.

results in serious inconsistencies in terms of financial user protection rules across the overall range of retail financial products. In particular, pension savings products – of critical importance to all financial services users and more generally to all EU citizens – are not properly addressed in our view by the ESFS. EIOPA is only in charge of occupational pensions, which are not covered by the investor protection rules of the MiFID (securities and funds) or IMD (insurance) Directives. The fate of non-occupational pension products is unclear in terms of European supervision responsibility. The same applies to the spot currency markets (the biggest financial markets in the world): no ESA seems to be in charge. The issue of whether 'it is appropriate to continue separate supervision of banking, insurance, occupational pensions, securities and financial markets' must indeed be addressed in the ESFS Review as required by article 81(2)(a) of the ESAs Regulations. On this issue, Better Finance supports the ESMA SMSG's recommendation to have a European Financial Conduct Authority cover all types of retail financial products, regardless of whether they are bank, insurance, securities or any other type of product.

5.3. THE EVENTS ORGANISED BY THE INTERNATIONAL PUBLIC FINANCIAL AUTHORITIES

Despite some recent improvements, the speakers invited by the public authorities to their events are overwhelmingly from the financial industry, and all too often there is not even one speaker from the user-side.

An example was the European Commission Public Hearing on the Review of the ESFS (European System of Financial Supervision) of 24 May 2013, which included several bankers and/or insurers as speakers but no retail user representative.[61]

One of the most striking examples of the discrimination against the user-side in the events of the public authorities dealing with financial services policy was the 2013 annual conference (18 September 2013) of IOSCO, the International Organisation of Securities Commissions, the public agency that includes and represents all national capital markets supervisors of the world:

- Although the public part of the IOSCO Conference was open to 'observers', individual investors were not considered as such by IOSCO, which lists all stakeholders as observers except individual investors and financial services

[61] <ec.europa.eu/internal_market/conferences/2013/0524-financial-supervision/docs/programme_en.pdf> accessed 19.10.2014 (one panel speaker was a member of the FSUG, but he is an academic, not a retail user representative, and all four speakers presented as ESAs' Stakeholder Group members were from the financial industry).

users: 'Observers (= public part attendees): Persons interested in meeting the regulators and IOSCO members as well as persons interested in the topics covered in the 4 panels: i.e. (mainly senior) representatives from financial entities such as banks, stock exchanges, management companies, asset managers, distributors, brokerage firms, specialised service providers, for example in the IT field, but also academics, officials from ministries of finance and embassies from various countries'.

- The registration fee for 'observers' was set at €2,100, in any case making it impossible for most individual investor representatives to attend (see section 4 above on resources), and obviously favouring industry participants.
- The IOSCO 2013 panels were of primary importance to individual investors and savers, especially the one on 'long term savings and pensions', as the recent research report published by EuroFinUse[62] shows. But there was not one representative of the user-side in these panels, despite the fact that they are the most exposed stakeholders in the dramatic pension issue.
- The IOSCO Conference had two of the biggest banking groups in the world as its main sponsors, raising issues about its economic independence from the financial industry it has the responsibility to supervise.

5.4. THE PARTICIPATION OF EU POLITICIANS AND EXECUTIVES TO OUTSIDE INITIATIVES AND EVENTS

Until some years ago, it was difficult for retail user organisations to get EU officers to participate in their rare events (annual conferences and the like). At the same time, the participation of EU executives at industry-sponsored events is systematic, and these events occur almost every week or several times a week.

An example is the 'European Parliamentary Financial Services Forum' (EPFSF)[63] which is managed by the European Banking Federation (EBF) and its membership consists of MEPs and financial industry institutions. Annual membership is €8,000, and 2012 expenses amounted to €351,000. It is chaired by an MEP and by the European Banking Federation (EBF) and organises events on financial regulatory issues in the European Parliament premises. Each time quite a few MEPs participate. Since 2012, Better Finance, BEUC, Finance Watch and FSUG have been able to obtain 'observer' status and get invited to these events, and sometimes to speak together with several industry speakers and typically one speaker from the Commission. The moderator is an MEP. However, retail

[62] EuroFinUse, *The Real Return of Private Pensions. A Research Report by EuroFinUse*, 2013 <www.betterfinance.eu/fileadmin/user_upload/documents/Research_Reports/en/Pension_Study_EN_website.pdf> accessed 19.10.2014.

[63] <www.epfsf.org> accessed 19.10.2014.

users are still massively outnumbered there, and there is not an even remotely equivalent process for MEPs to interact with the user-side.

Nevertheless, this has improved in recent times, as these two examples show:

- 16 March 2012: for the first time the Director General of the EC DG Internal Markets and Services spoke at a Better Finance event: Jonathan Faull delivered the keynote speech at the Better Finance International Conference in Brussels.
- 26 March 2013: for the first time the Internal Market and Services commissioner spoke at a Better Finance event: Michel Barnier delivered the closing speech at the Better Finance International Conference on the audit market reform. Three MEPs, as well as the EC Head of the Audit Unit, also spoke at this conference.

On the other hand, almost every week EU officials of equivalent levels or below participate in numerous industry-sponsored events, especially in lobbyists-laden Brussels. This is also an area where finding some balance is challenging. It would be interesting to direct academic research on quantifying this participation of EU policymakers in financial industry-sponsored events.

5.5. THE MEETINGS OF EU OFFICIALS WITH THIRD PARTIES

This is still an area of European public policy that remains very little known and researched: with which third parties are the EU financial services executives and officers meeting? Do they spend most of their meetings with industry lobbyists or not? In Sweden, ministers are required to disclose their meetings with third parties, but no such requirement exists to our knowledge for EU politicians and executives.

EU officials – Members of the European Parliament especially – are often besieged by industry lobbies. The MEP Rapporteur of the AIFMD[64] Directive once mentioned he received more than 1,800 amendment proposals – all from industry, none from the retail investor side, which was already busy trying to submit amendments to the parallel discussion of the ESFS Regulations. The AIFMD Rapporteur Jean-Paul Gauzes later became one of the founders of Finance Watch.

64 The Alternative Investment Fund Managers Directive – Directive 2011/61/EU of the European Parliament and of the Council of 8 June 2011 on Alternative Investment Fund Managers and amending Directives 2003/41/EC and 2009/65/EC and Regulations (EC) No. 1060/2009 and (EU) No. 1095/2010, OJ 2003 No. L 174/1 – entered into force on 22 July 2013.

Financial services user organisations often find it difficult to get appointments with EU executives, and suspect that besides their participation in third-party events (see above section 5.4), these executives spend significantly more time talking to industry and industry providers (i.e. paid by the financial industry) than with the user-side. However, as mentioned above we cannot provide substantial evidence for this at this stage. More transparency on the third-party meetings agendas of top EU executives would be welcome in that regard. This after all would provide a good yardstick for measuring the actual depth of EU democracy.

6. CONCLUSION: TIME FOR CHANGE

The financial crisis has had one side benefit: to make EU policymakers more aware of the imbalance of influence between the financial industry and the user-side.

This chapter identifies clear signs of this growing awareness.

The 2010 EU Regulations on Financial Supervision now require balanced representation between the financial industry and the retail users in the consultative bodies, and adequate compensation and support to the non-industry not-for-profit members of these bodies. These newly set legal principles represent significant progress in the direction of better involvement of civil society in EU financial policy design.

The European Commission, in particular under the impulse of the Internal Market and Services Commissioner Michel Barnier, revamped its user expert groups and launched the first call for proposals to fund retail users and other non-industry stakeholders' capacity building in the area of financial services policy in December 2011. On 27 March 2012, Michel Barnier summarised his views in an important speech on 'Making financial regulation serve society through civil society and consumer participation'.

But this chapter also points to further improvements that are necessary to ensure a more balanced representation of the interests of the user and civil society side in general in the design and implementation of European financial policies.

Furthermore, the recent improvements noted are not a given and could well be scaled back in this new era of 'financial repression'[65] against depositors and investors due to the combined actions of the central banks and the Governments. Those are confronted with a much-deteriorated financial climate. And the recent

[65] See for example 'The financial repression levy', *The Economist*, 23.03.2013.

handling of the Cyprus crisis and tax increases on savings (that now eat into more than 100% of the real return of households' savings in some Member States)[66] show that financial services user protection could easily be put on the back burner again, in favour of replenishing state coffers. The IMF is even proposing that governments seize 10% of the financial net worth of households to solve their public finance issues.[67] This would be terrible for the EU economy, for all European pension savers and overall for the European democracy, taking us back to the pre-crisis 'business as usual' between the financial industry and policymakers.

The future implementation of the most recent regulatory initiatives that are key to financial services user protection will help us tell which way we may be heading:

- The Review of the European System of Financial Supervision: the Report from the Commission to the European Parliament, due by 2 January 2014, is still awaited as of April 2014;
- The Regulation on the Key Information Document (KID) for investment products (known as the 'PRIIPs'[68] Regulation): for the very first time the EU authorities have issued a horizontal user protection regulation that applies to many retail investment products. Unfortunately, the European Parliament just (April 2014) voted on a text that still excludes equities, bonds, personal and occupational pensions and bank savings products from the scope of these harmonised and simplified disclosure requirements.

---

66 See examples in EuroFinUse, *The Real Return of Private Pensions. A Research Report by EuroFinUse*, supra note 62.

67 See Better Finance comment on this IMF proposal <www.betterfinance.eu/fileadmin/user_upload/documents/Press_Releases/en/Press_Release_Financial_Repression_Conference_EuroFinUse_18.10.2013.pdf> accessed 19.10.2014.

68 PRIPs: Packaged Retail and Insurance-based Investment Products.

Part II.2

The United States of America

FINANCIAL STABILITY REARTICULATED: INSTITUTIONAL REFORM, POST-CRISIS GOVERNANCE AND THE NEW REGULATORY LANDSCAPE IN THE UNITED STATES

David S. Bieri

The recent financial crisis was a powerful reminder that the inherent instability of the monetary-financial system is likely to entail serious consequences for the real economy. In the U.S., the monumental Dodd-Frank Wall Street Reform and Consumer Protection Act of 2010 ('Dodd-Frank Act') has provided legislation that aims to institutionalise several aspects of a new thinking on financial stability. In addition to the interagency Financial Stability Oversight Council ('FSOC'), the creation of the Consumer Financial Protection Bureau ('CFPB') marks an important departure from the U.S. regulatory tradition of de-centralized agencies whereby the institutional locus of financial oversight depended on the precise nature of the legal structure of and business activities pursued by individual financial intermediaries. In its mandate and institutional structure, the CFPB unifies both 'micro-prudential' and 'macro-prudential' principles of financial regulation to enhance overall financial stability. From an historical perspective, the creation of the CFPB does not change the regulatory landscape to the same extent as did the creation of the Federal Reserve after the Panic of 1907 or the creation of the FDIC after the 1933 Banking Crisis. At the same time, however, the CFPB represents an important historical shift in the policy focus of U.S. financial regulation away from bank stability to a broad notion of financial stability that recognises the increased financialisation of households' welfare.

1. OVERVIEW

The recent financial crisis was a formidable reminder of the inherent instability of the monetary-financial system and of the serious consequences for the real economy that this instability entails.[1] This chapter argues that the broad range of policy responses to the crisis in the United States are unified by a common theme, namely a shift in the policy stance away from monetary stability towards financial stability. On the one hand, this shift is characterised by an extension of the perimeter of financial regulation such that it puts the monitoring of systemic risk on an institutional footing. On the other hand, the U.S. regulatory stance has tilted away from traditional concerns over bank stability towards an institutional recognition that household decision making is increasingly financialised.

The monumental Dodd-Frank Wall Street Reform and Consumer Protection Act of 2010 ('Dodd-Frank Act') has provided legislation that aims to institutionalise several aspects that are emblematic of this new thinking on financial stability. In addition to the interagency Financial Stability Oversight Council ('FSOC'), the creation of the Consumer Financial Protection Bureau ('CFPB', 'Bureau') marks an important departure from the U.S. regulatory tradition of de-centralized agencies whereby the institutional locus of financial oversight depended on the precise nature of the legal structure of and business activities pursued by individual financial intermediaries. An independent regulatory agency of the United States government, the Bureau's mandate is to make 'consumer financial products and services work for Americans'. Its purview thus ranges from financial literacy education to financial regulation which includes banks, credit unions, securities firms, payday lenders, mortgage-servicing operations, foreclosure relief services, debt collectors and other financial companies operating in the United States. Despite its outwards appearance as a single-purpose regulator, the CFPB's mandate and institutional structure unifies both 'micro-prudential' and 'macro-prudential' principles of financial regulation to enhance overall financial stability.

The remainder of this chapter is structured as follows. The next section discusses the scope and limits of financial regulation, focussing on the shift from monetary stability to financial stability as an emergent policy paradigm in more recent years. In section 3, I examine the institutional arrangements and governance challenges of the U.S. regulatory and supervisory complex. I also investigate possible consequences of some of the shortcomings and compromises that have plagued recent regulatory reform. The CFPB as an institutional response to the crisis is explored in more detail in section 4. This section also highlights that the post-crisis U.S. regulatory landscape is defined by a historical shift in the policy focus away from bank stability to a broad notion of financial stability that recognises the increased importance of finance for households welfare. These new institutional realities pose very specific challenges for regulatory and supervisory

1 I use the term 'monetary-financial system' in keeping with Chandler's view that monetary institutions and financial markets now overlap to such a degree that they are best viewed as parts of a larger whole – L.V. Chandler, *The Monetary-Financial System*, Harper and Row Publishers, New York City, NY 1979.

accountability. Section 5 offers some concluding thoughts on the post-crisis regulatory landscape.

2. THE QUEST FOR FINANCIAL STABILITY

In contrast to monetary stability, there is a much broader spectrum of definitions and consensus only seems to exist in so far as financial stability is deemed a 'good thing' and that it is mostly noticed by its absence.[2] One of the earliest definitions of financial stability is given by Bagehot[3] who describes financial stability as '(...) not a situation when the Bank of England is the only institution in which people have confidence'. Despite much definitional progress in the century and a half since Bagehot, a firm consensus for financial stability has yet to emerge, albeit not for a shortage of efforts. The recent financial crisis has led to a veritable outpour of policy work, white papers and theoretical treaties, all attempting to pin down this elusive concept further.[4] The question remains whether financial stability requires just the soundness of institutions, the stability of markets, the absence of turbulence, low volatility, or whether it constitutes something more fundamental.[5]

Broadly speaking, one can distinguish between a systems approach - primarily linking financial stability to a well-functioning financial system - and a more narrow definition relating to the (excess) volatility of an observable financial variable, such as asset price volatility or interest rate smoothness. The debate around finding a suitable definition is more than a semantic one, particularly since any given definition predetermines the role assigned to specific institutions in contributing to financial stability.[6]

---

2 Consensus with regard to the definition of monetary stability has emerged during much of the 20th century and permits various notions ranging from stability of the (anticipated) value of money to price-level stability or even low levels of inflation.

3 W. Bagehot, *Lombard Street: A Description of the Money Markets*, 1st ed., Scribner, Armstrong, New York 1873.

4 The literature is far too voluminous to do full justice here, but some important milestones in the development of a cohesive body of knowledge in this area include M.D. Bordo and D.C. Wheelock, 'Price Stability and Financial Stability: The Historical Record' (1998) 80 *Federal Reserve Bank of St. Louis Review* 41; W.R. White, 'Past Financial Crises, the Current Financial Turmoil, and the Need for a New Macrofinancial Stability Framework' (2008) 4 *Journal of Financial Stability* 307; C.E. Borio and M. Drehmann, 'Towards an Operational Framework for Financial Stability: "Fuzzy" Measurement and its Consequences' (2009) *BIS Working Paper* No. 265; D. Mayes, R. Pringle and M. Taylor (eds.), *Towards a New Framework for Financial Stability*, Central Banking Publications, London 2009; R.E. Krainer, 'Regulating Wall Street: The Dodd-Frank Act and the New Architecture of Global Finance: A Review' (2012) 8 *Journal of Financial Stability* 121 and R.E. Krainer, 'Towards a Program for Financial Stability' (2013) 85 *Journal of Economic Behavior & Organization* 207.

5 G.J. Schinasi, 'Defining Financial Stability' (2004) *IMF Working Paper* No. 04/187.

6 D.S. Bieri, 'Regulation and Financial Stability in the Age of Turbulence' in R.W. Kolb (ed.), *Lessons from the Financial Crisis: Causes, Consequences, and Our Economic Future*, John

From an historical perspective, one can broadly outline a typology of financial market upheaval that distinguishes between three types of financial instability. First, there is volatility-based instability, such as the crises of the European Exchange Rate Mechanism in the 1980s and 1990s, the 1987 stock market crash, the 1994 emerging market bond market instability, the 1998 Russian default, the Argentinean default in 2001 and most recently, the US subprime crisis in 2007–08. A second type of instability is stress-based instability, which is often triggered by the default of an individual financial institution. Instances of stress-based instability include the insolvency of Credit-Anstalt in 1931, the collapse of Bankhaus Herstatt in 1974, the folding of the Bank of Credit and Commerce International in 1991, the Barings scandal in 1995, the failure of Long-Term Capital Management in 1998 and the most recent string of institutional failures, from Northern Rock to Bear Stearns, Lehman Brothers and the American International Group. Lastly, there are instances of crisis-based financial instability that are largely characterized by a triggering development that originates in the real economy or the financial system. Costly bank insolvencies and major adjustments in the level of asset prices tend to follow. During this type of financial instability, there is often a very strong (reinforcing) interaction between the financial sector and the real economy, with strong contagion effects both domestically and internationally. Aside from the Great Depression, the Scandinavian banking crisis in the late 1980s, the bursting of the Japanese asset bubble in the 1990s, the Mexican crisis (1994–95) and the Asian financial crisis all fall into this class of crises.

While no episode of financial upheaval neatly fits into any one of the three categories, a classification can be informative for policy purposes. The recent financial crisis is an important case in point; what started as distant volatility rumblings of market-based financial instability in the U.S. sub-prime market in mid-2007 eventually snowballed into a fully blown global crisis with major financial instability across several market and institutional segments, including upheavals in the government debt market in Europe.

From the perspective of policy makers, however, it is clear that some of the elements that might potentially harbour a threat to financial stability are actually very desirable for achieving the goal of monetary stability. Financial innovation, for example, has been key to making the transmission mechanism for monetary policy more effective. This apparent tension raises the question of a latent trade-off between monetary and financial stability with important implications for regulatory accountability that I discuss in more detail in section 4.[7] Despite the increasing interlinkages of globalized financial markets, the implementation

Wiley & Sons, Inc., Hoboken, NJ 2010, pp. 327–336.

7 See also D.S. Bieri – 'The Basel Process, Financial Stability and the Age of Turbulence' Mimeograph, Virginia Tech, Blacksburg, VA 2008 – for a more detailed discussion of this point.

of policy goals pertaining to both monetary and financial stability still rests almost exclusively with national institutions. The recent financial crisis was a forceful reminder of the increasing difficulties to obtain these objectives without coordinated efforts at the supranational level. The next section takes a closer look at the institutional division of labour for financial stability in the United States.

3. THE INSTITUTIONAL ARRANGEMENTS OF U.S. FINANCIAL REGULATION

Historically, the main policy focus of the U.S. financial regulatory system has been one of 'prudence'.[8] Beginning with the National Banking Acts of 1863 and 1864, the institutional emphasis of U.S. regulation has been placed on the twin objectives of bank stability and monetary policy. Most major regulatory reforms and institutional innovations of the U.S. regulatory landscape of the last 150 years followed in the wake of a financial crisis, either strengthening systemic bank stability or the implementation of monetary policy. Indeed, the creation of the Federal Reserve System in 1913 – a response to the Panic of 1907 – and the creation of the Federal Deposit Insurance Corporation ('FDIC') after the 1933 Banking Crash mark the most important events in this regard. While the creation of the CFPB perhaps does not change the regulatory landscape to the same extent as did the creation of the Federal Reserve and the FDIC, it represents an important shift in the policy focus of U.S. financial regulation away from bank stability and monetary policy to consumer protection.

3.1. MICRO-PRUDENTIAL ENTITIES

In characterising regulatory functions at the micro-prudential scale (i.e. focusing on individual types of financial institutions, functions or markets), it may be useful to distinguish between regulators that generally focus on prudence and regulators that generally focus on disclosure. Prudential regulation implies the monitoring and regulation of risks that a specific firm engages in, whereas regulatory disclosure monitors and regulates the information that firms and exchanges provide to potential market participants. Figure 1 provides an overview of the institutional arrangements of the U.S. regulatory context in this regard. Four federal agencies have prudential authority to regulate and supervise banks, thrifts, and credit unions (i.e. the Office of the Comptroller of the Currency, 'OCC'; the FDIC; the National Credit Union Administration, 'NCUA'; and the Federal Reserve).

[8] C.W. Calomiris and G. Gorton, 'The Origins of Banking Panics: Models, Facts, and Bank Regulation' in R.G. Hubbard (ed.), *Financial Markets and Financial Crises*, University of Chicago Press, Chicago, IL 1991, pp. 109–174 and C.W. Calomiris, *U.S. Bank Regulation in Historical Perspective*, Cambridge University Press, Cambridge, UK and New York 2000.

In addition to prudential regulators with an institutional focus, there are three prudential agencies with an activities-based mandate, regulating the farm credit system (Farm Credit Agency 'FCA'), the federal housing finance system via the Federal Housing Finance Authority ('FHFA' monitoring government sponsored entities, 'GSEs') and consumer financial products (CFPB), respectively. Among the disclosure-based regulators, two agencies oversee markets for financial contracts such as securities and derivatives (i.e. the Securities and Exchange Commission, 'SEC' and the Commodity Futures Trading Commission, 'CFTC').

Figure 1. The institutional arrangements of U.S. financial regulation

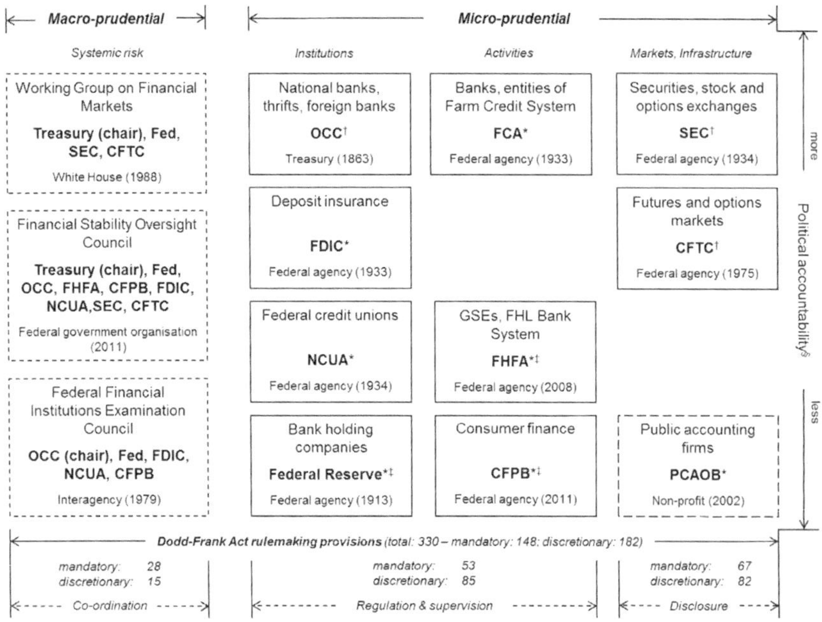

Source: Author.

Notes: * Independent federal agency with self-funding. Funding source is not only independent of Congress, but authority to use funds is not conditioned on congressional budgetary approval.
† Independent federal agency without self-funding. Accountability via budgetary appropriations process.
‡ 'For-cause' removal protection of director, commonly used to distinguish between independent and executive branch agencies.
§ Degree of political accountability is determined using a number of criteria, including the degree of self-funding, for-cause protection of the director, multi-member boards and the requirement for partisan balance on the board.

The policy problems and regulatory approaches of the agencies are listed in figure 1. For example, the prudential bank regulators and the FHFA examine firms with specific charters and monitor and limit the risks that their chartered firms engage in. Securities and derivatives regulators monitor exchanges that host the trading of financial contracts, oversee the disclosures that market participants provide, and enforce rules against deceptive or manipulative trading practices. Unlike prudential bank regulators, securities regulators generally do not monitor the composition of assets and liabilities of the firms participating in their markets.[9] These and other general differences may exist because of the various missions and risks to financial stability that the agencies each address individually.

3.2. MACRO-PRUDENTIAL FRAMEWORK

At the macro-prudential scale, there are three entities with an institutional mandate to act as an interagency coordinating forum. These entities are made up of the micro-prudential financial regulators with related duties or functions and facilitate communication and coordination among member agencies. In each instance, the creation of a coordinating entity is a policy response to an episode of systemic financial instability. The Federal Financial Institutions Examination Council ('FFIEC') was a regulatory response[10] to a spike in bank failures during the early 1970s, the President's Working Group on Financial Markets ('WGFM') a reaction to the stock market crash of 1987, and, most recently, the FSOC a reply to the recent financial crisis. While not tasked to address systemic risk in the same comprehensive manner as the FSOC, both the FFIEC and the WGFM are thus important institutional precursors to an emergent thinking about macro-prudential regulation that is now fully embodied in the FSOC.

Indeed, former U.S. Treasury secretary Tim Geithner's memoirs[11] document that the fragmentation of the U.S. financial system's main regulatory agencies encumbered co-ordination during the recent crisis as agencies appeared to lock horns over divergent political interests. As such, the Dodd-Frank Act may have failed to fix the fractured and fractious regulatory system of the United States. Indeed, one the Act's many imperfections is that the responsibility for monitoring systemic risk was lodged not inside the Federal Reserve, the one agency that had

---

9 Although the distinction between prudence-based regulators and disclosure-based regulators may be true in general, bank regulators can regulate the disclosures of their chartered firms and securities and derivatives regulators do have some prudential responsibilities. See M. Jickling and E.V. Murphy – 'Who Regulates Whom? An Overview of U.S. Financial Supervision' (2010) *CRS Report for Congress* No. R-40249 – and E.V. Murphy – 'Who Regulates Whom and How? An Overview of U.S. Financial Regulatory Policy for Banking and Securities Markets' (2013) *CRS Report for Congress* No. R-43087 – for more details on this point.

10 The FFIEC was established in 1979, pursuant to title X of the Financial Institutions Regulatory and Interest Rate Control Act of 1978 (FIRA) to curtail bank failures by regulating the banking industry more closely. See A.F. Garrison – 'The Financial Institutions Regulatory and Interest Rate Control Act of 1978, Federal Banking, and the Judiciary: The Struggle to Define the Limitation of Cease and Desist Order Authority' (1987) 44 *Washington and Lee Law Review* 1357 – for more details.

11 T. Geithner, *Stress Test: Reflections on Financial Crises*, Random House, New York 2014.

to pick up the pieces of a financial crisis, but with the FSOC which is made up of all those feuding agencies.

A distinguishing feature of the U.S. regulatory landscape is that – despite the existence of single-purpose regulators, such as the CFPB – the regulatory activities of individual agencies are not necessarily mutually exclusive. The creation of the CFPB also marks a departure from the U.S. regulatory tradition of de-centralized agencies whereby the institutional locus of financial oversight has long depended on the precise nature of the legal structure of and business activities pursued by individual financial intermediaries. For deposit-taking institutions, for example, this means that the Federal Reserve regulates bank holding companies, whereas national banks, state commercial and savings banks are supervised by the National Bank Supervisors, state bank supervisors and the FDIC, respectively. Similarly, federally chartered credit unions are regulated by the National Credit Union Administration, while state-chartered credit unions are regulated at the state level.[12]

In light of the fact that the post-crisis U.S. regulatory landscape is defined by a historical shift away from bank stability to a broad notion of financial stability that recognises the increased importance of finance for households welfare, the next section now focuses on the CFPB as an institutional response to the crisis in more detail.

4. THE CFPB AS A POST-CRISIS RESPONSE

The CFPB is an independent regulatory agency of the United States government with a mandate to make 'consumer financial products and services work for Americans'. Its purview ranges from financial literacy education to financial regulation which includes banks, credit unions, securities firms, payday lenders, mortgage-servicing operations, foreclosure relief services, debt collectors and other financial companies operating in the United States. In important ways, the creation of the CFPB recognises that the structural transformation of the financial system, characterised by technological change, financial innovation, and financial deregulation, has meant that an increasingly large component of the financial decision making that affects household welfare has been delegated to individual households themselves.

From managing their own pensions to taking important credit decisions to finance housing and other large-ticket consumption expenditures, the institutional

12 See J.R. Barth, T. Liy and W. Luy – 'Bank Regulation in the United States' (2010) 56 *CESifo Economic Studies* 112 – for more details on the historical evolution of U.S. banking regulation.

center of gravity for financial decision making no longer resides with financial professionals, but with the common household. This democratisation of access to credit and the larger participation of individual households in financial market activity have extended the policy boundary of the monetary-financial system. The financialisation of household decision making implies that concerns about financial stability no longer automatically just extend to concerns about the solvency and liquidity of banking institutions, but also extend to the financial stability of individual households.[13] Politically, thus, the creation of the CFPB was driven by a narrative of the crisis as one where consumer abuse in the financial sector was rampant as scrupulous financial predators took advantage of the financial needs of households, particularly of low-income and minority families.[14]

Legislation for the creation of the CFPB was authorized by the Dodd-Frank Wall Street Reform and Consumer Protection Act, the passage of which in 2010 was the most important regulatory response in the United States to the financial crisis of 2007–2008. The Bureau was formally established when Dodd-Frank was enacted, on July 21, 2010. After a one year 'stand up' period, the Bureau obtained enforcement authority and began most activities on July 21, 2011. The creation of the CFPB marks perhaps the most significant change to the post-crisis regulatory institutional landscape in the United States.

4.1. INSTITUTIONAL FOCUS AND POLICY MANDATE

In consolidating in one place responsibilities that had been scattered across various government agencies, the CFPB is intended to increase government accountability, while at the same time having additional responsibility for supervision and enforcement with respect to the laws over providers of consumer financial products and services that previously escaped regular Federal oversight. Primarily, however, the Bureau is intended to protect families from unfair, deceptive, and abusive financial practices. Focusing both on the demand side and

---

13 A. Lusardi and O.S. Mitchell – 'The Economic Importance of Financial Literacy: Theory and Evidence' (2014) 52 *Journal of Economic Literature* 5 – provide an overview of why financial literacy matters more for financial stability than ever.

14 E.g. M.S. Barr, *No Slack: The Financial Lives of Low-Income Americans*, Brookings Institution Press, Washington, DC 2012. At the same time, however, an equally plausible narrative is that of declining lending and underwriting standards across important segments in the credit markets in the run up to the crisis, suggesting that lenders' screening decisions, first and foremost in the subprime market for low-documentation loans, were becoming more lax during the upswing of the credit cycle (C. Mayer, K. Pence and S.M. Sherlund, 'The Rise in Mortgage Defaults' (2009) 23 *Journal of Economic Perspectives* 27; C.D. Anderson, D.R. Capozza and R. van Order, 'Deconstructing a Mortgage Meltdown: A Methodology for Decomposing Underwriting Quality' (2011) 43 *Journal of Money, Credit and Banking* 609; B.J. Keys, A. Seru and V. Vig, 'Lender Screening and the Role of Securitization: Evidence from Prime and Subprime Mortgage Markets' (2012) 25 *Review of Financial Studies* 2071).

on the supply side of financial services, the CFPB is intended to make regulations and issue guidance as clear and streamlined as possible, so providers of consumer financial products and services can follow the rules on their own.

Designed to overcome the historical regulatory fragmentation of the U.S. regulatory complex, the CFPB thus consolidates employees and responsibilities from a number of other federal regulatory bodies, including the Federal Reserve, the Federal Trade Commission, the FDIC, the NCUA, and even the Department of Housing and Urban Development. Technically, the CFPB is an independent unit located inside and funded by the Federal Reserve, with an interim affiliation with the U.S. Treasury Department.

Specifically, the CFPB's areas of activity can broadly be categorized into 'supervision, regulatory compliance and enforcement' and 'financial research and education'. In the first category, the Bureau's activities are comprised of: 1. Rule making, supervision and enforcement of federal consumer financial protection laws; 2. Enforcement of financial antidiscrimination legislation and other unfair treatment in consumer finance; and 3. Restriction of unfair, deceptive, or abusive acts or practices. At present, CFPB's most pressing concerns are mortgages, credit cards and student loans. In the second category, the CFPB focuses on: 1. Collection of consumer complaints; 2. Strengthening of financial education; 3. Research on consumer behaviour; and, 4. Monitoring of financial markets for new risks to consumers. Indeed, much of the Bureau's policy remit and scope are directly reflected in its organizational structure which is separated into six divisions: 1. Supervision, Enforcement, and Fair Lending; 2. Research, Markets, and Regulations; 3. Office of the Chief Operating Officer; 4. General Counsel; 5. Consumer Education and Engagement; and 6. External Affairs.

In terms of regulatory governance, the CFPB breaks important new grounds in that it relies on legal enforcement, rather than the traditional process of supervision that permits regulatory fine-tuning as part of ensuring compliance. While bank supervision is principally a forward looking process that resolves problems informally without sanctions for past violations, enforcement requires formal federal legal action. In contrast to her colleagues at other regulatory agencies, the CFPB examiner's influence and effectiveness thus depends on the agency's 'willingness to make a federal case out of financial misconduct'.[15]

In its mandate and institutional structure, the CFPB unifies both micro-prudential and macro-prudential principles of financial regulation to enhance overall

15 H. Beales, *The Importance of Financial Literacy and the Financial Crisis and the CFPB, Presentation on 'Reflections on the Federal Reserve and its Place in Today's Economy'*, George Washington University, Washington, DC 2012.

financial stability. Beyond protecting borrowers and investors that participate in financial markets, the CFPB contributes to achieving financial stability by possible disruptions to the broader economy that might emanate from the financial sector.

4.2. FINANCIAL STABILITY AS A PUBLIC GOOD

The rationale for financial regulation such as that contained in the CFPB's mandate ultimately rests on two objectives: 1. The desire to maintain financial stability by mitigating systemic risk, and 2. The desire to protect consumers (investors). Consumer protection and mitigation of systemic risk are mostly complementary, but they can also conflict. The recent crisis has shown that measures taken to protect particular market participants (e.g. home owners in the U.S. or depositors in the Eurozone) may sometimes have unintended consequences, which are increasing systemic risk.

Indeed, financial stability carries all the textbook hallmarks of a public good. First, it is non-rival as its benefits to one consumer are not limited by the simultaneous consumption by other consumers. Second, financial stability is non-excludable as its benefits are available to all economic agents, even to those who do not pay for it (i.e. entities that are not regulated, such as, e.g., shadow banks and other non-depository financial intermediaries). Lastly, individual agents cannot actively withdraw themselves from the influence of financial stability.

Public finance theory has long established that the private-sector production of public goods yields an under-supply with respect to its optimal quantity. For this very reason, financial stability has traditionally been produced by and provided by national governments. Globalization, however, has brought about a partial shift in the optimal locus of production, since financial stability is no longer a fully spatially delineated public good. Indeed, the importance of international public goods such as financial stability or an international regulatory level playing field, has considerably raised the stakes in the ordo-liberal challenge for well-coordinated international policy co-operation in the age of turbulence.

The economic theory of regulation pioneered by Stigler[16] stipulates that regulation often induces changes in behaviour which go against the very effects that regulation intended in the first place. During periods of investor exuberance and comparative regulatory complacency, these adverse effects of regulation are very likely to be muted if not invisible altogether. Any new regulation – from Dodd Frank at the

[16] G.J. Stigler, 'The Theory of Economic Regulation' (1971) 2 *Bell Journal of Economics and Management Science* 3

local level to Basel III,[17] the most recent international regulatory framework for banks, at the global level – will bring with it the so-called boundary problem of regulation, i.e. the problem that institutions in the regulated sector and those in the unregulated sector face different incentives. Supervisors must thus attempt to learn how the regulated are seeking to avoid the constraints placed upon them.[18]

During the Great Moderation, the boundary problem profoundly misaligned incentives across many agents in the financial sector as systemic financial imbalances accumulated in the run-up to the crisis. This induced large-scale regulatory capital arbitrage, e.g. in the form of securitization, which offset some or all of the intended regulatory effects. Regulation failed to take account of the risks that can emerge from the interaction between regulated and unregulated institutions, activities, and markets. In particular, bank regulation did not reflect risks from off-balance-sheet vehicles, monoline insurance companies, shadow banks or loan originators with weak underwriting standards. Equipped with the analysis from ratings agencies, even sophisticated investors could not be relied on to assess risk accurately on more complex financial products.

To be sure, it can be argued that is was the principal-agent problems in the public sector that enabled many of the principal-agent problems in the private sector that are so commonly blamed for the crisis. One of the immediate legacies of the crisis is a massive series of bailouts by public authorities in Europe and the United States that, according to work by Herring,[19] amounted to the equivalent of nearly one-fifth of world GDP in taxpayer funds. In turn, the sheer magnitude of the bailouts has created a new moral hazard in that it might lead to deeper and more frequent crises unless counteracted by more 'regulatory bite'.

4.3. REGULATORY GOVERNANCE AND THE ACCOUNTABILITY CHALLENGE

Despite the fact that the global financial system is increasingly interlinked, much of the international regulatory system still operates on a sectorial level. Indeed, as the financial landscape of the post-Bretton Woods era has changed, and banks, insurers, and securities firms have begun to offer similar or even identical products, central banks and regulatory authorities such as the CFPB have recognized the growing need for a central vehicle for coordinating their efforts.

17 BCBS, *International Regulatory Framework for Banks (Basel III)*, Basel Committee on Banking Supervision, Basel 2013.

18 C.A.E. Goodhart, 'The Boundary Problem in Financial Regulation' (2008) 206 *National Institute Economic Review* 48.

19 R.J. Herring, 'How Financial Oversight Failed And What it May Portend for the Future of Regulation' (2010) 38 *Atlantic Economic Journal* 265.

At the level of the global financial system, the various regulatory and supervisory initiatives of the Basel-based committees and their working groups form the core institutional building blocks of such a global coordination exercise. This global framework which is aimed at harmonizing regulatory and supervisory processes and standards is collectively known as the 'Basel Process'.[20]

4.3.1. Global governance

Among the plethora of regulatory efforts that address the new realities of financial globalisation, the Basel Process is uniquely positioned to provide policy makers with an institutional arrangement for regulatory coordination, governance and standard setting. The Bank for International Settlements ('BIS'), the world's oldest and perhaps least well-known international financial institution, provides the locational anchor for the Basel Process which has come to form the natural home for the global policy coordination among central bankers and regulators.[21] As the political geography of the world is still more or less organized around the building block of the nation state, central banks and other institutions involved in the Basel Process are inevitably going to be held accountable by the citizens of their nation states, even if their nature is not directly susceptible to democratic pressure.[22] The institutional responsibilities for financial stability are traditionally shared across different institutions, namely finance ministries, the central bank and regulators. While clearly defined accountabilities for each of the institutions involved is a sine qua non, the actual goal of financial stability can only be brought about by an effective coordination of these efforts. This is the role of the Basel Process.

While BIS and its central bank members have engaged in several initiatives to improve the transparency of decision-making processes, the Basel Process might not always be considered 'accountable' in the ways citizens might want. For example, Kane[23] argues that participants in the BCBS process lacked sufficient democratic accountability to reconcile the fundamental conflicts between bank, regulator and societal interests that arise in efforts to connect national safety nets. Referring to 'gaps in the cross-country regulatory contract', he explains how national differences in regulatory accountability made gaps in the cross-country deal more

---

20 D.S. Bieri, 'Financial Stability, the Basel Process and the New Geography of Regulation' (2009) 2 *Cambridge Journal of Regions, Economy and Society* 303.

21 Perhaps one of the most prominent recent initiatives arising out of this process is the most recent incarnation of the international regulatory framework for banks, commonly referred to as Basel III.

22 The 2006 Global Accountability Report assigns a relatively low 'accountability score' to the BIS in comparison to other international institutions (M. Blagescu and R. Lloyd, *2006 Global Accountability Report. Holding Power to Account*, One World Trust, London 2006).

23 E.J. Kane, 'Basel II: A Contracting Perspective' (2007) 32 *Journal of Financial Services Research* 39 and E.J. Kane, 'Connecting National Safety Nets: The Dialectics of the Basel II Contracting Process' (2007) 35 *Atlantic Economic Journal* 399.

easily tolerated in other BCBS countries than in the USA. More prominently, the 'Lamfalussy Process' on pan-European financial services legislation has incurred considerable public criticism as it allows some elements of bypassing accountable oversight by the Council of the European Union and the elected European Parliament.[24] This echoes similar concerns by Robinson[25] who argues that the international framework for governing globalization lacks accountability and is undemocratic, thus largely embodying a move away from representative, participatory democracy towards a state of technocratic governance.

Despite the fact that financial globalization has created rising interdependencies between institutions, markets and infrastructure and the co-operative efforts of the Basel Process in response, there remains a good deal of local and sectorial fragmentation in the international regulatory system. Official definitions of systemic risk leave out the role of government officials in generating it. To underscore and strengthen regulators' duty of accountability, Kane[26] calls for a series of informational reforms designed to measure systemic risk on an ongoing and less conflicted basis. This program has three components: 1. Expanding the types of information financial institutions generate and report; 2. Separating bureaucratic responsibility for measuring growth in the safety net from responsibility for limiting safety-net growth; and 3. Improving the tools and incentives of safety-net managers.[27]

4.3.2. National accountability

At the national level, the complex and multi-faceted interaction between accountability and governance issues in the U.S. regulatory system are evidenced by the fact that the Dodd-Frank legislation contains well over 300 explicit provisions that at least permit or require rule making. The bottom panel of figure 1 highlights how these rulemaking provisions are distributed across macro- and microprudential considerations for financial stability. Indeed, five years into the

---

[24] The Lamfalussy Process was created in 2001 in order to enhance flexibility for European securities legislation by reacting promptly to market developments and benefitting from expertise of national supervisory authorities. As part of this process, the EU institutions agreed to accelerate the passage of financial services legislation and began applying to securities legislation in 2002 and to banking legislation in 2004 (D. Alford, 'The Lamfalussy Process and EU Bank Regulation: Another Step on the Road to Pan-European Regulation?' (2006) 25 *Annual Review of Banking and Financial Law* 389).

[25] W.I. Robinson, 'Capitalist Globalization and the Transnationalization of the State' in M. Rupert and H. Smith (eds.), *Historical Materialism and Globalization*, Routledge, London and New York 2002, pp. 210–229.

[26] E.J. Kane, 'Redefining and Containing Systemic Risk' (2010) 38 *Atlantic Economic Journal* 251.

[27] See also P.A. Volker and R.W. Ferguson, Jr – *The Structure of Financial Supervision: Approaches and Challenges in a Global Marketplace*, Group of 30, Washington, DC 2008 – for a discussion of key organisational challenges for the design of global governance of financial regulation and supervision.

adoption of the legislation, it is still not clear – in fact technically unknowable – how many rules will ultimately be issued pursuant to the act, because most of the provisions are discretionary and agencies may or may not issue to rule, individual provisions might result in multiple rules, and some provisions provide rulemaking authority to agencies that technically already possess such authorities.[28]

Since passage of the Dodd-Frank Act, its initial 848 pages of statutory text have ballooned to more than 14,000 pages – testimony to an unimaginable explosion of administrative complexity compared to, for example, the decidedly anaemic 37 pages of 1934 Glass-Steagall Act.[29] Furthermore, over 80% of the provisions assigned rulemaking responsibilities or authorities to one of five federal agencies: the Federal Reserve, the FDIC, the SEC, the CFTC, and the newly-created CFPB. Dozens of other provisions in the act gave joint rulemaking responsibility or authority to two or more of these agencies.

In quantifying the extent of political accountability of an independent agency in the U.S. regulatory complex, one of the most agreed upon characteristics is what is termed 'for cause' removal protection, which is intended to provide a measure of independence from presidential direction and control.[30] The political fight over the CFPB's structure was largely focused on the Bureau's for-cause-protected, single-member head, which Congress combined with the Bureau's exclusion from the congressional appropriations process, because it was believed that self-funding would be essential to the CFPB's independence.[31] Indeed, while self-funded agencies are a rarity in U.S. administrative law, their freedom from both congressional budgetary approval and the congressional appropriations process

---

[28] C.W. Copeland, 'Rulemaking Requirements and Authorities in the Dodd-Frank Wall Street Reform and Consumer Protection Act' (2010) *CRS Report for Congress* No. R-41472. Washington Law Firm Davis Polk monitors monthly progress in the Dodd-Frank implementation using its *Regulatory Tracker*. As of December 2014, a total of 280 Dodd-Frank rulemaking requirement deadlines have passed. This is over 70% of the 350 some total rulemaking requirements, and 100% of the 280 rulemaking requirements with specified deadlines. Of the total rulemaking requirements, 230 (58%) have been met with finalised rules and rules have been proposed that would meet 94 (24%) more. Rules have not yet been proposed to meet 96 (24%) rulemaking requirements.

[29] E.J. Kane, 'Missing Elements in US Financial Reform: A Kübler-Ross Interpretation of the Inadequacy of the Dodd-Frank Act' (2012) 36 *Journal of Banking and Finance* 654.

[30] The heads of Cabinet departments and independent agencies generally serve 'at the pleasure of the President' and therefore can be removed at any time. In contrast, the heads of independent regulatory agencies, whether part of a multi-member board like the SEC or a single administrator like the CFPB, can only be removed by the President for some type of 'cause' (C.W. Copeland, *Economic Analysis and Independent Regulatory Agencies, White paper*, Administrative Conference of the United States, Washington, DC 2013).

[31] H. Beales, *The Importance of Financial Literacy and the Financial Crisis and the CFPB, Presentation on 'Reflections on the Federal Reserve and its Place in Today's Economy'*, supra note 15.

gives self-funded agencies potentially a unique degree of political independence.[32] The CFPB's unique structure thus gives the Bureau independence from direct Executive oversight in at least three ways: 1. The Bureau is headed by a for-cause protected director; 2. It has independent litigation authority; and 3. It is permitted to officially communicate with Congress without first obtaining approval from the Office of Management and Budget.

Indeed, figure 1 shows that the CFPB is at the very low end of the spectrum in terms of its degree of political accountability, even when measured – in addition to the for-cause protection of the director – using a much wider number of criteria, including the degree of self-funding, multi-member boards and the requirement for partisan balance on the board. Given this sizeable broadening of the post-crisis mandate of U.S. financial regulatory agencies, concerns have not only arisen in terms of regulatory accountability, but also in terms of the (unintended) economic burden that new regulatory legislation might entail. In fact, a number of individuals and organizations have recommended that independent regulatory agencies be required to prepare economic cost-benefit analysis before issuing certain rules.[33] A common argument for the introduction of such analysis is that it would bring much-needed transparency and accountability to the rule-writing process in the U.S. regulatory complex.[34]

Overall then, the creation of the CFPB tilts the post-crisis regulatory institutional landscape in the United States towards more regulatory independence in significant ways. As figure 1 illustrates, the Bureau's strong budgetary independence and relative insulation from political processes is on par, if not higher than that of the Federal Reserve and the FHFA, raising new challenges of accountability and regulatory governance.

---

32 C. Kruly, 'Self-Funding and Agency Independence' (2013) 81 *George Washington University Law Review* 1733. In line with the literature, I use the term 'self-funded' to describe an agency whose funding source is not only independent of Congress, but whose authority to use those funds is not conditioned on congressional budgetary approval. Congress has empowered a number of agencies to collect fees and fines that the agencies then use to fund their operations. However, not all form of self-funding provides the same degree of political independence. The Federal Communications Commission ('FCC'), for example, is self-funded in the sense that it funds its operations from the fees it collects. At the same time, the FCC may only collect and use fees in an amount authorized by Congress. In contrast, the Fed is simply authorized to 'levy semiannually upon the Federal reserve banks … an assessment sufficient to pay its estimated expenses and the salaries of its members and employees'. See C. Kruly – 'Self-Funding and Agency Independence', supra this note – for a more detailed discussion of this point.

33 C.W. Copeland, *Economic Analysis and Independent Regulatory Agencies, White paper*, supra note 30.

34 For example, the *American Enterprise Institute*, a conservative think tank, proposes a statutory requirement for economic analysis at federal financial regulators, modelled after the analysis required of executive branch federal agencies under executive orders (A. McCloskey and H. Peirce, *Holding Financial Regulators Accountable: A Case for Economic Analysis*, American Enterprise Institute, Washington, DC 2014).

5. REGULATORY LESSONS FROM THE RECENT FINANCIAL CRISIS

In very broad terms – as the global economy no longer stares into the abyss of a financial market fallout and the first green shoots of a tentative recovery are visible – the principal regulatory lesson is twofold. First, at a micro-prudential level, the regulatory perimeter needs to be strengthened and extended. It was excessive risk taking by global financial actors outside this very perimeter that lies at the origin of current crisis. Going forward, this implies both expanding the scope of regulation of institutions (improved disclosure, limits on leverage, liquidity requirements, governance standards) and a tighter regulation for markets and individual financial products.

Immediately in the aftermath of the crisis, the G-20 has called for a review of the scope of financial regulation, focusing on institutions, instruments and markets that are currently unregulated, along with ensuring that all systemically important institutions are appropriately regulated. This call reflects concern that the coverage of prudential regulation has been too narrow. Prudential regulation typically aims at minimizing the risk of failure by institutions (and settlement systems) that are viewed as critical to maintaining stability. Instruments of prudential regulation typically include minimum capital and liquidity requirements, supervisory inspection, mechanisms to require early intervention by regulators, deposit insurance, and similar safety nets, as well as special insolvency and resolution mechanisms. The scale of relevant activities outside the regulatory perimeter depends on the definition of regulation. For the United States, it has been estimated that the total assets of the 'shadow banking system' – i.e., bank-like entities not subject to bank-like prudential regulation – were roughly US$10 trillion in late 2007, about the same size as those of the banking system.[35] Indeed, the regulation of the shadow banking system has been one of the most active areas of regulatory reform efforts since the financial crisis. Despite some progress at strengthening the stability of the shadow banking system, progress to date has been uneven.[36]

---

[35] However, it is important to recognize that this total includes the assets of entities such as investment banks, which were subject to a degree of regulation, although this was often focused mainly on ensuring investor protection and appropriate business conduct (A. Carvajal, R. Dodd, M. Moore, E. Nier, I. Tower and L. Zanforlin, 'The Perimeter of Financial Regulation' (2009) *IMF Staff Position Note* No. SPN/09/03).

[36] E.g. G. Gorton and A. Metrick, 'Regulating the Shadow Banking System' (2010) 41 *Brookings Papers on Economic Activity* 261; T. Adrian and A.B. Ashcraft, 'Shadow Banking Regulation' (2012) 4 *Annual Review of Financial Economics* 99. In the context of shadow banking regulation, a key challenge is the potential for regulatory overlap when regulated banks actively participate in shadow financial system (S.L. Schwarcz, 'Regulating Shadow Banking' (2012) 31 *Review of Banking and Financial Law* 619).

At the same time, macro-prudential regulation ought to incorporate the fact that systemic risk is an endogenous component of the global financial system; the seamless monitoring of the growing interconnectedness of its various institutional building blocks forms a central part of this new regulatory paradigm. Much like the CFPB, the new financial supervisory framework for the European Union, the European System of Financial Supervision (ESFS), which was adopted in 2011, rests on a micro- and a macro-prudential pillar and envisions the establishment of a single supervisory mechanism for banks led by the European Central Bank.[37]

Yet better regulation such as Dodd-Frank and new institutions such as the CFPB or the ESFS will not be enough; complementary adjustments to macroeconomic policy frameworks are equally essential. These adjustments would call for a more symmetric response to the build-up and unwinding of financial imbalances. The BIS, for example, sees a need to explore how to incorporate credit and asset price booms and the associated risk-taking more meaningfully in monetary policy frameworks.[38] Likewise, additional consideration to the possible role of fiscal policy, including that of the tax system and fiscal balances, seem inevitable. Despite much progress on, much remains to be done. In its most recent annual report, the FSOC[39] reports on a number of key milestones in financial reform implementation, including finalization of the Volcker Rule, bank capital rules, a supplementary leverage ratio for the largest banks and BHCs, enhanced prudential standards for the U.S. operations of large foreign banks, and the advent of clearing, trading, and registration requirements for swaps markets. Furthermore, policy development needs to be pushed forward with proposed rule-makings on money market fund reform, risk retention for securitizations, and requirements for short-term liquidity coverage for large banking organizations.

In addition to this long punch-list of regulatory efforts, a number of critical issues for financial stability remain yet to be included on that list. For example, Kane[40] highlights the incentive conflicts that led creditors and internal and external supervisors to short-cut and outsource due diligence. The Dodd-Frank strategy of reform does not adequately acknowledge or address these conflicts. Without reforms in the practical duties imposed on industry and governmental officials and in the way these issues of governance are enforced, financial safety nets will continue to expand and their expansion will undermine financial stability by generating large rewards for creative and aggressive risk-takers.

---

37 L. Bini Smaghi, 'Going Forward: Regulation and Supervision after the Financial Turmoil' (2009) *Bocconi University Paolo Baffi Centre Working Paper* No. 2009–47; N. Véron, 'Europe's Single Supervisory Mechanism and the Long Journey Towards Banking Union' (2012) *Bruegel Policy Contribution* No. 2012/16.

38 BIS, *79th Annual Report*, Bank for International Settlements, Basel, Switzerland 2009 and BIS, *84th Annual Report*, Bank for International Settlements, Basel, Switzerland 2014.

39 FSOC, *4th Annual Report*, Financial Stability Oversight Council, Washington, DC 2014.

40 E.J. Kane, 'Missing Elements in US Financial Reform: A Kübler-Ross Interpretation of the Inadequacy of the Dodd-Frank Act', supra note 29.

THE FINANCIAL INDUSTRY REGULATORY AUTHORITY: NOT SELF-REGULATION AFTER ALL

Hester PEIRCE

The Financial Industry Regulatory Authority (FINRA) is the front-line regulator of broker-dealers in the United States. FINRA is not the self-regulatory organization some imagine it to be. A self-described 'independent' regulator, FINRA is a non-governmental, not-for-profit organization that wields considerable control over the daily activities of its member firms, their employees, and the investors they serve. The U.S. Securities and Exchange Commission (SEC) – the governmental regulator of the securities markets – oversees FINRA, but FINRA enjoys considerable independence. On the one hand, its governance structure means that it is not accountable to the industry it regulates in the way an SRO would be. On the other hand, FINRA's broad governmental powers are not paired with the public accountability measures to which governmental regulators are subject. Concerns about FINRA's lack of accountability loom even larger as FINRA seeks to regulate additional facets of the financial markets such as investment advisers and securities markets. Policymakers should reconsider its growing role in light of its lack of accountability to the industry it regulates and to the public it is supposed to serve.

The chapter proceeds as follows. Part 1 discusses the history and responsibilities of FINRA and its predecessor the National Association of Securities Dealers (NASD). Part 2 discusses FINRA's current functions. Part 3 sets forth the structure of accountability within which FINRA operates. Part 4 compares the mechanisms by which governmental regulators are held accountable to the public with FINRA's accountability structure. Part 5 discusses recent changes in FINRA's focus and aspirations. Part 6 concludes with a recommendation that FINRA's role in the regulation of the U.S. securities markets be reconsidered in order to achieve more effective and accountable financial regulation.

1. THE EMERGENCE OF FINRA

FINRA, which was formed in 2007, was built upon a long tradition of self-regulatory organizations (SROs) in the securities industry. FINRA's predecessor, the NASD, joined the ranks of SROs in the late 1930s. Self-regulating securities exchanges were already the industry norm when Congress created the Depression-era federal securities framework. They regulated member conduct and market activity and set standards for listed companies.[1] The Securities Exchange Act of 1934[2] (Exchange Act) recognized and relied on exchange SROs, such as the New York Stock Exchange (NYSE), to continue performing these regulatory functions.

Before the Exchange Act reached its fifth birthday, its self-regulatory provisions were expanded to include the over-the-counter (OTC) markets. Prior to this expansion, brokers working in these markets were not regulated by an SRO. Instead, in 1934, President Franklin Roosevelt approved a securities industry-developed 'code of fair competition' under the National Industrial Recovery Act (NIRA), which made the privately developed code legally binding on the industry.[3] The Supreme Court soon thereafter ruled NIRA unconstitutional,[4] and the securities industry code lost its legal force.

After NIRA's demise, the SEC worked with industry to fill the void. These efforts culminated in convincing Congress to pass the Maloney Act[5] in 1938.[6] The Maloney Act added new section 15A to the Exchange Act to allow any association of brokers or dealers meeting the statutory requirements to register with the SEC as a 'national securities association'.[7] To register, an association had to have rules that, among other things, ensured 'fair representation of its members', 'equitable allocation of dues', prevention of 'fraudulent and manipulative acts and practices' and 'unreasonable profits or unreasonable rate of commissions or other charges', promotion of 'just and equitable principles of trade', appropriate member discipline, and protection of 'investors and the public interest'.[8]

---

1 For a history of securities markets SROs, see K. Durr and R. Colby, *The Institution of Experience: Self-Regulatory Organizations in the Securities Industry, 1792–2010*, <www.sechistorical.org/museum/galleries/sro/index.php> accessed 14.04.2014.

2 15 U.S.C. § 78a et seq. (2012).

3 J.D. McGowan, *The NASD-Origins, Recent Developments, and Future Goals*, 1974, pp. 8–10 <http://3197d6d14b5f19f2f440-5e13d29c4c016cf96cbbfd197c579b45.r81.cf1.rackcdn.com/collection/papers/1970/1974_0801_NASDOriginsT.pdf> accessed 31.03.2014.

4 Schecter Poultry Corp. v. United States, 295 US 495, 541–42 (1935) (holding that 'code-making authority thus conferred is an unconstitutional delegation of legislative power').

5 Pub. L. No. 75–719, 52 Stat. 1070 (1938).

6 K. Durr and R. Colby, *The Institution of Experience: Self-Regulatory Organizations in the Securities Industry*, supra note 1.

7 15 U.S.C. § 78o-3 (2012).

8 15 U.S.C. § 78o-3(b) (1940).

The Maloney Act's voluntary national securities associations were to be the OTC market counterparts to the exchange SROs. As the SEC explained shortly after the Act's passage, the Act embodied 'the principle of conferring upon regulatory groups from business a primary responsibility for enforcing high standards of business conduct upon their members ... (by setting) up a system of regulation in the over-the-counter markets through the formation of voluntary associations of investment bankers, dealers and brokers doing business in these markets under appropriate governmental supervision'.[9] SEC Commissioner George Mathews predicted that the Maloney Act would serve as the basis for a long and productive shared regulatory relationship between the SEC and the industry:

> '(T)he cooperative program envisioned in the Act must of necessity be an evolutionary one. Ideally, the industry should eventually play the predominant role in its own regulation and development along sound economic and social lines. ... As spokesman for the Commission have repeatedly said, it is sincerely to be hoped that the ultimate role of the Commission will be a residual one in which its energies may be principally directed toward dealing with the submarginal element known to all industries which in the absence of coercion refuses to abide by either moral or legal standards. Admittedly, the fulfillment of this ideal requires time'[10]

A year later, the first step in the evolution began when the SEC approved FINRA's predecessor, the National Association of Securities Dealers (NASD), to be the first registered national securities association. Because no other associations registered with the SEC, the NASD was the only SRO for brokers and dealers in the over-the-counter markets.[11] In 1945 the NASD began requiring principal and customer-facing employees of broker-dealers to register with the NASD.[12]

In the early 1960s, the SEC recommended making NASD membership mandatory.[13] Instead, in 1964, Congress gave the SEC the authority to establish a regulatory framework for broker-dealer firms in the over-the-counter securities

---

9 SEC, *Fourth Annual Report for the Fiscal Year Ended June 30, 1938*, 1938, p. 33.

10 G.C. Mathews, Commissioner, SEC, *A Discussion of the Maloney Act Program*, Speech before the Annual Convention of the Investment Bankers Association of America, White Sulphur Springs, West Virginia, 23.10.1938, p. 2, <www.sec.gov/news/speech/1938/102338mathews.pdf> accessed 31.03.2014.

11 The National Futures Association subsequently registered as a limited purpose national securities association because of new regulatory powers over security futures products it acquired under the Commodity Futures Modernization Act of 2000. NATIONAL FUTURES ASSOCIATION, *The Value of Building Strong Relationships* <www.nfa.futures.org/news/newsLetterArticle.asp?ArticleID=535> accessed 31.03.2014.

12 For a contemporaneous discussion of the requirement, see W.H. Fulton, 'Executive Director's Report,' *NASD News*, February 1946, p. 3, <http://3197d6d14b5f19f2f440-5e13d29c4c016cf96cbbfd197c579b45.r81.cf1.rackcdn.com/collection/papers/1940/1946_0201_NASDNews.pdf> accessed 31.03.2014.

13 H.F. Owens, Commissioner, SEC, *The Securities Acts Amendments and the Investment Banking Community*, Speech before Texas Group Investment Bankers Association of America, San

markets that were not NASD members.[14] Under this authority, the SEC set up the so-called 'SEC Only' (SECO) program. In 1983, NASD membership became mandatory through legislation resulting from 'a joint effort with the NASD' that 'abolished the SECO program, under which the Commission staff has been directly supervising and inspecting 600 over-the-counter firms'.[15] The SEC staff later explained why the SEC recommended that Congress replace the SECO program with mandatory NASD membership:

> 'The Commission concluded that a direct regulatory program was not the most efficient use of the Commission's resources and that weak links in the program regarding rulemaking and data collection could not be improved without increased expenditures. The Commission determined that the benefits of retaining the SECO Program were minimal compared to the benefits to be derived from its elimination. The Commission noted that even if the program were abolished, the Commission would still retain general oversight authority over SRO actions. Because all its rules would be reviewed by the Commission, specific complaints concerning NASD performance would also be heard'.[16]

The decision to eliminate the SECO program and shift more responsibility to the NASD came after changes made by Congress in 1975 had taken hold. The 1975 amendments to the Exchange Act reflected Congress' mixed conclusion that '(t)he securities industry's unique system of self-regulation has shown great strength in some areas and, in general, has served the industry well (but) has also displayed serious deficiencies and has not operated as effectively or fairly as it should'.[17] Among other things, the 1975 amendments resolved the 'continuing controversy as to the precise scope of the SEC's power to amend the rules of a self-regulatory organization (by giving) the SEC clear authority to amend any self-regulatory organization's rules in any respect consistent with the objectives of the Exchange Act'.[18] By making this change and requiring SEC approval for SRO rules, the 1975 amendments 'greatly broadened the Commission's authority over the SROs, and

Antonio, Texas, 08.04.1965, p. 7 <www.sec.gov/news/speech/1965/040865owens.pdf> accessed 03.04.2014.

14 Pub. L. 88–467, 78 Stat. 565 (1964) (section 6 amended section 15 of the Exchange Act).

15 SEC, 49th *Annual Report of the Securities and Exchange Commission for the Fiscal Year Ended September 30, 1983,* 1984, p. vi <https://www.sec.gov/about/annual_report/1983.pdf> accessed 25.03.2014.

16 DIVISION OF MARKET REGULATION, SEC, *Market 2000: An Examination of Current Equity Market Developments*, 1994, p. VI-6.

17 COMMITTEE ON BANKING, HOUSING & URBAN AFFAIRS OF THE U.S. SENATE, *Summary of Principal Provisions of the Securities Act Amendments of 1975 S. 249*, 1975, p. 4 <www.sechistorical.org/collection/papers/1970/1975_0101_SummaryAmendments.pdf> accessed 25.03.2014.

18 Ibid., p. 8.

generally produced a much more substantial nexus between the Commission and the SROs'.[19]

The SEC exercised its authority over the NASD in a very public way in the mid-1990s in connection with the NASD's ownership of the National Association of Securities Dealers Automated Quotations (NASDAQ) electronic stock market. The NASD created NASDAQ in 1971, and, by 1994, it had 'surpasse(d) the NYSE in yearly share volume'.[20] In 1996, the SEC censured the NASD for failing to enforce its rules against Nasdaq market makers participating in anticompetitive pricing practices.[21] The offending practices included coordination to manipulate prices, harassment of nonconforming market makers, unauthorized sharing of customer order information, selective failures to honour quotes, and delayed trade reporting.[22] The SEC found that 'the consequences for the Nasdaq market of this failure were exacerbated by the undue influence exercised by Nasdaq market makers over various aspects of the NASD's operations and regulatory affairs'.[23]

Explaining that '(w)hile self-regulation benefits from the knowledge, insight, and expertise brought by industry participants, it must give primacy to the fundamental purpose of regulation of the securities markets: the protection of investors and the public interest',[24] the SEC required NASD to agree to certain undertakings. The NASD's undertakings included increasing the role of public members on the NASD board, augmenting staff autonomy and independence, chairing its disciplinary hearings with professional hearing staff, and adopting uniform guidelines to govern membership applications and regulatory activities.[25] Professor Barbara Black points to the NASD's 1996 settlement with the SEC as an important milestone in 'the NASD's transformation into a professional regulator largely independent of its membership'.[26] In 2000, Nasdaq members voted to separate Nasdaq from NASD and become a publicly held, for-profit company, and in 2006 the Nasdaq gained exchange status.[27]

---

19 R.L. Stone and M. Perino, 'Not Just a Private Club: Self-Regulatory Organizations as State Actors When Enforcing Federal Law' (1995) *Columbia Business Law Review* 453, 461.

20 NASDAQ OMX Corporate Timeline <www.nasdaqomx.com/aboutus/company-information/timeline> accessed 03.04.2014.

21 SEC, *Report Pursuant to Section 21(a) of the Securities Exchange Act of 1934 Regarding the NASD and the Nasdaq Market*, 08.08.1996 (hereinafter *SEC Report Pursuant to Section 21(a)*), p. 4 <www.sechistorical.org/collection/papers/1990/1996_0808_SECNASD_1.pdf> accessed 25.03.2014.

22 Ibid., pp. 2–3.

23 Ibid., p. 4.

24 Ibid., p. 44.

25 Ibid., pp. 44–45.

26 B. Black, 'Punishing Bad Brokers: Self-Regulation and FINRA Sanctions' (2013) 8 *Brooklyn Journal of Corporate, Financial & Commercial Law* 23, 36.

27 NASDAQ OMX Corporate Timeline, supra note 20.

Against the backdrop of the NASD's manifest conflicts of interest, U.S. securities markets were undergoing other important changes that led Congress, the SEC, and industry to consider the need for changes to the SRO model.[28] Concerns about conflicts of interest were not limited to the NASD. Exchanges were also SROs, and there was concern that 'the interests required of an SRO to regulate itself and its members are in conflict with its interests in promoting itself'.[29] Those concerns intensified as exchanges started to demutualize and become for-profit entities. Most notably, the NYSE merged with Archipelago – a major electronic market and became a publicly traded company in March 2006.[30] The changes raised concerns about whether the for-profit NYSE could effectively manage 'the conflicting goal of having to maximize profits while not compromising regulation'.[31]

In addition, the SEC, Congress, and industry were increasingly worried about regulatory duplication. Because there were multiple securities industry SROs, firms were subject to different, and sometimes conflicting, rules and duplicative examinations and disciplinary proceedings.[32] Approximately 180 firms were members of, and thus regulated by, both the NASD and the NYSE's regulatory arm.[33] The NASD and NYSE made efforts to coordinate their regulatory programs, but the industry still believed that 'duplication and redundancy will continue to occur as long as two separate entities regulate the same conduct of the same firms'.[34] The SEC likewise recognized that 'the existence of multiple SROs can result in duplicative and conflicting SRO rules, rule interpretations, and inspection regimes ... and redundant SRO regulatory staff and infrastructure across SROs'.[35]

---

[28] See, for example, *Self-Regulatory Organizations: Exploring the Need for Reform – Hearing Before the Subcommittee on Capital Markets, Insurance, and Government Enterprises of the Committee on Financial Services of the U.S. House of Representatives* – 109th Cong., 1st Session, 17.11.2005 (hereinafter SRO Hearing); SEC, *Concept Release Concerning Self-Regulation*, 69 Federal Register 71,256, 08.12.2004 (hereinafter *SEC SRO Concept Release*); SEC, *Fair Administration and Governance of Self-Regulatory Organizations; Disclosure and Regulatory Reporting by Self-Regulatory Organizations; Recordkeeping Requirements for Self-Regulatory Organizations; Ownership and Voting Limitations for Members of Self-Regulatory Organizations; Ownership Reporting Requirements for Members of Self-Regulatory Organizations; Listing and Trading of Affiliated Securities by a Self-Regulatory Organization*, 69 Federal Register 71126, 08.12.2004; Securities Industry Association, *White Paper: Reinventing Self-Regulation* (updated 2003) <www.sifma.org/workarea/downloadasset.aspx?id=21354> accessed 03.04.2014 (hereinafter *SIA White Paper*).

[29] *SIA White Paper*, supra note 28, p. 8.

[30] NYSE, *Stock of New Public NYSE Group, Inc. Begins Trading*, News Release, 08.03.2006, <www.nyse.com/press/1141729831759.html> accessed 31.03.2014; NYSE, *NYSE/Archipelago Merger Gains Final SEC Approval*, News Release, 08.03.2006 <www.nyse.com/press/1141083887100.html> accessed 31.03.2014.

[31] SRO Hearing, supra note 28 (statement of R.G. Glauber, Chairman and CEO, NASD), p. 3.

[32] *SIA White Paper*, supra note 28, pp. 9–10.

[33] SRO Hearing, supra note 28 (statement of R.G. Glauber, Chairman and CEO, NASD), p. 89.

[34] SRO Hearing, supra note 28 (statement of M.E. Lackritz, President, Securities Industry Association), p. 111.

[35] *SEC SRO Concept Release*, supra note 28, p. 71264.

In light of the substantial changes in the securities markets and the concerns about regulatory redundancy, the SEC offered seven reform options that ranged from modifications to the existing system to replacement of the SRO system with direct regulation by the SEC.[36] One option was the so-called 'hybrid model', under which there would be a 'Single Member SRO' to which all broker-dealers would belong. That SRO would set membership requirements for firms and their registered representatives, write rules related to financial condition, margin, customer relationships, supervision, and sales practices.[37] Exchanges would continue to operate as SROs, but only as it related to regulation of their own markets.[38] Another option posited by the SEC would have given a single SRO authority over all markets and firms, but a concern with this approach was the 'lack (of) market specific expertise'.[39] The industry's preferred approach was the hybrid model, because it would eliminate redundancies and conflicts in member regulation, while allowing for continued market-specific regulation:

> 'Enhanced regulatory efficiency will allow both the SROs and firms to use compliance resources more effectively. Regulatory accountability will be bolstered as a result of one entity being responsible for overseeing broker-dealer activity at the SRO level. Finally, the regulatory expertise of the SRO staff will expand as a single SRO gains the resources, power, and prestige to attract talented staff, and keeping the expertise close to the markets whose day-to-day activities it regulates. At the same time, the existence of multiple-market SROs, each with responsibility over those regulations applicable to its unique trading structures will keep market expertise where it is most useful'.[40]

A version of the hybrid model became a reality with the merger of the member regulation functions of the NASD and NYSE Regulation in 2007.[41] The result was FINRA – a more powerful successor to the NASD.[42] FINRA 'would provide member firm regulation for securities firms that do business with the public in the United States'.[43] Specifically, the new SRO was 'responsible for rule writing,

---

36 Ibid., p. 71275.
37 Ibid., p. 71277.
38 Ibid., p. 71278.
39 Ibid., p. 71280.
40 SRO Hearing, supra note 28 (statement of M.E. Lackritz, President, Securities Industry Association), p. 112.
41 FINRA, *NASD and NYSE Member Regulation Combine to Form the Financial Industry Regulatory Authority*, News Release, 30.07.2007, <www.finra.org/Newsroom/NewsReleases/2007/p036329> accessed 13.10.2014.
42 FINRA was created by amending the NASD's bylaws. SEC, *Self-Regulatory Organizations; National Association of Securities Dealers, Inc.; Order Approving Proposed Rule Change To Amend the By-Laws of NASD To Implement Governance and Related Changes To Accommodate the Consolidation of the Member Firm Regulatory Functions of NASD and NYSE Regulation, Inc.*, 72 Federal Register 42169, 01.08.2007.
43 Ibid., p. 42170.

firm examination, enforcement and arbitration and mediation functions, along with all functions that were previously overseen solely by NASD, including market regulation under contract for NASDAQ' and three other exchanges.[44] The SEC, in approving the consolidation, explained that it was 'intended to help streamline the broker-dealer regulatory system, combine technologies, and permit the establishment of a single set of rules governing membership matters, with the aim of enhancing oversight of U.S. securities firms and assuring investor protection'.[45] NYSE Regulation retained the responsibility for regulating its markets (as opposed to its member firms).

2. FINRA'S FUNCTIONS

Through the consolidation, FINRA solidified its role as a front-line regulatory force of almost equal weight with the SEC. At the end of 2013, FINRA regulated approximately 4,100 firms, 161,000 branch offices and 636,000 registered securities representatives.[46] FINRA has approximately 3,400 employees and a nearly $1 billion budget.[47] By comparison, the SEC has a staff of approximately 4,000 and a budget of approximately $1.3 billion.[48] Although not directly comparable given the different nature of the entities registered with the SEC, the SEC oversees more than 25,000 firms.[49]

FINRA's stated substantive objectives are:

> '(1) To promote through cooperative effort the investment banking and securities business, to standardize its principles and practices, to promote therein high standards of commercial honor, and to encourage and promote among members observance of federal and state securities laws;
>
> (2) To provide a medium through which its membership may be enabled to confer, consult, and cooperate with governmental and other agencies in the solution of problems affecting investors, the public, and the investment banking and securities business;

44 FINRA 30.07.2007 News Release, supra note 41.

45 SEC, *SEC Gives Regulatory Approval for NASD and NYSE Consolidation*, Press Release, 26.07.2007 <www.sec.gov/news/press/2007/2007-151.htm> accessed 14.04.2014.

46 FINRA, *FINRA 2013 Year in Review and Annual Financial Report*, 2014, p. 8 (hereinafter *FINRA 2013 Annual Report*).

47 Ibid., pp. 8–9.

48 SEC, *Fiscal Year 2013 Agency Financial Report*, 2014, pp. 10, 38.

49 M.J. White, Chair, SEC, Testimony on SEC Budget Before the Subcommittee on Financial Services and General Government, Committee on Appropriations of the United States House of Representatives, 07.05.2013 <www.sec.gov/News/Testimony/Detail/Testimony/1365171516034#_ftnref3> accessed 01.04.2014.

(3) To adopt, administer, and enforce rules of fair practice and rules to prevent fraudulent and manipulative acts and practices, and in general to promote just and equitable principles of trade for the protection of investors; (and)
(4) To promote self-discipline among members, and to investigate and adjust grievances between the public and members and between members. . ..'[50]

In carrying out these objectives, FINRA performs a wide range of functions. Broker-dealers doing business with the public and certain persons associated with them must register with FINRA. FINRA administers qualifying examinations for firms' principals and employees who perform securities functions (so-called 'registered representatives').[51] FINRA maintains a lengthy rulebook that governs the activities of member firms and their associated persons.[52] The rules cover all aspects of the securities business, including registration, continuing education, firm and member conduct, prohibitions against the use of fraudulent devices, 'know your customer' and suitability requirements, 'best execution' obligations for customer transactions, member firm supervisory responsibilities, communications with the public and with customers, financial condition, margin, operations, books and records, anti-money laundering responsibilities, and transactions with customers.[53]

As a registered securities association, FINRA enforces its own rules and the federal securities laws.[54] In addition, FINRA enforces the rules of another SRO, the Municipal Securities Rulemaking Board (MSRB), which writes rules for the municipal securities markets, but is not authorized to enforce these rules.[55] FINRA conducts routine examinations of member firms and branch offices and cause examinations that are motivated by a particular concern or tip. In 2012, for example, FINRA conducted more than 1800 routine firm examinations, 800 branch office examinations, and 5,100 cause examinations.[56] FINRA also conducts multi-firm sweep examinations, such as a targeted examination of

50 Restated Certificate of Incorporation of Financial Industry Regulatory Authority, Inc., 02.07.2010, <http://finra.complinet.com/en/display/display.html?rbid=2403&element_id=4589> accessed 13.10.2014.
51 FINRA, *FINRA Registration and Examination Requirements* <www.finra.org/industry/compliance/registration/qualificationsexams/qualifications/p011051> accessed 14.04.2014.
52 FINRA, *FINRA Rules* <www.finra.org/Industry/Regulation/FINRARules/> accessed 14.04.2014.
53 FINRA, *FINRA Manual* <http://finra.complinet.com/en/display/display_main.html?rbid=2403&element_id=1> accessed 13.10.2014.
54 15 U.S.C. §78o-3(b)(2) (2012).
55 MUNICIPAL SECURITIES RULEMAKING BOARD, *Market Regulation* <www.msrb.org/About-MSRB/Programs/Market-Regulation.aspx> accessed 15.04.2014.
56 *FINRA 2012 Year in Review and Annual Financial Report*, 2013, p. 8.

high-frequency trading in July, 2013 and a cybersecurity examination in January, 2014.[57]

When FINRA finds violations of its rules, MSRB rules, or the federal securities laws, it is authorized to bring disciplinary actions. FINRA's sanctions include censures, fines, restitution to harmed investors, suspensions, and permanent bars from the industry.[58] In 2013, FINRA brought 1,535 disciplinary actions.[59] Most disciplinary actions are settled.[60] Contested actions are heard by a panel composed of a professional hearing officer as chairman and two industry representatives.[61] FINRA's National Adjudicatory Council (NAC), a fourteen-member panel with equal numbers of public and industry members, hears appeals from hearing panel decisions.[62] FINRA's Board of Governors can choose to review the NAC's decision. As section 3 discusses, FINRA's disciplinary decisions are subject to SEC review. FINRA actively refers potential civil and criminal cases to governmental regulators.[63]

FINRA also performs a number of services ancillary to its primary tasks of registering, inspecting, and disciplining members. It administers the arbitration process through which firms and their investors and employees are required to resolve business disputes.[64] FINRA also administers a voluntary mediation program.[65] FINRA makes certain information it collects from broker-dealers and associated persons available to investors through BrokerCheck.[66] BrokerCheck also includes information about investment advisers and their associated persons.[67] On behalf of the SEC and the state securities administrators, FINRA developed and runs the Investment Adviser Registration Depository, an online registration and filing system for investment advisers.[68] FINRA is bidding to obtain the contract to implement the consolidated audit trail system for tracking

---

57 FINRA, *Targeted Examination Letters* <www.finra.org/Industry/Regulation/Guidance/TargetedExaminationLetters/> accessed 15.04.2014.

58 FINRA, *Sanction Guidelines*, 2013, pp. 9–11.

59 FINRA, *About FINRA* <www.finra.org/AboutFINRA/> accessed 15.04.2014.

60 B. Black, 'Punishing Bad Brokers: Self-Regulation and FINRA Sanctions', supra note 26, 47.

61 FINRA, *Adjudication* <www.finra.org/Industry/Enforcement/Adjudication/> accessed 25.03.2014.

62 FINRA, *National Adjudicatory Council* <www.finra.org/Industry/Enforcement/Adjudication/NAC/naccommittee/> accessed 25.03.2014.

63 FINRA made approximately 660 such referrals in 2013. FINRA, *About FINRA* <www.finra.org/AboutFINRA/> accessed 16.01.2015.

64 FINRA, *Arbitration Overview* <www.finra.org/ArbitrationAndMediation/Arbitration/Overview/index.htm> accessed 15.04.2014.

65 FINRA, *Mediation Overview* <www.finra.org/ArbitrationAndMediation/Mediation/Overview/> accessed 15.04.2014.

66 FINRA, *FINRA BrokerCheck® – Research Brokers, Brokerage Firms, Investment Adviser Representatives and Investment Adviser Firms* <www.finra.org/Investors/ToolsCalculators/BrokerCheck/> accessed 25.03.2014.

67 Ibid.

68 IARD, *What Is IARD?* <www.iard.com/WhatIsIARD.asp> accessed 25.03.2014.

equity and option orders and executions, which is currently being designed by a consortium of SROs.[69] FINRA's Trade Reporting and Compliance Engine (TRACE) collects and publicly disseminates data about OTC corporate bond transactions.[70] FINRA's subsidiary, the FINRA Investor Education Foundation, works on financial education initiatives.

FINRA is a not-for-profit Delaware corporation. It funds itself with a mix of fees and fines. The following table sets forth the sources of FINRA's revenue for fiscal year 2013.

Table 1. FINRA Revenues, Year Ended 31 December 2013

Source	**Amount ($ millions)**
Regulatory Fees: Include the Trading Activity Fee, which firms pay on the sell side of every transaction in a covered security, and other assessments on firms, their branch offices, and their associated persons.	414.6
User Fees: Include registration, examination and continuing education fees and fees for reviewing firms' advertising and proposed public offerings.	206.4
Contract Services Fees: Include fees charged for surveillance and examination services FINRA provides to NASDAQ, the NYSE, Trade-Reporting Facilities, and fees in connection with a FINRA-developed mortgage licensing system.	115.2
Transparency Services Fees: Include fees for TRACE and other reporting facilities.	58.4
Dispute Resolution Fees: Includes fees for arbitrations and mediations.	36.2
Other: FINRA's annual report does not specify what this category includes.	9.6
Fines: Includes sanctions for rule violations. Fines are not used for operating expenses, but are used for 'capital expenditures and regulatory projects'.	60.4

Source: FINRA, *FINRA 2013 Year in Review and Annual Financial Report*, 2014, pp. 13-14.
Notes: The table omits activity assessment fees, which FINRA pays to the SEC and then recoups from the industry.

In addition to its revenues, FINRA maintains a large investment portfolio – $1.7 billion at the end of 2013 – 'to support FINRA in fulfilling its mission of protecting investors and maintaining market integrity by providing FINRA with supplemental financial resources'.[71] Investment returns have been an important

[69] SEC Rule 613 Consolidated Audit Trail RFP Bid Submissions <http://catnmsplan.com/process/P469129> accessed 25.03.2014.
[70] FINRA, *Trade Reporting and Compliance Engine® (TRACE®)* <www.finra.org/Industry/Compliance/MarketTransparency/TRACE/> accessed 25.03.2014.
[71] *FINRA 2013 Annual Report*, supra note 46, p. 20.

source of income for FINRA, but have also been a source of losses.[72] FINRA adopted a lower risk investment strategy after the investment portfolio incurred large losses in 2008.[73]

3. FINRA'S ACCOUNTABILITY STRUCTURE

Avoiding the label 'SRO', FINRA refers to itself as 'the largest independent regulator of securities firms doing business with the public in the United States'.[74] The use of the term 'independent' in this context appears intended to convey its independence from both the securities industry and the government.

FINRA is independent from industry because it is overseen by a Board of Governors, the majority of whom are not representatives of industry. The Board currently comprises 24 governors, including FINRA's CEO, 13 'public' governors, and 10 industry representatives.[75] FINRA bylaws require the public governors to outnumber the industry governors.[76] Public governors cannot have any 'material business relationship' with a broker, a dealer, or another SRO.[77] To reflect the different types of firms affected by FINRA regulation, the industry governors must include a floor member governor, an independent dealer/insurance affiliate governor, an investment company affiliate governor, three small firm governors, one mid-size firm governor, and three large firm governors.[78] Industry members cannot outnumber public members of the nominating committee – which has primary authority to nominate replacement governors.[79] Small, medium, and large firms can petition to place a candidate on the ballot other than one nominated by the nominating committee.[80] The board structure, which is intentionally weighted away from the industry, is not consistent with self-regulation. An organization run by a board that is dominated by people who are not in the industry is not an SRO; it is a regulator with industry representation. The independence from industry extends beyond the board. Professor Dombalagian has documented the

---

[72] D. Jamieson, 'Finra Turns a Profit, Helped By Investments, Fee Increases', *Investment News*, 28.06.2013 <www.investmentnews.com/article/20130628/FREE/130629921> accessed 15.04.2014.

[73] FINRA, *2008 Year in Review and Annual Financial Report*, 2009, p. 29.

[74] FINRA, *FINRA 2013 Annual Report*, supra note 46, p. 35.

[75] FINRA, *FINRA Board of Governors* <www.finra.org/AboutFINRA/Leadership/P009756> accessed 25.03.2014.

[76] FINRA By-Laws, Article VII, Sec. 4(a).

[77] FINRA, By-Laws, Art. I, par. (tt).

[78] FINRA By-Laws, Article VII, Sec. 4(a).

[79] FINRA By-Laws, Article VII, Section 9(b).

[80] FINRA By-Laws, Article VII, Section 10.

trend away from SRO staff having deep industry expertise and its replacement with a bureaucratized staff.[81]

FINRA's primary outside accountability comes through SEC oversight. As explained in section 1, the SEC's role in monitoring and guiding SROs has increased over time, and now the agency has broad powers to influence FINRA's activities, including its rulemaking and disciplinary actions. FINRA is subject to SEC reporting requirements.[82] The SEC conducts routine and for-cause inspections of FINRA. FINRA files proposed rule changes with the SEC before they can take effect so the SEC can publish them in the Federal Register for public comment and decide whether to disapprove them.[83] The SEC can abrogate, add to, or delete FINRA rules through notice-and-comment rulemaking.[84] The SEC also has authority – of its own volition or through an appeal by the disciplined party – to review disciplinary actions once FINRA has had its last word.[85] The SEC can affirm, remand, or revise FINRA's sanction.[86] As the SEC's enforcement action against the NASD in 1996 illustrates, the SEC can force structural and governance changes through enforcement proceedings.

In practice, however, FINRA operates with substantial independence from the SEC. FINRA can set its own rulemaking and disciplinary agendas and budget without SEC input. The Government Accountability Office (GAO) found that 'SEC's oversight of FINRA's programs and operations varied, with some programs and operations receiving regular oversight and others receiving limited or no oversight'.[87] Among the areas over which the GAO found that the 'SEC has conducted limited or no oversight' is executive compensation, despite the comparatively high FINRA executive compensation packages.[88] Although the SEC has the power to approve or disapprove FINRA rules, the SEC's Division of Trading and Markets typically exercises this approval and disapproval authority through a delegation from the Commission.[89] In order to rescind the delegation,

---

81 O.H. Dombalagian, 'Self and Self-Regulation: Resolving the SRO Identity Crisis' (2007) 1 *Brooklyn Journal of Corporate Finance and Commercial Law* 317, 329–30.

82 See, for example, 17 CFR § 240.15Aj-1.

83 15 U.S.C. § 78s(b)(1) and (b)(2).

84 15 U.S.C. § 78s(c).

85 FINRA, *Adjudication* <www.finra.org/Industry/Enforcement/Adjudication/> accessed 25.03.2014; 15 U.S.C. § 78s(d) (2012).

86 15 U.S.C. § 78s(e) (2012).

87 GOVERNMENT ACCOUNTABILITY OFFICE, *Securities Regulation: Opportunities Exist to Improve SEC's Oversight of the Financial Industry Regulatory Authority*, 2012, p. 7.

88 FINRA's CEO earns approximately $2.5 million a year. FINRA, *Annual Report*, supra note 46, p. 24. This is more than the SEC chairman's salary of $165,300 and, according to a recent analysis, more than heads of securities industry SROs and securities industry trade groups. L. Hume, 'SEC Chair's Salary Far Below Group Execs Representing Firms, Individuals Overseen', *The Bond Buyer*, 03.09.2013 <www.bondbuyer.com/issues/122_170/sec-chairs-salary-far-below-firm-executives-overseen-regulated-1055210-1.html> accessed 14.10.2014.

89 17 CFR § 230.30–3(a)(12).

two commissioners must object in writing within five days of being notified of staff plans to disapprove a rule.[90] As a consequence, FINRA rules do not typically attract close attention from the SEC's commissioners. Because many FINRA disciplinary actions are settled, the SEC reviews only a small subset of disciplinary actions. The SEC's ultimate power over FINRA comes from its ability to revoke the SRO's registration as a securities association under the Exchange Act, but the 'drastic' nature of this remedy makes the exercise of this power unlikely.[91] There would be no nongovernmental organization to take FINRA's place as the statutorily requisite SRO, so FINRA has substantial leverage in its relationship with the SEC.

FINRA is subject to less SEC oversight than the Public Company Accounting Oversight Board (PCAOB), the non-profit, quasi-governmental regulator responsible for overseeing auditors of public companies and broker-dealers. The SEC, for example, approves the PCAOB's budget and appoints its board members. One commentator argues that, if the Supreme Court applied the same reasoning it used in its consideration of the PCAOB's constitutionality,[92] it would find FINRA as an entity to be unconstitutional because of the SEC's inability to remove its board members.[93] At a minimum, this inability limits FINRA's accountability to the SEC.

4. FINRA'S COMPARATIVE LACK OF ACCOUNTABILITY

FINRA's regulatory powers are similar to the SEC's, but its accountability structure is very different. Operating on the strength of a government mandate and carrying out a regulatory mission using government-like tools, FINRA is difficult to distinguish from its patron agency. As does the SEC, FINRA enjoys immunity from suit in carrying out its regulatory responsibilities.[94] As Professor Barbara Black documents, 'FINRA (including its predecessor, the NASD) has evolved from a membership association primarily responsible for enforcing industry norms to a regulator that enforces federal securities laws as an adjunct of the SEC'.[95] Professors Birdthistle and Henderson put the matter even more

---

90 Ibid.

91 M. Smythe, 'Government Supervised Self-Regulation in the Securities Industry and the Antitrust Laws: Suggestions for an Accommodation' (1984) 62 *North Carolina Law Review* 475, 483.

92 Free Enterprise Fund v. Public Company Accounting Oversight Board, 130 S. Ct. 3138 (2010).

93 J. McLaughlin, 'Is FINRA Constitutional?' (2011) 12 *Engage* 111, 113–14.

94 For a discussion of immunity as it has been applied in the SRO context, see R. Nafday, 'Comment: From Sense to Nonsense and Back Again: SRO Immunity, Doctrinal Bait-and-Switch, and a Call for Coherence' (2010) 77 *The University of Chicago Law Review* 847.

95 B. Black, 'Punishing Bad Brokers: Self-Regulation and FINRA Sanctions', supra note 26, 29.

starkly when they observe that 'financial SROs are transforming into a 'fifth branch' of government'.[96] Professor Onnig Dombalagian worries that SROs 'are likely to behave as if they are an extension of the Commission's own compliance and enforcement arms, with the added benefit that they are subsidized directly by industry fees and not constrained by the same statutory limitations on their power'.[97] FINRA is not subject to the same administrative procedures that hold government regulators accountable to Congress, the President, and the public.[98] In FINRA's case, rigorous administrative process is also important for ensuring accountability to investors[99] and to its own members.[100]

Governmental regulators are subject to a number of accountability measures to which FINRA is not subject. Agencies have politically accountable heads. The SEC, for example, is governed by a five-member, politically balanced commission. The Freedom of Information Act (FOIA) enables the public to obtain documents from government agencies.[101] Most federal agencies are subject to Congressional appropriations, which enables Congress to exercise some control over them. The SEC is no exception. Although the SEC receives fees on securities transactions to cover its costs, Congress determines how much the SEC may spend. The penalties and disgorgement collected by the SEC are used to compensate victims or are paid to the U.S. Treasury, and are not used to supplement the SEC's budget.[102] Regulatory agencies conduct their rulemaking under the constraints of the Administrative Procedure Act (APA), which requires agencies to take into account public comments on proposed rule.[103] Regulated entities and individuals can challenge the process by which a regulation was made. Multi-member regulatory agencies generally have to conduct their rulemaking meetings in public.[104] As part of the rulemaking process, agencies use economic analysis to understand the problem they are trying to solve, to identify potential alternative solutions, and to assess the costs and benefits of those solutions. In fact, the Exchange Act explicitly requires that:

---

96 W. Birdthistle and M.T. Henderson, 'Becoming a Fifth Branch' (2013) 99 *Cornell Law Review* 1, 5.

97 O.H. Dombalagian, 'Self and Self-Regulation: Resolving the SRO Identity Crisis', supra note 81, 330.

98 W. Birdthistle and M.T. Henderson, 'Becoming a Fifth Branch', supra note 96, 6.

99 S. Irwin et al., 'Self-Regulation of the American Retail Securities Markets – An Oxymoron for What Is Best for Investors?' (2012) 14 *University of Pennsylvania Law Review* 1055, 1071.

100 R. Karmel, 'Should Securities Industry Self-Regulatory Organizations Be Considered Government Agencies' (2008) 14 *Stanford Journal of Law, Business, & Finance* 151, 197.

101 5 U.S.C. § 552.

102 FINRA, as noted in Table 1 above, uses fines to cover capital expenditures. This practice gives the regulator an incentive to impose fines and thus potentially clouds its disciplinary discretion.

103 5 U.S.C. § 551–559.

104 5 U.S.C. § 552b.

'(w)henever pursuant to this title the Commission is engaged in rulemaking, or in the review of a rule of a self-regulatory organization, and is required to consider or determine whether an action is necessary or appropriate in the public interest, the Commission shall also consider, in addition to the protection of investors, whether the action will promote efficiency, competition, and capital formation'.[105]

Courts have interpreted that provision to require the SEC to perform economic analysis in its rulemakings.[106] The Exchange Act economic analysis requirement on its face applies to SRO rulemakings, but, to date, the SEC has generally not raised the issue. An exception occurred recently when SEC Commissioners Daniel Gallagher and Troy Paredes took the unusual step of dissenting from the approval of another SRO's rule because it lacked rigorous analysis:

'If there is any question as to the rigor of an SRO's analysis, then it is all the more paramount that the Commission not defer to the SRO's claims, conclusions, and judgments. The Commission has a fundamental oversight role with respect to SROs, and undue deference to an SRO in the SRO rulemaking process undercuts the basic structure of that regulatory relationship'.[107]

FINRA recently hired a chief economist and pledged to integrate his work into the rulemaking process.[108] Without support and scrutiny from the SEC, the chief economist's attempts to build rigorous analysis into the rulemaking process likely cannot succeed.

As a non-governmental regulator, FINRA faces some constraints in its disciplinary program that governmental regulators do not. While a firm or individual can appeal an SEC's decision with respect to a FINRA disciplinary action to a federal appellate court,[109] FINRA cannot. Nor can FINRA sue to collect its fines.[110] Because FINRA membership is mandatory for brokers doing business with the public, however, FINRA has significant leverage – the ability to bar and suspend – to force the payment of monetary sanctions.[111] The prospect of an industry bar also

---

105 15 U.S.C. § 78c(f).

106 See, for example, Business Roundtable v. SEC, 647 F.3d 1144, 1148 (D.C. Cir. 2011).

107 D.M. Gallagher and T.A. Paredes, Commissioners, SEC, *Statement Regarding Commission Approval of MSRB Rule G-17 Interpretive Notice*, 14.05.2012.

108 FINRA, *Jonathan S. Sokobin Named FINRA's Chief Economist*, News Release, 30.04.2013 <https://www.finra.org/Newsroom/NewsReleases/2013/P251015> accessed 25.03.2014; D. Michaels, 'FINRA Hires First Chief Economist to Boost Cost-Benefit Analysis,' *Bloomberg*, 30.04.2013.

109 15 U.S.C. § 78y(a)(1)(2012).

110 Fiero v. FINRA, 660 F.3d 569, 577 (2d Cir. 2011) ('Congress did not intend to empower FINRA to bring court proceedings to enforce its fines').

111 For a discussion of the degree to which FINRA exercises leverage, see J. Macey and C. Novogrod, 'Enforcing Self-Regulatory Organizations' Penalties and the Nature of Self-Regulation' (2012) 40 *Hofstra Law Review* 963, 963.

gives FINRA leverage to force individuals to answer questions during FINRA proceedings. An individual generally is unable to assert his Fifth Amendment right not to incriminate himself in a FINRA proceeding; he has to answer FINRA's questions or face getting kicked out of the industry.[112] An exception may be made in cases in which FINRA's proceeding is being carried on as part of a joint proceeding with a government agency.[113] State securities regulators contend that FINRA has withheld information from them in order to avoid being classified as a state actor.[114] By avoiding the state actor classification, FINRA has thus far managed to exercise governmental powers without governmental accountability.

5. FINRA'S REGULATORY ASPIRATIONS

Amid rising concerns about its lack of accountability, FINRA has actively sought opportunities to expand its regulatory authority. Most notably, in the wake of the crisis, FINRA argued that it should become the SRO for investment advisers.[115] FINRA also has gradually expanded its role as a regulator of securities markets. In addition, through the JOBS Act, Congress recently gave FINRA responsibility for registering and overseeing crowdfunding portals, the intermediaries through which companies will be able to raise small amounts of equity funding.[116] As FINRA expands its regulatory reach beyond broker-dealer oversight, it will look even less like an SRO and more like a governmental regulator.

State securities regulators and the SEC currently share regulatory responsibility for U.S. investment advisers. Reflecting a concern that the SEC was not examining investment advisers frequently enough, Dodd-Frank adjusted the division of labour by shifting additional small advisers from SEC to state oversight.[117] Despite this temporary reprieve, the SEC staff anticipates that as the number of advisers

112 United States v. Solomon, 509 F.2d 863, 872 (2d Cir. 1975).

113 See, for example, In the Matter of Justin F. Ficken, Exchange Act Release No. 54,699, 03.11.2006, p. 11 ('we consider the burden of demonstrating joint activities sufficient to render NASD a state actor to be high, and that burden falls on the party asserting state action'). For a suggested framework for deciding whether FINRA is a state actor, see M. Deshmukh, 'Is FINRA a State Actor: A Question that Exposes the Flaws of the State Action Doctrine and Suggests a Way to Redeem It' (2014) 67 *Vanderbilt Law Review* 1209.

114 S. Irwin et al., 'Self-Regulation of the American Retail Securities Markets – An Oxymoron for What Is Best for Investors?', supra note 99, 1068.

115 R. Ketchum, Chairman and CEO, FINRA, Testimony Before the Subcommittee on Capital Markets and Government Sponsored Enterprises of the U.S. House of Representatives, 13.09.2011 <www.finra.org/Newsroom/Speeches/Ketchum/P124416> accessed 15.04.2014.

116 Jumpstart Our Business Startups Act, Pub. L. 112–106 § 304(a) (2012); FINRA, *Jumpstart Our Business Startups (JOBS) Act: FINRA Requests Comment on Proposed Funding Portal Rules and Related Forms*, Regulatory Notice 13–34 (Oct. 2013).

117 Dodd-Frank Wall Street Reform and Consumer Protection Act § 410 (amending 15 U.S.C. § 80b-3a(a)).

rises, it will once again overwhelm the SEC's resources.[118] The staff suggested creating an SRO for investment advisers or allowing FINRA to examine its registrants under the Investment Advisers Act.[119]

FINRA has expressed a willingness to become the SRO for investment advisers. Particularly because many investment adviser representatives are also registered representatives under FINRA's jurisdiction, FINRA contends it is prepared to take over responsibility for investment advisers.[120] FINRA argues that 'given our experience operating a nationwide program for examinations and our ability to leverage existing technology and staff resources to support a similar program for investment advisers, we believe we are uniquely positioned to serve as at least part of the solution to this pressing problem' of inadequate investment adviser oversight.[121] FINRA cites its own failure to detect the Madoff fraud in support of its call to become the SRO for investment advisers. The special review committee that FINRA set up to investigate its failures in connection with the Madoff and Stanford frauds[122] recommended that FINRA 'proactively seek new jurisdiction from Congress to regulate activities under the Investment Advisers Act to give it more effective means to detect future Madoff-like situations'.[123] FINRA's use of the Madoff fraud as a justification for additional regulatory authority over investment advisers is puzzling because during most of the time period in which the fraud was ongoing, the firm was registered only as a broker-dealer and not as an investment adviser. Consequently, as Professor John Coffee has noted, FINRA arguably bears responsibility for not detecting the fraud.[124]

If FINRA succeeds in becoming the SRO for investment advisers, its status as an SRO will be further compromised as it tries to balance the needs of a new set of members. FINRA's rules-based regulatory regime is very different than the current investment adviser regime, which is based on the less precise, but some argue more demanding fiduciary duty standard. FINRA reportedly has been softening that distinction by 'stressing to brokerage firms to act in the best

118 STAFF OF THE DIVISION OF INVESTMENT MANAGEMENT, SEC, *Study on Enhancing Investment Adviser Examinations,* 2011, p. 38.

119 Ibid., p. 39.

120 B. Protess, 'A Regulator Moves to Expand Power Over Wall St.' *NYTimes.com*, 25.4.2011.

121 R.G. Ketchum, CEO, FINRA, Testimony Before the U.S. House of Representatives Comm. on Fin'l Servs., 06.06.12 <www.finra.org/Newsroom/Speeches/Ketchum/P126815> accessed 14.10.2014.

122 Stanford, a FINRA member firm, perpetrated a $7.2 billion fraud by selling foreign certificates of deposit. C.A. Bowsher et al., *Report of the 2009 Special Review Committee on FINRA's Examination Program in Light of the Stanford* and Madoff Schemes, 2009, pp. 2–4.

123 Ibid., p. 6.

124 J.C. Coffee, Testimony Before the U.S. Senate Comm. on Banking, Housing & Urban Affairs, 20.01.2009, p. 13 <http://banking.senate.gov/public/index.cfm?FuseAction=Files.View&FileStore_id=d3f6706f-2d65-4fad-a349-d839e04149e9> accessed 25.03.2014.

interests of their clients'.[125] If FINRA were to become the SRO for investment advisers, FINRA might seek to craft a single regulatory approach for broker-dealers and investment advisers. Combining two industry groups – albeit ones with overlapping functions – into a single SRO would lessen one of the advantages of self-regulation, namely the ability to apply the expertise from within the industry to design appropriate regulations for the industry. Given the tensions between the two groups, a joint SRO could also undermine the industry's trust in the regulator, another advantage of self-regulation.

FINRA also has sought actively to add additional market venues to its regulatory portfolio. Exchanges contract with FINRA to perform market regulation. Recently, with the addition of BATS Global Markets (BATS), FINRA will be responsible for monitoring ninety-nine per cent of the market of U.S. listed equities.[126] In the early 2000s, when different regulatory models were being considered, one of the justifications for the hybrid model was its ability to bifurcate member and market regulation in order to 'get centralized expertise ... for operations that are similar across the board at the member level (and) leave market-based surveillance, market-based expertise in the marketplaces'.[127] With the concentration of market and member regulation in FINRA, that distinction has been lost.

Even within its core jurisdiction of member regulation, FINRA is asserting itself more aggressively. In December 2013, it sought comment on a plan to require firms to provide specific retail customer information, such as account types and categories, investment profile, date of birth, details of account activities and balances, and descriptions of securities.[128] Subsequently, FINRA retreated and promised not to 'require the submission of information that would identify to FINRA the individual account owner, particularly, account name, account address or tax identification number'.[129] Nevertheless, FINRA's plan for such extensive data collection about individual accounts and transactions suggests a far-reaching regulatory vision.

---

125 M. Schoeff, Jr., 'Is FINRA Pulling Its Efforts to Be the SRO for Advisers?', *Investment News*, 13.04.2014.

126 FINRA, *BATS Global Markets, FINRA Enter Regulatory Service Agreement*, News Release, 06.02.2014 <www.finra.org/Newsroom/NewsReleases/2014/P443474> accessed 14.10.2014.

127 SRO Hearing, supra note 28 (statement of M.E. Lackritz, President, Securities Industry Association), p. 32.

128 FINRA, *Regulatory Notice 13-42: Comprehensive Automated Risk Data System* (Dec. 2013).

129 FINRA, *Update Regarding Comprehensive Automated Risk Data System* <www.finra.org/Industry/Regulation/Notices/2013/P451243> accessed 25.03.14.

6. CONCLUSION

FINRA has become a very powerful force in the securities markets. As its choice to characterize itself as an 'independent regulator' reflects, FINRA is not a self-regulator. Its members are not regulating themselves; they are being regulated by FINRA, just as they are regulated by the SEC. FINRA's status as a non-governmental regulator, however, enables it to avoid the scrutiny and procedural requirements to which a government agency performing the same tasks would be subject. Before FINRA succeeds in further expanding its regulatory footprint by taking on additional responsibilities, policymakers should revisit the long-debated questions about whether self-regulation works and what form it should take. One option could become to acknowledge that FINRA looks a lot like the SEC and accordingly fold FINRA into the SEC.[130] Alternatively, FINRA could be remade into an organization that is run by the industry it regulates. In other words, FINRA could become a true self-regulator. Competing SROs might emerge to tailor regulation to a particular group of firms, such as smaller broker-dealers. Another option would be to enhance FINRA's public disclosure and procedural obligations. Procedural requirements should include a clear requirement to conduct and document economic analysis and greater procedural protections in connection with disciplinary actions.

The shift from self-regulation to 'independent' regulation has been gradual and has been driven in part by legitimate concerns about conflicts of interest. As academics continue to point out, however, SROs offer real advantages over governmental regulators. Professors Birdthistle and Henderson lay out a number of these benefits: SROs have expertise, enjoy the trust of their regulated entities, are efficient, are better able to tailor rules, and are well-suited to handle minor missteps.[131] Moreover, a long history of self-regulation – in name at least – and practical considerations – the money and staff that the SEC would need to take over FINRA's work[132] – lead many to believe that 'self-regulation of the broker-dealer industry is here to stay'.[133] After decades of modifications, FINRA's version of self-regulation embodies a troubling independence from government, industry, and the public. Future modifications should be aimed at restoring accountability to this powerful regulator.

---

130 See, for example, letter from Danielle Brian and Michael Smallberg, Project on Government Oversight, to U.S. House of Rep. & Sen. Comms., 23.02.2010 <www.pogo.org/our-work/letters/2010/er-fra-20100223-2.html> accessed 25.03.2014.

131 W. Birdthistle and M.T. Henderson, 'Becoming a Fifth Branch', supra note 96, pp. 55–58.

132 This is a common argument in favor of self-regulation. But see M. Smythe, 'Government Supervised Self-Regulation in the Securities Industry and the Antitrust Laws: Suggestions for an Accommodation', supra note 91, footnote 10 ('Of course, the cost of self-regulation ultimately is passed through to brokerage firm customers in the form of higher fees, so a lessened burden on the taxpayer is accomplished at the expense of securities industry customers').

133 B. Black, 'Punishing Bad Brokers: Self-Regulation and FINRA Sanctions', supra note 26, 27.

Part II.3
Canada

WHY OPACITY IS JUST NOT GOOD ENOUGH: THE EFFECTIVENESS AND ACCOUNTABILITY OF CANADA'S OFFICE OF THE SUPERINTENDENT OF FINANCIAL INSTITUTIONS

Ian Roberge and Dona M. Dunea

This chapter considers the effectiveness and the accountability of financial services sector regulators by focusing on the Office of the Superintendent of Financial Institutions (OSFI), Canada's prudential regulator. We identify three broad measures of effectiveness – the overall regulatory framework, outcome, and adaptability – and, three measures of accountability – vertical accountability, the co-production of accountability, and the culture and value placed on being accountable. In the aftermath of the 2007–2008 global financial crisis, OSFI has been hailed as a very effective regulator. We argue, however, that OSFI's performance should be more critically assessed; there is a need, in particular, for greater transparency. This chapter pays particular attention to the difficult balancing act between opacity and transparency in financial services sector regulation.

The 2007–2008 global financial crisis highlighted anew the importance of a properly functioning financial system for the economy, and of good, effective and accountable supervision and regulation. The crisis was the result of both market failures, and political, legislative and regulatory failures. This chapter is specifically interested in the effectiveness and accountability of financial services sector regulators, and how to assess performance. As part of this discussion, we are particularly attentive to the relationship, and difficult balancing act, between opacity and transparency. Effectiveness is, in a way, closely associated with opacity; regulators can be more flexible in an opaque environment, at the same time, opacity makes it difficult to assess performance. Transparency, on the other hand, can impede effectiveness, though it also likely increases accountability. In this chapter, we consider the effectiveness and accountability of financial services sector regulators by studying the Office of the Superintendent of Financial Institutions (OSFI), Canada's prudential regulator.

How effective and accountable is OSFI? How does OSFI fulfill its mandate and stated objectives? How does it operate in practice? What are its accountability mechanisms? Following the 2007–2008 global financial crisis, OSFI has been frequently commended for its role in helping the country navigate through the crisis.[1] The IMF has been positive about Canadian supervision and regulation of financial markets.[2] Anand and Green suggest that OSFI has shown itself to be a very effective regulator.[3] Kelly et. al., studying insurance regulation, recognise OSFI for its ability to monitor system-wide issues.[4] We suggest, however, that OSFI's performance should be more critically assessed. Canadian success has tended to be overstated. Canada underwent the worst financial crisis in its history in 2007, one that is better known and referred to as the asset-backed commercial paper (ABCP) crisis.[5] This particular set of events – including Canadian banks operating as active players on the largely unregulated ABCP market – is seen to have transpired, in part, as a result of regulatory shirking.[6] Despite the rhetoric that Canadian banks did not need a bail-out during the financial crisis, they did receive governmental assistance to ensure liquidity.[7] There are good reasons to question, at the very least, the widely perceived effectiveness of Canadian regulatory authorities. We argue that there is a need, in particular, for greater transparency and openness in regulatory practices.

Canada is worth studying because, as just noted, it has generally been hailed as a success story coming out of the global financial crisis, the result of strong

1 See L. Savage, 'From Trial to Triumph: How Canada's Past Financial Crises Helped Shape a Superior Regulatory System' (2014) *University of Calgary School of Public Policy Research Paper* No. 7–15.

2 International Monetary Fund (IMF), 'Intensity and Effectiveness of Federal Bank Supervision in Canada – Technical Note' (2014) *IMF Country Report No. 14/70* <www.imf.org/external/pubs/cat/longres.aspx?sk=41406.0> accessed 14.08.2014.

3 See A. Anand and A. Green, 'Regulating Financial Institutions: The Value of Opacity' (2012) 57 *McGill Law Journal* 399.

4 M. Kelly, A. Kleffner and D. Leadbetter, 'Structure, Principles and Effectiveness of Insurance Regulation in the 21st Century: Insights from Canada' (2012) 37 *The Geneva Papers* 155.

5 J. Chant, *The ABCP Crisis in Canada: The Implications for the Regulation of Financial Markets*, Expert Panel on Securities Regulation, 2009 <www.expertpanel.ca/eng/reports/research-studies/index.html> accessed 19.04.2010.

6 S. Harris, 'The Global Financial Meltdown and Financial Regulation: Shirking and Learning – Canada in an International Context' in G. B. Doern and C. Stoney (eds.), *How Ottawa Spends 2010–2011*, McGill-Queen's University Press, Montreal/Kingston 2010, pp. 68–86.

7 See D. Macdonald, *The Big Banks' Big Secret*, Canadian Centre for Policy Alternatives (CCPA), Ottawa 2012 <www.policyalternatives.ca/publications/reports/big-banks-big-secret> accessed 16.10.2013.

and competent supervision and regulation.[8] Canadian performance may not be as straightforward as has been suggested, but it remains a good case for comparative purposes. Despite years of regulatory harmonisation, cooperation and collaboration, there remain important variations across states. Institutional legacies, jurisprudence, market organisation and practices, among many factors, all help explain cross-country differences. While a single regulatory model is not desirable – such a scenario could, in fact, increase the risk of regulatory failure – there is still a need for governments and regulators to learn from each other. Canada with a developed, and modern, financial services sector is an interesting case from which to learn, with strengths and weaknesses – too often unacknowledged – of its own.

The rest of this chapter is divided into three sections. The first section is a review of the literature on financial services sector regulator effectiveness and accountability that provides broad assessment criteria. The second section considers the Canadian case, focusing directly on OSFI. The final section of the paper outlines lessons learned from the case study. The research for this chapter is gathered from publicly available documents – governmental, press and academic.

1. THE EFFECTIVENESS AND ACCOUNTABILITY OF FINANCIAL SERVICES SECTOR REGULATORS

This section considers the two angles by which to analyse the performance of public organisations such as financial services sector regulators, effectiveness and accountability. Related to the good governance of the sector, regulatory effectiveness and accountability are central to ensure safe, secure, efficient and fair financial markets that properly facilitate the distribution of financial capital across the economy.

1.1. EFFECTIVENESS

The interest in financial services sector regulator effectiveness has surged in recent years as a result of a mix of financial liberalisation, the advancement of risk management techniques and of a series of fairly severe financial crises.[9] Effectiveness in the financial services sector can be understood as the move towards better proportionality between the benefits and the costs of insuring

8 M.D. Knight, 'Surmounting the Financial Crisis: Contrast Between Canadian and American Banks' (2012) 42 *American Review of Canadian Studies* 311.

9 See D.W. Arner, *Financial Stability, Economic Growth, and the Role of Law*, Cambridge University Press, New York 2007.

against systemic risk. The effectiveness and efficiency of regulators is, thus, contingent on the manner in which regulators impact the markets they regulate such that the overall outcome of the market is beneficial.[10] Financial institutions have obtained greater freedom as a result of financial liberalisation;[11] there is, as a result of deregulation, re-regulation and the creation of new financial products a higher incidence of contagion of financial fragility.[12] According to Das et al., the heightened interest is also the result of advancement in risk management techniques, which now permeate both the public and private sector.[13] Coupled with a riskier and more crisis-prone environment, there has been increased pressure on government to provide a sense – if only a semblance – of market safety and stability.

As to regulatory effectiveness per se, the central question remains how best to construct a 'good' and 'effective' regulatory regime. There are three central measures of effectiveness: the institutional framework, performance (outcome), and adaptability. We pay particular attention in the discussion below to the challenges of measuring outcomes. Much of the existing literature on effective and efficient regulatory regimes seems reluctant to distinguish between regulatory inputs and market outcomes, and as a result, focuses rather singularly on inputs, that is, without referencing whether the enforcement of said inputs is conducive to better market outcomes.[14] This tactic arguably produces ambiguous results regarding the relative merits and failures of regulators and says little of the overall impact of regulation on the market. How is effectiveness to be assessed? First, it is important to note that the very nature of financial regulation presents a challenge in such a discussion. Regulators provide a certain type of service (regulations) to various stakeholders, which is imposed and applied by administrative fiat rather than being supplied through a market process. As a consequence, the agent is 'unable to signal what is required or to indicate how much he or she is prepared to pay for the benefits of regulation'.[15] The absence of the market for regulatory service, thus, implies a very big and obvious inefficiency from the very start: there is a major loss of information about what type of regulation is needed for

---

10 See CRA International (CRA), *Assessing the Effectiveness of Enforcement and Regulation*, City of London Corporation, London 2009 <www.cityoflondon.gov.uk/business/economic-research-and-information/research-publications/Documents/research-2009/Assessing%20the%20Effectiveness%20 of%20Enforcement%20and%20Regulation.pdf> accessed 19.04.2010.

11 See M. Yokoi-Arai, 'The Regulatory Efficiency of a Single Regulator in Financial Services: Analysis of the UK and Japan' (2006) 22 *Banking & Finance Law Review* 1.

12 See A. Crockett, *International Standard Setting in Financial Supervision*, Lecture at the Cass/IEA Financial Services Regulation Seminar Series, 05.02.2003 <https://www.bis.org/speeches/sp030205.htm> accessed 19.04.2014.

13 U. Das et al., 'Does Regulatory Governance Matter for Financial Stability? An Empirical Analysis' (2004) *IMF Working Paper* No. 04/89 <https://www.imf.org/external/pubs/ft/wp/2004/wp0489.pdf> accessed 19.04.2014.

14 See supra note 10.

15 C. Goodhart et al., *Financial regulation*, Routledge, London 1998, p. 61.

stability and about how much the consumer is willing to pay. The result is that there is a tendency to favour a cost-benefit analysis to assess the merits of financial regulation. Goodhardt et al. argue that there are notoriously few studies that measure the costs of financial regulation; likewise, benefits are hard to quantify, but are suggested to be nonetheless real.[16] At least one study argues that there are benefits whenever regulation enhances transparency in competition through information disclosure.[17] A cost-benefit analysis is nevertheless very difficult to achieve successfully in real life, most importantly because assessments, even those of internal scope and purpose, are rarely presented transparently to the public for analysis. As such, this method is, as of yet, not properly attuned to providing stable indicators of regulatory effectiveness.[18]

To assess the efficiency and performance of a regulator, there is research that suggests that it is necessary to evaluate more concretely the vectors influencing the calibration of the regulatory framework.[19] To this end, Yokoi-Irai and Mwenda identify, above all other considerations, that institutional structure – in tandem with clear objectives; independence, accountability, integrity and adequate resources; transparency; effective enforcement powers; comprehensiveness of regulation; and cost-effectiveness – has a large impact on the overall efficiency of regulation and supervision.[20] Invoked for evaluation of different regulatory regime structures are the OECD Guiding Principles for Regulatory Quality and Performance (2005; cf. the newer version Policy Framework for Effective and Efficient Financial Regulation: General Guidance and High-Level Checklist, 2010) and the APEC-OECD Integrated Checklist on Regulatory Reform 2005.[21] Another set of indicators and variables are employed in Barth et al. in order to determine what regulatory institutional structure reflects the highest potential for effectiveness and efficacy in financial services regulation.[22] All in all, the

16 Ibid.

17 National Economic Research Associates (NERA), *Costs and benefits of Securities and Investment Board's Proposals to Improve and Commission Disclosure in Life Assurance: A Report prepared for the SIB*, NERA, London 1994.

18 See supra note 15.

19 J. O'Brien, *Redesigning financial regulation*, John Wiley & Sons, Chichester, England 2007.

20 M. Yokoi-Arai, 'The Regulatory Efficiency of a Single Regulator in Financial Services: Analysis of the UK and Japan' (2006) 22 *Banking and Finance Law Review* 23; See also, K.K. Mwenda, *Legal aspects of financial services regulation and the concept of a unified regulator*, World Bank, Washington, D.C. 2006.

21 Organisation for Economic Co-operation and Development (OECD), 'Policy Framework for Effective and Efficient Financial Regulation: General Guidance and High-Level Checklist' (2009) 97 *Financial Market Trends*; also, OECD, *OECD Guiding Principles for Regulatory Quality and Performance*, 2005 <www.oecd.org/gov/regulatory-policy/recommendations-guidelines.htm> accessed 14.05.2014; Organisation for Economic Co-operation and Development (OECD) and Asia Pacific Economic Cooperation (APEC), *APEC-OECD Integrated Checklist on Regulatory Reform*, 2005 <www.oecd.org/gov/regulatory-policy/recommendations-guidelines.htm> accessed 14.05.2014.

22 J.R. Barth, G. Caprio, Jr and R. Levine, 'Bank Regulation and Supervision: What Works Best?' (2004) 13 *Journal of Financial Intermediation* 205.

institutional structure of regulators is a recurring theme in the academic literature on efficiency, manifestly because it poses some significant considerations that go well beyond minor bureaucratic matters. However, Goodhardt et al. warn against exaggerating this significance stating that, 'institutional structure does not in itself guarantee what really matters: the effectiveness of regulation in achieving its objectives in an efficient and cost-effective manner' and that, 'without a clear analytical foundation based on the rationale and objectives of regulation, any institutional structure is likely to be ad hoc and arbitrary'.[23] In this analysis, the focus should rather be placed on the careful circumscription and definition of regulations, realistic expectations of outcomes, endorsement of information asymmetry linked with transparency and accountability (facilitated by credible mechanisms), all glued together by a regulatory staff of well-qualified, well-paid individuals.[24]

The sum and substance of financial regulation is the manipulation of regulated institutions' behaviour. The efficiency and performance of regulators in this industry should not be assessed on whether the regulation succeeds in changing this behaviour, and enforcing a new one – that it does so is indisputable, since regulation by default is here to generate incentives for the regulated parties to act in different ways. What is essential for determining whether a regulator is effective in its performance or not is determining whether the regulator is reinforcing (and not replacing) market discipline, that is, whether its objectives reward good performance and penalise reckless behaviour.[25] As such, the focus on the outcome as a key indicator of effectiveness in regulation and enforcement (where 'effectiveness' is identified as low cost of equity, size and liquidity of markets, valuation premiums, listings and market cleanliness, etc.) should inform all analysis.[26] To this end, there is a final method identified in the literature for measuring the effectiveness of regulators – that is, their impact on final market outcomes. The CRA report proposes a causality tree methodology to evaluate efficiency and performance of regulators in light of different transmission channels that link inputs to outcomes.[27] In doing so, the causality tree builds hypothetical impacts that are expected from certain inputs provided by regulators, and thus enables the researcher to understand what information and data is necessary to assess whether regulators and their regulations reach anticipated impacts on the market (ergo, if they are efficient and effective).

---

23 Supra note 15, pp. 147 and 181.

24 A discussion on this topic is expanded in H.E. Jackson, 'Variation in the Intensity of Financial Regulation: Preliminary Evidence and Potential Implications' (2005) *Harvard Law and Economics Discussion Paper* No. 521.

25 Supra note 15, p. 61.

26 See supra note 10.

27 Ibid.

The performance of regulators becomes in this way tied to market outcomes; by the same token, the performance of markets reflects the legal and regulatory frameworks that supervise them. The assessment of effectiveness through a causality tree – a logic model – should be exercised carefully. Greitens and Joaquin argue that in the lead-up to the global financial crisis, the evaluation of regulators in the United States was correlated with the performance of the market – that is, if the market performed strongly, the regulator was deemed to be effective.[28] Regulators, therefore, had an incentive to ensure continued market growth, irrespective of the sources generating this growth. Regulatory effectiveness, thus, is built on a circular argument: the regulator is effective because the market is stable or growing, and the market is stable or growing because the regulator is effective. The market could self-correct and be stable, without regulatory interference. The market could also be quite unstable, even with good supervision and regulation. There are intervening variables, many that are uncontrollable, that affect market activity – minimally, the causal chain between inputs and outputs is hard to determine. At the very least, the causality tree emphasises outcomes as a central component of performance.

A correct measurement of effectiveness is, thus, challenging to arrive at successfully, especially when inputs and activities are difficult to link to medium and long-term outcomes. There is a long history of financial crisis; regulators must predict, prevent and contain crisis when they erupt. The best regulated financial market is still extremely likely to encounter a crisis – though, the crisis impact can be minimised if prevention measures are in place, and with an appropriate policy response. Effectiveness, as such, also includes policy learning, adaptation and change. Regulators that stand still, that are un-flexible, and that have a hard time adapting may well get caught flat-footed.

1.2. ACCOUNTABILITY

This sub-section considers accountability of financial services sector regulators. Accountability, at a broad level, is broken down into two components: to assume responsibility for performance, and to justify and explain actions taken or not taken.[29] There are three factors that need to be considered: vertical accountability, the co-production of accountability, and the culture and value placed on being accountable – the relationship between opacity and transparency.

---

28 T. Greitens and E. Joaquin, 'Perceptions of Performance in US Financial Regulatory Programs' (2012) 25 *International Journal of Public Sector Management* 444.

29 See P. Iglesias-Rodriguez, *The Accountability of Financial Regulators: A European and International Perspective*, Kluwer Law International, Alphen aan den Rijn, The Netherlands 2014.

Vertical accountability refers to the relationship between the organisation to be held accountable and the organisations and persons to whom it is accountable for its performance. The constitutional, legislative, administrative and regulatory framework sets out the formal mechanism of accountability. Within Westminster style democracies, regulatory agencies, such as financial services sector regulators, are generally accountable to citizens through Parliaments via the Minister responsible. The institutional structure affects accountability – as it does effectiveness – as regulators across countries can range in status from public organisations to more or less independent regulatory agencies. OSFI, for instance, is an independent regulatory agency; the organisation enjoys a great deal of leeway in determining how best to achieve its mandate for stable, fair and efficient markets.

The second factor is the co-production of accountability, which refers to the relationship between the organisation and other stakeholders. To consider the co-production of accountability, it is necessary to study the relationship between regulators and market actors, as well as citizens. The inter-connectedness of regulators and firms is note-worthy. For instance, large banks, under international banking regulation (Basel II and III) can set up their own risk models. Regulators, as such, depend on the firm itself to obtain the information it needs for prudential supervision. In such situations, the risk of regulatory capture or even regulatory arbitrage – as happened in the United States in the lead-up to the global financial crisis – is real. Clearly, the performance of the regulator can be affected if the relationship is too close. Under public and/or political pressure, regulators have a crystal clear incentive to try and avoid – and, maybe even to simply avoid taking responsibility for – market failures. The tight knit relationship implies that regulators are very likely to be influenced by the subject of regulation – a heavy influence of avoiding grasping the nettles when times are rough and gamble on the same chip of market resurrection.[30]

The third factor refers to the importance placed by the organisation on the value of accountability. Transparency is generally assumed to be an important component of accountability especially in the public sector. There are limits, however, to the benefits of transparency, especially in finance. What is the appropriate balance between confidentiality and the public need for transparency to ensure trust and confidence? There is an argument to be built against excessive transparency, and in favour of opacity. Transparency can preclude government bodies from acting efficiently. Transparency, it is argued, connotes normative and utilitarian concerns that can only lead to fewer efficacies. This line of thought suggests that full, free and easy access to state information by the public will ultimately not

[30] See supra note 15.

create an informed and engaged public that will hold officials accountable,[31] but might actually pose constitutional threats, security breaches, higher fiscal cost, and greater opportunity for regulatory capture,[32] as well as incur majoritarian preferences that prevent substantive public policy debates. Transparency, within this stream, is perceived as a mere paperwork exercise that provides the appearance of public intervention with little substantive impact, rather than providing a new means to achieve public ends, it represents a retreat from the regulatory field.[33] This particular literature, as such, constructs a case in favour of opacity. Anand and Green build on this strand of thought in their research on OSFI; they suggest that the organisation's success – a largely standalone assumption based on a survey about private sectors' satisfaction with the regulator – can largely be explained because of the opaqueness that surrounds the organisation.[34] A layer of opacity, in some cases, is justifiable. Regulators might be able, for instance, to better ensure the fair and equal treatment of firms through its control of information. Making public too much information could impact market stability. The problem, however, with opacity is that it becomes impossible to hold actors to account due to a lack of information and the situation is rendered worst when performance is not straightforward. Opacity gives regulators a pass – or requires complete confidence, which in practice is rarely warranted – because without information it is very difficult to determine how well they are performing, and the costs and implications of the actions that were taken. Lack of transparency in this policy field could actually be used to hide agency inefficiency and incompetence.[35] The real question is not whether regulatory arrangement should be opaque or transparent, but about the appropriate level of secrecy versus disclosure.

There is a last component that is worth mentioning and that complicates accountability for financial services sector regulators, especially *vis-à-vis* the public: financial services sector regulatory agencies operate in very technical fields. The nature of their activity, as such, makes it harder to hold them to account, and, in fact, opens the door to the possibility of capture or arbitrage. Most consumers of financial regulation simply accept the type of regulation chosen by the authorities just because it provides them with benefits both in a direct (prevention of losses) and in an indirect (no need for diligence in researching solvency and reputational capital of firms) manner, an expertise which the consumer does not need to attain to participate in the market. The globalisation of finance, alongside de-pillarisation, the creation of new financial products and the

31 M. Fenster, 'The Opacity of Transparency' (2006) 91 *Iowa Law Review* 885.
32 R.E. Barkow, 'Insulating Agencies: Avoiding Capture through Institutional Design' (2010) 89 *Texas Law Review* 15.
33 D. Weil, *The Benefits and Costs of Transparency: A Model of Disclosure Based Regulation*, 2002 <http://ssrn.com/abstract=316145> accessed 02.08.2014.
34 See supra note 3.
35 See E.J. Kane, *Foundations of Financial Regulation*, Boston College, January 1997, mimeo.

rise of new information technologies have all made supervisory and regulatory oversight extremely difficult. Financial markets are competitive and fluid – which theoretically is highly desirable – and policymakers and regulators must have the knowledge and skills necessary to keep up with this market innovation. There is also a sense – though this may be more evident in the United States than elsewhere – that regulators may find it difficult to compete for talent, due to the natural pull of the market for qualified candidates.

2. CANADA

The Canadian financial services sector regulatory landscape is complex and multi-layered. Policy in this field in Canada is divided between jurisdictions, as the federal government is responsible for chartered banks, and parts of the insurance sector (solvency of firms) and the provinces are responsible for the supervision and regulation of securities markets, trusts, and parts of the insurance industry because they have responsibility over contract law. There are, thus, multiple regulatory bodies both at the federal and provincial level. Federally, the regulators are OSFI, the Canadian Deposit Insurance Corporation (CDIC), and the Financial Consumer Agency of Canada (FCAC). In addition, provinces have their own regulatory bodies. For instance, Ontario, which is home to Toronto, the country's main financial services sector centre, has the Ontario Securities Commission and the Financial Services Commission of Ontario. The effectiveness and accountability of financial services sector regulators are not mute subjects in Canada, simply when considering the number of agencies under examination.

2.1. EFFECTIVENESS

As noted above, there are three key measures of effectiveness: the institutional framework, performance (outcome), and adaptability. The observations below demonstrate that the effectiveness in the Canadian case should not be taken for granted.

The institutional framework discussion in the Canadian context must go beyond OSFI to the effect of federalism on regulatory effectiveness. OSFI operates within the institution of federalism, which restricts – to an extent, at least – its scope of activity. Does federalism facilitate or impede regulatory effectiveness? One important consequence of the de-pillarisation of Canadian finance in the 1980s was that it effectively blurred the lines of jurisdictional authority. Coleman argues that the federal government – OSFI – became more powerful since Canadian banks came to dominate across pillars.[36] The reality may be more complex and there may be, in fact, a need for actors across levels of authority to work together better. The 2007 ABCP crisis certainly revealed gaps in the Canadian regulatory regime and strengthened the perceived need for change. As Roberge and Williams point out:

> 'Perhaps even more important (in hindsight) was that the banks' takeover of the securities industry facilitated the emergence of securitized finance. Products like the asset-backed commercial paper – at the center of the 2007 crisis – could now be created by a provincially regulated securities firm (perhaps a bank subsidiary), rated by a provincially regulated bond rating agency, guaranteed and marketed by a federally regulated bank (subject to a banking regulator, not a securities regulator) and then sold to a provincially regulated or managed pension fund'.[37]

Federalism is often assumed to lead to duplication and overlap, though in the financial services sector it has clearly led to important gaps and serious supervisory and regulatory shortcomings. A recent example that has emerged to this effect is that there is no supervisory and regulatory oversight of the Canadian Dealer Offered Rate (CDOR), the inter-bank rate of exchange in Canada.[38] OSFI is not technically responsible for this void since this is not a prudential issue, and provincial regulators are equally not responsible because the CDOR is independently set by banks. To remedy part of the situation in regards to the perils of federalism in the financial services sector, the federal government has attempted to create a national securities regulator, but at the time of writing all efforts have so far failed.[39] Opponents, in fact, have suggested that the current system is quite effective, and that there is very little evidence to the contrary.[40] Canadian federalism practices suggest, minimally, that the assessment of regulatory effectiveness is not straightforward.

---

36 W.D. Coleman, 'Federalism and Financial Services' in H. Bakvis and G. Skogstad (eds.), *Canadian Federalism: Performance, Effectiveness and Legitimacy,* Oxford University Press, Toronto 2002, pp. 178–96.

37 I. Roberge and R.A. Williams, *Path Dependency in Canadian Financial Services Regulation: Increasing Returns or the Logic of Appropriateness,* 1st International Conference on Public Policy, Grenoble, 2013.

38 J. Greenwood, 'Canada's LIBOR Apparently Going without Regulation' *National Post,* 12.03.2014.

39 I. Roberge, 'Politics over Policy: Multilevel Public Management of the Financial Services Sector in Canada' in D. Cepiku, D.K. Jesuit and I. Roberge (eds.), *Making Multilevel Public Management Work: Stories of Success and Failure from Europe and North America,* CRC Press, Boca Raton 2013, pp. 103–118.

40 For an example of this, see T.J. Courchesne, 'The Economic Integration Continuum and the Canadian Securities Industry: In Praise of the Status Quo' in J. Bickerton and B.G. Peters (eds.), *Governing Essays in Honour of Donald J. Savoie,* McGill-Queen's University Press, Montréal 2013, pp. 306–330; also, P. Lortie, *Securities Regulation in Canada: The Case for Effectiveness,* Institute for Research on Public Policy, Montreal 2011 <www.irpp.org/pubs/IRPPstudy/IRPP_Study_no19.pdf> accessed 14.03.2014.

Canada's success coming out of the global financial crisis is on the whole assumed to show the effectiveness of a system that breaks away from the traditional model often claimed to be best personified by the U.K. approach. In contrast to the orthodox tradition championed by the U.K. model of business/marketplace regulation and transactional-level consumer protection, Canada embodies a new approach that focuses predominantly on prudential regulation and institutional safety and soundness.[41] This focus on the individual institution, coupled with the presence of solely one integrated regulator – OSFI – is supposed to have augured a systemic (albeit largely but not fully successful) perspective to catching risk-bubbles on the Canadian regulatory radar screen. To this end, Canada's Auditor General suggested that the Canadian response to the financial crisis was well-coordinated and effective.[42] It is also noteworthy that OSFI, by virtue of its tight-knit one-on-one relationship with individual regulated institutions, was willing to be flexible in regards to the application of its guidelines as part of its approach to oversight. For instance, when Manulife got into trouble due to a loss of value resulting from stock market guarantees in late 2008, OSFI adjusted its Minimum Continuing Capital and Surplus Requirements to ensure the firm had the credit needed to avoid major financial difficulties.[43] Though concerns have been raised that OSFI's acted without full consideration of disclosure requirements,[44] there is no denying that flexibility was necessary especially when faced with the extraordinary circumstances on global markets in the fall of 2008. Snyder refers to this type of action as 'the common sense of regulators'.[45] Canada likely escaped the worst of the crisis through such 'common sense' interventions.

As we noted in the introduction, however, there remain important concerns. Canada and OSFI's performance can be interpreted differently and success is relative. As noted previously, Anand and Green posit that the Office is a good regulator – an affirmation largely based on a survey of financial services sector firms that could be found on the regulator's website.[46] Firms may be satisfied with a lax regime, but this does not give a prescient analysis of OSFI effectiveness. At best, the results suggest that OSFI and private sector actors profit from a strong relationship (more on this issue below). The ABCP crisis should also be a cause for alarm, since OSFI and provincial regulators blamed each other for this major

---

41 See supra note 1, p. 39.

42 Office of the Auditor General of Canada, *2010 Fall Report of the Auditor General of Canada to the House of Commons*, 2010 <www.oag-bvg.gc.ca/internet/English/parl_oag_201010_e_34282.html> accessed 11.03.2014.

43 T. Perkins, 'Shaken Manulife Goes to Banks for Loan', Globe and Mail, 07.11.2008 <www.theglobeandmail.com/report-on-business/shaken-manulife-goes-to-banks-for-loan/article662809> accessed 14.03.2014.

44 J. Hymas, 'OSFI and the Third Pillar', *Advisor's Edge Report*, December 2008 <www.himivest.com/media/advisor_0812.pdf> accessed 14.03.2014.

45 L. Snyder, 'Accommodating Power: The "Common Sense" of Regulators' (2009) 18 *Social and Legal Studies* 179.

46 Supra note 3.

market disruption. Finally, there is also the view suggesting that Canada's success is explained through the market's structure, rather than regulatory design.[47] From this perspective, it can be derived that Canada was more lucky than prudent.

The last point to consider is whether Canada and OSFI have demonstrated the ability to learn, especially coming out of the financial crisis. There has not been a major reform of Canadian legislation, or of regulatory arrangements, in the financial services sector in Canada in over ten years. The last major legislative revision goes back to 2001 to help the industry adapt to globalisation, and to manage the possibility of bank mergers. As just noted, the federal government tried to create a national securities commission, but federal-provincial politics have so far precluded the creation of this office. Williams, in fact, is strident: Canada has not learned from the crisis and is likely not ready for another major disruption on markets.[48] From a prudential standpoint, OSFI has sought to implement the Basel Accords and, in fact, claims to have already implemented Basel III years before the deadline. The regulator also launched in the summer of 2014 a consultation on 'systemically important financial institutions'.[49] Though the tinkling that has taken place can be seen as important, it certainly does not reflect a fundamental rethink in regards to current arrangement. Indeed, the discourse of success that followed the global financial crisis, and governmental inaction, suggests a certain satisfaction with the current set-up. This is certainly made evident by the fact that, even though the Canadian system has obvious, visible weaknesses, there appears to be little appetite for reform.

2.2. ACCOUNTABILITY

For accountability, there are also three variables to consider: institutional and formal mechanisms of accountability, co-production or the relationship to stakeholders (market actors) and citizens, and transparency versus opacity.

The institutional and formal accountability arrangements for an organisation such as OSFI are, from a Canadian perspective, fairly standard. OSFI was created in 1987 by merging the previously existing Office of the Inspector General of Banks and the Department of Insurance. It is an independent agency with the mandate to supervise federally regulated financial institutions. Plainly speaking,

---

47 L. Ratnovski and R. Huang, 'Why are Canadian Banks More Resilient?' (2009) IMF Working Paper No. 09/152.

48 R.A. Williams, 'The Limits of Policy Analytical Capacity – Canadian Financial Regulatory Reform' (2012) 25 *International Journal of Public Sector Management* 455.

49 Department of Finance of Canada, *Taxpayer Protection and Bank Recapitalization Regime: Consultation Paper*, 2014 <www.fin.gc.ca/activty/consult/tpbrr-rpcrb-eng.asp> accessed 14.08.2014.

OSFI is Canada's prudential, or solvency, regulator. The 1997 OSFI Act indicates that OSFI's mandate is to supervise federally-regulated financial institutions to determine if they are sound and in compliance with the law; advise management if this is not the case and require remedial action; promote the adoption of risk-control policies and procedures; promote the adoption of risk control policies that may negatively affect the financial condition of institutions; and, administer federal legislation under the bank insurance trust and loan companies, co-op credit associations and pension benefits acts. Pursuant to its mandate, OSFI is responsible (at the time of writing) for the regulation and supervision of 82 banks, 64 trust and loan companies, 285 insurance companies, 7 cooperative credit associations and over 1300 federally registered private pension plans. OSFI is to determine whether these institutions are in sound financial condition and whether they meet minimum plan funding requirements, governing law, and supervisory requirements. OSFI must advise firms if there are material deficiencies, and if there are, it is to require management and boards of directors to take necessary corrective measures expeditiously.

The Superintendent is appointed formally by the Governor in Council, in practice by the Cabinet, and has a renewable mandate of seven years. The Superintendent may appoint one or more Deputies, of which there are two and an Assistant Superintendent. OSFI's staff members are not a part of the civil service; there exist different pay bands that seek to align to remuneration in the financial sector. It aims to pay at the 75th percentile of salaries for posts of similar level in the financial industry. The government Chief Actuary is also part of OSFI. The total number of OSFI employees is around 550 with close to half working in Supervision. OSFI has three main sectors: Supervision (Deposit-Taking Group, Life Insurance Group, Property and Casualty Group, Specialist Support Group, Supervisory Practices Division, Supervision Support Office), Regulation (Accounting Policy, Actuarial, and Capital requirements, Legal Services, Research, and Private Pension Plans) and Corporate Services (Human Resources and Administration, Communications Division, Finance and Corporate Planning Division, Information Management and Information Technology, Data Management).

OSFI's supervision of federally regulated financial institutions is in a very general sense principles (and risks)-based – vs. rules-based – meaning that it outlines a minimum expectation for regulated entities rather than a set of prescriptive requirements. While OSFI is in charge of applying existing legislative and regulatory requirements, most of the time it relies on devising guidelines that are not legally binding; OSFI uses Memoranda of Understanding to ensure compliance. The system implies constant interaction and negotiation between the regulator and firms on whether or not the latter meet the minimum expectations of the former.

There are various legal mechanisms to ensure accountability. OSFI is accountable to Canadians through Parliament; under the OSFI Act, OSFI is an independent, self-financing agency that reports to Parliament through the Minister of Finance. The Superintendent submits the regulator's annual report to the Minister of Finance, who presents it in turn to Parliament. Officials must appear before parliamentary committees to provide information on topics of concern. Second, OSFI interacts with the executive branch of government policy and regulatory issues through two advisory committees: the Senior Advisory Committee (SAC) which advises on policy, and the Financial Institutions Supervisory Committee (FISC), in charge of regulatory matters. The SAC is chaired by the Deputy Minister of Finance and the FISC is chaired by the Superintendent of Financial Institutions. It is also worth noting that under the Bank Act, OSFI is required to report on individual deposit taking institutions to the Minister. The Minister of Finance can also request public disclosure of information for the purposes of analysis. OSFI is subject to the Auditor General and it must also submit financial statements and related control processes to an annual external audit.

The second component is the co-production of accountability via the network structure. The key financial services sector network actors are the Canadian Bankers Association and the country's six large banks, as well as a handful of large life and health insurance firms. OSFI regularly consults with industry, other government agencies and subject matter experts on issues and proposals pertaining to prudential guidelines and regulations. OSFI keeps industry insiders abreast of development through such publications as its newsletter, the *OSFI Pillar.* OSFI has a statutory obligation to report on the disclosure of information by banks and in describing the progress made in enhancing the disclosure of information in the financial services industry. As well, OSFI is supposed to conduct anonymous surveys of knowledgeable observers on its operations on individual activities, and on broader issues such as its contribution to public confidence, and how it compares to other regulators, participating in reviews to determine whether it is meeting internationally established standards for prudential regulators. Consultation processes are public, as are relevant documents. OSFI's website provides detailed and technical information for stakeholders. Savage goes so far as to argue, 'We believe that in the financial sector especially, the degree to which industry and governments in Canada have worked together in the public interest is relatively unique and is an important contributing factor to Canada's record of financial stability'.[50]

There are, however, some grey areas in terms of this 'close-touch' approach. There is much interaction that is informal. Savage describes the process for intervention as follows:

---

[50] See supra note 1, p. 35.

> 'The first step would be for the regulator to bring the situation to the attention of management and to require a well thought-out plan to address the issue. If the plan is not effective or is not followed, the regulator would follow up, perhaps by meeting directly with the board, and insisting that steps be taken to get the problem under control. If there continues to be no effective action, the regulator might consider other possible interventions, such as requiring the institution to increase its capital base to offset the higher level of risk, or requiring that the institution bring in new management with respect to the area of concern'.[51]

Dickson – the outgoing Superintendent – suggested in an interview that when faced with a difficult situation she could reach all network participants over the phone in a matter of hours.[52] Though flexibility can be seen as a positive, the intervention process appears fairly opaque. The justness of an intervention in such a context is hard to ascertain. There is an apparent lack of clarity about what happens when actors are not acting properly, or as to what measures OSFI actually devises when a firm falls flatly outside the established guidelines. OSFI appears to obtain compliance through regular interactions with private sector actors, but much of it takes place behind closed doors. The IMF even recognises that OSFI processes should be clarified.[53] The tightness of the relationship between the regulator and the regulated also raises concerns about regulatory capture. Though Anand and Green (2012) dismiss such considerations as being irrelevant in Canada – the so-called Wall St.-Washington complex is a fixture of American debates on the financial services sector –[54] the confidential nature of much interactions makes it hard to determine if the 'line has ever been crossed'.

The discussion as such comes back to whether opacity is desirable. OSFI states that confidentiality is vital to public confidence in that public awareness of a state regulator's dealing would create a self-fulfilling prophecy of failure that would harm consumers as well as other parties. It is also deemed of paramount importance because 'publicity would force state regulators to reveal the subjective basis of their judgments, which would have the effect of forcing them back into more objective tests that are less effective from their viewpoint'.[55] The problem, as noted previously, is that opacity provides no means by which to assess performance. Could opacity help OSFI hide its inefficiencies? Full disclosure as the basis for

---

51 Supra note 1, p. 29.

52 See C. Freeland, 'View from the Top: Julie Dickson, Superintendent OSFI', *Financial Times*, 21.12.2009 <www.ft.com/cms/s/0/e3aa59ca-edcf-11de-ba12-00144feab49a.html> first accessed 14.05.2010.

53 International Monetary Fund (IMF), 'Intensity and Effectiveness of Federal Bank Supervision in Canada – Technical Note', supra note 2.

54 See, for instance, S. Johnson and J. Kwak, *Thirteen Bankers: The Wall St. Takeover and the Next Financial Meltdown*, Pantheon Books, New York 2010.

55 R. Ericson, A. Doyle and D. Barry, *Insurance as Governance*, University of Toronto Press, Toronto 2003, p. 149.

regulation appears to be consistent with the notion that markets require a free flow of information to operate normally. As Le Pan, the former Superintendent, acknowledges, lack of information leads to confusion and unclear expectations which do not help either a) the authorities to achieve their goals, or b) the market participants to 'anticipate the actions of authorities and to adapt their behaviour in response'.[56]

The paradox in Canada is between the lack of transparency and the high level of trust from Canadians; the public has bought into the political discourse about the country's success during the financial crisis, and while it may not like the big banks, it has generally trusted the country's financial institutions. Even this trust may not be warranted – consumers have often been dealt the short end of the stick[57] – Canadians have not really sought to hold regulators, or market actors, to account. Banks and other financial firms, in turn, may be quite happy to let 'sleeping dogs lie'. OSFI will claim that its accountability is rendered through its performance and output legitimacy – Canadian markets are fair, stable and secure, and Canadian banks are profitable. Further turmoil on Canadian markets, of the kind seen with the ABCP crisis in 2007, could, however, damage the public's trust. In essence, it is important to keep in mind that opacity and transparency lie on a continuum, where neither of the extreme is particularly useful. Now, the current balance in the Canadian case weighs on the opacity side, when free flow of information through a more transparent screen could be a better answer to solidifying market confidence.

3. KEY LESSONS

This paper has been concerned with the effectiveness and accountability of financial services sector regulators, focusing on Canada's OSFI. This public organisation, as noted, holds an intrinsically close relationship with market actors, which is seen as essential to ensure market stability. OSFI's actual performance, though, remains difficult to ascertain. Formal mechanisms of accountability are respected – there is no reason to believe otherwise, and there is also no reason to believe that there is political interference in the affairs of OSFI – they provide, though, limited satisfaction to those who believe that the Canadian marketplace is not as well-functioning as is often assumed.

56 N. Le Pan, 'Look Before You Leap: A Sceptical View of Proposals to Meld Macro and Microprudential Regulation' (2009), *C.D. Howe Institute Commentary* No. 296 <www.cdhowe.org/look-before-you-leap-a-skeptical-view-of-proposals-to-meld-macro-and-microprudential-regulation/4536> accessed 14.03.2014.

57 See B. Livesey, *Thieves of Bay Street: How Banks, Brokerages and the Wealthy Steal Billions From Canadians*, Random House, Mississauga 2012.

There are two main lessons that emanate from the discussion on effectiveness and accountability. The first is that trying to gauge and verify the effectiveness and accountability of a financial sector regulator is like looking through nebulous glass. For OSFI, the lack of transparency is entrenched in its organisational approach. Financial services sector regulators are public organisations and the cost of policy failure in this field is high. There needs to be serious considerations given on how to obtain the right balance between opacity and transparency. Part of the answer likely lies in finding ways to ensure citizens – consumers or users – are able to participate in the regulatory process. In Canada, OSFI interacts with private sector actors, and informs consumers of its activities, but there is no public input into the regulatory process. The FCAC exists, but its mandate is to increase consumer awareness and financial literacy, similar to the Consumer Financial Protection Bureau in the United Sates. The European Commission created in 2010 the Financial Services User Group (which replaced FIN-USE) to advocate for consumers in regulatory affairs. McKeen-Edwards suggests that FIN-USE was able to exercise influence over the policy agenda, though she admits the committee had little sway over decision-making and implementation.[58] The advent of users' committee in various jurisdictions appears to be a step in the right direction, and is something that should be considered in Canada.

The second consideration relates to policy learning and the political rhetoric. The rhetoric of success in Canada following the global financial crisis has prevented further consideration for substantive improvement to policy, supervision and regulation. There should, however, be some flexibility to the regulatory infrastructure, and regulatory organisations should have the capacity, beyond politics, for introspection. The obvious policy recommendation, as such, for the Canadian case is that it is time for a major review of Canadian financial services sector policy and supervisory and regulatory infrastructure, with a view to regulatory effectiveness and accountability. For instance, there is no regulator in Canada in charge of systemic risk. The aforementioned SAC and FISC facilitate a system-wide approach, but there is not a specific actor responsible for systemic risk similar to what has come to exist in other jurisdictions like the US and the EU. Beyond the infrastructure and the scope of intervention, there is a need to come back on the guiding principles of supervision and regulation. The outgoing Superintendent of Financial Institutions defines OSFI's mandate in the following way:

[58] H. McKeen-Edwards, 'Integrating User Voices into the European Financial Services Policy Process' in D. Cepiku et al. (eds.), *Making Multilevel Public Management Work: Stories of Successes and Failures from Europe and North America*, CRC Press, Boca Raton 2013, pp. 51–65.

'Often when I speak about supervision, I use a sporting analogy so as to help the audience understand the concept of what supervision is. I explain that supervision is not about the rulebook; rather it is all about how the game is played, about refereeing and making tough calls, about how much latitude each player is given and, for excitement, about players jumping up and down in disagreement'.[59]

The sport analogy suggests a minimalist role for OSFI, where its main mandate is to ensure a level playing field between players. Could and should OSFI be a more pro-active public organisation? This is an important question for Canadian policymakers to consider.

Canada has been hailed as an example to follow in the aftermath of the 2007–2008 global financial crisis. There are lessons to be learned from the Canadian case, but this does not suggest that the Canadian model should be emulated *as is*. Could it be the reverse, in fact, and that Canada itself has something to learn from other jurisdictions? As the Canadian experience demonstrates, the virtues of opacity should not be exaggerated, and regulators need to give serious considerations to processes of accountability and transparency. Striking the appropriate balance is both 'science' and 'art' and it is no easy task.

59 J. Dickson, *Remarks by Superintendent Julie Dickson to the International Institute of Finance*, Madrid 21.05.2012 <www.osfi-bsif.gc.ca/Eng/osfi-bsif/med/sp-ds/Pages/jd20120522.aspx> accessed 18.03.2014.